Supplying The New Model Army

Logistics, arms, ammunition, clothing, victuals and the matériel of war, 1645–1646

Andrew Abram

'This is the Century of the Soldier', Fulvio Testi, Poet, 1641

Helion & Company

Helion & Company Limited
Unit 8 Amherst Business Centre
Budbrooke Road
Warwick
CV34 5WE
England
Tel. 01926 499 619
Email: info@helion.co.uk
Website: www.helion.co.uk
X (Twitter): @helionbooks
Visit our blog https://helionbooks.wordpress.com/

Published by Helion & Company 2024
Designed and typeset by Mach 3 Solutions (www.mach3solutions.co.uk)
Cover designed by Paul Hewitt, Battlefield Design (www.battlefield-design.co.uk)

ISBN 978-1-804515-49-5

British Library Cataloguing-in-Publication Data.
A catalogue record for this book is available from the British Library.

Contents

Acknowledgements

In completing this book, I would like to thank the staff of several archives, both national and regional, for their unstinting assistance. I am also indebted to Simon Frame for sharing his wide knowledge of seventeenth century swords and supplying photographs from his personal collection to be used in the present volume. Appreciations are also due to Rosie Sales and Alan Larson for providing valuable insight on cavalry saddles, and Charles Singleton for alerting me to the muster list of Sergeant Major Thomas Smith's company.

This book is dedicated to my fellow former British Army, Commando, Royal Marines and Royal Navy logisticians.

List of Abbreviations

A&O	*Acts and Ordinances*
BL	British Library
Bodl. Lib.	Bodleian Library
CJ	*Journals of the House of Commons*
CRO	Cheshire Record Office/Cheshire Archives
CSPD	*Calendar of State Papers Domestic*
ECWT	*English Civil War Times*
HMC	Historical Manuscripts Commission
HR	*Historical Research*
JSA	*Journal of the Society of Archivists*
JRUSIDS	*Journal of the Royal United Services Institute for Defence Studies*
JSAHR	*Journal of the Society for Army Historical Research*
LA	Lancashire Archives
LJ	*Journals of the House of Lords*
MH	*Midland History*
ROP	*Royalist Ordnance Papers*
JCA	*Journal of Conflict Archaeology*
JAAS	*Journal of the Arms and Armour Society*
TJTH	*The Journal of Transport History*
TLCAS	*Transactions of the Lancashire and Cheshire Antiquarian Society*
TLH	*The Local Historian*
TNA	The National Archives
TT	Thomason Tracts (in the British Library)
WSL	William Salt Library

Explanatory Notes and Conventions

Although dates prior to 1752 are recorded with the year beginning 25 March, modern dating is used throughout, with the New Year being taken to start on 1 January. Spellings in contemporary manuscripts and printed sources (which varied considerably during the seventeenth century) have been modernised, while where appropriate, current forms of punctuation have been added to period accounts.

Contemporary values have been quoted throughout, following the Imperial system.

Finance: 12 pennies (12d.) = 1 shilling (1s.); 20 shillings = one pound sterling (£1) and thus £1 = 240d.

Lengths and distances are given in inches, feet, yards, ells and miles; weights in pounds (lb), 112lb = a hundredweight (cwt), 20cwt = 1 ton.

NB an ell was 45 inches in England, 37 inches in Scotland, and between 21½ inches and 29½ inches (depending on the town or province) in The Netherlands. Similarly, it varied across the rest of the Continent.

Lord General Sir Thomas Fairfax

Introduction

The following book provides a substantial assessment of the topic of supplying the New Model Army under the command of Sir Thomas Fairfax in 1645 and 1646 with ordnance, ammunition, victuals, horses, arms, clothing, and other warlike materials by closely examining the procurement, storage, distribution, and logistical operation behind it. The breadth and detail of the primary manuscript sources – much of which remain unpublished – in addition to printed material in the form of Parliamentary documents and contemporary newsbooks – allows an in-depth approach and broader appreciation of the logistical operation underpinning the army. For instance, it is never enough to simply quote supply contracts (the record of which is occasionally haphazard and incomplete) without considering Treasury Warrants and Receipts, which record what the army received from suppliers, either in full or in part of contracts, and when, and in what quantities, it received them. Lists of stores, along with the means and destination of their transport also place the New Model's munitions and matériel in time and place, while providing evidence of the nuts and bolts of its logistical machinery.

Researching and writing this study has been a lengthy, detailed, and at times complex, process, especially given the enormous quantity of primary sources, mainly in manuscript form. Reflecting the New Model's nature as a national and in many respects centrally administered military force, the bulk of these form a part of the Commonwealth Exchequer Paper (SP28) and War Office (WO) series in The National Archives, Kew. A large amount of related material is also deposited in various other archives, including the British Library, the Museum of London, the Bodleian Library, and elsewhere. Such material is wide-ranging, although some of its content is contradictory, fragmentary, and unsystematic. There is no doubt, however, that its extent is formidable in both quantity and scope, although as is always the case, such material should be seen in context and in some cases treated with caution.

Researchers have gleaned something of the understanding of the supply of arms, ammunition, clothing, and equine equipment to the New Model Army from the transcripts of contracts notified to the Ordnance Office (ML, Tangye Collection Ms 46 78/708, published by Gerald I. Mungeam as 'Contracts of the Supply of Equipment to the New Model Army'). While an important resource, this composite volume, assembled in the nineteenth century, is fragmentary in nature, and although indicative of other material is better used in conjunction with other Ordnance Office books. Much of the material in Ms 46 78/708 is also found in the minute book WO47/1 in The National Archives, although many of the corresponding documents differ in terms of dating. There are also other minute books covering the period at Kew

(WO55/1660, WO55/1646–7, WO55/1662–4), which have received little attention by historians. Such volumes contain additional material on the supply and logistics of Fairfax's Army, including receipts of supplies brought in by contractors for examination and storage at the Ordnance Office, in addition to warrants for deliveries of war matériel to both commissaries and military units. Hence, these manuscript books are most important.

Also of great value to the present study are TNA, SP28/140/3, being an Ordnance Office book recording receipts of military stores between 1646 and 1649, and SP28/352 which consists of warrants for payments to army contractors during a similar period. Furthermore, SP28/29–41 are largely volumes of Treasury Warrants, mainly signed by Sir Thomas Fairfax on behalf of the Committee for the Army, for the use of the New Model Army between April 1645 and December 1646. These are especially important as they record the actual dates and methods of delivery, as well as identifying merchants and the sums paid to them. Such records also contain incidental, but relevant, material covering things such as the reduction of the Earl of Essex's and Earl of Manchester's regiments, in addition to the operations of the Ordnance Office. Other material includes lists of clothing in the Reading magazine for transportation to Portsmouth; 'An account of moneys disbursed by Edward Orpin, Commissary General of Victuals' (extensive lists of the preparation of clothing and rations – consisting mainly of substantial quantities of cheese and biscuit, in addition to the hiring of carts and draught animals for carrying stores from Lyme to various magazines along the line of march of the army in the West Country). Another group of documents (SP28/123/1–4) consists of schedules of batches of (named) recruits to the New Model Army in 1645–6.

Elsewhere, British Library Add. Ms 35332 consists of an Ordnance Office book of deliveries, with corresponding warrants, between 1646 and 1650, with part of a document covering the early months of 1646. In the William Salt Library in Stafford is Ms Salt 463, a mainly unknown warrant book of 1645–46. This includes 350+ folios pertaining to the completion of the equipping of Fairfax's Army and some garrisons by the Ordnance Office, the logistics of the New Model, its campaigns, and partial re-equipping of military units. The first third of the manuscript's folios cover the formative period of the army's existence, and this volume has been rarely noticed by historians and has been referred to in few published studies. Corresponding with Ms Salt 463 and largely in the same hand, are 3 contemporary Ordnance Office books in the Bodleian Library in Oxford. Ms Add. C247 lists war materials delivered to the army between 4 April and 2 May 1645. Ms Eng. hist. C14 consists of certificates from the Ordnance Office for the receipt of stores contracted for and supplied to Fairfax's forces between 24 March 1645 and 4 March 1646, whereas Ms Eng. hist. C244 forms a register of receipts for arms and supplies received into the Tower stores, mainly for the use of the New Model Army from 1646 to 1649. Again, these manuscripts and their valuable contents – which include material included nowhere else – have been almost entirely missed by researchers.

The orthodox view of writers that armies of the seventeenth century relied upon plunder and free quarter is highly pervasive, and to some degree based upon practices during the Thirty Years' War on the European Continent. Martin Van

Creveld's *Supplying War: Logistics from Wallenstein to Patton* went some way to highlighting the consequences that logistical requirements had on military strategy and battlefield effectiveness.[1] Similarly, Geoffrey Parker in his book *The Army of Flanders and the Spanish Road* focussed on the extensive supply needs of armies and the administrative organisation of logistics.[2] Nevertheless, recent research suggests that during the British Civil Wars there were increasing changes to this custom. Glenn Price's innovative study of military logistics and transportation – taken from his doctoral thesis – establishes how crucial land and water transport, recruitment, and provisioning were to armies of the period. He points out particularly a certain level of 'disinterest, or perhaps a lack of awareness of logistics and supply' among historians of the British Civil Wars, although in regard to the emerging shift away from battlefield reports and lists of officers, Price asserts that, 'focussing on issues such as logistics and supply, which connect military history to wider historical themes, could be one way in which the field of military history might be revitalized at the same time as reinforcing its connection to concepts of war and society.'[3]

The creation, politics, religious identity, officer corps and military campaigns (especially the Battle of Naseby) of the New Model Army have been the focus for various writers, nonetheless, little attention has been paid to the supply and logistics of Fairfax's command. The result has been a critical gap in the understanding of the recruitment, victualling, ordnance, ammunition, clothing, arming, and logistics employed by the Committee of the Army in both the initial establishment of the army and its subsequent campaigns. The methods of sustaining this military force of around 17,000 men in the field necessarily called for a system which operated at an increasingly considerable physical distance from London and the army's headquarters at Reading. The prevailing view is that provisions (for soldiers and horses) were obtained from local sources during 1645 and 1646, nevertheless, the army increasingly relied on an organised system of supply from London by commercial means.

In discussing Sir Thomas Fairfax's Army in England various writers have made rather casual assumptions about its supply and logistical capability, though at times this has been undertaken by employing, in some cases, a limited range of source material. According to Mark Kishlansky:

> in its composition and organization as much as in its material condition of pay and supply, the New Model Army exhibited few dissimilarities from the old armies. In the first 15 months of its existence the Army was continually engaged in battle or siege and its military concerns were paramount. The most frequent statements from the Army, Rushworth's letters

1 Martin Van Creveld, *Supplying War: Logistics from Wallenstein to Patton* (Cambridge: Cambridge University Press, 2004).

2 Geoffrey Parker, *The Army of Flanders and the Spanish Road 1567–1659: The Logistics of Spanish Victory and Defeat in the Low Countries' Wars* (Cambridge: Cambridge University Press, 1972)

3 Glenn W. Price, *Soldiers and Civilians, Transport and Provisions: Early modern military logistics and supply systems during the British Civil Wars, 1638–1653* (Solihull: Helion & Co., 2023), p.xiii.

> to Parliament, or the reports of victories by various messengers focussed the Army's logistical problems.[4]

Glenn Foard described the New Model in Northamptonshire as having been mostly supplied by the county committees from local resources, employing evidence from the Civil War Loss Accounts of local parishes, albeit from very early in the Naseby campaign.[5] Moreover, Ian Gentles asserted that, except for bread and cheese, the New Model, like other forces of the period 'procured a good 90 percent of [its] consumption locally.'[6] Such comments can be challenged, however, in the light of the available broader documentary material, much of which is relatively obscure. Undoubtedly, the formation, composition and maintenance of the army, begun in earnest in spring 1645, was an extraordinary administrative, logistical and military achievement, despite its political detractors, initial discontentment of nominated officers, and constant recruiting problems.

In terms of its origins, Kishlansky argued that 'far from being the revolutionary new army that many have described it, the New Model Army was the conglomeration of pre-existing forces that had themselves already undergone organisational changes and the New Model Army should be seen as much as a continuation as a change.'[7] However, as Foard suggested, by mid-June 1645:

> The New Model represented a complete rebuilding of the Parliament's forces based to a high degree upon Cromwell's experience with the Eastern Association. It comprised regiments of horse which were almost up to strength, well-trained and most of them highly committed, and just 8 regiments of foot [at Naseby]. Despite the views of many Royalists and Parliamentarians, most of the officers … had proved themselves in several years of Civil War, indeed it is too easy to overlook the degree to which the New Model was in reality an old army reborn and expanded.[8]

In the days after the New Model's advance from Oxford in spring 1645 it was clear that requisitioning from the countryside was ineffective as provisions from Buckinghamshire had not been forthcoming, although a small amount of food was supplied by the Newport Pagnell garrison. Contemporary Continental armies travelled with large supply trains which allowed them to extend beyond their own central stores.

Yet as Aryeh Nusbacher in his important 2000 article on victualling remarked, 'There is no supply evidence to support the existence of a full-blown commissary train [belonging to the New Model] transporting staples and baking its bread and

---

4 Mark A. Kishlansky, *The Rise of the New Model Army* (Cambridge: Cambridge University Press, 1979), p.70.

5 Glenn Foard, *Naseby: The Decisive Campaign* (Barnsley: Pen & Sword, 2004 edn), pp.169–175.

6 Gentles, Ian, *The New Model Army in England, Ireland, and Scotland, 1645–1653* (Oxford: Blackwell, 1992), p.45.

7 Kishlansky, *Rise of the New Model Army*, p.74.

8 Foard, *Naseby*, p.207.

brewing its beer on the march, after the fashion of Continental armies.'[9] But as the army under Sir Thomas Fairfax was too large to live off the local economy, and no evidence has emerged to suggest that it supplied its own food – other than bread/biscuit and cheese (in modern terms 'iron rations') – it seems that a 'market which is appointed to follow the armies with provisions' trailed in its rear. Although evidence for this is slight, the assumption must be that through a system of contractors and victuallers the army drew most of its foodstuffs, even though the transport capability was sufficient to move bulk quantities between London and various magazines.

As noted, in sustaining the New Model Army, the development of a supply system ensured that supplies were procured and stored in magazines, such as Reading and Windsor, and transported via internal routes and by sea. The idea of a 'magazine of victuals' was well known in 1645, and the 'magazine' was utilised by the Committee of Both Kingdoms to describe storage of bulk stores in garrisons. Hence, during the campaign of 1645–6 a series of magazines were established at centres such as Portsmouth and Lyme, which sent out convoys to supplied troops at the right place and the right time with recruits, provisions, clothing, arms, ammunition, and money, initially in support of the relief of Taunton, then as the army advanced deep into the Southwest. In achieving this the Committee for the Army utilised established civilian transport networks and routes, both to and from the army's headquarters and London, as well as those in local areas. In describing the system of procurement used by the Committee for the Army and the New Model Army Gentles stated, 'The system of provisioning was administered efficiently and, by delivering the matériel to the army when it was needed, was instrumental in achieving the victories of 1645. Based upon prompt payment in cash, this new centralised system soon supplanted other schemes for equipping the army.'[10]

Most modern thinking and doctrines of warfare place supply and logistics at the core of military operations. Fought some 8,000 miles from the UK, the Falklands War of 1982 emphasised the importance of the integration of combat operations and logistics, whereas had the logistics plan failed, victory for the British Taskforce would have been impossible. Hence, 3 Commando Brigade was sustained by the Commando Logistics Regiment RM, which provided dedicated logistic support. At the time (and for some considerable period afterwards) this was a unique military unit. Integral to this was the Ordnance Squadron, whose primary operational role was to hold and distribute 30 days' worth of first-line stocks of ammunition, rations, and fuel in a ship to shore operation, before external resupply. The Commando Logistics Regiment also established and maintained multiple supply areas, which gave flexibility to brigade operations.[11]

9 Aryeh J. S. Nusbacher, 'Civil Supply in the Civil War: Supply of Victuals to the New Model Army on the Naseby Campaign, 1–14 June 1645', *English Historical Review*, 115 (2000), pp.145–160, (p.149).

10 Gentles, *New Model Army*, p.41, note 10.

11 Kenneth L. Privatsky, *Logistics in the Falklands War: A Case Study in Expeditionary Warfare* (Barnsley: Pen & Sword, 2014), pp.47–50; Adams, Valerie, 'Logistics Support for the Falklands Campaign', *Journal of the Royal United Services Institute for Defence Studies* (September 1984), pp.43–49.

Conversely, when Russia invaded Ukraine on multiple fronts in February 2022, military operations were expected – both by Russian leadership and outside observers – to be extremely brief. Nonetheless, the assault failed to achieve its stated objectives, partly due to inadequate planning, and lack of capacity in logistics and sustainment. Russia's assumption was that light opposition would allow fast movement and reinforcement, with little necessity for logistical support. Contingency plans are unlikely to have considered the logistical challenges of supporting other types of operation, partly because of Soviet era concepts that built on the echelon principle of resupply. Additionally, Ukrainian tactics of targeting Russian logistics resources have significantly reduced Russian fighting power in particular locations.[12]

12 Alex Vershinin, 'Feeding the Bear: A Closer Look at Russian Army Logistics and the *Fait Accompli*', *Texas National Security Review* (21 November 2021) https://warontherocks.com/2021/11/feeding-the-bear-a-closer-look-at-russian-army-logistics

1

The New Model Army: origins and composition

The New Model Army, or as contemporaries understood it, the 'Parliament's Army New Modelled' or 'Sir Thomas Fairfax his Army', was created out of the disorder, missed opportunities and recriminations of the autumn of 1644 when the military forces of the Eastern Association, the Earl of Essex and Sir William Waller failed to crush the numerically inferior Royalist army at the Second Battle of Newbury. Between February and April 1645, the requisite legislation for a new force – a standing army, raised and wholly maintained by State taxation and enforced City loans, and supplied predominantly from London sources – was passed by Parliament. Hence, the New Model Ordinance combined the three armies into one. In addition, the Self-Denying Ordinance, which began on 3 April 1645, disqualified MPs and peers from holding military commands, though with an option of being reappointed should circumstances require it. On 21 January 1645, the 32-year-old Sir Thomas Fairfax was commissioned as commander-in-chief of the New Model Army. In part, his commission read:

> At a free conference of both Houses, reasons being given by the Commons for the speedy passing the ordinance commissioning Sir Thomas Fairfax, the Lords returned to their House and passed the same without any alterations. The purport of which ordinance was to constitute Sir Thomas Fairfax, commander-in-chief of the army, and them to lead against all rebels, traitors, and other common enemies, and them to kill and slay all such as by force oppose them. Also giving him power to exercise martial law, according to the Rules of War, and the Laws and Ordinances confirmed this present Parliament, which were to be read in the head of his army. Likewise, that he should have command over all castles, garrisons, or towns fortified, or to be fortified, not removing or displacing the governors. That he should have power to nominate a provost marshal, or marshals for the executing his commands, and to command waggons, carts or boats, for the carriage of his ordnance, ammunition or provisions, as there shall be occasion.[1]

1 *LJ*, VII, p.209; John Rushworth, *Historical Collections of Private Passages of State* (London: D. Browne, 1721), VI, p.12.

Sir Thomas had campaigned with his father, Ferdinando, Lord Fairfax, in Yorkshire during 1643 and 1644, while his leading role at Nantwich (January 1644) and Selby (April 1644), established a reputation as an audacious cavalry officer, a stern disciplinarian, and a skilled commander. Joshua Sprigge contended that Sir Thomas Fairfax was chosen to command the New Model, 'to which trust and honour he was preferred upon no other grounds, that the observation of his valour, and all answerable abilities for the same, testified in many notable services done by him in the North, while he was yet in a lower sphere.'[2] There is little space within the current study to consider more fully the reasons why Fairfax was appointed, suffice to say that some popular accounts have depicted a simplistic figure who was 'well-liked and trusted on all sides'.[3] Furthermore, more recent scholars have significantly questioned assumptions about his supposed lack of political acumen and ambition, and role within the army. As Andrew Hopper notes:

> A closer investigation of why and how Fairfax was appointed commander-in-chief challenges such views. It fell to Fairfax, not Cromwell, to structure the new army, appoint its officers and overcome political hostility in Parliament before taking the field. Fairfax was better equipped than Cromwell to do this. His concept of honour that stressed humility and shrank from personal advancement helped undermine hostility to his appointment. Yet his lack of ambition should not be interpreted as evidence that he was divorced from Westminster politics.[4]

On 11 January 1645 the initial establishment of the New Model Army was revised to 22,000 men, comprising 6,600 horse, 14,400 foot and 1,000 dragoons.[5] There would, it was intended, be 11 regiments of cavalry, each with 6 troops of 100 troopers, plus commissioned and non-commissioned officers; 12 infantry regiments, each with 10 companies and a nominal strength of 1,200 men; and one regiment of dragoons of 10 companies, each of 100 men, besides officers. Of these, three cavalry regiments and four of foot came from Essex's Army, nine of horse and four of foot from the Eastern Association, and the remaining two regiments of foot from Sir William Waller's forces. It has been assumed that the cavalry regiments were already up to strength, however, the documents recording the addition of recruits, and the supply of horses, saddles and weapons to the various regiments do not bear this out. The New Model was overseen by the Committee for the Army, specially established in March 1645 under the chairmanship of Robert Scawen MP. He was also concerned with the administration of the Ordnance Office, located within the Tower of London.[6] The Committee was authorised to procure all the arms, ammunition, equipment, and

2 Joshua Sprigge, *Anglia Rediviva or England's Recovery* (London: 1647), p.7.
3 For instance, see Maurice Ashley, *Cromwell's Generals* (London: Jonanthan Cape, 1954), pp.14–16.
4 Andrew Hopper, *'Black Tom': Sir Thomas Fairfax and the English Revolution* (Manchester: Manchester University Press, 2007), p.54.
5 *CJ*, IV, pp.16–17; *CSPD 1644–1645*, p.205.
6 TNA, WO47/1, ff. 96r–97v.

clothing required for the army and the train of artillery as the Commons should direct or as itself thought fit.[7] Additionally, it would receive into its charge and prove all munitions, and other military stores which had been contracted for. The Ordinance establishing the New Model, permitted Fairfax to choose his own officers 'out of any forces under the command of Parliament', although these came almost entirely from the armies of Manchester, Essex and Waller.[8]

The initial list of colonels for Fairfax's Army was agreed on 21 January 1645, but a bitter wrangle ensued, partly in relation to the preferred religious makeup of the officer corps. However, the new establishment could not embrace all serving officers from previous armies, and 6 originally nominated colonels stood down or were changed. Colonels James Holbourne and Edward Aldridge resigned – Holbourne obeying instructions from the Scottish government that he was not to serve in the New Model because of the radical religious beliefs of some of the English officers, while Aldridge was unsatisfied with the officers he had been allotted. Colonel Edward Aldridge began his military service as lieutenant colonel in Colonel Rochford's regiment of foot in the Earl of Essex's Army. In 1643 he succeeded Sir John Meldrum as colonel of the regiment first raised and commanded by Viscount Saye and Sele. The regiment was wearing blue coats in 1642, though it may not have benefitted from the issue of red and grey garments to Essex's foot at Gloucester in August the following year as it was garrisoning Aylesbury at the time.[9] At Sir Thomas Fairfax's request, Aldridge remained in post for a few weeks but left in early May 1645.

Aldridge's regiment was then given to Colonel Walter Lloyd, who was subsequently killed at the relief of Taunton. On 28 March 1645 Aldridge wrote to Sir Thomas Fairfax:

> In the interim of my coming to Reading, your letter being sent down and returned to London, and back again hath delayed my answer (I fear) too long; I much marvel at the nomination of the list of my regiment. I shall humbly desire if possible my former list might stand with the addition of a more able major and captains as my list may inform you, for having made inquiry I perceive some to be put to me of weak resolutions, so as I cannot conceive, it will be both dishonourable for me to engage with them, as also may prove prejudicial to the cause and service we undertake, yet my lieutenant colonel in my absence hath given notice to all according to your commands, but cannot hear of Captain Smith, I have enclosed a list of my officers now standing, with the number of soldiers as also my opinion in two lists concerning the new and old officers which appears to me so great concernment (besides the love of the soldiers which must be looked upon) that if not rightly stated, I shall humbly desire (though my resolutions to

7 *CJ*, IV, p.78; *A&O*, I, p.828.

8 *LJ*, VII, p.209.

9 Wood, *Life and Times*, pp.66–67; *A Perfect Diurnall of Passages of the Souldiers, that are under the Command of the Lord Say in Oxford* (London: 1642). TT, E122[13]; *Exceeding Joyfull Newes From the Earl of Essex Being a true and reall Relation of His incompassing the Kings Army neare the Citty of Oxford, Decemb. 7* (London: 1642). TT, E124[33].

> be proceed) to desist rather than engage with dishonour, which of necessity must follow, I leave all to your noble consideration being your humble servant to be commanded.

On 9 April Fairfax replied,

> I received your letter and what you desire in it I do very well approve of but shall entreat you for three or four days to stay with the regiment till I can dispose of it, which I think will be to your lieutenant colonel whom I hear much worth of. Sir, I cannot but give you thanks for so fair an advertisement and shall ever remain your assured friend to serve you.[10]

The initial list of officers did not include a colonel of dragoons, and it is possible that individual companies were to be attached to each cavalry regiment, or to operate as independent units. Nevertheless, on 3 March 1645 Parliament resolved that 'the dragoons shall be formed into a regiment. The colonel and officers of dragoons were all reported and approved.'[11] Fairfax may have considered Lieutenant Colonel John Lilburne of the Earl of Manchester's dragoons, for the colonelcy, but he refused to sign the Solemn League and Covenant, which was required of New Model Army officers following the alliance between Parliament and the Scots. The colonelcy instead went to John Okey, a London drayman and stoker, who had previously served as captain of dragoons and horse under Essex and Lord Brooke.[12] The first and second lists of officers represented a diverse mix of officers, some of whom had served together before. However, the lists differ markedly, and it is evident that by June 1645 there had been a change in half of the senior officers. The strength of the New Model's dragoon regiment remained a concern to Sir Thomas Fairfax, and he continued to find ways of reinforcing it.

Command of the New Model Army's foot went to Sir Philip Skippon, who had performed the same role in Essex's Army. A Norfolk gentleman, he was a professional soldier of Continental experience and was highly respected by his men, though he received a serious wound at Naseby in June 1645. According to the list provided by Joshua Sprigge, chaplain to Sir Thomas Fairfax and the army's 'official historian', the commanding officers of the 12 regiments of foot in May 1645 were:

> Sir Thomas Fairfax
> Sergeant-Major Sir Philip Skippon
> Colonel Sir Hardress Waller
> Colonel Robert Hammond
> Colonel Richard Fortescue
> Colonel Richard Ingoldsby
> Colonel Thomas Rainborowe

10 Bodl. Lib., Ms Tanner 60/1, ff. 33r, 34r.
11 *CJ*, IV, pp.65–67.
12 TNA, SP28/144/2, ff. 1r–7r; SP28/143/1, f. 27r; E121/2/3/43A/1; Wanklyn, *Reconstructing*, I, pp.50, 60, 71.

Colonel Ralph Weldon
Colonel Edward Harley
Colonel Edward Montague
Colonel Walter Lloyd

Overall command of the cavalry was given to Colonel Bartholomew Vermuyden, nonetheless he resigned his commission on 8 June, whereupon Sir Thomas Fairfax ignored the House of Lords' refusal to permit him to appoint Oliver Cromwell as Lieutenant General of the horse and colonel of Vermuyden's regiment, thus making him one of the few exceptions to the Self-Denying Ordinance. As Member of Parliament for Huntingdon Cromwell was also a highly experienced cavalry officer in the Earl of Manchester's army, and had notable successes at Gainsborough and Marston Moor.

Commanding officers of the 11 regiments of horse:

Sir Thomas Fairfax
Colonel Thomas Butler
Colonel Thomas Sheffield
Colonel Charles Fleetwood
Colonel Edward Rossiter
Lieutenant-General Oliver Cromwell
Colonel Nathaniel Rich
Colonel Sir Robert Pye
Colonel Richard Graves
Commissary General Henry Ireton
Colonel Edward Whalley[13]

Having received his commission Fairfax began the task of reducing the armies of Essex, Manchester and Waller, although his immediate priority was the formation of the New Model's foot and train of artillery. One key question concerns the actual strength of the New Model Army in May and June 1645. Peter Young, in his book on Naseby suggested 6,400 foot, 7,200 horse and 1,000 dragoons, a total of 14,600 as being present; Maurice Ashley estimated 8,000 foot and 7,000 horse, a total of 15,000, which may, or may not, include Okey's dragoons. More recently, Glenn

13 Sprigge, *Anglia Rediviva*, pp.328–331. For an in-depth discussion of the early formation and composition of the regiments of the New Model Army, see C. H. Firth, and Godfrey Davis, *The Regimental History of Cromwell's Army*, 2 vols (Oxford: Clarendon Press, 1940); Ian Gentles, *The New Model Army in England, Ireland, and Scotland, 1645–1653* (Oxford: Blackwell, 1992), chapters 1 & 2; Barry Denton, *Cromwell's Soldiers: The Moulding of the New Model Army 1644–1645* (Privately published: 2005); Glenn, Foard, *Naseby: The Decisive Campaign* (Barnsley: Pen & Sword, 2004 edn), chap. 3; Malcolm Wanklyn, 'Choosing Officers for the New Model Army, February to May 1645', *JSAHR*, 92 (2014), pp.109–125; *Reconstructing the New Model Army Volume 1: Regimental Lists April 1645 to May 1649* (Solihull: Helion and Co., 2015), *passim*. Due to the range of archival material, especially that among the Commonwealth Exchequer Papers, now available to study, but to which Firth and Davis had limited access, some of their conclusions have been updated more recently.

Foard thought fewer than 8,720 foot, 7,200 horse and 1,000 dragoons, a total of about 17,000. Though useful, such computations are difficult to achieve because precise strengths of units are rarely found in contemporary documents. Moreover, there are chronological gaps in the records, and during the Naseby campaign a New Model brigade consisting of 3,000 infantry and one cavalry regiment (Graves' – formerly the Earl of Essex's) was detached from the main army to aid the besieged garrison of Taunton. David Blackmore's 'educated estimates' of the strengths of regiments presented in surviving pay warrants are most useful, in that they are based on the theoretical rates of pay for officers and soldiers, as well as the assumption – largely from the army's establishment – that each unit contained 10 commissioned officers in its ranks.[14] Hence, with some approximation, we might suggest that the following, amounting to a total of just over 14,600 men were present at Naseby on 14 June 1645:

Regiments of Foot:

Fairfax's	1,397	Harley's	1,151
Skippon's	1,533	Montague's	1,025
Waller's	560	Lloyd's	93
Hammond's	788	Ingoldsby's	63
Rainborowe's	888	Fortescue's	
Pickering's	1,126	Weldon's	
			8,624

Regiments of Horse:

Fairfax's	489	Rossiter's	565
Cromwell's	542	Rich's	545
Ireton's	426	Pye's	616
Butler's	535	Walley's	506
Sheffield's	541	Graves'	
Fleetwood's	473	Lifeguard	50
			5,288

Colonel John Okey's Regiment of Dragoons, excluding officers:

Okey's company	75	Captain Farr's	55
Sergeant Major Moore's	65	Captain Bridge's	46
Captain Farmer's	105	Captain Wogan's	72
Captain Mercer's	82	Captain Skirmager's	53
Captain Abbot's	80	Captain Turpin's	61
			694

Although Lloyd's and Ingoldsby's regiments of foot were part of the brigade sent to relieve Taunton, some of the former marched with Skippon's, while a detachment from the latter accompanied Harley's regiment.[15] Given such numbers for the foot,

14 David Blackmore, 'Counting the New Model Army', *ECWT*, 58 (2004), pp.3–5.

15 TNA, SP28/30/2, ff. 412r, 427r, 451r, 453r, 506r, 509r.

horse and dragoons we must ask whether the New Model Army was created as a single field force, or was it constantly to be divided into brigades? Sprigge mentioned that Colonel Thomas Rainborowe commanded a brigade at Bristol in September 1645, which contained his own, Skippon's, Harley's and Hammond's regiments.[16] It worth noting that besides Weldon's regiment, which came from Waller's forces, Fortescue's, Lloyd's and Ingoldsby's regiments originated in Essex's Army. In terms of the New Model cavalry, Colonel Richard Graves' regiment was absent in the West Country in mid-1645 and during 1645 and 1646 only operated with the main forces on one occasion.

Furthermore, the 8 regiments of New Model foot at Naseby probably formed two brigades. In his schema of the battle Robert Streeter depicted a front line of five regiments, supported by a second, 'reserve', line of three regiments. Streeter was not present at the battle, however, and his interpretation is misleading. The eye-witness account of George Bishop, who *was* there, stated:

> The infantry was thus ordered: in the right wing the General's, Colonel Montague's, Colonel Pickering's and Colonel Sir Waller's regiments; in the left, Major General Skippon's, Colonel Bartlett's [Harley's, commanded by Lieutenant Colonel Thomas Pride], Colonel Rainborowe's and Colonel Hammond.[17]

This is supported by Sprigge, who stated that initially 'The General, together with the Major-General, put the several brigades of foot into order.'[18] Once in position, Skippon redeployed his own regiment further forward to lengthen the army's frontage and in order to outflank the Royalists' shorter line. Consequently, the second line or 'reserve' consisted of (r-l) Harley's/Pride's, Hammond's and Rainborowe's, with a small body of foot to the rear – Pride's command was split into two divisions to cover the ground vacated by Skippon.

On 14 April Skippon reported to the Commons, 'Tomorrow, if the Lord will, I shall reduce and settle Colonel Weldon's and Colonel Holborne's regiments of foot, which were with Sir William Waller, and now quartered at Wokingham.'[19] Weldon's was selected for the New Model Army, 'in regard of the good service and good affection to the Parliament shown by the Committee of Kent, this House being confident they will be very good and able men.'[20] The regiment passed into service practically unchanged, although Parliament initially objected to some of its officers. Given the number of soldiers who re-enlisted into the New Model's foot, almost 7,000 men needed to be made up by conscripts from the county quotas which had

16 *A Narration of the Expedition to Taunton: The Raising the Siege before it, and the Condition of our Forces, and the Enemies, at this present in the West. Sent from a Commander in the Army, and dated at Chard, May 18. 1645*. TT. E285[10].

17 *A More Particular and Exact Relation of the Victory obtained by the Parliament's forces under the command of Sir Thomas Fairfax* (London: Richard Cotes, 1645). TT, E288[38].

18 Sprigge, *Anglia Rediviva*, pp.34–5.

19 Vicars, *Burning-Bush*, pp.133–4.

20 *LJ*, VII, pp.266, 279.

been previously set. Yet despite Fairfax's best efforts, there remained a shortage of infantrymen and his authority to impress recruits was repeatedly extended until mid-1646.

The Moderate Intelligencer reported for 18 April 1645:

> This day Sir Thomas Fairfax went to begin the taking on of the horse, he begins with Colonel Vermuyden, and goes on with that party that was under the command of the noble Earl of Manchester, no doubt the next week will reduce them also, and the horse as well as the foot, under the commanders appointed by the Lords and Commons.[21]

Hence, Manchester's own regiment mustered at Amersham Heath on 25 April and was absorbed into the New Model, with its former lieutenant colonel, Nathaniel Rich, taking command.[22] Cromwell's double regiment was divided into two, six troops went into Fairfax's own and another six into Colonel Edward Whalley's. However, Captain Margery, Cromwell's 'plain russet coated captain', was transferred to Sir Robert Pye's regiment of horse, whereas another troop went into Rich's regiment. Vermuyden's and Fleetwood's regiments also entered into the New Model.[23] Of the Earl of Essex's regiments, on 14 April 1645 Skippon wrote, 'Yesterday and this day all His Excellency's horse are reduced and settled into Colonel Graves', Sir Robert Pye's, and Colonel Sheffield's regiments, except Colonel Dalbier's and Colonel Beurs' regiments, which are commanded to Gloucester.[24]

Table 01: New Model Army Regiments, May-June 1645[25]

Horse

Colonel	Origin	Notes
Sir Thomas Fairfax	Army of the Eastern Association	6 troops from Cromwell's double regiment. Lifeguard originally added as sixth troop but removed
John Butler	Army of the Southern Association	Originally intended for Lt Gen. John Middleton. Formerly Sir Arthur Haselrige's regiment
Thomas Sheffield	Army of the Earl of Essex	Originally commanded by Colonel James Sheffield, succeeded by his brother. 3 captains formerly of Sheffield's regiment; 2 from Essex's regiment; 1 from Sir Arthur Balfour's regiment

21 *The Moderate Intelligencer*, 17–24 April 1645. TT, E278[26].
22 TNA, SP28/29/1, f. 285r.
23 TNA, SP28/29/1, f. 172r.
24 John Vicars, *The Burning-bush Not Consumed. Or, The Fourth and Last Part of the Parliamentarie-chronicle* (London: 1646), p.133.
25 Firth and Davies, *Regimental History, I, pp.317–452; II, pp.398–453; Malcolm* Wanklyn, 'Choosing Officers for the New Model Army February to April 1645', *JSAHR*, 92 (2014), pp.109–25; *Reconstructing*, I, pp.23–64.

Colonel	Origin	Notes
Charles Fleetwood	Army of the Eastern Association	5 captains from Fleetwood's former regiment; 1 from Waller's Southern Association regiment
Edward Rossiter	Army of the Eastern Association	Regiment transferred to the New Model Army in spring 1645
Oliver Cromwell	Army of the Eastern Association	Vermuyden's former regiment. 4 captains from Vermuyden's regiment; 1 from Sir John Norwich's regiment; 1 (Captain John Reynolds) unknown
Nathaniel Rich	Army of the Eastern Association	Earl of Manchester's regiment. Originally intended for Colonel Algernon Sidney. 4 troop commanders from Manchester's regiment; Captain Thomas Ireton from Cromwell's regiment; Captain William Bough from Waller's regiment in Southern Association
Sir Robert Pye	Army of the Eastern Association	Originally intended for Rich. All troop commanders from Manchester's army; Captain Ralph Margery from Cromwell's double regiment; junior officers and rank and file of Pye's own troop mainly from Essex's Army
Edward Whalley	Army of the Eastern Association	6 troops from Cromwell's double regiment
Richard Graves	Army of the Earl of Essex	Earl of Essex's regiment
Henry Ireton	Army of the Southern Association	Initially led by Sir Michael Livesey, who had commanded it in Waller's army

Dragoons

Company commander	Origin/notes
Colonel John Okey	Captain in Colonel Richard Browne's dragoons, Lord Brooke's regiment of horse, captain and sergeant major in Haselrige's regiment of horse in Waller's Army
Sgt Major Nicholas Moore	Captain in Sir William Waller's regiment of foot/dragoons
Captain John Farmer	Captain in Sir William Balfour's regiment of horse in Essex's Army
Captain Christopher Mercer	Captain in Manchester's/Lilburne's regiment of dragoons in Eastern Association Army
Captain Daniel Abbot	Captain in Manchester's/Lilburne's regiment of dragoons in Eastern Association Army
Captain Ralph Farr	Lieutenant to Okey in Haselrig's horse
Captain Tobias Bridge	Captain in Manchester's/Lilburne's regiment of dragoons in Eastern Association Army
Captain Edward Wogan	Captain in Waller's regiment of foot/dragoons
Captain Harold Skirmager	Captain in Waller's regiment of foot/dragoons
Captain William Turpin	Captain in Waller's/Holborne's regiment of dragoons

Foot

Colonel	Origin	Notes
Sir Thomas Fairfax	Army of the Eastern Association/ Earl of Essex	8 captains from Eastern Association (including 5 from Manchester's regiment), 1 from Essex's regiment, 1 (Richard? Cooke junior) unknown but he had served in the London garrison in early 1645
Sir Phillip Skippon	Army of the Earl of Essex	Amalgam of Skippon's old regiment, and 2 weak regiments of Manchester's army – Sir Thomas Hogan's and Sir Miles Hobart's
Sir Hardress Waller	Army of the Southern Association	Originally intended for Colonel James Holborne. Companies moved *en bloc* into Waller's regiment
Robert Hammond	Army of the Eastern Association	Originally commanded by Maj. Gen. Lawrence Crawford. 4 captains from Crawford's Eastern Association regiment, 2 from Manchester's regiment, 3 from Colonel James Hobart's disbanded regiment, 1 (John Boyce) unknown, but had served in Manchester's
Richard Fortescue	Army of the Earl of Essex	Passed *en bloc* into the New Model Army
Richard Ingoldsby	Army of the Earl of Essex	Probably formed from drafts of the 5 reduced regiments of Essex's Army. 5 company commanders from Ingoldsby's own regiment, 2 from Essex's regiment, 1 from Lord Robartes' regiment; 2 – Sergeant Major Richard Cromwell's and Captain Francis Allen's unknown, though Cromwell had probably been in Picking's regiment of Manchester's army
Thomas Rainborowe	Mixture	Originally intended for Colonel Thomas Ayloffe of the Abingdon garrison. Command given to Rainborowe, a colonel in the Eastern Association but not in Manchester's field army. Contained no company commanders from Rainborowe's old regiment. In May 1645 3 were from Ayloffe's, 3 from other regiments in Manchester's army, 2 had served in Essex's Army; the origins of the lieutenant colonel and Captain John Edwards are uncertain
Ralph Weldon	Army of the Southern Association	7 (possibly 8) company commanders from Weldon's Kentish regiment, origins of 2 captains uncertain, although John Munday had served in Devon
Edward Harley	Army of the Eastern Association	Originally intended for Colonel Harry Barclay. Harley did not serve in 1645, as he was still recovering from wounds; regiment commanded by Lt Colonel Thomas Pride
Edward Montague	Army of the Eastern Association	Passed *en bloc* into the New Model Army

Colonel	Origin	Notes
Walter Lloyd	Army of the Earl of Essex	Originally intended for Colonel Edward Aldridge. Regiment an amalgam of 3 others from Essex's Army: 6 companies from Aldridge's old regiment, 2 from Colonel William Davies', 2 from Lord Robartes'
John Pickering	Army of the Eastern Association	Passed *en bloc* into the New Model Army, though reinforced with drafts from Colonel Ayloffe's reduced regiment

Also included in the establishment of the New Model Army's horse was Sir Thomas Fairfax's Lifeguard. This was originally intended to form a troop in his regiment, but on paper it remained separate. Both Captain Charles Doyley and Captain Lieutenant Henry Hall, had previously served in Essex's Lifeguard. Troopers or gentlemen were paid '3s. per day each more than an ordinary trooper', while on 25 April 1645 '28 fine plunket coats' (plunket being a blue-grey or sea-green colour), were purchased from Richard Downes, costing £1 19s. 3d. each. The Lifeguard also received 40 pairs pistols and holsters, 40 saddles and '40 able horses, geldings and mares at £9 apiece'.[26]

26 TNA, SP28/29/2, f. 254r; SP28/140/7, f. 276v; WO47/1, f. 242v.

2

The Committee for the Army, the Ordnance Office, and the Train of Artillery

The Committee for the Army

When the New Model Army was formed in spring 1645, a single monthly assessment on all counties under Parliamentarian control was to be paid into the central treasury in London. Additionally, the City of London provided a loan of £80,000 secured on future assessment revenues to finance the cost of equipping Sir Thomas Fairfax's forces.[1] In terms of procurement and supply the New Model was overseen by the Committee for the Army, specially established in March 1645 under the chairmanship of Robert Scawen MP. He was also concerned with the internal administration of the Ordnance Office, located within the Tower of London.[2] Sir Walter Erle, Lieutenant of the Ordnance from 1644 to 1645, and 1647 to 1648, was also one of its leading members. In 1645 the Army Committee was authorised to contract for all victuals, arms, ammunition, clothing, horses, and other necessaries required for the summer's campaign, that is, for the New Model Army, in addition to the train of artillery as the Commons should direct or as the Committee should think fit.[3] On 24 March 1645 the Committee for the Army ordered the Officers of the Ordnance to receive into their charge and to prove all munitions, and other military stores which had been contracted for. The Committee's powers were renewed on 15 January 1646.

Fundamentally, the Committee for the Army oversaw a largely integrated logistical endeavour that comprised 2 mutually compatible elements: the train of artillery, whose primary responsibility – save for the movement and maintenance of the New Model Army's ordnance capability – was to hold and distribute 'front line' stocks of ammunition and victuals (in the form of cheese and biscuit), in addition to quantities of clothing, weapons and tools, directly to regiments, troops and companies in the field. Moreover, the Office of the Ordnance, guided by the Committee, operated a supply system based upon the utilisation of land and maritime transportation of stores, in which the army's Waggonmaster General, chartered civilian carriers and waggons, and military commissaries sustained Sir Thomas Fairfax's forces during its operations of 1645 and 1646. This it did from its central base in

1 *A&O*, I, p.656.
2 TNA, WO47/1, ff. 96r–97v.
3 *CJ*, IV, p.78; *A&O*, I, p.828.

London, in addition to the army's logistical centres at Reading and magazines along the New Model's line of march.

The Ordnance Office

The origins of the Office of the Ordnance can be traced to the early part of the reign of Edward I (1239–1307) when the Privy Wardrobe began to act as an itinerant armoury for the Royal Household during the Welsh Wars. However, it was in the Tudor period that major reforms occurred within the Office. As military conflict became increasingly apparent during the summer of 1642, both King and Parliament sought possession of the Ordnance Office and the Tower stores, being the country's principal magazine, in addition to the allegiance of its employees. The Ordnance Office also supplied castles, garrisons, and magazines under its jurisdiction, but additionally, if desired, county forces. During August 1642 Parliament took effective steps to secure control of the Office, and in August 1642 Parliament ordered the Lieutenant of the Ordnance 'not to permit any ordnance, arms, ammunition, or other warlike provisions, to be shipped or carried from Tower Wharf, or any other wharf belonging to the jurisdiction or liberty of the Tower, without his licence, and the House being first acquainted therewith.'[4] The Commons subsequently barred from the Tower those officers who refused to submit to its authority, and on 24 August Parliament was reported to be in possession of the Ordnance Office.[5] In late 1642 its personnel comprised the Lieutenant of the Ordnance, the Surveyor of the Ordnance, the Clerk of the Ordnance, the Keeper of the Stores, the Clerk of Deliveries, the Master Gunner, the Keeper of the Small Guns, the Keeper of the Rich Weapons, 7 clerks, 11 artificers belonging to the ordinary or salaried establishment – including a plumber, a ladle maker, a smith, a carpenter, a wheelwright, a fletcher, a bowyer, 1 cooper, 2 furbishers, and one Proof Master – a messenger, and 20 labourers.[6] There were a few fluctuations in this number, but overall it remained fairly static. The personnel employed by the Ordnance Office also included, in some instances, deputies, apprentices and a casual labour force when required urgently. The Committee of Both Kingdoms issued a warrant to the Officers of the Ordnance on 22 April 1645 to 'called to be impressed 8 carpenters and wheelwrights to be employed by Thomas Bateman, wheelwright, and 6 smiths to be employed by Thomas Hodgkins, smith' in making carriages for the New Model Army's train of artillery.[7]

Following the outbreak of war in 1642 the King's Office of the Ordnance was relocated from the Tower of London to Oxford, where a new establishment was overseen by William Legge, the Master of the Armouries. The provision of ordnance, ammunition, and firearms for the Royalist army during the early months of the conflict was a matter of immediate concern, particularly as his forces had very little

4 *CJ*, II, p.699.
5 TNA, WO55/1754, f. 1r.
6 TNA, WO54/14-16, *passim*.
7 TNA, WO47/1, f. 227v.

access to London's manufacturing industries.[8] The importance of the Ordnance Office was emphasised by Edward Chamberlayne, who wrote in the 4th edition of *Angliæ Notitia, or the present state of England together with divers reflections upon the antient state thereof*:

> Within the Tower is kept the office of her Majesty's Ordnance, which has always been an office of great account and importance, as being the only standing and grand magazine of the principal preparatives, habiliments, utensils and instruments of war, as well as by sea and land, for the defence and safety of the Kingdom. And consequently has influence in the navies, forts, castles and armies thereof, having the superintendence, ordering and disposing as well of the grand magazine lodged in the Tower as at the Minories, Woolwich, Chatham, Windsor, Portsmouth, Hull and elsewhere, wherein is ammunition at all times for as many land and sea forces as may not only defend England, but be formidable to all our neighbours.[9]

Contracts

The Committee for the Army agreed numerous contracts involving the procurement of large quantities of munitions and other stores during 1645 and 1646. These were notified to the Officers of the Ordnance in advance, but entries in the books of receipts show that such notifications could range between months to single days in some cases. The Committee continued to make contracts on behalf of the Army until the end of the Civil Wars. During 1648 it assumed responsibility for procuring ammunition, weapons and ordnance for certain garrisons, including Hereford and Chester as well. The contracts made by the Committee with suppliers – mainly from London – were generally sent to the Ordnance Office in batches, accompanied by instructions to the officers to 'take notice hereof and see that the provisions be answerable to the agreements, and for as many provisions as they shall receive in and allow to certify the same unto this Committee.' Hence, one set was notified to 'the Honourable Committee for the Army' by Erle and Thomas Hammond, the Lieutenant General of the Ordnance, on 10 January 1646. According to 'the order and direction of the Committee' they had agreed with 7 suppliers – including 'John Wallington and John Coate, turners', and 'Joshua Foote, ironmonger' – to provide various tools and accessories for the train of artillery.

They added, 'these provisions are to be brought into the stores by the first day of March next', although two Ordnance Office officials, Robert Baddeley and Everard Walton, testified *Vera Copia* ('A true copy') of the original indenture and *Exam*

8 Ian Roy (ed.), *The Royalist Ordnance Papers, 1642–1646*, I (Oxfordshire Record Society, 1964), introduction; H. C. Tomlinson, *Guns and Government: The Ordnance Office under the Later Stuarts* (London: Royal Historical Society, 1979), pp.1–4.

9 Edward Chamberlayne, *Angliæ Notitia, or the present state of England together with divers reflections upon the antient state thereof* (London: 4th edn, 1673), p.224.

per nos ('Examined by us'). On 20 January, the Committee for the Army issued a warrant, in which it approved 'these contracts and do desire that the Officers of the Ordnance will take notice thereof and carefully see that the provisions be answerable to the agreements. And for as many of the provisions as they shall receive in and allow to certify the same unto this Committee.'[10] Thus, following the receipt and scrutiny of the stores at the Tower, the supplier was issued with a bill. Upon presentation of this bill, a debenture was produced by the Officers of the Ordnance and a copy subsequently entered in the book of debentures. It was not uncommon for formal notification of a contract to reach the Ordnance Office after the proscribed items had been delivered into the stores. Thus, a contract for the supply of muskets and pistols agreed on 22 November 1645 was received at the Office on 19 December, 11 days later than the date of the receipt of the stores. Another letter from the Committee dated 16 January 1646, giving details of contracts for the supply of muskets, pistols, and pikes was received by the Surveyor on 19 March, by which time some of the arms had already been brought in. From December 1645 the Officers of the Ordnance were required to mark each batch of munitions delivered to the Army magazine with a serial number for identification purposes and perhaps also to ensure that the oldest stocks were issued first.[11]

When the Officers of the Ordnance were themselves responsible for agreeing indentures, they usually did so at the instigation of either the Committee for the Army or the Committee of Both Kingdoms. However, the officers seem to have exercised the right to make contracts for the cleaning and repair of weapons. These were agreed both with the furbishers employed at the Ordnance Office, as well as gunsmiths and cutlers in the City.[12] The overall pattern of contracting was such that clothing, gunpowder, match and shot were supplied in the main by a limited number of substantial contractors who were often contracted with for large quantities. Sometimes they were required to deliver in various batches over an extended period, sometimes when not all the agreed sums of money were available, or as much as a particular merchant could produce with the materials at their disposal. For instance, on 7 April 1645 John Berisford – a substantial supplier of munitions to the New Model Army – was contracted for 130 barrels of English gunpowder at £4 10s. per barrel, one-half in hand, the rest at 3 months. He delivered 65 barrels on 14 April, for which he received the sum of £292 10s. the following day, and the remaining amount upon completion of the agreement.[13]

Such large and expensive contracts were, however, outnumbered by the usually smaller agreements for the supply of arms and equipment which involved a range of individuals acting in a consortium or partnership. Thus, the London merchants Stephen Estwick, Thomas Player, Tempest Milner, Maurice Gethin, and John Pocock

10 TNA, WO47/1, ff. 208r–211r, 289r–290v; WO55/460, unfol.; ML, Ms 46 78/108, ff. 29r–31v.

11 TNA, WO55/1662, f. 77v; WO55/1663, *passim*; MS 46 78/708, *passim*.

12 TNA, WO47/1, ff. 1r, 20r, 177r.

13 TNA, WO47/1, f. 233v; SP28/29/1, f. 130r; SP28/140/1, f. 6v; MS 46 78/708, f. 42r; Bodl. Lib., Ms Eng. hist. C14, f. 16r. An undated notification of a contract for a similar item exists in MS 46 78/708, f. 42r, although the entry has '5 months' instead of 3; this possibly relates to the WO47/1 debenture, and the date was entered incorrectly, or it could relate to a different contract entirely.

furnished 4,500 coats, breeches, shirts, and pairs of stockings costing 17s. per set on 9 February 1646. An acquittance signed by Estwick for £2,339 1s. 3d. demonstrates that they received half this amount on 6 March, and the remainder 21 days later.[14] Importantly, although the total amounts delivered by such partnerships were relatively extensive, the quantities stipulated in individual contracts were often quite small. The result was a proliferation of minor suppliers – in some cases tradesmen and women combined either in their craft guild or in private groups – who were able to share the market with more substantial merchants and manufacturers.

The Train of Artillery

On 10 March 1645 Scawen reported from the Committee at Grocers Hall an estimate of the arms to be provided for the Ordnance Office magazines, in that the sum of £31,989 should be provided for furnishing a magazine of arms for horse and foot, and clothes for the foot of the New Model Army. He also demanded that £4,406 be provided for the supply of the New Model Army's train of artillery. The following day, Sir Thomas Fairfax authorised by the Lords and Commons:

> for the more speedy raising, perfecting, and completing of the army whereof he is appointed commander-in-chief, shall have power to take into the same all such lieutenants, sergeants, and other under-officers and soldiers as he shall think fit, as well of horse as foot, now or late in the several armies under the immediate commands of the Lord General the Earl of Essex, the Earl of Manchester, and Sir William Waller; and likewise all gunners, gentlemen of the ordnance, and other officers and soldiers belonging to the several Trains of Artillery in the said several armies.[15]

The establishment for the New Model Army train of artillery was proposed by the Committee for the Army and passed by the Commons on 5 March 1645. An alternative scheme, entitled 'A list of the Train of Artillery consisting of 30 pieces of ordnance with an estimate how many horses will draw the ordnance waggons and utensils belonging to such a train, also how many waggons, carts and tumbrels etc.' aimed at reducing the number of personnel, horses, vehicles, and overall costs was presented by the Committee of Accounts but was rejected.[16] The train was commanded by Lieutenant General Thomas Hammond, uncle to Colonel Robert Hammond – commander of a regiment of foot in the New Model – and a highly experienced officer, having served on the Continent in the Thirty Years' War, then later as Lieutenant General of the Ordnance to the Eastern Association Army, and commander of the regiment of firelocks guarding its artillery train.[17] However, most

14 TNA, SP28/140/3, unfol.; Bodl. Lib., Ms Eng. hist. C14, f. 78v.
15 *CJ*, IV p.76.
16 TNA, SP28/145, ff. 60r–63v; SP28/225, unfol.
17 *CSPD 1644*, p.224; Sprigge, *Anglia Rediviva*, pp.326–327, 329–330.

of the operational management of the artillery in the field appears to have been undertaken by Captain Richard Deane, the Comptroller of the Ordnance.

In describing the enormously responsible and complex role of the 'General of the Ordnance', Elton wrote:

> his duty and care must be in the day of battle, to see that the ordnance be well placed; for at such time his wisdom is most discerned, keeping (with the assistance of his lieutenant) the Train of Artillery together in good order. He must have a vigilant eye upon all accidents that may fall, and make choice of such ground for their planting, as the general of the army and he shall think most fit and convenient. He must be careful that all things be in a readiness, putting the master, gunners, gentlemen of the ordnance, and commanders in mind of their duty, that they do their best endeavours, and acquit themselves like men. It is likewise partly his charge to see that the whole army be well provided with ammunition, because the ammunition marches under his train. He must also be near the general of the army upon all occasions, to receive his directions and commands, and to know from him after what manner he will make his battle, that he may plant his ordnance accordingly, finding out hills and heights to play over his own men. And when the enemy shall present himself, and come up to charge, he must draw, and plant his ordnance as near their horse as possible may be, to hinder them from breaking in upon the divisions of foot, taking along with him sailors, and pioneers, to help to draw up the ordnance, and sufficient guards to defend them.[18]

The Earl of Essex's train was reduced in early April 1645 with most of its officers and artificers receiving a fortnight's pay before being discharged. At this point it was fragmented across three locations, with 99 of those at Reading (about one-third of the total present) being paid £528 by Captain Deane on 6 April and disbanded the next day. This was followed by those at Windsor on 9 April, and finally the bridge of boats detachment at Colnbrook – along with the Earl of Manchester's train of artillery – were stood down on 14 April. Four days later, Matthew Martin, paymaster to the train, received £330 2s. 9d. for 14 days' pay 'for the officers, artificers, firelocks, pioneers and horses belonging to train according to the muster taken at Colebrook the 15th day instant.'[19] At least one of those reduced at Reading, the engineer John Lyons, served in the New Model Army during 1645 and it is possible that others were returned to service, especially those at Windsor, wherein George Tompson as Gentleman of the Ordnance, Master Carpenter Thomas Hammond, Gunner James Dyer, Matrosses Thomas Boswell and George Arnold, Master Miner Isaiah Clothey, and 12 carters were brought into the new formation.

On 3 April 1645, a warrant was issued by the Army Committee to 'pay Lieutenant General Hammond £100 for removing that part of the Earl of Manchester's train that is at Cambridge and is to be employed under Sir Thomas Fairfax, and to pay the

18 Elton, *Complete Body*, p.175.

19 TNA, SP28/29/1, f. 30r; SP28/29/3, ff. 325r–326v, 344r–334v, 379r.

quarters of the draught horses as they come to the rendezvous from several counties.'[20] Moreover, on 23 April the same Committee ordered that all the ordnance, ammunition and equipment belonging to Manchester's former train, which had been sent from Cambridge, be delivered into the Tower stores. On the following day 5 field pieces, a mortar, ammunition, carts, gunners' implements, tools, and other accessories were brought into the Tower and Minories.[21] Although the personnel belonging to Essex's bridge of boats – consisting of 6 craft, transported on 6 carriages, with a further 9 carrying joists and planks – were disbanded, it was retained on the establishment of the New Model's train, even though the Accounts Committee had argued against it. Ninety horses were required for this task.[22] Fairfax's troops employed the bridge of boats during siege operations at Oxford in 1645 and 1646, and during their assault on the fortifications at Bridgwater on 11 July 1645, while each infantry soldier had cut a faggot, which he carried in addition to his musket or pike, Lieutenant General Hammond 'a gentleman of approved fidelity and of the most dextrous, and ripe invention' supervised the assembly of 8 moveable bridges 30–40 feet long. However, 'the difficulty of laying a bridge over the river [Parrett] through the violence of the current (which yet was necessary for the maintaining a communication between our quarters on both sides) hindered that design.'[23] Rushworth noted that 'carts with boats' were captured amongst the Royalist train at Naseby, whereas the newsbook *The Moderate Intelligencer* reported for 26 June 1645:

> The Royal boats taken in the late fight were sent to Gloucester. They are of excellent use to pass rivers which way soever the Army passes, but their being not many rivers except Severn in the West, and that being the border, they will be most useful there and so Gloucester the fittest place for them.[24]

A 'List of the officers, artificers and others of the Train of Artillery' agreed by Parliament lays out the function and pay rates of its personnel (amounting to 1,079 men), in addition to the number and type of ordnance (4 demi-culverins, 6 long sakers, 20 ordinary sakers and 2 mortars), the 'front line' stocks of powder and ammunition to be carried, as well as waggons, horses, tools and assorted warlike matériel. In mid-April one Parliamentarian-leaning newsbook declared, 'the artillery are coming up, and as brave a Train as in Christendom'.[25] According to a muster taken on 31 May 1645 the train of artillery, including officers, artificers, firelocks, pioneers and draught horses received five days' pay totalling £338 7s. 11d.[26] Integral to the train of artillery was its firelock guard. The establishment of the two firelock companies was 240 men 'with their officers in all'. At Reading on 29 April 1645, 7 days' wages were distributed to Lieutenant General Hammond 'for pay for 28 men

20 TNA, SP28/29/1, fol. 172r.
21 TNA, WO47/1, f. 229r; WO55/1664, ff. 21r–23v.
22 TNA, SP28/145, ff. 60r–63r.
23 Sprigge, *Anglia Rediviva*, p.69.
24 Rushworth, *Historical Collections*, VI, p.70.; *The Moderate Intelligencer*, 26 June–3 July 1645. TT, E288[37].
25 *The Moderate Intelligencer*, 10–17 April 1645. TT, E278[14].
26 TNA, SP28/30/4, f. 530r; SP28/145, ff. 61r–61v.

of his company of firelocks and 64 in Captain Deane's company, added to their companies as recruits since the last muster ... according to the muster taken from 28 April instant, the time of their first entry, to make them equal with the rest of the train.'[27] It is possible that the New Model's firelocks never reached their establishment strength of 240. When the Army mustered at Saffron Walden in May 1647 the 2 companies contained 22 commissioned and non-commissioned officers, and 166 soldiers between them.[28]

Treasurers' warrants provide further details of how the firelocks were equipped. On 11 April Hammond received money to furnish his regiment with 2 colours at £4 3s. apiece, 2 partizans at £1. 4s., and 4 halberds at £1. 4s. Similarly, the Committee for the Army ordered the Ordnance Office on 27 April to 'deliver to Lieutenant General Hammond, or his absence, Commissary Phipps, 4 drums out of the stores provided for Sir Thomas Fairfax his Army to furnish the firelocks of the train of artillery. Four days later, Phipps took delivery of 120 snaphaunce muskets for the supply of the train, in other words, to be issued to the firelock guard.[29] According to a list of the officers, artificers and others of the train proposed by the Committee for the Army in early March 1645, the firelocks should consist of 'men of as much use as of any other companies in the army, for without them there must be two or three other companies to guard the train, which by reason of their march may be very dangerous in regard of the powder, and so have better these than musketeers.'[30] This echoed Richard Elton's advice that 'Those who are ordained for their guard to be firelocks or to have snaphaunces for the avoiding of the danger that might happen by the coal of a match.'[31]

The New Model's firelock guard acquitted itself well at Naseby when the train they were protecting came under attack from Rupert's cavalry, an engagement which Foard suggests was 'a fierce engagement.'[32] Rushworth, who was with the train during the battle, documented the following eye-witness account of the opening stage of the encounter:

> A party of theirs broke through the left wing of horse, came quite behind the rear to our Train, the leader of them being a person somewhat in habit like the General, in a red Montero, as the General had, he came as a friend; our commander of the guard of the Train went with his hat in his hand, and asked him how the day went, thinking it had been the General; the cavalier whom we since heard was Rupert, asked him and the rest, if they would give quarter, they cried no, gave fire and instantly beat them off.[33]

27 TNA, SP28/29/1, f. 89r.

28 C. H. Firth (ed.), *The Clarke Papers: Selections from the Papers of William Clarke* (London: Royal Historical Society, 1992), I, p.19.

29 TNA, SP28/29/1, f. 209r; WO47/1, ff. 227r, 235r; WO55/1646, unfol.; Ms Salt 463, unfol.

30 TNA, SP28/145, ff. 60r–63v.

31 Richard Elton, *The Compleat Body of the Art Military* (London: Robert Leybourn, 1650), p.145.

32 Foard, *Naseby*, p.281.

33 *An Ordinance of the Lords and Commons assembled in Parliament ... Obtained against the Kings forces, nere Knasby in Northampton-shire the fourteenth of this instant Iune* (London: 16 June 1645). TT, E.288[26].

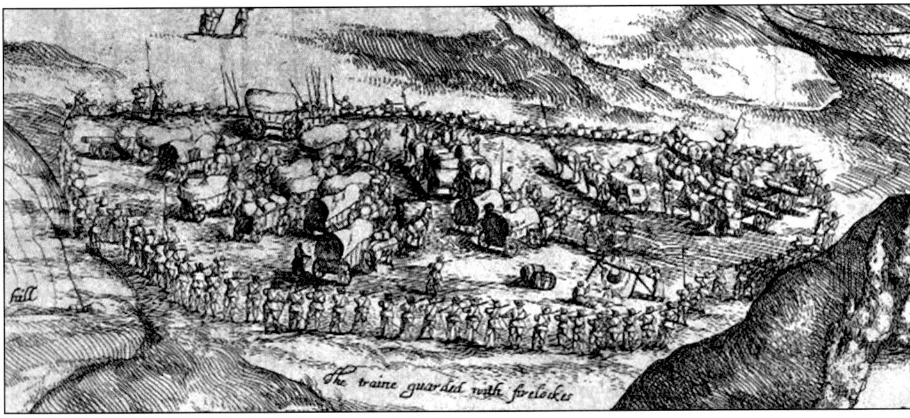

Streeter's depiction of the Firelocks guarding the Train of Artillery at Naseby.

The encounter was also reported by others, who wrote that during what appears to have been a sustained assault by Rupert, 'the firelocks, and rearguard left for that purpose ... fired with admirable courage on the Prince's horse.'[34] Among those listed among the New Model as seriously wounded during the Battle of Naseby are 'William Wells belonging to Train'; 'John Skidmore, Provost Marshall to the Train'; 'Isiah Clothey, Master of the Minories'; Thomas Benton, carpenter to the carriages'; 'Jeremiah Williams, waggonman'; 'Robert Gilbert, matross who lost his hand'; and 'Thomas Britton belonging to the carriages'. Moreover, Captains Potter and Cooke, both commissaries, later died of their wounds.[35] Sprigge also gives Robert Wolsey, Assistant to the Quartermaster General of Foot as receiving a wound.[36] By comparison, a pictorial plan drawn up by Fitz-Payne Fisher of the Battle of Dunbar in 1650 depicts the Scots baggage train placed behind the army.[37] Pulled tightly together, the waggons are secured by infantry or firelocks positioned around the perimeter. The entire train was captured by the victorious Commonwealth army commanded by Lieutenant General Oliver Cromwell.

On 5 May 1645 the Committee of Both Kingdoms wrote to Sir Thomas Fairfax:

> We send you a copy of the intelligence we have now received of the juncture of the Princes' forces with those of Goring now at or about Oxford. Considering the party left behind not to be sufficient, as we conceive, to oppose their motions and defend the Associations, we desire that Colonels Lloyd, Fortescue, Ingoldsby, and Weldon, with their regiments of foot, and Colonels Graves and Sheffield, with their regiments of horse, and such a train of artillery as you shall judge necessary, do with all possible expedition either by day or night march for the relief of Taunton, not delaying on their march. You will take order to put this party in such a way of command as may be best

34 Sprigge, *Anglia Rediviva*, p.38; *The Weekly Account*, 11–18 June 1645. TT, E4[18].
35 TNA, SP28/173/1, unfol.
36 Sprigge, *Anglia Rediviva*, p.38
37 Ashmolean Museum, University of Oxford, WA.Suth.C.3.293.1.

> for the service. We desire you and Major General Skippon, with the rest of the forces, upon intelligence held with Lieutenant General Cromwell, to join in such place as may be most for the advantage of the service.[38]

Various disbursements were also made during this period to the train of artillery, which offer clues to its composition and operations, part of which involved a portion of its capability being sent to support the New Model Army's operations to relieve the Parliamentarian garrison at Taunton. On 3 May 1645 the sum of £521 4s. 4d. was paid to Captain Richard Deane 'for 11 days' pay for the officers, artificers, firelocks, pioneers and horses appointed to go out in this present expedition to even their pay with the regiment [Colonel Richard Fortescue's regiment of foot] that go out with the same party'. Eleven days later Deane received a further £205 4s. 9¼d. 'for seven days' pay for the officers, artificers, firelocks, pioneers and horses belonging to part of the Train now at Whitchurch [13 miles south of Newbury] … commencing this day.' Similarly, a warrant issued on 18 May ordered the disbursement of £274 13s. 10d. for 14 days' pay 'for that part of the train of artillery that went to Taunton in the brigade commanded by Colonel Weldon, according to a muster taken 14 May last, commencing the same day.'[39] On 20 May the sum of £382 13s. 8d. was distributed to Matthew Martin, paymaster to the train for the segment mustered by Messrs Herbert and Leighton at Garsington, roughly 5 miles southeast of Oxford. This comprised 9 days' pay, commencing the day before 'to make them even with the rest of the train, and likewise for 14 days' pay for 622 draught horses mustered at Newbury and at Garsington by the said Commissioners of Parliament.' The next day, another £141 10s., was issued 'for 7 days' pay for the officers belonging to that part of the Train' mustered by Mr Herbert … the 17 May at Newbury commencing this present day.' The same was repeated on 22 May, whereas on 31 May 1645 it mustered again and was paid the sum of £338 7s. 11d. for 5 days' salary.[40]

Officers of the Train of Artillery, May 1645
Lieutenant General of the Ordnance: Thomas Hammond
Comptroller of the Ordnance: Captain Richard Deane
Chaplain to the Train: Master Hugh Peters
Engineer General: Peter Manteau van Dalem
Engineer Extraordinary: Captain Hooper
Chief Engineer: Eval Tercene
Engineers: Master Lyon, Master Tomlinson
Master Gunner of the Field: Master Francis Furin
Paymaster to the Train: Master Matthew Martin
Firelocks: Captain Lieutenant Desborough, Captain Lieutenant Brent

Officers of the Train of Artillery, December 1646
Lieutenant General of the Ordnance: Thomas Hammond

38 *CSPD 1644–5*, pp.458–9.
39 TNA, SP28/30/2, f. 213r; SP28/30/3, f. 200r; SP28/30/4, f. 530r.
40 TNA, SP28/30/2, f. 159r; SP28/30/3, ff. 215r–216v.

Comptroller of the Ordnance: Captain Richard Deane
Chaplain to the Train: Master Hugh Peters
Engineer General: Peter Manteau van Dalem
Engineer Extraordinary: Captain Hooper
Chief Engineer: Eval Tercene
Engineers: Master Lyon, Master Tomlinson
Master Gunner of the Field: Master Francis Furin
Paymaster to the Train: Master Matthew Martin
Firelocks: Captain Lieutenant Desborough, Captain Lieutenant Brent[41]

Table 02: Committee for the Army's proposed Establishment for the New Model Army Train of Artillery, March 1645[42]

Lieutenant General of the Ordnance	1	Pioneers	120
Comptroller	1	Master Smith	1
Comptroller's Clerks	2	Master Smith's Mates	2
Chief Engineer	1	Smiths	6
Chief Engineer's Clerk	1	Master Wheeler	1
Engineers	2	Master Wheeler's Mates	2
Conductors of Trenches	6	Wheelers	8
Chaplain	1	Master Farrier	1
Chaplain's Man	1	Farriers	6
Paymaster	1	Provost Marshal	1
Paymaster's Clerks	2	Provost Marshal's Man	1
Commissary for Ammunition	1	Gunmaker	1
Commissary for Ammunition's Clerks	2	Gunmaker's Men	2
Master Fireworker	1	Master Armourer	1
Assistant Fireworkers	4	Master Armourer's Men	3
Commissary Draught Horses	1	Basketmakers	4
Battery Master	1	Ladlemaker	1
Quartermaster	1	Ladlemaker's Mate	1
Waggonmaster	1	Cooper	1
Waggonmaster's Assistants	2	Cooper's Mate	1
Conductors of Ammunition	10	Tentmakers	2
Surgeon	1	Tentmaker's Mates	4
Surgeon's Mates	2	Master Ropemaker	1
Gentlemen of the Ordnance	14	Master Ropemaker's Man	1
Master Gunner	1	Master Collarmaker	1
Gunners	46	Master Collarmaker's Men	2
Matrosses	160	Bridgemaster (carpenter)	1
Master Miner	1	Bridgemaster's Assistant	1
Miners	4	Wheeler (for bridge of boats)	1
Master Carpenter	1	Wheeler's Mate	1
Master Carpenter's Mates	2	Boatwright	1

41 Sprigge, *Anglia Rediviva*, pp.326–327, 329–330.
42 TNA, SP28/145, ff. 61r–61v.

Carpenters	10	Boatwright's Mate	1
Captains of Pioneers	2	Watermen	10
Lieutenants of Pioneers	2	Quartermasters for draught horses	10
Overseers of Pioneers	2	Carters	246
Total 719			

A list of the Train of Artillery consisting of 30 pieces of ordnance with their officers, artificers and attendants, and an estimate of how many horses will draw the ordnance, waggons and utensils belonging to such a Train, also how many waggons, carts and tumbrels, etc.[43]

Demi-culverins	4	Horses to draw	60
Long sakers	6		54
Ordinary sakers	20		120
Powder 200 barrels; each waggon consisting of 6 horses and 15 barrels in one waggon, because that if 3 horses be waggons close 14 horses appointed for one man to look to, you must not put two men to one team and so by consequence there must be 6 horses to every draught			
Match 10 tons		Waggons open 13	Horses 78
Bastard musket bullet 10 ton		Tumbrells close 14	Horses 84
Cannon shot 150 for every piece amounts to Some two mortar pieces, the one 80lb shot the other some 12lb shot Two block carriages		Tumbrells open 22	Horses 126 Horses 12 Horses 6
Two gynnes with appurtenances 1cwt grenadoes for each mortar piece Petards 8 hand grenadoes		Carts open 2 Close waggons 4	Horses 12 Horses 24
Fireworks with appurtenances 2,000 materials with shovels, spades and 2,000 moulds to make bullets 1 dozen of 1lb, 6 dozen of bastard musket bullets with nippers, pots and ladles		Close waggons 2 Open carts 6 Close waggon 1	Horses 12 Horses 36 Horses 6
Candles 10 dozen, links [torches] 5 dozen, lanterns 3 dozen of wood, dark lanterns 1 dozen, canvas 200 ells		Close waggon 1	Horses 6
To carry pitch, oakum, tar, carpenter's and wheeler's tools and small bolts, etc.		Close waggon 1	Horses 6
For artificers:			
Carpenters with their nails, spikes and all kind of tools Smith with all his tools Wheelers with 6 hand screws, and all their tools and appurtenances Farriers with their tools and physic for horses 1,000 spare horseshoes and nails for store Armourers and gunmaker with all tools and necessaries Basket makers and coopers with all their tools Ladel makers and rope makers with their ropes and utensils Tent makers and collar makers as also 200 small tents for the Train to be disposed of presently		Close waggon 1 open cart 1 Close waggon 1 Close waggon 1 Close waggon 1 Close waggon 1 Close waggon 1 Close waggon 1 Close waggon 1 Close waggon 1	Horses 12 Horses 6 Horses 6 Horses 6 Horses 6 Horses 6 Horses 6 Horses 6 Horses 6

43 TNA, SP28/145, ff. 60r–63v.

For the officers of the Train:		
Lieutenant General of the Ordnance	Close waggon 1	Horses 6
Comptroller of the Ordnance	Close waggon 1	Horses 6
Engineers	Close waggon 1	Horses 6
Gentlemen of the Ordnance	Close waggon 1	Horses 6
Master Gunner and mates to put cartridges in	Close waggon 1	Horses 6
Commissary of Ammunition	Close waggon 1	Horses 6
Commissary of Draught Horses	Close waggon 1	Horses 6
Waggon Master and conductors	Close waggon 1	Horses 6
Surgeon of the Train	Close waggon 1	Horses 6
Paymaster, captains and officers of the firelocks and pioneers	Close waggon 1	Horses 6
To carry the surgery chest, spare arms and ammunition of every [foot] regiment	Close waggons 12	Horses 72
For 10 conductors and the waggon master's assistants to ride to perform their service		Horses 12
The whole draught besides the ordnance is with 6 boats and appurtenances	Close waggons 59 Open waggons 19 Open carts 18 Tumbrells 36	
For the regiments and all the total in draughts		132
Horses to draw them		792
For the ordnance		234
For the conductors		12
Total of horses		1,038

A list of the officers and artificers with other attendants as is thought fit to attend a Train of Artillery fit for an army of 15,000 foot, 6,000 horse and 1,000 dragoons[44]

	£	s.	d.
Lieutenant General of the Ordnance £1 10s. per diem, 2 clerks 2s. 6d. per diem	1	15	00
Comptroller 10s. per diem, 2 clerks each 2s. 6d. per diem		15	00
Chief Engineer 10s. per diem, 1 clerk 2s. 6d. per diem		12	06
2 other engineers each 8s. per diem		16	00
6 Conductors of trenches, fortifications and approaches each 2s. 6d. per diem		15	00
Chaplain 8s. per diem and his man 8d. per diem		08	08
Paymaster 5s. per diem, 2 clerks 2s. per diem		09	00
Commissary of the Ammunition 5s. per diem, 2 clerks 2s. 6d. per diem		10	00
Master fire worker and petardier per diem 8s.		08	00
4 assistants to go out with petards each 2s. 6d. per day		10	00
Commissary of the Draught Horses 4s. per diem and his man 2s. 6d.		06	06
Battery Master per diem 5s.		05	00
1 Quartermaster per diem 4s.		04	00
1 Waggon Master per diem 5s., 2 assistants each 2s. 6d. per diem		10	00
10 Conductors of Ammunition each 2s. per diem	1	00	00

44 TNA, SP28/145, ff. 60r–63v.

	£	s.	d.
1 Surgeon 5s. per diem, 2 mates each 2s. 6d. per diem		10	00
14 Gentlemen of the Ordnance each 4s. per diem	2	16	00
1 Master Gunner 6s. 8d. per diem		06	08
6 other gunners each 2s. 6d. per diem		15	08
40 other gunners each 2s. per diem	4	00	00
150 matrosses to attend the guns each 12d. per diem	7	10	00
10 matrosses to attend the Commissary each 12d. per diem		10	00
1 Master of the Minories 4s. per diem, 4 men each 12d. per diem		08	00
1 Master Carpenter 4s. per diem, 2 mates each 2s. per diem		08	00
10 other carpenters each 1s. 6d. per diem		15	00
1 Master Smith 4s. per diem, 2 mates each 2s. per diem		08	00
6 other smiths each 1s. 6d. per diem		09	00
1 Master Wheeler 4s. per diem, 2 mates each 2s. per diem		08	00
8 other wheelers each 1s. 6d. per diem		12	00
1 Master Farrier 4s. per diem, 6 other farriers each 1s. 6d. per diem		13	00
1 Provost Marshall 3s. per diem, 1 man 12d. per diem		04	00
1 Gunmaker 3s. 6d. per diem, 2 men each 2s. per diem		07	06
1 Master Armourer 3s. 6d. per diem, 3 men each 2s. per diem		09	00
4 Basket makers each 2s. 6d. per diem		10	00
1 Ladle maker 2s. 6d. per diem, 1 mate 2s. per diem		04	06
1 Cooper 2s. 6d. per diem, 1 mate 2s. per diem		04	06
2 tent makers each 1s. 6d. per diem, 2 mates each 12d. per diem		05	06
1 Master Ropemaker 2s. 6d. per diem, 1 man 1s. 6d. per diem		04	00
1 Master Collarmaker 2s. 6d. per diem, 4 men each 2s. per diem		10	06
1 Bridge master 4s. per diem, to assist him being a carpenter 3s. per diem		07	00
1 Wheeler for the carriages of the boat bridge 3s. per diem, 1 mate 2s. per diem		05	00
1 Boatwright 3s. per diem, 1 mate 2s. per diem		05	00
10 Watermen each 12d. per diem		10	00
2 Captains of pioneers each 5s. per diem		10	00
2 Lieutenants each 3s. per diem		06	00
2 Overseers each 2s. per diem		04	00
60 pioneers to each company, in all 120 each 12d. per diem	6	00	00
1 Drum-major of the whole train 1s. 6d. per diem		01	06
Brought from the other side	31	03	10
Per diem	41	00	10
Per mensem	1149	03	04
2 companies of firelocks for the guard of the train, being 240 with their officers, in all	11	00	00
Per mensem	308	00	00
10 Quartermasters for to take charge of the draught horses Each quartermaster 100 in his charge 2s. 6d. per diem	1	05	00
346 Carters, each man 3 horses 1s. 6d. per diem each man	25	19	00
1038 draught horses at 7¼d. per diem for meat and shoeing	31	07	01½
Per diem	58	11	01½

	£	s.	d.
Per mensem	1639	11	06
The officers, artificers and attendants for the train	41	10	00
The firelocks with their officers	11	00	00
The draught horses with the quartermasters and carters	58	11	01½
Per diem	110	11	01½
Per mensem	3096	14	10

Reasons why the Lieutenant General's Assistant is omitted, viz. because the Comptroller if he being an able man having two clerks may very well perform the place.

Why one engineer more is added, viz. because if one be left upon service at any place, the other two is as little as may be to serve the army, and two conductors to each engineer have hard duty in time of service, in that they are to watch every other night, and for this pay they have served, and under, if you will not get any able engineers to serve.

If there be but one commissary of the ammunition of necessity there must be two clerks, for one of them must attend night and day to deliver out ammunition.

The chaplain had never less than 8s. per diem, and his man 8d., and scarce can you get an honest and able man who will serve for that.

14 gentlemen of the ordnance are required, for there must go one with every regiment to look to the guns, and two is as little as can stay in the train.

Tent makers four is as little as can be for making and placing of tents, without which the gunners and others will never attend their charge, former lists having allowed 10 or 12.

For pioneers 100 or 120 is as little as may be for making the ways for the guns and carriages with one part, the other to cut the hedges that the foot and horse may march on both sides of the Train without retarding it, by which means the march may be advanced four or five miles in a day; former lists having allowed 400 and at the least 160, for upon a day of battle they cut ways and hedges, which have been found by experience to be of exceeding use.

For the firelocks they are men of as much use as of any other companies in the army, for without them there must be two or three other companies to guard the train, which by reason of their march may be very dangerous in regard of the powder, and so have better these than musketeers.

For the quartermasters for the horses, 10 is as little as may be each having 100 horses to see to.

For the carters three horses to one man is as much as he can look to, which is the reason we put six horses in a team and load the harder, whereof if we should put but five a man should have two horses in a team and one in another, which he could not look after, but now being all six together their drivers can the better go on with them.

For the purveyor we think him needless, for if there be money issued out for anything to be bought, the Lieutenant General or the Comptroller may employ one of their clerks to do it.

Lastly, where it is said by the List given in to the Committee that the gunners being few, they may be supplied with matrosses, but that cannot be well as scarce one of 20 of them can load a piece, or at the best can do no more than load her, what good can then be expected from them in point of service with a piece.

And they by that List shall not be above one and a quarter to a gun, but that defect, they say, should be supplied by pioneers who understand less than the former, but these pioneers should be firelocks also to guard the train, the guns perhaps planted in a day of service a mile from the train and musket shot, one from another in the heads of regiments and places of advantage, so that by this means the train should be guarded and men of no good knowledge employed to use the guns.

The wages of the several officers and artificers in this is in every particular conformable to what has been in former lists.

Memorandum: there is omitted which should afore been inserted, 1000 horse harnesses near 200 whereof should be full harnesses.

Read and assented unto 5 March 1645

A list of the Train of Artillery consisting of 30 pieces of ordnance with an estimate how many horses will draw the ordnance waggons and utensils belonging to such a Train, also how many waggons, carts and tumbrels etc.[45]

	Waggons	Horses
4 demi-culverins requiring to draw each of them 12 horses		48
2 long sakers requiring 7 horses to draw them		14
24 ordinary sakers requiring each 5 horses		120
200 barrels powder requiring	13 close	65
10 ton of match in fatts, 2 fatts in each wagon	10 open	60
10 ton of bastard musket shot requiring	12 tun	60
100 round shot for each piece of ordnance of all sorts of cannon shot	12 open	60
2 mortar pieces of 80lb and 12lb two carriages		8
2 block carriages each 6 horses		12
2 gynnes with appurtenances	2 open	10
For 100 grenadoes to each mortar piece requiring	4 close	24
For 8 petards and 10c[wt?] hand grenadoes, fireworks and other materials	2 close	10
For materials, pickaxes, shovels, ropes, etc.	5 open	25
For the smith's iron and coals	2 close	10
For clouts, nails, grease, etc.	1 close	6
For the carpenters and material, and the wheelers	2 close	10
For the farrier to carry his ingredients and the gunsmith's tools	1 close	5
For the smith to carry his tools, bullet moulds and other necessaries	1 close	5
The collarmaker for spare harness and tents	2 close	10
The Lieutenant General of the Ordnance	1 close	5
The Master Gunner and his mates to put in cartridges	1 close	5
The surgeon, paymaster and chaplain	1 close	5
To carry the surgeons' chests and spare arms of every regiment	12 close	60
For horses for 10 conductors		10
For 8 quartermasters, one for every hundred horses		8
To carry the arms to be gathered up	1 close	6
For the commissioners	1 close	4
Sum total	87	670

If the horses be not provided by the State, then their day at 2s. per diem for each horse hired and their drivers

If provided by the State then to have for each horse 7¼d. per diem per horse comes to £20 4s. 9½ per diem; £566 13s. 2d. per mensem

Memorandum: if there be no Lieutenant General, then the waggon allowed for him to serve for the commissary of the ammunition, and to carry candles, links and lanterns

In case there be a Lieutenant General then the collarmaker to have but one waggon and the other allotted to him to serve for the commissary of ammunition

Reasons given by the Committee of Accounts why they do not concur in the establishment of the Train of Artillery delivered by Mr Scawen:

45 TNA, SP28/225, unfol.

Whereas there are 15 horses appointed to draw every demi-culverin we humbly conceive 12 horses sufficient, our reason being grounded both upon precedents and experience. According to precedents there is allowed one horse to every 300lbs brass, besides equipage, and according to these precedents the Earl of Manchester never had more than 10 horses to draw a demi-culverin of 32cwt, which is the most any demi-culverin does weigh and has drawn them from York to Reading through the northern counties, which conceive to be as bad way for a carriage as any is in England and yet notwithstanding we have allowed 12 horses to each, whereas they had but 10, because we could not allow less than in reason and experience should be thought to be needful, but rather more and according to the same proportion we allow for the rest of the ordnance.

For the powder we allow but 13 waggons allotting after the rate of 15 barrels to each waggon, and 5 horses to each waggon we conceive as much as ever was allowed by former precedents to draw 16cwt, and conceive it more wisdom to allow 2 carters to 5 horses, than to have 6 horses, only because there be 2 drivers as is alleged and so put the Kingdom to an unnecessary charge of one horse in every team extraordinary, which will be very considerable in the whole

Whereas there is put down 150 rounds to each piece of ordnance we cannot find any precedents here in England or Ireland that there were ever allowed 100 rounds to each piece, but on the contrary, we find in his Majesty's Establishment but 30 rounds to each great gun, notwithstanding we thought to set 15 or 16cwt to each tumbrel

For the bullet moulds, nippers and the like to be carried in one of the smith's wagons, being allowed 4 waggons to carry his tools, iron, coals, clouts and grease

A list of such officers and artificers with other attendants as is thought fit to attend a Train of Artillery fit for an army of 15,000 foot, 6,000 horse and 1,000 dragoons, and presented by the Committee of Accounts[46]

	Per diem		
	£	s.	d.
1 Lieutenant General of the Ordnance at	1	00	00
2 Clerks at 2s. each		04	00
1 Comptroller at		06	08
1 Clerk at		02	00
1 Chief Engineer		06	08
1 Clerk		02	00
2 other Engineers		08	00
1 Chaplain		05	00
His man		01	00
1 Paymaster		05	00
His clerk		02	00
A Commissary of the Ammunition		04	00
His Clerk		02	00
A Commissary of draught horse		04	00
His man		02	00
1 Quartermaster of the Train		04	00
1 Principal Conductor instead of the Waggon Master		04	00
10 Conductors of Ammunition each 2s. per diem	1	00	00

46 TNA, SP28/145, ff. 63r–63v.

	Per diem		
	£	s.	d.
1 Surgeon		04	00
2 Surgeon's mates at 2s. each		04	00
14 Gentlemen of the Ordnance at 3s. per diem	2	02	00
1 Master Gunner		06	00
2 gunner's mates at 2s. 6d.		05	00
15 q[uarte]r[?] gunners at 2s. apiece	1	10	00
25 gunners at 1s. 6d. each per diem	1	17	06
104 matrosses, viz. to each delivered culverin 6; to the long saker 4; and to each other piece 3 at 1s. per diem	5	04	00
1 Master Miner at 3s. per diem		03	00
1 Master Carpenter		03	00
2 mates at 2s. per diem		04	00
10 other carpenters at 1s. 6d. per diem		15	00
1 Master Smith at		03	00
1 mate at		02	00
4 sergeant smiths at 1s. 6d.		06	00
1 Master Wheeler at		03	00
2 mates at 2s. each		04	00
6 other wheelers at 1s. 6d. each		09	00
1 Master Farrier		02	00
4 other farriers at 1s. 6d.		06	00
1 Provost Marshall		03	00
1 man		01	00
1 Gunsmith at		03	00
4 under gunsmiths at 1s. 6d.		06	00
1 basket maker		02	00
1 ladle maker		02	00
1 cooper		02	00
His man		01	06
1 tentmaker		01	06
A ropemaker		02	00
A collarmaker		02	00
4 men at 1s. 6d.		06	00
1 boatwright		02	06
3 captains of pioneers and firelocks at 5s. per diem		15	00
3 lieutenants at 2s. per diem		06	00
3 overseers or ensigns at 1s. 6d. each		04	06
70 pioneers to each company to serve both for firelocks and pioneers 10d. per diem for the 3 companies for 210 men	8	15	00
8 Quartermasters of the draught horses at 2s. 6d. each	1	00	00

	Per diem		
	£	s.	d.
If the State provides draught horses, then the drivers to have each 1s. per day constantly paid, viz. for every 3 horses 1 driver, in all per diem 220 drivers	11	00	00
2 drummers at 1s. per diem		02	00
Total	43	12	10

Edward Byworth, Carriage master to the Office of the Ordnance, desires allowance for his servants, horses and carts, being employed in the carrying and recarrying of munitions and other habiliments of war belonging to the Train of Artillery, for Sir Thomas Fairfax, to and from His Majesty's Stores and other places beginning on 17 April 1645 and ending on 5 May then next following:[47]

For 37 loads to and from Mr Bateman's to the Tower at 16d. per load	2	15	6
For 20 loads from the Minories to the Tower at 16d. per load	1	6	8
For 10 loads from Mr Pitt's to the Tower at 16d. per load	0	10	0
For drawing 2 demi-culverins in their carriages from the crane to the end of the wharf	0	4	0
The like for 4 sakers	0	4	0
For drawing 10 field carriages from the Mint to the crane at Tower Wharf	0	10	0
Total	5	10	2

We whose names are hereunto subscribed do certify that this work was done and performed according to the bill of the particulars above written:

John Pitt

Thomas Hodgson

Thomas Bateman

Artillery

When the New Model Army was created in 1645 it was provided with a powerful complement of artillery, its establishment being 4 demi-culverins, 6 long sakers, and 20 ordinary sakers. Artillery in the form of cannon and mortars were an increasingly important (and mobile) form of warfare during the seventeenth century. By comparison, the Royalist Ordnance Papers provide no indication of cannon and ammunition allotted to the King's Oxford Army during the Naseby campaign of 1645. Letters and diaries, however, show that the Council of War decided upon a smaller and perhaps more mobile train of artillery.[48] The King chose only 14 field

47 TNA, SP28/30/3, f. 248r.
48 John Hodgson (ed.), *Original Memoirs, written during the great Civil War; being the life of Sir Henry Slingsby, and memoirs of Capt. Hodgson* (London: Ballantyne, 1807), p.142; Eliot Warburton (ed.), *Memoirs of Prince Rupert, and the Cavaliers* (London: Richard Bentley, 1849), III, p.100.

pieces, yet the difficulty of providing sufficient transport could have influenced his decision. The cannon proved effective at the siege of Leicester in May, though at Naseby every gun and most of the military supplies of the army were lost.[49] Though their effects were firepower and destruction, ordnance logistics (the production, supply and storage of gunpowder, shot, grenadoes, petards, fuses and match, not to mention carriages, waggons and large numbers of draught animals) taxed most armies.[50] There were a great many sizes of cannon, the heavier types being regarded as 'siege or battering pieces'; those of smaller bore being more readily transportable, and regarded as 'field pieces'.

Table 03: Principal Types of Ordnance (William Eldred, *The Gunner's Glasse*, 1646)

Artillery piece	Calibre in inches	Weight of gun (lb)	Length of piece (feet)	Shot weight (lb)
Cannon Royal	8.0	8,000	8	63
Cannon	7.0	7,000	10	47
Demi-Cannon	6.0	6,000	12	27
Culverin	5.0	4,000	11	15
Demi-Culverin	4.5	3,600	10	9
Saker	3.5	2,500	9.5	5.25
Minion	3.0	1,500	8	4
Falcon	2.75	700	6	2.25
Falconet	2.0	210	4	1.25
Robinet	1.25	120	3	0.75

An important omission from the above is the drake, which fired a ball of about 3lbs and operated as light artillery. By the time the Civil War broke out these had become the standard infantry support weapon among Parliamentarian armies.[51]

According to Gentles:

> ...powder, match, shot, and shells consumed a considerable amount of money, but the New Model is known to have purchased no more than 3 pieces of artillery during its first year. The small attention paid to ordnance does not reflect a failure to appreciate its importance, but rather the fact that a good deal of ordnance had been inherited from the 3 armies that went out of existence in 1645.[52]

49 Sprigge, *Anglia Rediviva*, p.40; Sir Edward Walker, *Brief Memorials of the Unfortunate Success of His Majesty's Army and Affairs in the Year 1645* (London: 1705), p.115.

50 Stephen Bull, *'The Furie of the Ordnance': Artillery in the English Civil War* (Woodbridge: Boydell, 2008), chapter 3.

51 Bull, *'Furie of the Ordnance'*, p.141; Simon Marsh, 'A Case of Drakes – James Wemyss and Artillery Innovation in the Civil War', Serena Jones (ed.), *A New Way of Fighting: Professionalism in the English Civil War*, Proceedings of the 2016 Helion and Company 'Century of the Soldier' Conference (Solihull: Helion & Co., 2017), pp.91–107.

52 Gentles, *New Model Army*, p.43.

On 22 April Parliament ordered that, '2 brass demi-culverins, and eight brass sakers, formerly made use of in the Navy, and now lying upon the Tower Wharf, shall be taken thence, and employed towards the Train of Artillery in the army under the command of Sir Thomas Fairfax.'[53] These were transported by barge to Fairfax's headquarters at Windsor. John Streeter depicted in his schema of the battle 14 field pieces and 3 siege pieces deployed among the New Model Army's infantry regiments at Naseby. He was not present, however, but to some extent based it upon eye-witness accounts. Of more certainty, though, are those found in the warrants and receipts books pertaining to the Ordnance Office.

On 28 April 1645 John Phipps, Commissary for the Train of Artillery received from Thomas Bateman, John Pitt, and Thomas Hodgkin, 'Field carriages with fore carriages complete, coloured in oil for 2 demi-culverins, 8 sakers (except one fore carriage for saker). Also, one carriage bound with iron for one saker without wheels or fore carriage; in all, which several particulars I have indented for in my Office of the Ordnance.' Additionally, on 9 May Commissary Phipps received from Bateman 3 field carriages for sakers and drakes complete, whereas a warrant to pay Richard Ward the sum of £10 was drawn up on 26 May 1645, 'towards the charges of fitting the 2 whole culverins and 1 demi-culverin of brass now at Northampton for the service.' Furthermore, a 'summary of equipment received and remaining in store' by Phipps, dated May 1645, included '3 sakers with transportation carriages complete; ready in the Minories', with 1 mortar piece, 16 closed waggons, 11 open waggons, and 8 tumbrels remaining in the Tower.[54]

In late April or early May 1645, the guns, gun carriages, and spare wheels ready to be delivered to the New Model's train were painted in 'lead coloured oil' at the Tower stores by the Ordnance Office painter Anthony Hancock. According to his bill he was owed the sum of £7 13s. 6d., itemised as £1 2s. 'for painting lead colour in oil two demi-culverin travelling field carriages'; £4 for 8 sakers; 11s. for 1 long saker; £1 7s. for 3 saker carriages; 4s. for 2 fore carriages for demi-culverins; 3s. 6d. 2 fore carriages for sakers; 3s. for a carriage for a mortar piece; and another 3s. for painting a pair of spare wheels and 2 carriages.[55] As the accounts of Sir Edward Peto record, the Earl of Essex's train in 1643 painted its waggons using Spanish colour (a browny red colour) and red lead in linseed oil.[56] It is likely that the ordnance and carriages in Fairfax's forces were similarly painted, as that was the 'colour' available. Lead colour does not necessarily equate to grey and can refer to the use of lead oxide as a drying agent within the paint that also provided a robust coating to protect carriages and waggons from the elements.

On 1 May 1645 the following were delivered by the Tower officials to Commissary John Phipps for the train of artillery: 2 demi-culverins of brass, mounted upon field carriage with fore carriage upon shod wheels complete; 20 sakers of brass mounted

53 *CJ*, IV pp.74, 117; *LJ*, VII, p.330.

54 TNA, SP28/30/3, ff. 244r–244v, 251r; SP28/30/4, f. 361r. Minories was an administrative area that took its name from the Abbey of the Minoresses of St Clare without Aldgate, located to the east of, and outside, of London's former defensive walls.

55 TNA, SP28/30/3, ff. 236r–236v, 239r.

56 Shakespeare Birthplace Trust, Special Collections D98/1704, ff. 57r–58r.

upon field carriages complete; 1 brass mortar piece of 12 inch diameter; 20 grenadoe shells for the mortar piece; 6cwt 56lbs round shot for demi-culverin; ½ ton 5cwt 43lbs round shot for saker; 1 ton of hand grenadoes; 1 block carriage complete; 30cwt corn powder; 9 ton 5cwt 21lbs match; 5 tons lead shot; 400 shovels; 400 spades; 400 pickaxes; 200 tents furnished; 26 closed waggons; 7 open waggons; 1 closed cart; 3 long carts; 7 tumbrels; 1 pair of shafts; 10 handspikes; 1 ginn; 1 rammer head with brass scourer; and 3 field tampions. Eleven days later he received 1 mortar piece mounted and 60 grenadoe shells, while on 28 May Phipps took possession of '4 petards fixed, 6 grenadoe shells, and 200 steel spades'.[57] Moreover, a warrant was issued for the payment of £32 to John Petty on 18 June for 'a demi-cannon new field carriage complete at Windsor'.[58]

The Committee of Both Kingdoms directed the Officers of the Ordnance on 9 August 1645 to issue out of the stores at the Tower of London 200 shot of 24lbs; 200 of 12lbs; 300 of 9lbs; 300 of 6lbs; 60 barrels of powder; 200 grenadoe shells of 10" inch diameter; 600 shovels and spades; 200 axes helved. The Committee's warrant further related, 'These are to will and require you upon sight hereof to deliver unto Bartholomew Stileman or whom he shall appoint. All which are to be employed against Basing.' These stores were duly delivered 2 days later.[59] Likewise, it was reported for 14 August, 'Sir Thomas Fairfax, as by letters this day from the West, of the 11th, is yet before Sherborne; he has at last 1 whole cannon, and a demi-cannon come, which are planted ... the recruits are come likewise, which is good though not so good as was expected.'[60] Like the substantial quantities of stores for the supply of the New Model Army, such as small arms, ammunition, and clothing, sent to Commissaries Thomas Futter and Martin Pinder at Lyme during Fairfax's advance westwards, on 1 September he received the following by ship: 1 whole cannon of brass (possessing a 7-inch bore and shot weight of 47lbs); 1 ladle; 1 field tampion; 2 formers; 1 wad hook; 8cwt of round shot for cannon; 200 24lb bullets; 300 demi-culverin shot; 300 demi-cannon shot; 2 ginns for mounting the great cannon; 1 new mortar piece; and 'a new carriage belonging to the demi-cannon that came from Windsor and a draught rope in the stores as serviceable to the demi-cannon.'[61]

Due to the speed of the opening phases of the fighting, the guns of the New Model did little service at Naseby. The opening bombardment before the two forces came to close quarters was brief, with one Parliamentarian observer reporting, 'the ordnance began to play, but that being found at Marston Moor and other places but a loss of time, we resolved not to want daylight as usual, but charge with the first.'[62] Similarly, the Royalist Sir Edward Walker stated, 'Presently our forces advanced up the hill, the rebels only discharging 5 pieces at them, but over shot them, and so did their musketeers.'[63] However, during their next major engagement, at Langport on 10 July

57 TNA, WO55/460, unfol.; WO55/1647, unfol.; WSL, Ms Salt 463, unfol.
58 TNA, SP28/30/5. f. 639r.
59 TNA, WO55/1647, unfol.; WSL, Ms Salt 463, unfol.
60 *The Moderate Intelligencer*, 14–21 August 1645. TT, E297[12].
61 TNA, WO55/460, unfol.; WO55/1647, unfol.
62 *A True Relation of a Victory Obtained over the Kings Forces* (London: 1645). TT, E288[22].
63 Sir Edward Walker, *Brief Memorials of the Unfortunate Success of His Majesty's Army and Affairs in the Year 1645* (London: 1705), p.115.

1645, Sir Thomas Fairfax's gunners played an important role in the Army's victory. Sprigge reported, 'our ordnance began to play (a good while before the foot engaged) doing great execution upon the body of the enemy's army, both horse and foot, who stood in good order upon the hill (about musket shot from the pass) and forcing them to draw off their ordnance, and their horse to remove their ground. Another source added, 'Our cannon did very good service, and made the other side of the hill so hot that they could not come down to relieve their men.'[64] The efficient siege artillery of the New Model Army bore fruit during the south-western campaign. At Sherborne Fairfax's gunners blew holes in the walls after just 2 days, whereas before Winchester in November 1645 the Royalist garrison was overrun when a breach wide enough for 30 men to enter abreast had been forced.[65]

Waggons

The train of artillery also required substantial quantities of waggons for its supplies. According to its establishment, the New Model was assigned 132 waggons and tumbrels (2-wheeled carts pulled by a single horse or ox), drawn by 792 horses, while each of the 12 regiments of foot had 1 close waggon for its 'surgery chest [and] spare arms'. 21 close waggons and 11 open waggons were purchased from Thomas Bateman at £13 and £12 apiece respectively, 6 close for the use of Sir Thomas Fairfax, and another 2 for Sergeant Major General Skippon.[66] Moreover, when the 10 pieces of ordnance were dispatched from the Tower of London to the Army's headquarters at Windsor on 29 April they were accompanied by '12 waggons and carriages, comprising 5 loads of match, 2 loads of bullets, and 6 carriages for the ordnance.'[67] In autumn 1644 Bateman had delivered into the stores for Essex's new train of artillery almost 50 waggons, carts and tumbrils, in addition to wheels, axletrees, fore carriages and barrows. In April and May 1645, he provided a further 32 waggons for the New Model Army.[68] These vehicles were not necessarily made exclusively by him, but were probably assembled alongside smiths, carpenters and wheelwrights.

Tools and Equipment

As might be expected with the train of artillery, which directly provided the ordnance and logistical support to the New Model, both during field operations and

64 Sprigge, *Anglia Rediviva*, p.72; *An Exact and Perfect Relation of the Proceedings of the Army under the Command of Sir Thomas Fairfax … Dated at Sir Thomas Fairfax's Quarters at Middlesey July 11* (London: 1645). TT, E.292[28].

65 *Sir Thomas Fairfax's letter to the Honorable William Lenthall Esq: Speaker of the House of Commons; concerning the taking of Sherborn Castle* (London: 15 August 1645). TT, E297[3]; Sprigge, *Anglia Rediviva*, pp.128–9.

66 TNA, WO47/1, ff. 167v, 209r; Bodl. Lib., Ms Eng. hist. C14, ff. 12v, 20r; MS 46 78/708, f. 114v.

67 *The Moderate Intelligencer*, 23–29 April 1645. TT, E337[20].

68 TNA, WO49/82, ff. 62r, 91r–92v.

siege conditions, large quantities of tools and technical equipment was procured from specialist suppliers. On 15 April 1645 John Gace of Eastcheap, a turner and former Master of the Turners' Company, delivered to the Ordnance Office 800 shovels and spades at 1s. 3d. apiece 'according to the contract made with the said Committee, amounting to £50' to the Ordnance Office, with a further 100 spades at 3s. (probably metal-shod at that price) on 17 June. Gace was contracted mainly for the supply of bandoliers, shovels and spades for the New Model Army, and between April and September 1645 he provided 1,700 shovels and spades. Furthermore, with John Wallington he supplied 1,400 'ordinary shovels and spades', and 100 Flemish spades on 10 February 1646. A total of 199 of the latter had been issued to the train the previous May.[69] Late medieval depictions of these tools in Flemish manuscripts, such as the Book of Hours illuminated by the Master of Guillebert de Mets in 1440, in the Bodleian Library Oxford, suggests they were akin to mattocks with broad rounded blades.[70] Another supplier, Thomas Hodgson, the master smith at the Tower, furnished 500 pickaxes helved at 2s. 8d. apiece on 18 June 1645, according to the contract made with the Committee of the Army. He contributed ironwork, metal implements, and tools, including the 1,400 pickaxes and 2 tons of iron for the New Model Army between April and September 1645.[71]

Table 04: Accounts of Sir Walter Erle, Lieutenant of the Ordnance, 1645 (TNA, SP28/140/1, ff. 3r–3v)

Paid by Sir Walter Earle, Knight, for several items of provisions by him bought for the service of the Army under the command of Sir Thomas Fairfax by his appointment and direction of the Committee for the Army

Provisions for the Master of the Fireworks:

			£	s.	d.
14/4/45	Chisels and priming irons	William Evans	0	3	0
	Canvas 50 ells at 1s. 2d. per ell	Alderman Burrows	2	18	6
	Hand irons 2 and scissors 1 pair	Joshua Foote	0	2	10
	A copper pan and brass skillet	William Bromwich	0	15	0
	Chests 2	Richard Gearing	0	14	0
	Paper 2 reams	Thomas Batt	0	16	0
	Brass scales and weights	Richard Playford	0	17	1
16/4/45	White soap and oakum	William Terrill	3	12	1
	Packthread needles	William Rumball	0	1	4
	Materials for fireworks	Robert Hill	9	15	0
18/4/45	Cases of several sorts	Thomas Hall	11	10	0
19/4/45	[damaged] for fireballs 150	Thomas Hodgkinson	5	12	0
21/4/45	[damaged] and bellows	John Gace	1	1	0
	[damaged] for powder 1	Thomas Flower	1	5	0

69 TNA, WO47/1, f. 211r; SP28/29/1, f. 123r; SP28/30/5, ff. 636r-v; Bodl. Lib., Ms Eng. hist. C14, ff. 11r, 24v, 27v, 78v.

70 Bodl. Lib., Ms Buchanan e. 8.

71 TNA, WO49/82, ff. 7r, 55r, 57v; SP28/30/5, f. 638r.

			£	s.	d.
28/4/45	Copper plates 8, copper nails 2,000 and brass moulds 2 – 1 for the ladle maker	William Bromwich	12	3	4
	Iron [damaged] for demi-culverin and saker 2	Thomas Oldfield	3	0	0
	Lanterns ordinary 2 dozen at 1s. 6d. and black lanterns at 2s. 2d. apiece	John Gace	2	9	0
	Ladles for demi-culverin 2 at 13s. apiece, sponges for sakers 2 at 11s. apiece, wad hooks 15 at 9s. apiece, hand irons 15 at 3s. 2d. apiece	Richard Ward	17	9	6
28/4/45	Powder bags 50 at 2s. apiece	[damaged]	12	0	0
	The Minories' tools: Chisels 2, hatchets 2, dark lanterns 1	Joshua Foote	0	9	0
	Auger with 2 bitts for the Minories 1	Richard Aukey	0	3	0
	Wheeler's tools as the bill of particulars	Joshua Foote	10	3	6
	Wheeler's tools as the bill of particulars	Thomas Bateman	10	9	4
	Gunsmith's tools as the bill of particulars	Joshua Foote	15	3	10
	Ladle maker's tools as the bill of particulars	Joshua Foote	4	11	7
	Hatchets helved 250 at 1s. 6d. apiece	Joshua Foote	18	5	0
	Bills helved 250 1s. 8d. apiece	Joshua Foote	20	6	8
	Clouts 40 dozen at 5s. per dozen	Joshua Foote	10	0	0
	Clout nails 5,000 at 6d. per thousand	Joshua Foote	1	10	0
	Dray rope 1 and several lines 150 fathoms	Joshua Foote	1	14	0

Tents

Included in the establishment of the train of artillery were 2 tentmakers and 4 tentmaker's mates. These were classed as artificers and paid 1s. 6d. per day, and 1s. per day respectively. These appear to have been employed in constructing tents for the artillery, as it was recommended that 'tent makers, 4 is as little as can be for making and placing of tents, without which the gunners and others will never attend their charge.'[72] Nevertheless, on 3 April 1645 the Officers of the Ordnance were notified of a contract with the tentmaker John Snow for '200 tents for the Train'. These were specified as being '7 foot long, 7 foot broad and 6 foot high of good lockram according to the patterns, and with fir staves, lines and pins, and other appurtenances according to the best trench tents at 20s. per tent.' These were delivered by Snow on 18 April, and duly supplied to Commissary Phipps of the Train on 1 May.[73] Snow subsequently became master tentmaker to the army in Ireland during the Commonwealth.[74] Among his observations, the professional soldier Roger Boyle, Earl of Orrery, wrote,

72 TNA, SP28/145, f. 61v.

73 TNA, WO47/1, f. 211r; SP28/29/1, f. 124r; SP28/30/5, f. 639r; MS 46 78/708, fol. 112r; Bodleian Lib., Ms Eng Hist C14, f. 13r.

74 *CSPD Interregnum 1649–50*, p.591.

'I lay encamped several years, and in all tents; not so large as these sorts of huts, yet I allowed every 6 foot soldiers but 1 trench tent, and every 3 troopers but 1 trench tent (because of their saddles and furniture) and with this they were satisfied.'[75]

Known as 'trench tents' (or possibly 'entrenched-tents') – primarily intended for use at sieges and in harsh conditions – it appears unlikely that tentage was widely employed amongst the New Model Army in 1645–1646 because its soldiers were largely quartered in buildings or in the open. During the first march to relieve Taunton in May 1645 Sir Thomas Fairfax ('a commander in the army') reported 'for the most part we took barns and hedges for our night's repose, after our hard and hot days, until within the compass of 8 days'.[76] Moreover, when the bulk of the New Model lay in echelon near Piddington in Northamptonshire on 11 June, most of its troops were described as 'lying in the fields'.[77] Between April 1645 and June 1646, a total of 2,400 tents were procured from Snow. Except for the 200 received in April 1645, the remainder were procured in mid-1646, and quickly distributed to Fairfax's troops besieging Oxford.[78] Similarly, following the arrival of a brigade of New Model infantry before Royalist-held Worcester in July, it was recorded, 'White tents to hold four set up at Barbon House and on the side of the hill beyond the Windmill Hill looking towards Mistress Andrews' for the soldiery, and some huts. Colonel Rainborowe's quarters at Mistress Andrews' of the hill.'[79] In general, during the Civil Wars there is some evidence for the construction of temporary shelters or huts by troops on campaign, although no references to blankets being issued to, or purchased by, soldiers are known.

The use of tents by the forces of the Commonwealth in Ireland and Scotland, where for much of the time accommodation for soldiers was uncertain and the weather poor, was far more extensive. Consequently, among the warrants issued by the Council of State for payment of money to merchants, Richard Thorogood received the sum of £91 4s. 8d. in August 1649 for '1,508½ ells of tent canvas for Ireland'. Additionally, in January 1651 he provided '5,995 ells of vitry [a light durable canvas] for tent cloth for soldiers in Ireland' at a cost of £353 9s. 10d. (including portage) and was paid £516 14s. 7d. for '8,012½ ells of hall cloth for tents'. On the same date, George Waterman received £58 13s. 9d. for ropes, tape, and thread for tent making, whereas on 21 May 1650 Edward Tench supplied '800 sets of tent poles, pins, and mallets for Scotland' and was paid the sum of £43 6s. 8d.[80] Fisher's schema of Dunbar, which is based on first-hand accounts of the battle, shows Cromwell's tented camp to the north of the Broxburn, complete with panes and guy ropes.

75 Roger Boyle, Earl of Orrery, *A Treatise of the Art of War dedicated to the King's Most Excellent Majesty* (1677), p.84.

76 *A Narration of the Expedition to Taunton: The Raising the Siege before it, and the Condition of our Forces, and the Enemies, at this present in the West. Sent from a Commander in the Army, and dated at Chard, May 18. 1645*. TT. E285[10].

77 TNA, SP28/173, unfol.

78 BL, Ms Add. 35332, f. 7r; Bodl. Lib., Ms Eng. hist. C14, f. 13r; Ms Eng. hist. C244, ff. 17v–18r, 19r–19v; WSL, Ms Salt 463, unfol.

79 Worcs Archives, BA 1714/899 (Townshend's Ms), f. 591r; Stephen Porter, Stephen K. Roberts and Ian Roy (eds), *The Diary and Papers of Henry Townshend, 1640–1663* (Worcestershire Historical Society, New series, 25, 2014), p.249.

80 *CSPD Interregnum 1649–50*, pp.571–600.

3

Powder, Match and Shot

In September 1645, a few days after the fall of Bristol to the New Model Army, Commissaries Harcourt Leighton and Thomas Herbert reported to William Lenthall, Speaker of the House of Commons, 'The General has desired Colonel Pindar [Quartermaster General of the City of London] to speed to Lyme, Taunton and Bridgewater to furnish us here with what powder and other ammunition their magazines can spare for the dispatch of this business. Pray hasten money to pay the army.'[1] It was on 1 March 1645 that the Commons had directed that the Commissioner of Excise be reimbursed for a loan and advance of £4,000 to Sir Walter Erle, Lieutenant of the Ordnance, 'for furnishing the public stores with ammunition, match, and bullet as by Ordinance of 17 December 1644 is directed.'[2]

On 3 September 1645 the Committee of Both Kingdoms informed Sir Thomas Fairfax, the commander-in-chief of the New Model:

> There is at Reading for the use of your army £30,000 in money, besides 100 barrels of gunpowder with match and bullet proportionable, and 60 draught horses with carriages, and by reason that Colonels Graves and Whalley with their horse that were here are ordered to march after the King wherever he shall go, we have not here a fit convoy for these provisions, and therefore desire to appoint such convoy from thence as you shall think fit for bringing these provisions up to you.

At this point Sir Thomas was with his army before Bristol and preparing a major assault on the city. Arrangements were made with the London Horse and civilian carriers, to transport and guard these items by convoy to the Parliamentarian garrison at Malmesbury, some 25 miles or so northeast of Bristol, for collection by Fairfax's troops. Therefore, on 11 September the Committee ordered that

> the City horse and dragoons shall convey the provisions from Reading to Malmesbury where a convoy from Sir Thomas Fairfax's Army shall meet it, for which orders are to be given. That the foot at Reading shall accompany the convoy to Malmesbury and so up to the army, for which orders are to be

1 *CJ*, IV, p.270.
2 *CSPD 1644–5*, p.330.

> given. To signify this unto Sir Thomas, and desire him to send a convoy to meet the provisions at Malmesbury.[3]

This was confirmed on 23 September in a letter from the Earl of Northumberland to Sir Henry Vane, senior:

> Since the taking of Bristol our army has stayed in expectation of a convoy which is now going to them with money, ammunition, and some recruits of foot, which go very cheerfully to that service. The General [Sir Thomas Fairfax] is now about the Devizes, what course he will take to employ that army is not yet known, but most here incline to his going further west, where the King's only body of an army is, and likewise with reference to the relief of Plymouth, which is at this time pressed, and suffers many inconveniences.[4]

Large quantities of powder, match, and shot were supplied by him not only to Sir Thomas Fairfax's Army in 1645 and 1646, but also to Parliamentarian regional forces and garrisons. Thus, 60 barrels of gunpowder with match proportionable was issued by the Ordnance Office for Sir William Brereton's army in Cheshire on 25 March 1645, and during the following month, 16 barrels of powder, 20 barrels of corn powder (for priming muskets and cannon), and 30cwt of match purchased in the capital by Brereton's London agent, Richard Worrall, were included in a consignment of arms and equipment dispatched by sea to Liverpool for the use of his forces.[5] Brereton's forces also obtained powder, match, and musket shot from manufacturers in Manchester, in addition to large quantities of artillery ammunition from foundries in Staffordshire.[6] From March 1645 onwards, Owen Rowe, one of the chief agents for the Committee of Safety distributed various quantities of munitions out of the Ordnance Office to a number of garrisons, such as Aylesbury, Pembroke, Evesham, and Worcester. He had previously supplied arms and ammunition to the Earl of Essex's Army, in addition to other forces.[7] However, due to shortages in the Ordnance Office's stores, during July 1645 these supplies of gunpowder were borrowed from the Navy stores.[8] By 1647 military operations on land had subsided, and the Committee of the Navy cancelled two contracts agreed with Samuel Cordwell in December 1646 and April 1647 for the supply of a total of 360 barrels of powder. This was re-allocated to the Navy stores.

In February 1645, the Commons had directed the Navy Committee to consider the report of the Committee of Both Kingdoms concerning deficiencies in the magazine at the Tower, and to introduce an ordinance for the regular supply of

3 *CSPD 1645–47*, pp.108, 131.
4 *CSPD 1645–47*, p.149.
5 WSL, Ms Salt 463, unfol.; CRO, DDX/428, ff. 45r, 79v–80r.
6 TNA, SP28/35/5, ff. 751r, 754r; SP28/36, f. 405r; SP28/128/10, ff. 4r–5v; BL, MS Harley 2130, ff. 99r–99v.
7 TNA, WO49/82, ff. 114r–116v, 291r, 321r, 329r; WSL, Ms Salt 463, unfol.; *CSPD 1644–5*, pp.365, 367, 605, 609, 622, 625.
8 TNA, WO49/82, ff. 295r, 297r, 299r, 309r–309v.

powder and ammunition for land and sea service.[9] It seems that the logistical system employed by Parliament in 1645 was more flexible than in the past. There are no recorded borrowings from the Navy stores for any of the main Parliamentarian armies before this, and in effect there were no reserves of powder, meaning that they had to await the next consignment from contractors (or in the case of the Earl of Manchester's forces, to obtain stocks from the Low Countries). Probably reflecting the value of the increasing association between the two departments, on 31 March 1645 the Committee of the Navy ordered Sir Walter Earle to 'pay George Taylor, John Faulkner and John White, Officers of the Ordnance, for an extraordinary allowance for £50 for one year to each of them and £20 to nine clerks usually allowed to their predecessors.'[10] The deficiency of gunpowder for land service is also reflected in the borrowings from the Navy stores during 1646, though not all the warrants for powder which were directed to the Navy Committee could be met in full out of their magazine. On 17 January 1646 the Committee of Both Kingdoms requested the Committee of the Eastern Association to provide ammunition to the Scarborough garrison because none was available in the public stores.[11]

The various receipts books belonging to the Ordnance Office record that the Committee for the Army procured, received into the land stores, and paid for the following between March and December 1645: 4,825 barrels of powder; 143 tons 14cwt of match; 70 tons 10cwt of musket shot; and from John Browne, founder of iron ordnance to the Office of Ordnance, 6,420 round shot and 2,335 mortar shells. Of these totals, during the same period 919 barrels of powder; 49 tons 10cwt of match; 16 tons 6cwt and 153 barrels of musket shot; 6,161 round shot, 270 mortar rounds, and 1,000 hand grenadoes were supplied directly to the New Model Army from the stores. Likewise, in 1646 2,290 barrels of powder; 164 tons of match; 37 tons of musket shot; in addition to 3,825 round shot and 500 mortar shells were brought into the land stores. From the same stores the New Model received 1,093 barrels of powder; 41 tons 16cwt of match; 22 tons and 31 barrels of musket shot; 4,000 round shot, and 150 mortar rounds during this time.[12] It is likely, however, that other quantities of gunpowder, match and shot were procured from other sources, and used by Sir Thomas Fairfax's forces, including stocks captured from the Royalists. It was reported by Parliamentarian sources that in addition to all the King's ordnance, 12 waggons, 40 barrels of powder and match proportionable, in addition to large quantities of ammunition were captured with his train of artillery by the New Model Army at Naseby.

Also taken were between 5,000 and 10,000 arms (including 50 loads of muskets, pikes, powder, match and bullet), with 200 horses with saddles and pistols.[13] Correspondingly, Sprigge related upon the fall of Bridgewater on 23 July 1645 'about

9 TNA, WO47/1, f. 169v; WO49/82, ff. 84r–85v.
10 TNA, SP28/29/1, f. 142r.
11 BL, Ms Add. 35332, ff. 19v, 28r, 41r–42v; *CSPD 1645–7*, p.444.
12 TNA, WO47/1, *passim*; WO49/82, *passim*; WO55/1662, ff. 28v–29v; SP28/140/3, ff. 144r–147r; BL, Ms Add. 35332, *passim*.
13 *The Kingdomes Weekly Intelligencer*, 10–17 June 1645. TT, E284[26]; *Mercurius Civicus*, 12–18 June 1645. TT, E286[12]; Rushworth, *Historical Collections*, VI, pp.81–2.

44 barrels of powder, 1,500 arms, 44 pieces of ordnance, and 400cwt of match' was seized; while 'about 100 barrels of powder already come to our hands, with a good quantity of shot, ammunition and arms' (amounting to 2,000 to 3,000 muskets) were delivered up to Fairfax's troops after they had seized Bristol two months later.[14] It seems the collection and distribution of enemy weapons was anticipated, because among the proposed establishment for the New Model's train of artillery was a closed waggon 'to carry the arms to be gathered up', drawn by 6 horses.[15]

During 1648 there was a noticeable improvement in the quantities of ammunition made available from the Ordnance Office land stores to Sir Thomas Fairfax's forces since the previous year – when 373 barrels of powder were received into Ordnance Office stores from three manufacturers, though no musket shot and match – particularly in respect of powder and musket ammunition.[16] Fairfax's regiments operating in Kent and Essex against Royalist revolts were particularly well supplied with munitions, no doubt because they were in close proximity to London. On 10 May and 13 June 1648, a total of 750 barrels of powder, 80 tons of match, 17 tons of musket bullet, besides a quantity of small arms were delivered out of Ordnance Office, whereas deliveries, of large ordnance and shot, were made during the Army's siege of Colchester in July and August.[17] That part of the Army which went with Lieutenant General Cromwell to South Wales in April 1648 does not appear to have received anything from the Ordnance Office stores at that time, although he did request munitions from the Derby House Committee. There were difficulties in supplying these at such a distance and some use was made of local sources.[18] On its march to Wales Cromwell's forces were provided with a small quantity of powder, match and shot from the stores at Gloucester, which was subsequently replaced out of the Ordnance Office stores.[19]

Some cannon belonging to the train of artillery, left at Oxford after the siege of 1646, was sent by land and sea and eventually reached Cromwell at Pembroke at the start of July 1648. Moreover, on 16 September the Committee for the Army 'very earnestly recommended' that Cromwell's forces were sent 'clothes for the foot and pay for the General's [Sir Thomas Fairfax's] regiment, and that £1,400 may be sent down to Newcastle for provision of bread'. Likewise, a large consignment of powder, match and musket shot was shipped to the North on 26 October for the use of the Parliamentarian forces there.[20] Nonetheless, between February 1648 and October 1649 a total of 3,810 barrels of gunpowder, 101 tons 2cwt of musket shot, and 182 tons 13cwt 14lbs of match were received into the Ordnance Office stores from eight dealers – Judd, Berisford, Andrews, Cardwell, Steventon and Freeman, who had supplied the New Model Army from 1645 onwards – in addition to John Simms

14 Sprigge, *Anglia Rediviva*, pp.73, 117.
15 TNA, SP28/225, unfol.
16 TNA, SP28/140/3, unfol.
17 TNA, WO55/461, ff. 1r, 11r, 14v; BL, Ms Add. 35332, ff. 24r–28v.
18 Andrew Barclay, Tim Wales, John Morrill (eds), *The Letters, Writings, and Speeches of Oliver Cromwell* (Oxford: Oxford University Press, 2022), I, pp.505–506 & 515–520.
19 BL, Ms Add. 35332 f. 79r.
20 TNA, WO55/461, f. 9r; SP28/55, f. 267r; SP28/57, f. 300r; BL, Ms Add. 35332, f. 108v; *CSPD 1648–9*, pp.237, 282.

and John Semagne, who delivered 100 barrels of powder apiece in June and August 1648 respectively.[21] Not all the arms and munitions going to Ireland, however, were supplied by the Ordnance Office. On 26 February 1649 the Council of Sate informed the Committee for the Army:

> there is a great quantity of powder and match being made at Manchester, which lie in the hands of particular men, and may perhaps be bought up by such as will use it to the prejudice of the Commonwealth. We therefore desire you that it may be bought for the use of the State, and delivered into the custody of Lieutenant Colonel Venables, Governor of Liverpool, as a supply for Ireland; also 1,000 muskets with some bandoliers and swords, to be contracted for with Browne, of Manchester. We also desire you to certify your contract to us, that we may know the quantities, and how to dispose thereof, and all with speed, because of an absolute necessity of supplies for Ireland.

Venables was also to take into his care various quantities of weapons captured from the Scottish Engagers in Lancashire, at Preston and Winwick, during the previous August, 'and cause them to be made fit for the service of Ireland. If this order be effectually prosecuted, it will save much charge, and be a very ready provision for Ireland.' A total of 600 muskets, swords, and bandoleers, and 400 pikes and swords were duly issued to Colonel Robert Tothill's regiment, which was waiting to embark at Chester for Dublin. Similarly, in May 1649 it was ordered that pikes, swords, and bandoliers be sent to the magazine at the latter for Venables' own regiment, which was about to cross to Ireland, although their muskets were to be supplied to them at Chester. Moreover, the city's mayor was ordered 'to take care that the arms still wanting for Colonel Venables' regiment be brought and furnished to him there, and provide shipping and victuals for their transportation, and their month's pay when on board.'[22]

Gunpowder

The establishment of the Committee for Powder, Match and Shot was foreshadowed in June 1644 when the Committee of Both Kingdoms resolved to inform the Commons of the shortage of gunpowder, and to request the setting up of a committee with power to contract for powder. By then the question of gunpowder for land service had become critical, for reserves were virtually nonexistent and new supplies were being pre-empted for the most urgent needs of the moment. On 27 January 1645 the Committee of Both Kingdoms – the body established by Parliament for the administration of its war effort – advised the Commons to expedite the ordinance for the provision of powder and other ammunition.[23] Hence, on 6 February the Commons

21 TNA, SP28/140/3, unfol.; BL, Ms Add. 35332, ff. 24r–25v.

22 *CSPD 1649–50*, pp.20–21, 38, 96, 136–137, 169. On 27 June 1649 1,000 coats and pairs of breeches were also delivered by the Officers of the Ordnance to Venables' regiment at Chester (BL, Ms Add. 35332, f. 132r).

23 *CSPD 1644*, p.232; *CSPD 1644–5*, p.275.

ordered that the report of the Committee of Both Kingdoms concerning the replenishment of the stores be referred to the Navy Committee which was to bring in an ordinance for 'the constant supply and furnishing the Stores with all provision both for sea and land'. Accordingly, the Navy Committee asked the Officers of the Ordnance to certify what munitions 'are fit to be furnished into the Stores for the year according to last year's proportion', and what stores for this purpose were already in the Tower. The officers were also to make an estimate of the sums needed for the stores that would have to be purchased.[24] Such an approach was more relevant to the needs of the Navy than to those of the armies. An ordinance for the appointment of a committee authorised to contract for powder, match and shot and charged with overseeing the Ordnance Office was passed by the Commons on 30 June 1645, and approved by the Lords on the following day.[25]

On 31 July 1645 the new Committee for Powder, Match and Shot had put into effect its powers to supervise the receipt and issue of munitions at the Tower by instructing the Officers of the Ordnance to state how many of the 678 barrels of powder received from Samuel Cordwell since the second of that month had already been issued and for what purpose. In future, the officers were to present weekly summaries of the issues of ammunition in order that adequate provision for the magazine could be made. There was, however, a precedent for such regular checks. In January 1641 the Storekeeper was ordered to provide a monthly return of the amount of gunpowder in store.[26] The Committee was primarily engaged in the business of dealing with gunpowder manufacturers. Although it was in theory responsible for the provision of any kind of munitions that might be required, in fact the supply of powder, match and shot remained its principal concern. The Committee remained in existence until the end of the Second Civil War.[27]

An indication of the large amount of munitions used by a seventeenth century army is revealed in a national inventory of the ordnance and ammunition required for a field army of 10,000 men, drawn up on 28 March 1642. The foot regiments were allocated 7½ tons of powder, 7½ tons of musket shot, and 10 tons of match. The artillery train, comprising 10 field pieces and 60 small guns, was apportioned 10 tons of powder and 10 tons of cannonballs.[28] Between 20 September and 16 December the Cheshire Parliamentarian forces expended 140 barrels of powder with bullets proportionable, in addition to 20 tons of match, 'besides what ammunition has been spent at this time at Tarvin and Beeston, and at the battle in Wales [Denbigh on 1 November] with the enemy.'[29]

On 31 July 1645 the Committee ordered the Office of the Ordnance to provide 'a particular account of what gunpowder, match, and bullet has been received and issued since 2 July 1645 to this present'. The Officers attested that a total of 793 barrels of powder, 19½ tons of match, and 14½ tons of musket shot had been received

24 TNA, WO47/1, ff. 169r & 325r.
25 *CJ*, IV, pp.190–191.
26 *CSPD 1640–1*, pp.449–450.
27 TNA, WO49/82, ff. 35v–36r, 79r–89v; WO55/461, fol. 16v; BL, Ms Add. 35332, f. 17r.
28 TNA, SP16/489/99.
29 BL, Ms Add. 11333, f. 25r.

for land service, whereas 669 barrels of powder, 19½ tons of match, and 14½ tons of musket bullet had been distributed from its stores for the same purpose, including 200 barrels of powder to the Parliamentarian garrisons in the West and 20 barrels for the Derbyshire forces. Additionally, between 1 and 18 July 169 barrels of powder were delivered for sea service. This left a total of 124 barrels in the stores, although this included 100 barrels of powder earmarked for the Scottish Army, leaving no stock.[30] The manufacturers of ordnance, gunpowder, match, and shot were some of the most important contractors supplying the Ordnance Office. Thus, the most prominent of these – men such as John Freeman, Thomas Steventon, John Berisford, Samuel Cordwell, and the plumber Daniel Judd – were former holders of patents from the Crown who were obligated to enter agreed contracts with the Parliament if they wanted to retain control of their works, preserve access to the London market and receive payment of monies owed to them by the State.

In the seventeenth century the ingredients of gunpowder were saltpetre, charcoal, and sulphur in the ratio of 17:15:10 respectively, although depending upon the circumstances of its production and availability of some elements this may have altered.[31] Such great demand for powder during the British Civil Wars forced Parliament to intervene in the production of saltpetre. On 22 May 1643 an Ordinance 'for the better making of gunpowder, and taking of saltpetre, for the furnishing of the Navy, forts, and land forces with stores of powder' nominated saltpetre manufacturers to supply powdermakers, given that great quantities were needed and the foreign saltpetre and powder available was generally of an inferior standard.[32] Another Ordinance for the provision of saltpetre and munitions, introduced on 7 December 1644, referred both to the appointment of saltpetre men and to the purchase of foreign saltpetre from William Curteen and William Toombs, importers from the East Indies.[33]

On 4 April 1644 the Commons ordered that some of the saltpetre obtained from Curteen 'sufficient to make 600 barrels of powder for the Navy be delivered to Sir Walter Erle [Lieutenant of the Ordnance]'.[34] Receipts of the Ordnance Office 'in his Majesty's stores for the supply of Sir Thomas Fairfax his Army', include one of 1 April 1645, which records the sum of £665 due to Samuel Cordwell 'for 148 barrels of good and serviceable English powder made of foreign saltpeter by the said [Cordwell] and brought it his Majesty's stores within the Ordnance Office, for which he moved by order of the Committee for the Navy, 19 March 1645 after the rate of £4 10s. per barrel'. Cordwell also received £675 on 4 April for purchasing saltpetre and powder, 'being 150 barrels of good and serviceable English gunpowder made of foreign saltpetre', whereas Berisford was paid £429 for providing 104 barrels of the same to the Ordnance Office.[35]

30 TNA, WO49/82, ff. 329r–331r; *CSPD 1645–7*, p.292.

31 A. G. Crocker, G. M. Crocker, K. R. Fairclough and M. J. Wilks (eds), *Gunpowder Mills: Documents of the 17th and 18th Centuries* (Surrey Record Society, 2000), p.135.

32 *CJ*, III, p.97.

33 *A&O*, I, pp.578–579.

34 *CJ*, III, pp.364–5; *CSPD 1644*, p.129.

35 TNA, SP28/29/1, ff. 121r & 144r.

Exodus of the Spanish army from Maastricht, 1632, illustrating an artillery train, Jan van de Velde. (Rijksmuseum, Amsterdam)

Caldwell and Berisford were the leading gunpowder makers in England, although the latter also supplied match and shot to the Ordnance Office, and in turn to the New Model Army and other Parliamentarian forces. The other major source of supply was represented by merchants who purchased powder on the Continent, chiefly in the Netherlands. On 3 May 1645 the Committee of the Navy was informed that a consignment of gunpowder had been obtained from the Spanish ambassador, 'which upon proof they were found to be worth but £2 15s. per barrel, which the said ambassador is content to accept for the same'. Accordingly, on 30 June the Treasury paid Francisco Bernardi, the ambassador's agent, the sum of £150 7s. 6d. 'for 60 barrels and 15lbs of Dutch powder received into his Majesty's Stores out of the prize ship *Rigor*. By order of the Committee of the Navy each barrel 100lb nett'.[36] Gunpowder made in England from foreign saltpetre was somewhat more expensive than that made from English saltpetre, on average by about 5s. or 6s. a barrel. Records of deliveries of foreign gunpowder to the Ordnance Office stores are not abundant, but they indicate that barrel for barrel such powder cost about the same as English powder, although some foreign powder sold to the Committee of Safety during 1643 was about 5s. a barrel cheaper than its English counterpart.[37] According to two comprehensive Ordnance Office books in the Bodleian Library – one 'containing certificates by the Officers of the Ordnance for the receipt of certain materials of war contracted for and supplied for Fairfax's Army, from 24 March 1645 to 4 March 1646', and a 'Register of receipts for arms and supplies received into

36 TNA, WO/49/82, f. 283r; SP28/30/6, f. 643r.
37 TNA, SP28/264, ff. 27r–28v, 309r, 310v, 371r.

the King's Stores, mainly for the use of Sir Thomas Fairfax's Army, 1646–1649' – by far the most prolific supplier of gunpowder, John Berisford delivered 2,130 barrels between 14 April 1645 and 17 July 1646.[38]

Table 5 records the gunpowder contracted, paid for, and received by the Ordnance Office in 1645 and 1646. Though every effort has been made to match up the notification of indentures, pay warrants and entries in the receipts books, some gaps remain.

Table 05: Gunpowder Supplied to the Ordnance Office for the NMA (TNA, WO47/1; WO/49/82; SP28/29/1-32/3; SP28/140/1; Bodl. Lib., Ms Eng. hist. C14)

4/4/45	John Berisford	Paid £429 for 104 barrels of good and serviceable English gunpowder made of foreign saltpetre.
7/4/45		Contracted for 130 barrels of English gunpowder at £4 10s. per barrel, one half in hand, the rest at 3 months; payment 25/4/45 for same £585. Undated notification of contract of similar item in ML, 46–78/709, thought the entry has 'five months'; this possibly relates to the WO47/1 debenture and the date was entered incorrectly, or a different one entirely. 130 barrels delivered on 14/4/45; paid in part £292 10s. 15/4/45.
28/6/45		Paid £30 for repairing and making serviceable 24 barrels of gunpowder.
30/6/45		Contracted for 200 barrels of powder at gunpowder at £4 10s. per barrel, one half in hand, the rest at 3 months. 200 barrels delivered on 1/7/45.
17/7/45		Warrant: In pursuit of an order of the Committee for the Army for contracts for ammunition of 16 July, I have contracted with Mr John Berisford for 100 barrels of powder at the rates of £4 10s. per barrel, which you are to receive into the stores, and to certify the receipt and proof thereof to the Committee. Walter Erle. ML, 46-78/709 gives this as '200 barrels'. 100 barrels delivered 25/7/45.
26/7/45		100 barrels delivered 25/7/45. Paid in full of his contract for 200 barrels of English powder at £4 10s. per barrel, the sum of £625 at 3 months' end, beginning 25 July instant.
12/8/45		Paid £441 in full for 200 barrels of powder.
13/8/45		Contracted for 100 barrels of best English powder. 100 barrels delivered 16/8/45.
25/8/45		Contracted for 100 barrels of English powder at £4 10s. per barrel; 28/8/45 paid in full of his contract, the sum of £225 at 3 months' end, beginning 26 August instant. 100 barrels delivered 26/8/45.
3/9/45		Paid for 100 barrels of English corn powder at £4 10s. per barrel. 100 barrels delivered 9/9/45.
20/9/46		Paid £445 10s. for 100 barrels of powder delivered.
29/9/45		Contracted for 100 barrels of best English corn powder at £4 10s. per barrel.
21/12/45		200 barrels of powder delivered.

38 Bodl. Lib., Ms Eng. hist. C14, ff. 16r, 31r and 41r, 45r–45v, 46v, 52r 57r, 78r, 85r; Ms Eng. hist. C244, ff. 10r, 16v 19v, 21v.

26/12/45		Contracted for 200 barrels of English powder at £4 10s. per barrel to be forthwith sent into the stores of the Tower for the use of Sir Thomas Fairfax his Army. 200 barrels delivered 9/2/46.
11/12/45		My contract with the Committee for the Army for 1,000 barrels of powder; received this contract from Mr Hutchinson 5 April 1646. This might be the 'defective contract for gunpowder from Berisford' noted above the previous folio. Delivered by Berisford: 3/3/46 200 barrels 4/4/46 200 barrels 26/5/46 200 barrels 5/6/46 100 barrels 20/6/46 200 barrels
17/7/46		Delivered 200 barrels.
4/4/45	Samuel Cordwell	Paid £675 for buying saltpetre and powder, being 150 barrels of good and serviceable English gunpowder made of foreign saltpetre.
13/6/45	Daniel Judd	50 barrels delivered to Weymouth garrison.
9/9/45	Christopher Webb	Received 10 barrels of corn powder.

Musket, Carbine and Pistol Shot

During the early stages of the Civil Wars various sizes of musket bullets were used, which created both practical and logistical problems. In 1677 the Anglo-Irish soldier Roger Boyle, Earl of Orrery, who fought in the Irish Confederate Wars and later during the Cromwellian conquest of Ireland recommended that:

> All our muskets be of one bore, or at most of two sorts of certain bores; the bigger for the stronger, the lesser for the weaker bodies; for want of this, seen much hazard undergone; for generally our musket shot is of one certain size, and the bores of muskets are of various sizes, whereby having been once engaged in a fight, which by reason of the many enclosures in which we fought, the musketeers were to be supplied with more shot than they carried in their Pouches, and barrels of musket bullets being opened, few of the shot in them would fit the muskets, but were a size too large, whereby we had like to have been worsted; for the soldiers were forced to gnaw off much of the lead, others to cut their bullets; in which much time was lost, the bullets flew a less way, and more uncertainly; and, which was worse, so many pauses, animated the enemy, by making him think our courages cooled. If there be two sizes of muskets, and shot, on both ends of the barrels, which hold the shot, should be written lesser, and bigger, that in the hurry of a fight there might be no mistake, but that bullets be distributed according to the bores of the muskets.[39]

39 Orrery, *Treatise*, pp.29–30.

The practicality of this system is unclear, however, and it must be remembered that generally logistics and supply for Irish forces was not of the highest quality.

The Ordnance Office plumber, Daniel Judd, was contracted with mainly for lead shot and match. He was the principal supplier of musket bullets during the Civil Wars, nonetheless he also supplied a considerable amount of match. His contracts included those for 7 tons of lead shot and nearly 4 tons of match in July 1644.[40] Between June and December 1645 Judd delivered to the land stores 43 tons of musket shot, one ton of pistol shot, 36½ tons of match, 200 coats and 200 pairs of breeches. On 20 March 1646 he delivered 10 tons of match and on 5 February 1648 a debenture was made out to him in respect of 30 tons of musket shot and 30 tons of match.[41] Judd and others provided both 'musket shot', equating to 12 bore or .729 inches in calibre, and 'bastard musket shot', being 14 to the pound or .511 inches in calibre. The 10 tons of shot carried by the New Model's train of artillery as its 'front line' ammunition stocks consisted solely of bastard musket bullets, with 6 dozen moulds for making bastard shot.[42] One supplier, John Pembury, was contracted, before 3 April 1645, for '5 tons of musket shot of 14 to the pound at £16 10s. per ton for the use of the army, to be delivered within 14 days'. This order was delivered three weeks later, and he received payment of £82 10s. in full on 1 May.[43] Both Pembury and Judd provided this type of ammunition, which suggests a continuity in bullet size for bastard musket shot with that used by the Earl of Essex's Army between 1642 and 1644.[44] As Simon Marsh asserts, 'If this is the case and the New Model received the intended 10 tons of bastard musket shot proposed for its establishment, bastard musket bullets would have accounted for almost double the weight of musket shot ordered in 1645'.[45] The most common calibre of musket balls recovered from the site of the Battle of Edgehill (1642) is 14 to the pound, while a survey of Langport (1645 and a New Model Army engagement), by the Battlefields Trust revealed that of the 12 musket type balls recovered, 10 were of bastard musket size 'with at least seven of those probably originally intended for a 14-bore weapon'.[46] Moreover, among the slightly smaller sample of bullets found on the battlefield of Winwick (1648), the mean diameter is 13mm and of a typical weight of 1.1oz. (14 bore) weapon'.[47]

The combat effectiveness of the lighter bastard muskets, as opposed to those of a heavier calibre, were made clear by Francis Markham, who in 1622 wrote:

40 TNA, WO49/82, ff. 2r, 5r; BL, Ms Add. 25585, ff. 69r–69v.

41 TNA, WO49/82, f. 96r; WO55/1662, ff. 76v–77v; WO55/1663, f. 83r.

42 TNA, SP28/145, f. 60r; WO47/1, f. 210r.

43 TNA, WO47/1, f. 211r; WO55/1662, f. 44v; SP28/30/4, f. 337r; Bodl. Lib., Ms Eng. hist. C14, f. 18r.

44 TNA, WO55/1937, f. 31r; SP28/145 f. 34v.

45 Simon Marsh, 'Of Muskets and Bastard Muskets: Use of Lighter Muskets in Civil War England', *Battalia: The Journal of the Battlefields Trust*, 2 (2024), pp.12–26, (p. 22).

46 D. P. Miller, D. Allsop and D. J. Carr, 'The ballistics of seventeenth-century musket balls', *Journal of Conflict Archaeology*, 14 (2019), pp.25–36; Glenn Foard, 'History from the Field: The Edgehill Battlefield Survey' (2005) https://www.battlefieldstrust.com/media/558.pdf; Battlefields Trust, Langport Battlefield Survey Report (2023) https://www.battlefieldstrust.com/resource-centre/battleview.asp?BattleFieldId=20

47 Currently in the possession of the Battle of Winwick Society.

> The bastard musket (which differ nothing from the full musket, but in the bore only, and the charges which must be made suitable to the bore) they are of excellent use, for they carry as far as the full musket, and pierce as deep (thought their bore be less) and their lightness and nimbleness to those that are weaker, and of much less abler bodies, is such an ease and comfort, that they are able both to hold out in marches and in service.[48]

Injuries inflicted by the low-velocity soft lead projectiles of seventeenth century firearms are reflected in some of the wounds received by officers of the New Model Army in 1645. At Naseby Sir Phillip Skippon, Sergeant-Major General of foot, was accidently 'shot through the right side under the ribs, through armour, and coat, but not mortal', while the colonel of horse, John Butler, received 'a brace of bullets in the thigh [and] gallantly charged both the Princes before he came off'.[49] Moreover, at Bristol on 10 September Fairfax launched an assault against the line from Prior's Hill Fort down to the Frome. Colonels Thomas Rainborowe and Robert Hammond attacked round the Fort, the latter gaining the defences, which had been broken down by the pioneers, and made a way for the horse to enter. Nonetheless, Hammond:

> received a shot with two pistol bullets, which broke his arm, by means of this entrance of Colonel Hammond they did storm the Fort on that part which was inward; and so Colonel Rainborowe's and Colonel Hammond's men entered the Fort, immediately [and] put almost all the men in it to the sword.[50]

The New Model Army possessed its own means of manufacturing musket ammunition, thus to an extent making it self-sufficient in the field, especially during siege operations and when regular supplies were slow in arriving. On 5 March 1645, the Commons agreed that amongst the 'fireworks with appurtenances' distributed between 3 close waggons and 6 open carts of the train – under the auspices of the Commissary of Ammunition – were to be '2,000 moulds to make bullets 1 dozen of 1lb, 6 dozen of bastard musket bullets with nippers, pots and ladles', for the express use of the ladle maker William Bromwich.

Other equipment required specifically for the casting of musket shot, including 12 melting ladles at 3s. apiece, 24 dipping ladles at 6d. each, and 2cwt of sheet lead, is laid out in the partially damaged accounts of Sir Walter Erle, the Lieutenant of the Ordnance, along with the entire purchases for the New Model Army's train of artillery between April and June 1645.[51] Another suggestion listed 'for the smith to carry his tools, bullet moulds and other necessaries 1 close waggon with 5 horses',

48 Markham, *Five Decades of Epistles of Warre*, p.36.

49 George Bishop, *A More Particular and Exact Relation of the Victory obtained by the Parliament's forces under the command of Sir Thomas Fairfax* (London: Richard Cotes, 1645). TT, E288[38].

50 Sprigge, *Anglia Rediviva*, pp.115–116; Barclay, Wales, Morrill (eds), *Letters*, I, p.135.

51 TNA, SP28/140/1, ff. 3r–6v.

in addition to 'for the bullet moulds, nippers and the like to be carried in one of the smith's waggons, being allowed 4 waggons to carry his tools, iron, coals, clouts and grease.'[52] The latter proposal was not accepted, though, and it is likely that it was absorbed into the first. Nevertheless, on 17 May Commissary Phipps received from the Ordnance Office 'for the service of the army under the command of Sir Thomas Fairfax' 6 iron moulds for 1lb bullets and 12 for ½lb projectiles, in addition to other items of artillery equipment, such as 'spare field carriages for a saker, one demi-culverin, 3 ladles and sponges for sakers, 3 wad hooks, and 10 tilts of hair.'[53] Similarly, a brass falcon mould, along with 2 tons of flat iron and other equipment was delivered to Richard Fenner and Henry Jarman on 26 July 1645 for the New Model, 'by warrant from the Committee for the Army'.[54] No falcons were included in the initial establishment of the train, although they were light guns, with a calibre of 2.75 inches and shot weight of 2.25lbs, of limited value to a field army.

Quantities of cartridges – sealed paper tubes, containing a measure of powder and with a bullet at one end – must have been made up, perhaps locally by members of the train of artillery, for the use of the New Model Army's dragoons, cavalry troopers and possibly the firelock guard. In his report of the Battle of Naseby on 14 June 1645 Colonel John Okey recounted that prior to deploying his regiment of dragoons to secure the left flank of the army, he 'was half a mile behind in a meadow giving my men ammunition'.[55] Given that his soldiers had been supplied with cartridge boxes two months previously, the use of the term 'ammunition' here must imply cartridges. Writing in 1616, the German professional soldier Johann Jacobi von Wallhausen maintained that harquebusiers should either use powder flasks and bullets from a bag or, alternatively, cartridges.[56] Likewise, John Cruso, writing in 1632, agreed that only paper cartridges were used as ammunition for both cuirassiers and harquebusiers.[57] In 1644 the other cavalry practitioner John Vernon wrote in his manual:

> if you use cartridges, you shall find in your cartridge case a turned wooden pin which you must take, having cut lengths of white paper something broader than the pin is in length, and roll the paper on the pin, then twist one end of the paper, and fill it almost full of powder, then put the bullet on top of the powder, twisting that end also, then put it into your cartridge case, now when you come to load your carbine or pistol with these cartridges, you must bite off that end of the paper where the powder is, pouring it into your carbine or pistol, then put in that bullet, and some of that paper will serve as a wad after it, and ram home, but always observe that your bullet be not too big,

52 TNA, SP28/145, f. 61r; SP28/225, unfol. The entire purchases for the New Model Army's train of artillery between April and June 1645 are detailed in the (partly damaged) accounts of Sir Walter Erle, the Lieutenant of the Ordnance (SP28/140/1).

53 TNA, SP28/30/3, fol. 245r.

54 TNA, WO55/1647, unfol.; Bodl. Lib., Ms Eng. hist. C14. f. 40v; WSL, Ms Salt 463, unfol.

55 *A More Particular and Exact Relation of the Victory obtained by the Parliament's forces under the command of Sir Thomas Fairfax* (London: Richard Cotes, 1645). TT, E288[38].

56 Wallhausen, *Kriegskunst zu Pferd* (Frankfurt: 1616), p.35.

57 Cruso, *Militarie Instructions*, pp.37–42.

> but that it may roll home to the powder, for if there be any distance between the bullet and powder, it is like to break the barrel of your carbine or pistol. But if you use a flask, which in my judgement is far better than cartridge, because that many times the trotting of your horse in long march, shakes out all the powder of your cartridges and thereby causes you to be unprovided for the sudden charge of the enemy, you must gauge your flask and so lade your carbine and pistol with powder and bullet as before, but never prime before you have spanned. Now the quantity of the powder usually required for the loading of either carbine or pistol is half the weight of the bullet.[58]

In a similar fashion, Monck suggested that musketeers marching at the vanguard of an army 'ought to have two pairs of bandoliers furnished with powder and bullet, and in case you have no bandoliers, let there be provided for each musketeer … twelve cartridges, which they ought to carry in their righthand pocket, and twelve bullets apiece in their pockets besides'.[59]

Table 06: Musket and Pistol Shot Supplied to the Ordnance Office for the NMA (TNA, WO/49/82; SP28/30/4-32/3; SP28/140/1; Bodl. Lib., Ms Eng. hist. C14)

14/6/45	Daniel Judd	Delivered musket shot 3 tons at £17 per ton apiece according to the contract made with the Committee of the Army, notified 14/6/45. Paid in full £51 17/6/45.
17/7/45		Contract for 4 tons of musket shot at £16 10s. per ton to be delivered in 6 days. Delivered 22/7/45.
25/7/45		Contract for 4 tons of bastard musket shot for Pembrokeshire garrisons and 5 tons for the Scotch army.
12/8/45		Contract for 7 tons of bastard musket shot at £17 per ton, well sized and gauged.
12/9/45		Paid £87 for 11 tons of bastard musket shot at £17 per ton.
4/10/45		Contract for 5 tons of musket shot at £18 10s. per ton.
22/11/45		Contract for 10 tons of bastard musket shot and 1 ton of pistol shot at £17 each ton weight, to be delivered into the stores at the Tower of London before 1 January next, for the use of Sir Thomas Fairfax his Army – notified to Thomas Pury at the Ordnance Office on 19 October 1645.
8/12/45		Delivered 10 tons of musket shot and 1 ton of pistol shot.
3/4/45	John Pembury	Contract for 5 tons of musket shot of 14 to the pound at £16 10s. per ton for the use of the army, to be delivered within 14 days. Received 24/4/45; paid £82 10s. in full 1/5/45.
17/7/45		Contract for 4 tons of musket bullet at £16 10s. per ton to be delivered in 6 days. Delivered 22/7/45.

58 Vernon, *Young Horse-Man*, pp.8, 10.
59 Monck, *Observations*, p.150.

Match

Match cord, or slow match, used by musketeers, some dragoons, and gunners to ignite their charges, was made by steeping hemp cord or tow in saltpetre and limewater (vinegar being a substitute), then immersing it in sulphur. The principal suppliers of match for land service to the Ordnance Office were John Freeman and Thomas Steventon. In March 1645 they agreed with the Committee for the Army to provide 8 tons of match, and a further 4 tons in June 1645. Freeman also provided some gunpowder for the Ordnance Office and for the Committee of Safety.[60] Between 7 October and 8 November 1644, he brought in over 11 tons of 'good and serviceable English match to be supplied to Essex's train of artillery'. In April and July 1645, he delivered a further 11 tons for the New Model Army, including the 2½ tons of English match at £34 per ton that he was paid for on 10 July.[61] Steventon was contracted with for 7 tons of match on 6 September 1644 and thereafter he was a regular supplier of that commodity. Between April and August 1645, he provided 11 tons for the New Model Army. Amongst the debentures made out to him are one for '68cwt of English match in fatts' and 12cwt of Spanish match. On 1 June Steventon received a payment of £34 for 1 ton of match 'made up in fatts, by him provided and by him brought into his Majesty's stores for the service at Farnham Castle.' By 11 July he had delivered 2½ tons of English match and the like of Spanish, and on 2 August, provided 39cwt 4lbs of English match at £1 13s. per cwt and 3 tons 19lbs of Flemish at £3 per ton for Fairfax's Army, for which he had £155 19s. 6d.[62]

Before 12 April 1645 Freeman had agreed to provide 13 tons 10cwt of English match and 10cwt of 'Spanish' (i.e., purchased in the Spanish Netherlands) match in fatts, although by then he had already brought in various quantities. Various quantities of gunpowder and saltpetre (potassium nitrate) manufactured on the Continent were imported by both Parliamentarian and Royalist agents between 1644 and 1648. The names of the former remain unknown, though two merchants, Richard Hill and William Pennoyer, maintained an agent at Dunkirk for the importation of munitions for Charles I's forces.[63] Where it is possible to tell from the meagre entries in the documents, like powder, Dutch or Flemish match was roughly the same price, or sometimes cheaper than its English counterpart, although any true comparison of the cost of domestic and imported ammunition needs to consider the extra expense involved in procurement and transportation from abroad. One warrant, dated 1 April 1645, records 'received into his Majesty's stores for the supply of Sir Thomas Fairfax his army' from John Freeman for '3 tons of English match at £30 per ton and 1cwt of Dutch match made up the English way', while another drawn up on 17 June ordered payment to 'John Freeman [in receipt of] 1 ton of English match in fatts, for which he is to have by contract £34; also 1 ton of Dutch match in fatts made up in the English way £31 according to the contract made with the Committee of the Army'.

60 TNA, WO47/1, ff. 206v, 267r; WO55/1660, f. 7r.
61 TNA, SP28/31/5, f. 516r; Bodl. Lib., Ms Eng. hist. C14, ff. 10v, 35r.
62 TNA, WO/47/1, f. 99v; SP28/31/3, ff. 327r & 331r; SP28/31/5, f. 517r.
63 Edwards, *Dealing in Death*, p.203.

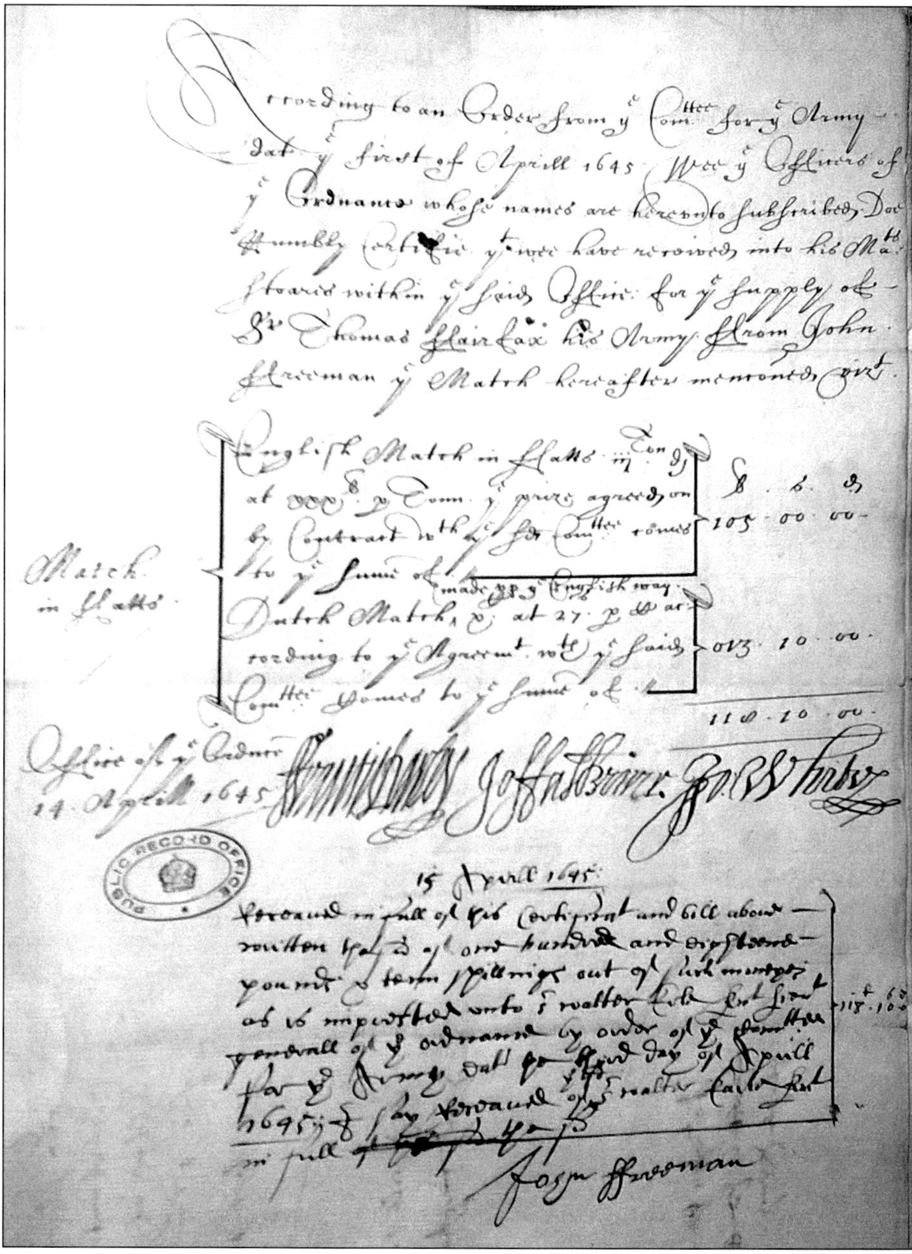

According to an Order from ye Comttee for ye Army dat ye first of Aprill 1645 Wee ye Officers of ye Ordnance whose names are hereunto subscribed Doe humbly Certifie yt wee have received into his Mats Stoares within ye said Office for ye supply of Sr Thomas Fairfax his Army from John Freeman ye Match hereafter menconed vizt.

Match in ffatts

	li	s	d
English Match in ffatts iij Ton at xxxli p Ton ye price agreed on by Contract wth ye said Comttee comes to ye sume of	105	00	00
Dutch Match made up ye English way j C at 27 p C according to ye Agreemt wth ye said Comttee comes to ye sume of	013	10	00
	118	10	00

Office of ye Ordnce 14 April 1645

15 Aprill 1645

[illegible]

John Freeman

Receipt from the Officers of the Ordnance Office, 1 April 1645, 'for the supply of Sir Thomas Fairfax his army from John Freeman for 3 tons of English match at £30 per ton and 1cwt of Dutch match made up the English way.' (TNA, SP28/29/1, fol. 120r)

He also supplied 2½ tons of English match and 2½ tons of Flemish match to the Scots army on 8 August at a cost of £157 10s.[64] Steventon and Freeman also operated in partnership. On 18 June 1645 they delivered 2 tons of English and the same of Flemish match, and a further 5 tons of each on 8 July.[65] A certain amount of match was also provided by Daniel Judd of the Ordnance Office. From mid-1645 onwards he brought in substantial quantities of match and shot, including 26 tons of English match and 7 tons of bastard musket shot on 16 and 26 July; 6 tons of match and 7 tons of bastard shot delivered before 1 August; in addition to supplying 11 tons of shot on 12 September; 10cwt of musket bullet and 6cwt of match on 19 September; and 5 tons on 10 October. The Committee for the Army notified the Ordnance Office of a contract with Judd on 18 December 1645 for the provision of 50 tons of match over the ensuing six months. By the following June he had supplied 56 tons, embracing '16 tons of English match in fatts and 10 tons musket shot' on the 25th of the month.[66] According to recommendations for the establishment of the New Model's train of artillery, agreed to by Parliament on 5 March 1645, when it began the campaign in April-May 1645 it was to be holding 10 tons of match in 20 fatts, transported in 13 waggons.[67]

On 10 January 1645 the Officers of the Ordnance Office had issued the following warrant, stating:

> There is due unto Richard Birch and William Franklin, two of the yeoman warders of the Tower of London, the sum of £20 each to them, payable upon the estimates for the last summer's fleet, viz. as well as for themselves 38 of their fellow warders for their extraordinary service in attending the Byward Gate daily and hourly upon all occasions, in letting in and out ammunition and provisions for land service from 19 January 1644, being one whole year, for which service they are allowed, according to former precedents in the Office of the Ordnance the said sum of £20.[68]

Similarly, on 12 April 1645 12 tons of match were furnished by the Ordnance Office to Commissary Thomas Phipps, another 5 tons of match in fatts and 1 ton of match 'without fatts' five days later, whereas a further 4 tons were received on 29 May. Similarly, a warrant was issued on 10 October 1645 for the payment of £78 3s. 6d. to William Wybert at New Fish Market Hill, who had previously supplied the army with 2 tons of match, for the delivery of 46¼cwt of match at £1 12s. per cwt, 'and for 8 demi-fatts and packing them £3 16s., and for carts to the ship and loading them 7s.'.[69]

64 TNA, SP28/29/1, f. 120r; SP28/30/5, f. 637r; SP28/31/3, f. 329r.

65 Bodl. Lib., Ms Eng. hist. C14, f. 9r, 10v, 29r, f.35r.

66 TNA, WO55/1663, ff. 73v, 83v; SP28/31/4, f. 441r; SP28/32/1, f. 7r; SP28/32/3, ff. 250r, 352r; SP28/140, ff. 114r & 119r; Bodl. Lib., Ms Eng. hist. C14, f.42r; Ms Eng. hist. C244, ff. 7v, 14v, 20v, 21r, 22r.

67 TNA, SP28/145, f. 60r.

68 TNA, SP28/29/1, f. 148r.

69 TNA, SP28/30/3, ff. 245r, 249r, 251r; SP28/31/4, f. 11r.

Warrants for the supply of powder, ball and match to Sir Thomas Fairfax's Army do not indicate the quantities issued to individual musketeers. In 1677 Sir James Turner recommended that 'a musket requires the half the weight of her ball in fine powder, and two thirds of common powder, that is, one pound of fine powder to two pounds of lead, and two pounds of ordinary powder for three pounds of lead.'[70] Orrery recounted that corporals were issued with an unspecified quantities of skeins (120 yards in length) and distributed to individual soldiers several links (being slightly under 8 inches). He also suggested that 'it might also do well, if the soldiers tied their links of match about their middle, and under their coats, and doublets, instead of tying them to their bandolier belt, or collar; for by that means, the match would be kept dryer, and fitter for service, in time of action'.[71] On 4 December 1643 Lieutenant Richard Colonel Brooke, the Parliamentarian governor of Halton in Cheshire instructed the constables of Aston to assist in seizing, taxing and levying of arms and ammunition upon their township, 'allowing for every musket 24 bullets and 2lb of powder'. A fortnight afterwards his brother, Captain John Brooke, directed the same officials to:

> ...gather moneys for the buying of ammunition according to 3lb of powder, 12 yards of match, 60 bullets for every musket ... you shall be provided after the rates of 1s. 6d. powder the pound, match 8d. the pound, now for the better gathering of this money you are to understand that every whole plough, and every two half ploughs are to find a man, musket, sword and bandolier, and for you to gather proportionately.[72]

Such warrants were issued in response to the general muster of Parliamentarian forces faced with the recent disembarkation of Royalist troops from Ireland in Cheshire and North Wales. Notably, Lieutenant Colonel Brooke's soldiers were mainly garrison troops, whereas his brother's company were mustered for field service (being 'equipped and trained in martial discipline'), thus suggesting that the 3lb of powder, 12 yards of match and 60 bullets was the most common issue during operations of an undefined period, without the expectation of resupply.

Going by the specifications given in contracts and the details of receipts, the powder contracted by the Committee for the Army in 1645 and 1646 appears to have been the same, both in terms of quality and price. Moreover, the bandoliers procured for the New Model appear to have had the same size boxes or charges, as no different sizes are indicated. This suggests that each full bandolier box equated to a single charge for a musket, and that powder was issued by volume. Even though the evidence for filling bandolier boxes is limited, the Earl of Newcastle's drill manual of 1642 stated, 'A measured charge shall be given to every musketeer that holds just so much powder as half the bullet weighs at 10 bullets in the pound, to fill

70 Sir James Turner, *Pallas Armata: Military Essays of the Ancient Grecian, Roman, and modern art of war written in the years 1670 and 1671* (London: 1683), p.175.

71 Orrery, *Treatise*, p.32.

72 Andrew Abram, *More Like Lions than Men: Sir William Brereton and the Cheshire Army of Parliament, 1642–46* (Solihull: Helion & Co., 2020), pp.309–311.

their bandoliers withal.'[73] This further suggests that during the British Civil Wars the issue of powder was frequently by use of a measure, although the varying power of some quantities, produced by disparity in quality and percentage of ingredients, in addition to differences in grain size and moisture content, probably affected its performance and reliability. In distributing powder, each day the corporals of divisions or squadrons of shot were required to issue rations and ammunition to sentinels. According to Richard Elton:

> He must advise his sentinels how to demean themselves upon the discovery of an enemy, either to give an alarm, or else to give notice without making a noise. And if upon his guard he shall either observe or be advertised by his sentinels of the approach of the enemy, then he is to have his men in readiness with bullets in their muskets, and their matches lighted; himself secretly coming in, giving intelligence unto his captain, or other superior officer, whereby they may all be in a readiness before the alarm be given. He is likewise to distribute victual, powder, bullet and match, unto his squadron, and to take notice of the best experienced men, and accordingly to employ them upon action upon the watches.[74]

Table 07: Match Received by the Ordnance Office for the NMA and Dates of Payment to Contractors (TNA, WO47/1; WO/49/82; SP28/29/1–32/3; SP28/140/1)

12/4/45	John Freeman	3 tons 8cwt of English match in fatts at £30 per ton £102; Spanish match made up the English way in fatts 12cwt at £27 per cwt £16 4s. Paid in full (including cartage) £118 10s. 14/4/45
17/6/45		1 ton of English match in fatts, for which he is to have by contract £34; also 1 ton of Dutch match in fatts made up in the English way £31 according to the contract made with the Committee of the Army. Paid in full (including cartage) £34 14s. 18/6/45
2/8/45		Paid £157 10s. for the supply of the Scots army English match in fatts 2½ tons and Flemish match in fatts 2½ tons
14/4/45	Thomas Steventon	Paid in full (including cartage) £118 4s. for 4 tons of English match
1/6/45		Paid £34 for 1 ton of English match made up in fatts, by him provided and brought into his Majesty's Stores for the service at Farnham Castle
18/6/45		1 ton of English match made up in fatts by contract £34; Dutch match in fatts made up the English way by contract £31. Paid in full (including cartage) £34 14s. 18/6/45
2/8/45		Paid £155 19s. 6d. English match 39cwt 4lbs at 33s. per cwt and Flemish match 3 tons 19lbs at £3 per ton
1/4/45	Freeman and Steventon	Contract for 8 tons of match at £30 per ton, Dutch made up the English way in fatts

73 Anonymous, *A True Description of the Discipline of War both for Horse and Foot* (n.d.), p.2.
74 Richard Elton, *The Compleat Body of the Art Military* (London: 1650), p.179.

2/7/45		Contract for 5 tons of English and 5 tons of Flemish match
25/7/45		Contract for 2½ tons of match for Pembrokeshire garrisons
26/7/45	John Berisford	Delivered 200 barrels of English match into the Ordnance Office stores, at a cost of £4 10s.
18/6/45	Daniel Judd	Paid in full (including cartage) for 4 tons of English match £138 12s. 6d.
11/7/45		Contract for 6 tons of match at £34 per ton
17/9/45		Paid £18 8s. for 6 cwt of English match at 33s. the cwt the sum of £9 18s., and for 10cwt at 17s. the sum of £8 10s.
12/8/45		Contract for 7 tons of match, 5 tons English and 2 tons Flemish new trimmed made English in fatts
17/9/45		Paid for 6cwt of English match at 33s. the cwt the sum of £9 18s., and for 10cwt at 17s. the sum of £8 10s. In all amounting to £18 8s.
18/12/45		Contract for 50 tons of match at £30 per ton to be delivered into the stores of the Tower of London before the end of July 1646, and at least 10 tons each month, beginning in March next ensuing
25/7/45	William Wybert	Contract for 2 tons of English match at £32 per ton
3/8/45	Alderman Andrews	Contract with Mr Alderman Andrews for 4½ tons of Flemish match in fatts at £30 per ton. If the dates involved in this agreement are at all reliable, this was notified to the Ordnance Office on 18/9/45
20/10/45		Contract for 4 ton and half three quarters 110lbs of Flemish match in fatts at £30 per ton
20/12/45	John Young & Richard Arnold	Contract for 5 tons of Flemish match to be made up English fashion at the price of £30 per ton, to be in fatts

On 13 July 1645 the Committee of Both Kingdoms advised Francis Allen, one of the army's treasurers:

> We are informed that [Fairfax's] army is in very great want of match and gunpowder, being disappointed of some which they expected to have found at Lyme Regis. We desire you to take care that 6 tons of match and 100 barrels of gunpowder be instantly sent to Portsmouth and thence to Weymouth for the army. We will take care that it shall be paid for.[75]

Consequently, on 14 July 100 barrels of powder, 100 barrels of musket shot, 300 demi-culverin round shot, and 6 tons of match were collected from the Tower stores by Michael Herring, who transported the whole consignment 'to Lyme for the service of Sir Thomas Fairfax his Army', and there delivered it to Commissary Captain Vincent Potter on 21 July 1645. Two days before, he had been paid the sum of £20 'upon account to defray the charges for transporting arms and ammunition to Lyme

75 *CSPD 1645–7*, p.18. Allen was first paid as one of two treasurers to the New Model on 10 April 1645, the other being John Orthick (TNA, SP28/29/1, f. 19v).

for the service.'[76] It was perhaps for this order that Herring received payment of £23 8s. on 21 August 'for the charges of shipping and freight of ammunition to Lyme'.[77] Potter replaced his brother John following his death at Naseby on 14 June, where he and another commissary, Captain Cooke were 'sore wounded in diverse places', and subsequently died.[78]

More substantial quantities of ammunition and other warlike stores for the supply of the New Model quickly followed. On 23 July the Ordnance Office was ordered to deliver 'unto Henry Jermin, Richard Farmer, and Alexander Kinsey, or any two of them', 200 grenadoe shells (possibly for mortars); 100 barrels of gunpowder; 6 tons of match; 4 tons of musket bullet; 300 saker shot; 200 horse harnesses; 1,000 snapsacks; 1 falcon mould; 200 ells of canvas; 2 tons of flat iron; and an unspecified amount of haircloth tilts. Moreover, 100 grenadoe shells were issued to Commissary Thomas Futter three days later 'to be by him put aboard the *Rose* of Lyme, to be there delivered to Captain Potter.'[79] Various other warrants for the payment of army commissaries and officials employed in the logistics of transporting and storing munitions during July and August 1645 offer some insight to the personnel involved. On 1 July it was ordered that 56 days' salary be disbursed 'for the use of Colonel Martin Pinder, Harcourt Leighton, Vincent Potter, and Thomas Herbert for them and their clerks, beginning from 29 April last past inclusive.' A further 56 days' pay was received by them on 22 August for service since 24 June. Similarly, on 23 August the sum of £170 was ordered to be disbursed to Humphrey Lower, keeper of stores for the Army at Reading magazine, at 5s. per day, for himself and 2s. 6d. for his clerk, 'being to take the charge of such ammunition as shall be sent for the army to Lyme.'[80]

Some deliveries of munitions and other stores were made to New Model Army regiments and Parliamentarian-held garrisons for direct distribution to the troops. On 20 June 1645 one warrant from the Committee for the Army ordered the Officers of the Ordnance to deliver to Colonel William Herbert's regiment of foot (formerly commanded by Walter Lloyd, who had been killed at Taunton) a barrel of powder with match and bullet proportionable, in addition to 60 matchlock muskets, 60 snaphaunces and the same number of swords.[81] On 5 July 1645 Captain Lieutenant Edmund Hamden received £10 'for the conveying of arms and ammunition for the recruiting [supplying] of Sir Robert Pye's regiment in the west', while on 29 July Colonel Nathaniel Rich – who at the time was leading siege operations at Bath – obtained the sum of £30 for the transportation of the same to his troopers.[82] On 14 February 1646 Thomas Richardson, Waggon Master General to the New Model delivered 12cwt of match, 6 barrels of powder, 6 barrels of musket bullet, along with 1,500 suits; 1,500 shirts; 1,500 pairs of shoes; 650 pikes; 1,350 muskets with bandoliers; and 2,000 snapsacks, 'to clothe and arm the new recruits at Newport

76 TNA, SP28/31/4, f. 523r; WA, CR2017/9, f. 40r.
77 TNA, WO49/82, f. 307v; SP28/31/5, f. 465r; *CSPD 1645–7*, p.18.
78 TNA, SP28/173, unfol.; *LJ*, VII, p.496; Bishop, *Relation*. TT, E288[38].
79 TNA, WO49/82, ff. 309v, 315v.
80 TNA, SP28/31/5, ff. 468r–478v; SP28/202, unfol.
81 TNA, WO49/82, f. 271v; WO55/460, unfol.
82 TNA, SP28/31/5, ff. 491r & 545r; Sprigge, *Anglia Rediviva*, p.76.

Pagnell for the supply of Sir Thomas Fairfax's Army'.[83] Sir William Brereton's Parliamentarian army in Cheshire obtained match in large quantities from various sources. In January 1645 Mr Marsh of Stafford supplied an unknown amount at a rate of £2 6s. 8d. per cwt.[84] Agreements were also reached between Richard Worrall – one of Brereton's London treasurers – and various suppliers of match there in 1645 and 1646. On 24 November 1645 he disbursed £125 5s. to Freeman for 72cwt of English match 'sent down to the Leaguer [of Chester]'.

Artillery Ordnance and Ammunition

Ordnance, round shot, and gunpowder were generally manufactured outside London. Production of artillery ammunition, both before and during the Civil Wars was concentrated in the hands of a small number of manufacturers, and by the location of the principal works in the Weald district of Sussex and Kent. Nonetheless, only a small proportion of ironworks were capable of casting guns, although virtually all of them would have been able to make shot. Iron gun founding was also conducted in Worcestershire, Shropshire, Denbighshire, Staffordshire, and the Forest of Dean, however, their furnaces and forges were sometimes put out of commission if they worked for the Royalists or were utilised by local Parliamentarian forces.[85] Hence, in addition to musket and pistol ammunition, Sir William Brereton's army obtained large supplies of artillery ammunition ordnance, normally manufactured by provincial foundries. In March 1644 shot and mortar rounds were received by the Nantwich garrison from nearby Hough furnace, near Stafford.[86] Similarly, during the siege of Chester in October 1645, the sum of £16 2s. was disbursed to Richard Hopkins of the Mereheath foundry in Staffordshire for 23cwt of cannon balls at £14 per ton, with an additional £4 'for the workmen that made them, and for making the mould they were cast in'. A further 30cwt was provided from the same source on 14 November at a cost of £26.[87]

The principal supplier of round shot and other ordnance to the New Model Army was John Browne, who operated furnaces at Cowden, Barden, Brenchley, and Horsmonden in Kent. On 11 April 1645 he was paid for delivering into the Ordnance Office 250 round shot for demi-culverin, and 1,000 saker shot, amounting to £40 3s. 7d., in addition to an unspecified quantity of 'hand grenades for sakers', costing £125. Similarly, on 25 May Sir Walter Erle, Lieutenant of the Ordnance, advised his officers, 'You are to take notice that Richard Pearson, agent unto Mr John Browne, gun founder, is contracted with for 300 grenadoe shells for the greater mortar piece in Sir Thomas Fairfax his Train of Artillery, at the rate of £2 2s. per

83 TNA, WO55/1646, unfol.; WSL, Ms Salt 463, unfol.

84 TNA, SP28/137, f. 12v; SP28/225/4, f. 697v.

85 Edwards, *Dealing in Death*, pp.96–98; Peter Edwards, 'Turning Ploughshares into Swords: The Arms and Military Equipment Industries in Staffordshire in the First Civil War, 1642–1646', *Midland History*, 27 (2002), pp.52–79.

86 TNA, SP28/36, f. 405r.

87 TNA, SP28/35/5, ff. 751r & 54r.

cwt, which accordingly are to be received into the stores'. A further indenture with Pearson, notified on 30 June, was for the supply of 300 demi-culverin shot, 300 saker shot, and 210 grenadoe shells of 12-inch diameter. These were duly delivered on 1 August 1645.[88] It is unlikely, however, that such large amounts were obtained expressly for land service, although the warrant for the payment of £82 13s. 7d. to John Berisford, who also supplied powder, match and shot to the Ordnance Office, on 15 April 1645 for 66¾cwt 24lbs of round shot for demi-culverins and sakers, and 100 hand grenades for sakers expressly states that these items were for the supply of the New Model Army.[89] Far greater quantities of munitions were received from 1645 onwards, when procurement was mostly in the hands of the Committee for the Army and the Committee for Powder, Match and Shot. During the period March 1645 to April 1646 the value of the known, yet largely incomplete, contracts notified to the Officers of the Ordnance amounts to £59,206 0s. 10d.[90] Nevertheless, there were considerable quantities of some kinds of ammunition, particularly ordnance and shot, which were already in store in 1642 and consequently available for distribution during the earlier periods of the Civil Wars, although these stocks were essentially depleted by 1644.

On 23 May 1645 the House of Commons gave the Committee for the Army orders to 'make provision for such money and necessaries for the siege of Oxford, as they have or shall receive directions for from the Committee of Both Kingdoms, not exceeding the sum of £6,000'. Moreover, it had previously been agreed that £10,000 was to await Fairfax at Windsor, along with the following provision for a siege:

> 2 demi cannons and 3 whole culverins (ready at Windsor and Northampton)
> 1,200 spades and shovels
> 500 pickaxes
> 300 steel spades
> 200 scaling ladders
> 500 barrels of gunpowder
> 40 tons of match
> 30 tons of bullet
> 300 great grenadoe shells
> 300 small grenadoe shells
> 1,000 hand grenades
> 20 carriages for provisions
> 200 horse harnesses[91]

88 TNA, SP28/29/1, f. 137r; WO/49/82, f. 317; ML, 46–78/709, ff. 65r, 95v.
89 TNA, SP28/29/1, f. 226r.
90 TNA, WO47/1, *passim*; ML, 46–78/709, *passim*.
91 *CJ*, IV, pp.151–2.

Table 08: Receipts of Consignments of Artillery Ammunition, Ordnance and Equipment by the Ordnance Office for the NMA (Bodl. Lib., Ms Eng. hist. C14)

1 April 1645

Ordered that the Officers of the Ordnance shall receive the particulars above contracted for and give certificates to the parties for what they received, and the officers are to view the arms.

Robert Scawen

Receipts of consignments brought into his Majesty's Stores from the several artificers hereafter mentioned, being for the supply and furnishing of the Army, under the command of Sir Thomas Fairfax by virtue of the abovesaid order:

f. 4v	5/4/45	250 round shot for demi-culverin 1,000 round shot for saker 1,000 hand grenades for saker	John Browne Paid £82. 10s. for consignment 15/4/45[92]
f. 16v	14/4/45	56 round shot for demi-culverin 2,831 round shot for saker 20 grenado shells 13" diameter 1 ton 5cwt 2 quarters 1lb match	Cambridge – formerly belonging to the Eastern Association's train
f. 18v	26/4/45	350 round shot for demi-culverin 1,000 round shot for saker 1 brass mortar piece	John Browne Paid £45 for shot 3/6/45[93]
f. 40v	23/7/45	1 falcon mould of brass	Thomas Oldfield
f. 40v	24/7/45	300 ells canvas	Henry Pettit
f. 41r	24/7/45	2 tons flat iron	Thomas Hodgkins
f. 42v	26/7/45	20 tilts of hair	Joshua Foote
f. 43r	1 & 28/7/45	300 round-shot for demi-culverin 300 round-shot for saker 240 grenadoe shells of 12" diameter	Richard Pearson
f. 45r	18/8/45	1 field carriage for whole cannon with wheels and fore carriage shod with iron 1 mortar piece carriage with fore carriage and wheels shod with iron and hind axletree 3 gynns furnished with rope 3 pairs of slings	John Pitt, Master Carpenter
f. 47r	12/9/45	Brass mortar piece of 13" diameter 600 round shot for demi-culverin 1700 round shot for saker	John Browne
f. 54v	7/8 & 7/11/45	125 grenadoe shells for 12" diameter	John Browne
f. 83r.	27/2/46	1 doz. ladle staves 11ft long 1 doz. ladle staves 12ft long 1 doz. ladle staves 13ft long	Richard Ward
f. 84r	2/3/46	6 doz. Sheepskins	Michael Reynolds
f. 84v	2/3/46	Rammer, ladle, etc.	Thomas Hall

92 TNA, SP28/140/1, f. 6r.

93 TNA, SP28/140/1, f. 6v.

Table 09: Deliveries of Artillery Ammunition, Ordnance and Equipment from the Ordnance Office to the NMA (TNA, WO55/1647; WSL, Ms Salt 463)

Warrant Book of the Ordnance Office (deliveries), 1645–1646			
unfol.	10/4/45	250 round shot for demi-culverin 1,000 round shot for sakers Hand grenadoe shells for sakers 8 tons match in fatts 2,391 muskets	Warrant to deliver by indenture to John Phipps, Commissary to the Train of Artillery under the command of Sir Thomas Fairfax, the several parcels of munitions hereafter mentioned for the supply and furnishing of the said Army. Robert Scawen
	17/4/45	From my Lord Manchester's Train: 1,986 muskets 25cwt 2 stone 1lb match 56 demi-culverin shot 20 grenadoe shells for mortar pieces	At the Committee for the Army, 24/4/45: Warrant to deliver by indenture to Commissary Phipps the particulars abovementioned for the use of Sir Thomas Fairfax his Army. Scawen
	18/4/45	10 hair cloths 100 barrels powder 2,000 muskets 2,000 bandoliers 400 horse harness 5 tons musket shot	Warrant to deliver by indenture the proportion of the arms and ammunition to Mr Phipps to be sent to the Army. Scawen
	28/4/45		Warrant to deliver unto Commissary Phipps 30 barrels of powder over and beside the 100 already delivered him, 200 tents, all your waggons, carts, tumbrels, ordnance, mortar pieces with their equipage, and such other utensils and necessaries which are supplied or come from Cambridge. And carriage for the 10 guns taken to the wharf and the waggons provided by Mr Bateman and Mr Pitt, with the harness for draught horses, [and] spare wheels. And all other things that are provided for the guns and carriage for the use of Sir Thomas Fairfax his Army. Scawen
	1/5/45	2 demi-culverin of brass, mounted upon field carriage with fore carriage upon shod wheels complete 20 sakers of brass mounted upon field carriages complete 1 brass mortar piece of 12" diameter 20 grenadoe shells for the mortar piece 6cwt 56lbs round shot for demi-culverin ½ ton 5cwt 43lbs round shot for saker 1 ton hand grenadoes	Delivered to Commissary Phipps

	2/5/45	4 petards armed	Delivered out of his Majesty's Stores unto Sir Thomas Fairfax's Train
	5/5/45	500 minion shot for the use of the town and garrison of Taunton	Warrant to deliver to Commissary Hawkins
	9/5/45	Brass saker shot 6cwt 14lbs of 1lb shot 6cwt 13lbs of 2lb shot 6cwt 66lbs of 3lb shot	Delivered to Commissary Phipps
	12/5/45	1 mortar piece mounted 60 grenadoe shells	Delivered to Commissary Phipps
	28/5/45	4 petards fixed 6 grenadoe shells	Delivered to Commissary Phipps
	29/5/45	1 mortar piece of brass 60 grenadoe shells for the mortar piece	Warrant to deliver to Commissary Phipps for the use of the Commissary of the Victuals
	14/7/45	300 demi-culverin round shot	Warrant to deliver to Michael Herring to be sent by him to Lyme for the service of STF his Army, and there to be delivered to Captain Potter, one of the commissioners of the Army
	26/7/45	120 grenadoe shells 12" dia. 400 saker shot 1 falcon mould brass 2 tons flat iron	Warrant to deliver to Richard Fenner and Henry Jarman for Sir Thomas Fairfax's Army 'by warrant from the Committee for the Army' 23/7/45
	6/8/45	300 whole culverin shot 300 demi-cannon shot	Delivered to Thomas Foote for Sir Thomas Fairfax's Army
	9/8/45	200 shot of 24lbs 200 of 12lbs 300 of 9lbs 300 of 6lbs 60 barrels powder 200 grenadoe shells 10" dia. 600 shovels and spades 200 axes helved	Warrant from COBK to the Officers of the Ordnance Office: 'These are to will and require you upon sight hereof to deliver unto Bartholomew Stileman or whom he shall appoint. All which are to be employed against Basing'
	15/8/45	40 grenadoe shells	Warrant ordering that the Officers of the Ordnance do deliver unto Thomas Futter, to be sent by him to Lyme for the service of Sir Thomas Fairfax his Army
	18/8/45	700 saker shot 600 demi-culverin shot	Warrant ordering that the Officers of the Ordnance do deliver unto Thomas Futter, messenger to this Committee [for the Army] from the Navy stores, to be sent to Lyme for the service of Sir Thomas Fairfax his Army
	19/8/45	200 shot of 24lbs 200 culverin shot	Delivered to Daniel Judd for use at Basing

	19/8/45	600 saker shot 600 demi-culverin shot 40 grenadoe shells of 12" dia	Warrant to deliver unto Thomas Futter
	19/8/45	1 whole cannon of brass 1 ladle for cannon 1 field tampion 2 formers 1 wad hook 8cwt round shot for cannon 200 24lb bullets 300 Dutch culverin shot 300 demi-cannon shot 2 gynns for mounting the great cannon	COBK to Ordnance Officers to deliver unto such persons as the Committee for the Army shall appoint … for the service of Sir Thomas Fairfax's Army. Note to Officers 28/8/45 to 'deliver the particulars mentioned to Mr Thomas Futter to be sent to Lyme'; items delivered to Futter 1/9/45
	20/8/45	New gynn	Order to Ordnance Office to deliver to Thomas Futter the new gynn in case it will serve the new mortar piece
	21/8/45	New gynn	That the Ordnance Office do take care for the making of 1 new ginn more, and do also deliver to Futter … the old mortar piece with their complete appurtenances to be sent to Lyme
	23/8/45	New mortar piece	Scawen ordered Committee to deliver to Thomas Futter the new mortar piece
	29/8/45	500 pickaxes 2 rammer heads 2 prs slings 2 prs ginn ropes	Warrant to deliver to Thomas Futter for Sir Thomas Fairfax's Army
	29/8/45	New carriage which belonged to the demi-cannon that came from Windsor and a draught rope in the stores as serviceable to the demi-cannon	Warrant to deliver to Thomas Futter for Sir Thomas Fairfax's Army … which are to be transported to Lyme for the service of Sir Thomas Fairfax's Army
	6/9/45	50 fire pikes	Warrant to deliver to Daniell Judd or whom he shall appoint … which are to be employed in the service against Basing
	13/9/45	1,100 saker shot	Delivered … to be sent to Lyme for the use of Sir Thomas Fairfax his Army
	9/10/45	200 round shot for demi-cannon 300 round shot for culverin 200 round shot for demi-culverin 25 cross shot for demi-cannon 25 cross shot for demi-culverin	Delivered to Daniell Judd to be employed in the service against Basing

4

Victuals: Feeding the Army

The procurement, organisation, accounting, and transportation of provisions (victuals and other foodstuffs) for seventeenth century armies was essential to military operations, in addition to the maintenance of good health, effective performance and high morale among the rank and file. Not only did soldiers need to be fed and provided with beverage, but horses and draught animals required large amounts of fodder. During the seventeenth century Continental armies travelled with huge supply trains – of both ammunition and victuals – the latter controlled by the Commissary General of the Victuals, with assistant commissaries and clerks, as well as bakers, butchers, and other victuallers. Even though troops in garrisons might fare better than those in marching armies, benefitting from a more varied and plentiful diet, much depended upon the resources of the locality, in addition to the attitude of the inhabitants who proffered them. There was a distinction between the types of food which were suitable for storage in garrisons and transportation with an army in the field; the professional soldier, Francis Markham, who had been in the Dutch service, noted, 'if it be in marching or journeying, then he [the commissary] shall give them the victuals which is most easy for carriage, and the longest lasting, as biscuit, beef ready boiled, cheese and the like.'[1] As to the source of victuals, Price suggests:

> The common thread of food supply for early modern warfare in Europe was the lack of daily rations issued by the army's governing authority at the authority's own expense. Soldiers were instead expected to buy their food themselves. Even when the authorities supplied food directly out of magazines, the soldiers' pay would be subsequently docked to cover the costs, usually above the value of the food to reflect attendant costs of storage and transportation. This represented the ideal more than the reality as on occasion, soldiers had to make do with only 'two pound of bread' to last them all week.[2]

When, on 5 June 1645, the New Model Army – minus a brigade of foot and a regiment of horse, which had been previously detached for the relief of Taunton – was

1 Francis Markham, *Five Decades of Epistles of Warre* (London: Augustine Matthew, 1622), p.103.

2 Price, *Soldiers and Civilians*, p.155.

ordered to leave the siege of Oxford and march north to confront the King's Army, its strength was between 14,000 and 15,000. It also included most of the train of artillery, in addition to the commissioned and non-commissioned officers from the regiments of horse, dragoons, and foot, and large quantities of horses (both for riding and draught animals). Such numbers, while not precise, offer an indication of the extent of the Army's logistical challenge in providing victuals to men and horses. Gentles describes Fairfax's regiments during the Naseby campaign as 'more or less at full strength', but this ignores the evidence of pay warrants and narrative accounts which suggest otherwise.[3] Estimates of the strength of the New Model infantry alone indicate that on 14 June Sir Hardress Waller's regiment fielded 560 common soldiers, while Colonels Hammond's and Rainborowe's mustered 788 and 888 respectively, all significantly below strength.

Among the Protestant forces in Ireland during 1642 and 1643, soldiers' rations consisted of salt beef, herrings, cheese, butter, and wheat and other cereals (such as rye) baked into biscuits. Such a diet was, however, blamed for the poor health of the men; the Earl of Cork remarking that salted beef, biscuit, and butter without drinking water was only good for 'a rich churchyard and weak garrison'. Biscuits made this way seem to have been standard practice, and one which retained its calorific properties and made it easier for soldiers to carry on the march. An estimate for provisioning 2,000 troops with a daily ration of 1lb of bread and ½lb of cheese, records that instead of the latter, '1lb more of biscuit is needful for each man per day'. Nevertheless, it was also stated that 'when this country did afford (in the time the soldiers were on the march) some provision, then 1lb of biscuits per man per day (and a pint of salt per man for a ten-day march) did well serve.'[4] On 7 February 1642 Parliament ordered the Commissary of Victuals to:

> as much speed as conveniently you can, provide victual for 10,000 men for 3 months, after the rate of 4d. the day for every man, in bread, beef, butter, and cheese. Wherein you shall be careful of the goodness and wholesomeness of the provision; and likewise of the prices, that they be as cheap as the markets will afford. You shall, as near the prices will bear, provide for every man after the proportion of 1lb of bread, 1lb of beef, or, in lieu thereof, ½lb of cheese, or fish, as near the value thereof as you can; and ¼lb of butter, for every day.[5]

This corresponds with instructions given for the victualling of the Royalist garrison at Worcester in January 1645, which stated, 'every common soldier's allowance per day is 1lb of biscuit and ½lb of cheese'.[6]

3 Gentles, *New Model Army*, p.55.

4 James Hogan (ed.), *Letters and Papers Relating to the Irish Rebellion Between 1642–46* (Dublin: Stationery Office, 1936), pp.25, 119, 135.

5 *CJ*, II, p.417.

6 Worcs. Archives, BA 1741/899/192, ff. 519r–523v; Stephen Porter, Stephen K. Roberts and Ian Roy (eds), *The Diary and Papers of Henry Townshend, 1640–1663* (Worcestershire Historical Society, 2014), p.184.

On 1 November 1642 the Lords and Commons in Parliament ordered that 2,000cwt of biscuit, 400cwt of cheese (provided by London cheese mongers), 100 quarters of malt, 500 quarters of oats, and 500 quarters of wheat, be transported to Ireland 'into the province of Munster for relief of the forces there.' Similarly, among a list of commodities contained in a report made by the Committee for the Affairs of Ireland 'concerning what present supply of victuals and other necessaries are fit to be sent to the Fort of Gallway in the province of Connaught in Ireland, for relief of the soldiers and strengthening of the fort', were 50 butts of beer, 30 quarters of malt, 30 quarters of wheat, 50,000cwt of biscuit, 30 hogsheads of peas, and 20 hogsheads of oatmeal. Moreover, on 9 July 1643 a warrant was issued for the payment of £563 2s. 6d. to Thomas Prince, cheesemonger, of London 'for 400 cwt of Suffolk cheese, containing 2,981 cheeses at the rate of 28s. the hundred, by him sold and delivered on shipboard the *Edmund and John* of London, for the relief of his Majesty's army in Munster, according to an account thereof remaining with the Committee for the Affairs of Ireland.[7] The accounts of Edward Orpin, Commissary of Victuals to the New Model Army record a delivery from the magazine at Lyme made on 20 November 1645 and shipped to the garrison of Youghal in county Cork. This consisted of 165cwt of cheese; 180 bags of biscuit; 20 hogsheads of beef; 200 yards of stuff to make bags for biscuits; and 3lbs of packthread. Additional payments were made for 'weighing and loading beef into the waggons', 'weighing and carrying of the cheese', '4 seams of straw to lay under the cheese', 'loading 180 bags of biscuit into the waggons and carrying it to the Cobb', '1 seam of faggots to lay under the biscuit in the ship', and a man 'to help in the business, and for horse hire and horse meat'.[8]

On the victualling of armies, Monck wrote:

> In marching with an army to fight with your enemy, you ought to carry with you as much bread, cheese, or cattle and salt as you may conveniently; for it is impossible that soldiers should find bread to be bought everywhere. And if it be possible to be done with safety, lie with your army between your enemy and his provisions, being better furnished with provisions than your enemy. For lying near your enemy with safety, and without fighting, will in the end surely discourage your enemies soldiers by their necessities, or force them to fight upon disadvantages, or at last put them to a retreat. And then the victory is more than half won, if any of these things happen unto your enemy. An army may be divided into four parts, namely, the cavalry, the infantry, the artillery, and the victuals. If you are to march with an army into a country where you think the inhabitants will fly before you, then ought you to carry hand mills, and baking pans along with you, that each company upon occasion may be able to grind their own corn and provide themselves bread.[9]

7 Bod. Lib., Ms Rawlinson A/110, ff. 11v–12v & 59v–60r.
8 TNA, SP28/147/2, ff. 352r–357r.
9 Monck, *Observations upon military and political affairs*, pp.82–3.

Sir Thomas Fairfax's commission as commander-in-chief of the New Model Army, issued on 1 April 1645, stipulated 'That he should have power to nominate a Provost Marshal, or Marshals for the executing his commands, and to command, waggons, carts or boats, for the carriage of his ordnance, ammunition or provisions, as there should be occasion'.[10] Provost Marshals were remunerated 5s. per day, though in the New Model their 'respited' pay amounted to 3s. 4d.[11] According to Sir James Turner, writing in the 1670s:

> Every army should have a General Proviant-master; and truly I conceive him to be an officer as necessary and useful, if not more, in the fields, where mostly our modern armies are entertained with proviant, as either a general commissary, or a treasurer. His charge is to provide victuals, corn, flesh, wine, bread and beer; he has the inspection of them, and should see them equally and proportionably divided to the regiments according to their several strengths; for which purpose he should have all the rolls and lists by him, which his secretaries should carefully keep. He hath no power to sell any proviant under what pretence soever, without the generals express warrant. All mills where the army comes are under his protection, and he is obliged to protect them. He has the ordering of all the magazines for victuals, and to him belongs the care of seeing the garrisons, and fortified places sufficiently provided with such meats and drinks as are most fit to preserve ... This General Proviant-Master has under him a lieutenant, a secretary, a clerk, a smith, a waggon master, and a waggon-maker, a quartermaster, and some officers who are called directors.[12]

Of the Commissary of Victuals or Victual-Master, Francis Markham wrote in *Five Decades of Epistles of Warre*:

> The next officer ascending in this warlike legend (and with which I am to account in this Epistle) is that of the Victual-Master, Proviant-Master or Purveyor of Victuals for the whole body of the army, and is indeed a principal and eminent person holding a place both of great trust, care and estimation; his general dependence is upon the army and the General's especial commandments, but the particular looks most at the treasurer; for he supplies all those necessities which he is not able to furnish. The election of this man ought to be out of the best sort of gentlemen, having in him both the dignity of blood and the glory of virtue, with the one to feel and pity mens' wants and extremities, and with the other to give a speedy, honest and an wholesome remedy: he ought to be endued with three especial virtues, as first wisdom (which he is to exercise in making his provisions) then temperance (which is to govern him in the expense of his commodities according to order), and lastly frugality (by which to increase and keep

10 Rushworth, *Historical Collections*, VI, p.12; *LJ*, VII, p.299.
11 TNA, SP28/130/3, unfol.; *LJ*, X, p.70.
12 Turner, *Pallas Armata*, p.201.

good his store in an honest, profitable, and thrifty manner) he should be a man of years and great experience both in the natures of men, the necessities of the wars, and the proportioning of allowances; but especially he must be a man notably well seen in all manner of household provisions, knowing both the rates of all manner of victuals, the places where best to find them, and the safest and wholesomest way how to keep and preserve them, he must not in any wise be a beggar, for he that hath neglected to feed himself, will either little regard how he feeds others, or else so extremely feed himself first, that other men will starve while he is in surfeiting. To conclude, he must in no wise be a hard hearted or covetous person, for covetousness is the mother of many vices, and if this officer, either to gain at cheap rates by unsound and insufficient victuals, or to keep them (till the extremity of times do compel the soldier to accept them) store them till they rot and turn to putrefaction, and then force them on those where denial cannot be heard nor relieved; then believe it, this man doth his Prince and country most wicked service; hath the curse of the living and the blood of many slaughtered souls hanging at his elbow, for from this ground (above others) doe mutinies and divisions amongst soldiers arise, which is seldom appeased but with death; and from hence in mine own experience I have observed two such insurrections, that they started the whole army with amazement ... he is to make provision for the army of all kind of victuals whatsoever, carefully and faithfully, and for that purpose is to have at every rendezvous or place of garrison, a fit and convenient storehouse, in which to pile up and accommodate the same, whether it be bread, biscuit, cheese, butter, fish, beef, bacon, meal, Pease or any other provision; which according to warrants from the superior officers (nominating the number of men in list of every company) he shall deliver out proportionably according to such a rate for every man *per diem*, and being still assured to keep his proportions within the compass of the soldiers common allowance of ordinary lendings, as for example: If the soldiers lendings be after the rate of 3s. by the week, then shall the victual-master allow him victuals at the rate of 4d. by the day and 1d. for drink, which amounts to 2s. 11d. the week, the remainder when the captain comes to reckon with the treasurer, by the victuallers certificates shall (or at least should) be an arrearage due to the soldier; and thus according to the proportion of any wages, and in this expending of victuals it is to be supposed that every victual-master ought to accommodate his victuals unto the place in which they are spent; as if it be in garrison or settled camp, then he shall spend those victuals which are worst for carriage and most troublesome for the soldier to dress; as butter, bread, fish or the like, except his plenty be great, and then he may let them have two days flesh, as ether beef or bacon, for Sundays and Thursdays; two days butter as on Monday and Tuesday; one day cheese as Wednesday; and two days fish as Friday and Saturday.[13]

13 Francis Markham, *Five Decades of Epistles of Warre* (London: 1622), pp.101–104.

Considerable quantities of victuals were shipped to Commonwealth troops in Flanders, Ireland, and Scotland, perhaps the more so because locally procured foodstuffs were liable to be less forthcoming. On 9 July 1658 the Governor of Dunkirk, Colonel William Lockhart, provided the following account of his measures for victualling the recently garrisoned port. It was cheaper, he thought, to buy provisions in Flanders that to have them sent from England:

> I shall go about the buying of wheat and rye, to make bread for the present subsistence of the forces, and shall keep the month's provision of biscuit in store, least at any time, either by siege or otherwise, we should be put to a pinch; and once in a year, the magazine of bread, I mean the month's biscuit for 4,000 men, must be renewed, and the old given out, and rebated of the soldiers pay; but before the old stock of biscuit so laid in be meddled with, the new stock to the same quantity must be first in store; and so this place will never want six week's provision of bread, which is the staff of man's life. If I find the butter and cheese may be kept without spoiling, I shall likewise save it; but I think, for provisions that are not to be made use of save once in a year, all cheese, or at least salt beef and bacon, or pork in lieu of the butter will be best.[14]

The Committee for Irish Affairs agreed a contract in April 1649 with Daniel Wybrantz, a merchant of Dublin, to supply cheese, biscuit, salt, corn, and other foodstuffs 'to be bought by him in Holland, for the use of our forces in Ireland'. On 25 December another arrangement stated that, 'on a provision of cheese needed for the army in Ireland, they treated with William Harris, Lucas Lucy and partners for 200 tons of 'Tuninghen', alias Holland cheese, and considering the goodness of the cheese, and the rates that that commodity now affords, they recommend the propositions to Council for approbation.' The commander-in-chief of the squadron in the Downs was informed on 8 June 1649 that there are three ships laden in the Thames, 'being the *James of London*, with wheat and rye, bound for Dublin, the *Elizabeth of Yarmouth*, with wheat, powder, match for Chester, and the *Constant* of Yarmouth, with wheat for Liverpool.' The following month (amongst other consignments) Francis Smith was commissioned to ship 300 quarters of rye, and 100 quarters of wheat to Sir Charles Coote, for the garrison at Derry.[15] Another essential element of a soldier's diet was ale or beer (usually small beer), although purchases by commissaries or local officials appear rarely in documents, probably since brewing was often a localised activity and the product would be consumed quickly. Nevertheless, beer was sent to Ireland in large quantities. For instance, in July 1649 one commissary was paid £400 on account for 450 tuns of beer for Ireland, whereas on 13 August he received £800 for double the amount.[16]

---

14 Thomas Birch (ed.), *A Collection of State Papers of John Thurloe, Esq; Secretary to the Council of State* (London: 1742), VII, p.216.

15 *CSPD 1649–50*, pp.111, 126, 178, 186, 224, 454.

16 *CSPD Interregnum, 1649–50*, p.585–587.

Beginning in April 1645 the Committee for the Army procured substantial quantities of cheese and biscuit (double-baked bread of a higher calorific value than ordinary bread, and highly transportable) in increasing amounts for the use of the New Model Army. The soldiers were supplied by a commissariat which purchased such items from London cheesemongers and merchants, who had it transported to the army's principal magazine at Reading for onward distribution. Instead of building a commissariat from scratch, the Committee for the Army exploited an existing trading system by procuring wholesale foodstuffs in bulk for the supply of the New Model via seaports and established road transport networks.[17] Gentles observed that 'Almost 90,000lbs of Suffolk and other cheeses, and 1,503cwt of biscuit were distributed [to the New Model Army] during the first two months. After that the men were on their own'.[18] This may be challenged, though, as it fails to take into consideration the regular supplies of such rations over a much longer period. Warrants for the payment of deliveries of cheese and biscuit for the army show that on 22 April 1645 Thomas Ross and his partner received £299 4s. for 1,777 Suffolk cheeses containing 272cwt at 22s. per cwt; on 23 May John Chestman, Thomas Prince, and Thomas Rose were paid the sum of £367 3s. 9d. for 2,182 cheeses containing 312cwt and 2 quarts weight at 23s. per cwt; whereas the same partners brought in 287cwt and 2 quarts of cheese at 36s. per cwt, and for 292cwt and 2 quarts of cheese, for which they were paid £713 3s. 9d. on 20 June.[19]

According to Markham, the Commissary of Victuals should:

> ...if it be in marching or journeying, then he shall give them the victuals which is most easy for carriage, and the longest lasting, as biscuit, beef ready boiled, cheese, or the like. Now for the proportions how much conveniently may sustain a man a day (though they must be rated according to the plenty of the store and the prizes by which they are attained) yet for example sake, and according to the experience of those wars which I have seen, half a pound of biscuit, and half a pound of butter hath been at fit day's proportion for one man, or a pound of bread and half a pound of beef or else bacon; a full day's proportion, or otherwise half a pound of biscuit and a pound of cheese; likewise a pound of biscuit and a Poor-John between two men for one day, or two pound of biscuit and a haberdine between four men for one day is a great proportion, half a pound of biscuit and four herrings is one man's allowance for one day, and so is a quart of peas boiled, or a pint of rice with the ordinary allowance of biscuit.[20]

17 T. S. Willan, *The Inland Trade: Studies in English Internal Trade in the Sixteenth and Seventeenth Centuries* (Manchester: Manchester University Press, 1976), pp.7–10; Dorian Gerhold, *Carriers and Coachmasters: Trade and Travel before the Turnpikes* (Chichester: Phillimore, 2005), pp.10–11.

18 Gentles, *New Model Army*, p.44.

19 TNA, SP28/29/1, f. 242r; SP28/30/4, ff. 363r & 371r.

20 Markham, *Five Decades of Epistles of Warre*, p.104.

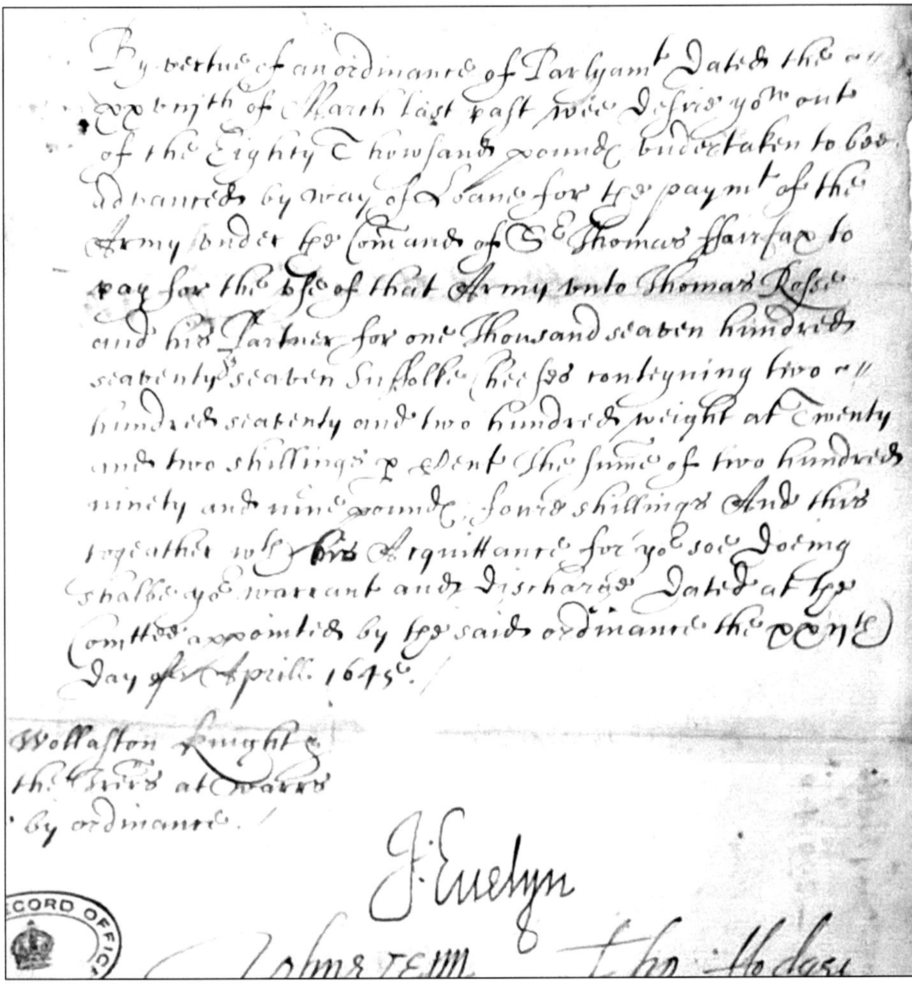

By vertue of an ordinance of Parlyam^t dated the [illegible] of March last past wee desire you out of the Eighty Thousand pounds undertaken to bee advanced by way of Loane for the paym^t of the Army under the Comand of Sr Thomas ffairfax to pay for the use of that Army unto Thomas Rosse and his Partner for one Thousand seaven hundred seaventy seaven Suffolke cheeses conteyning two hundred seaventy and two hundred weight at twenty and two shillings p Cent the sume of two hundred ninety and nine pounds foure shillings And this togeather wth his Acquittance for yor soe doeing shalbe yor warrant and discharge Dated at the Comittee appointed by the said ordinance the xxii^th Day of April 1645.

Wollaston Knight
the Treasurers at Warre
by ordinance.

J. Evelyn

Warrant to pay Thomas Ross and partner £299 4s. for 1,777 Suffolk cheeses containing 272cwt at 22s. per cwt, dated 22 April 1645. (TNA, SP28/29/1, f. 242r)

In March 1645 Sir William Brereton sent 51 tons of Cheshire cheese to Kinsale and 10 tons 9cwt to London, while a second batch for London consisted of 495 locally produced cheeses. Such shipments amounted to over 60 tons of cheese, with at least seven thousand individual cheeses weighing from 8lbs to 12lbs.[21] Moreover, among the vast number of cheeses recorded as being issued to the Parliamentarian forces in Cheshire by the sequestrators of various hundreds are 14½cwt of cheese worth £20 10s. provided by Bucklow to Commissary John Miller in March 1643 'for the use of the army in part sent from Dutton demesne'. Likewise, in mid-1644 240 measures of oats and 5cwt of cheese was received from Tabley, while the sum of 1s. 1d. was

21 CRO, DDX/428, ff. 40v–41r.

paid on 19 November 1644 'for carrying 629lb weight of cheese to the garrison of Northwich from Mr Allan in Netherleigh'.[22] Suffolk cheese, which had been supplied to soldiers in Ireland in large quantities, was commonly consumed by armies. The production of which, according to Stuart Peachey, involved

> taking the skimmed milk from the previous night's milking and adding to the full fat milk from the morning milking, producing a reduced fat cheese. Lower fat content made the cheese harder. Reproductions based on Tudor descriptions produce a cheese which stored without refrigeration for two years without notable degeneration, other than becoming very hard. It would be an ideal cheese to transport as it would be very resistant to breaking up (or chewing).[23]

As mentioned, large quantities of biscuit – transported in large canvas bags, sewn up with pack thread – were purchased for the New Model Army. Thus, on 22 April 1645 £60 was paid to John Jarvis for '112 bags of biscuit containing 100cwt at 12s. per cwt, and for 112 biscuit bags at 12d. per bag the sum of £65 12s.'; the following day Thomas Flood received £65 12s. for the same, while £87 5s. was paid 'to Gilbert Cornelius for 149 bags containing 133cwt at 12s. per cwt the sum of £79 16s. 0d., and for 149 bags at 12d. per bag the sum of £16 9s.'. Also, on 23 May 1645 Cornelius, Flood and Jarvis delivered 625 cwt of biscuit at 12s. per cwt, and 700 biscuit bags at 12d. per bag, for which they got £410. A week later, Cornelius and Flood received £246 for '75 cwt of biscuit at 12s. per cwt, and for 420 bags at 12d. per bag'.[24] By comparison, vast quantities of biscuit were sent to Ireland during the Commonwealth period. On 27 June 1649 200,000lbs of biscuit with 2,500 quarters of wheat were waiting in the Thames to be shipped to Ireland in 10 days' time. Additionally, Flood was paid £1,380 6s. on 7 August for biscuit and biscuit bags, while a fortnight later one of the treasurers at war, Francis Smith, laid out the sum of £2,948 11s. for 300,000lbs of biscuit.[25]

In addition to this, the New Model's victories of 1645 and 1646 saw large amounts of victuals falling into its hands. John Rushworth, Sir Thomas Fairfax's secretary, wrote that following their victory at Naseby on 14 June 1645 the New Model troops seized 'carts with boats, and great store of biscuit and cheese (a seasonal refreshment for our soldiers that had marched so hard, and the night before had not a bit of bread to a regiment for their refreshment).'[26] Sprigge noted that when Berkley Castle surrendered to Colonel Thomas Rainborowe in September 1645, 11 pieces of ordnance and 'provision of victuals for six months' were taken. Moreover, among the substantial amounts of warlike stores captured at Winchester on 5 October were the following victuals: 38 hogsheads of beef and pork; 16,800lbs of cheese; 800lbs of

22 BL, Ms Harley 2137, ff. 55v, 95v, 105v, 199r, 152v–153r.
23 Peachey, *Soldier's Life*, p.172.
24 TNA, SP28/29/1, ff. 244r–245r; SP28/30/4, ff. 364r, 371r.
25 *CSPD 1649–50*, pp.209–10; *CSPD Interregnum, 1649–50*, p.585–87.
26 *An Ordinance of the Lords and Commons ... with two exact Relations of the said Victory* (London: 1645). TT, E288[26].

butter; 140 quarters of wheat and meal; 3 hogsheads of French wine; 10 quarters of salt; 20 bushels of oatmeal; 14 sheep; 4 quarters of fresh beef; 7,840lbs of biscuit; and 112 hogsheads of strong beer. Such an acquisition was probably well-timed, because Sprigge also reported that Fairfax arrived in Lyme on 8 October and the following day 'came back from Lyme to Chard, where he received intelligence that Goring intended to break through with his horse'.[27] When Royalist-held Basing House fell to New Model troops commanded by Cromwell on 14 October 1645, it was reported to the House of Commons by the army's chaplain, Hugh Peters – who played an important part in the campaigns of 1645–1646 – that,

> the rooms before the storm (it seems) in both houses, were all completely furnished, provisioned for some years, rather than months; 400 quarters of wheat, bacon divers rooms full (containing hundreds of fliches), cheese proportionable, with oatmeal, beef, pork, beer, divers cellars full and that very good.[28]

Military biscuit, used by both armies and navies, was not necessarily fresh and must have been durable enough to survive transportation. Wheat, barley, rye, oats, pea flour or ground malt, either singly or in combination, produced a wide variety of products. The Parliamentarian colonel, John Birch recounted that 'black rye bread' was consumed in Herefordshire, although quantities of rye and wheat were sent to Ireland, presumably for baking into bread or biscuit.[29] Instructions for the victualling of Worcester in January 1645 specified,

> it is desired by the commissary that 1,000 quarters of wheat be laid in at 30s. per quarter, which is 3s. 9d. per strike. Of which 500 quarters to be baked in biscuit, the rest in bread. A quarter of wheat, which is 8 strike will make 3 cwt of biscuit in the hands of a good workman; which after 30s. a quarter per wheat, the biscuit is after 10s. per cent weight. [Also included was] coarse canvas at 9d. per ell, and 2 ells to make a sack to put in the biscuits of which there must be 1,000 sacks £100. The making of them £20.[30]

Though in essence the New Model in 1645 and 1646 was a mobile field army, various sets of accounts detail the quantities and type of victuals delivered by the Committee of the Militia to the Parliamentarian garrison of Windsor Castle, commanded by Colonel John Venn and comprising 12 companies of foot. Such supplies were transported from London via Thames barges.

27 Sprigge, *Anglia Rediviva*, pp.124–125, 128, 134, 138.
28 *The full and last relation, of all things concerning Basing-House: with divers other passages; represented to Mr Speaker, and divers members in the House* (London: 1645). TT, E.305[8].
29 T. W. Webb (ed.), *Military Memoir of Colonel John Birch* (London: Camden Society, 1878), p.28.
30 Worcs. Archives, BA 1741/899/192, ff. 519r–523v; Porter, Roberts and Roy (eds), *Diary and Papers*, pp.184–185.

Sent to Windsor for the victualling of the castle, 29 October 1642:
Biscuit (brown) 412 bags containing each 100lbs of biscuit at 12s. per cwt £220 14s. 3d.
For carriage from the lighter at Bull Wharf £1 19s. 6d.
Biscuit (white) 3 bags at 18s. per cwt £2 8s. 2d.
Carriage from Tower Hill to Bull Wharf 1s.
Bags 415 at 12d. per bag £20 15s.
Cheeses 1,122 containing 81cwt 15lbs at 52s. per cwt £211 8s.
Butter 60 firkins at 22s. per firkin £66
For cordage of 12 loads of butter and cheese from Botolph Lane to Bull Wharf at 20d. per load £1
For portage of it into the barges 2s. 6d.
For wharfage for the whole 10s.
To Mr Taylor 10cwt of cheese, which he put aboard the boats with the soldiers when they went to Windsor.
Total expenditure £535 18s. 5d.[31]

A note of 'victuals provided by the Militia in the City of London by the Lords and Commons, sum to be paid by them to Mr Walter Frost (Commissary for Victuals) who made them' includes the entry, 'Together with the goods there was advice sent to issue the biscuits at 1½d. the pound; the cheese at 3d.; the butter at 5d., which was as cheap a rate as they could at that time buy anywhere. The butter and cheese being of the very best sort of Suffolk'.[32]

Moreover, among the various warrants issued in 1643 for the supply of the Windsor garrison are the following:

26 April 1643
By warrant of the Committee for 80 cwt of cheese, 70 firkins of butter and 140 bags of biscuit sent to Windsor for the use of Colonel Venn's regiment £357 15s. and to the bargemen for carriage £5 13s. 4d.

21 September 1643, there was sent to Windsor for the relief of the army 149 bags of biscuit, and for cartage and other carriage £82 14s.

30 October 1643 sent to Colonel Venn at Windsor cheese, butter and biscuit with charges £180.[33]

As detailed in the accounts of Commissary Orpin, various quantities of cheese and biscuit were received at the magazine in Lyme between August and October 1645, where they were stored, trimmed, turned, bagged, and distributed to the New Model Army. Similarly, during December a total of 40,000lbs of cheese and 80,000lbs of biscuit arrived from London aboard the vessel *Elizabeth and James*;

31 TNA, SP28/262/2, f. 219r; SP28/263, f. 76r.
32 TNA, SP28/263, f. 70v.
33 TNA, SP28/16/2, ff. 171r–171v.

both commodities were transported onwards by waggon and packhorse from Lyme to forward bases in the Southwest of England.[34] As previously noted, in addition to draught horses, substantial numbers of packhorses and pack boards were hired by Orpin, mainly for the transportation of clothing, cheese and biscuit for Fairfax's Army. For instance, on 23 January 1646 a total of 2,598 coats; 2,952 pairs of breeches; and 2,082 shirts were forwarded from Tiverton to Chudleigh on 100 packhorses, while £1 15s. was paid for 'cords, packthread and needles to pack them up'.[35] Before the advent of the railway in Britain packhorses were often preferred as the main means of transport by professional carriers, including those operating along routes in Southwest and Northern England, and from Wales, often carrying cloth and other easily transportable goods.[36]

In February 1644, the Committee of Both Kingdoms resolved that 'the supplies to be now sent to Gloucester shall be sent by horse and not by waggon', and the county committee was ordered 'to provide 60 horses with panniers and saddles for the conveyance of provisions'.[37] Moreover, Sprigge described that in January 1646 Sir Thomas Fairfax's Army used packhorses as it advanced into Cornwall, where reliable roads were rare.[38] Some indication of the distances and timings of packhorse routes is that of Shrewsbury to London. During the 1620s the distance of 156 miles could be achieved in around 7 days (covering 22 miles per day with no rest days assumed), although there were complaints that they sometimes took longer.[39]

Table 10: An Account of Moneys Disbursed by Commissary Orpin, Commissary General of Victuals for the use of the State, 1645[40]

		£	s.	d.
At the Magazine at Windsor:				
23/8/45	Paid to one labourer 10 days @ 8d. per day for mending two locks		7	10
24/8/45	For freight of 938 coats, 800 pairs of breeches, 270 shirts, 190 pairs of stockings and 118 pairs of shoes from Windsor to London, and there shipped to Lyme	1	10	0
24/8/45	For two labourers to pack and load them and for cards to make up stockings and shirts		2	8
24/8/45	For packthread and carrying them to the waterside		1	2
16/9/45	For one labourer 18 days @ 8d.		12	0
16/9/45	For three baskets to use in the magazine and for nails		1	3
16/9/45	For brooms and paper			10

34 TNA, SP28/147/2, ff. 352r–357r.
35 TNA, SP28/147/2, f. 356v.
36 Dorian Gerhold, 'Packhorses and Wheeled Vehicles in England, 1550–1800', *The Journal of Transport History*, 14 (1993), pp.1–26, (p. 13); Rob Stuart, *Wagons, Carts and Pack Animals 1580–1660* (Bristol: Stuart Press, 1996), p.15.
37 *CSPD 1644–5*, p.24.
38 Sprigge, *Anglia Rediviva*, p.174.
39 Thomas Mendenhall, *The Shrewsbury Drapers and the Welsh Wool Trade in the XVI and XVII Centuries* (Oxford: Oxford University Press, 1953), p.35.
40 TNA, SP28/147/2, ff. 352r–357r.

		£	s.	d.
	For mending the magazine door, and a lock and nails for the same		3	10
At the Magazine in Lyme:				
16/8/45	For three men to rub and pack cheese [for] two days		6	0
17/8/45	For charge of a horse to Taunton and Sherborne three days		4	6
19/8/45	For one iron bar and two staples for the cellar window		1	8
19/8/45	For three men to cut biscuit for three days		6	0
19/8/45	For four men to scrape and rub cheese one day		4	0
27/8/45	For a horse to carry a packet of letters from Lyme thereunto Colonel Pindar[41]		2	6
6/9/45	For charges for a horse to the Leaguer at Bristol and back to Lyme, being 10 days		7	6
6/9/45	For charges for a horse to Taunton two days		3	6
6/9/45	For two men at Hisby about the provisions there		1	4
10/9/45	For ink and paper, 200 packs, thread and needles		2	0
10/9/45	For two labourers two days and straw to rub cheese		5	0
24/9/45	For boards and nails to mend the store chamber		3	0
27/9/45	For two men three days to cut biscuit		6	0
4/10/45	For one labourer 3 days to scrape and scrub cheese		3	0
7/10/45	For sending warrants into the country for ploughs [carts?] to carry provisions to Chard		1	0
8/10/45	For two men to help weigh and sand 90cwt of cheese		3	0
8/10/45	For three men to help load 180 bags of biscuit		4	6
14/10/45	For charges of a horse 14 days at several times about sending provisions to the army	1	2	0
16/10/45	For charges of a horse to Chard		1	4
16/10/45	For three men to turn biscuit at Chard		1	6
21/10/45	For three men to scrape and scrub cheese 10 days at Lyme	1	10	0
11/11/45	For wood to air the rooms		1	6
11/11/45	For a horse to Taunton to look to the provisions		4	6
14/11/45	For a horse to Chard		1	6
15/11/45	For two men to turn the biscuit there		1	0
25/11/45	For 20 yards of cloth to make biscuit bags		10	0
25/11/45	For 1lb of packthread			8
27/11/45	For three men three days to cut biscuit and for mending the bags		9	0
27/11/45	For two men three days to cut biscuit, and to scrape and scrub cheese at Lyme		6	0
27/11/45	For one man four days to pack cheese		4	0

41 Quartermaster General to the City of London (CSPD 1644, pp.263, 270).

		£	s.	d.
20/12/45	For charges of a horse to look after the clothes by the General's order and back again to Lyme		8	0
21/12/45	Paid Mr Hazelwood, master of the *Jonas* for waiting for 3 days in earnest for the hire of his ship to bring the clothes to Lyme, being informed they were come to Weymouth by Mr Edwards but were not	[blank]		
In the army:				
25/10/45	For carrying of provisions from Silverton to Stoke, paid six men that brought in enough provisions		7	6
25/10/45	For pay			8
25/10/45	Paid James Thorne and John Ascot, carriers 3 days' pay		5	0
25/10/45	For sending warrants into the country		1	0
26/10/45	Paid William Walton and John Farrow each for watching and looking to the fat oxen 14 days		14	0
26/10/45	For hay for said oxen at Crediton		5	0
2/11/45	For hay for 18 fat oxen at Topsham [near Exeter]		4	0
3/11/45	For paper and a paper book		2	6
3/11/45	For sending warrants into the country from Broadcliffe		1	0
5/11/45	For a shop there to sell meat in			8
5/11/45	For a guide to conduct a waggon from Broadcliffe to Mary Autrey			6
5/11/45	For 2 quires of paper		1	0
18/11/45	Paid William Walton and John Farrow each for watching and looking to the fat oxen 24 days and nights	1	4	0
4/12/45	For extreeing of the wagon and shoeing the wagon horses		6	0
At Lyme for charges of provisions:				
20/11/45	Delivered to Sir William Fenton by warrant from the General and shipped to Youghal in Ireland, viz: 165cwt of cheese and 180 bags of biscuit, and 20 hogsheads of beef by Colonel Ceely, Governor, viz: For 200 yards of stuff to make bags to put the governor's biscuit in For 3lbs of packthread and making of them For weighing and loading beef into the waggons For weighing and carrying of the cheese For four seams of straw to lay under the cheese For loading 180 bags of biscuit into the waggons and carrying it to the Cobb For one seam of faggots to lay under the biscuit in the ship For one man to help in the business, and for horse hire and horse meat	5	0 6 3 16 16 7 18	0 0 6 2 10 10 9 0
	In the army:			
2/11/45	For 12 horseshoes for the waggon horses		6	0
2/11/45	For 6 removes		1	0
2/11/45	For three clouts for the wagon		1	0
2/11/45	For grease and nails for the wagon			8

		£	s.	d.
2/11/45	For a spoke for the wheel		1	4
2/11/45	For one pack of salt to powder the meat at Chard		1	6
2/11/45	Paid Benjamin Gardner 6 days' pay as waggoner, ending 29 September at 18d. per day		9	0
9/12/45	Paid William Walton and John Farrow each for watching and looking to the fat oxen 21 days and nights, for hay and grass for 13 oxen and five waggon horses at Mary Autrey 28 days		2	10
8/12/45-13/12/45	At the magazine in Lyme for charges of 80,000lbs of	3	15	0
	biscuit and 40,000lbs of cheese received from London			
	by the *Elizabeth & James* for 15 labourers five days to			
	stow it in several rooms	4	0	0
	For carrying it from the Cobb:	1	0	0
	Paid Henry Pittock and Christopher Lamberton for			
	labouring 10 days in the storehouses			
	Paid to five messengers at several times to fetch the		5	0
	carriages from their quarters			
	For ½lb of packthread			4
	For two door locks and nails		2	10
	For three staples and hasps, and six hinges		1	0
	For mending of a waggon		4	10
	For mending of a chamber, it broke down with the			
	weight of the biscuit, viz: for nails and a beam to bear		6	6
	the joists		9	0
	For a door and four double quarters			9
	For rafters 4s., carpenters' work 5s.		1	6
	For a paper book			
	For cradle and one seam of straw			
			6	0
	In the army:		3	0
	For 12 shoes for the waggon horses		2	0
	For bleeding and drenching my six horses		7	0
	For ½ bushel of malt for mast		12	0
	Paid John Fairweather for looking to eight fat oxen 14		1	0
	days			6
	For hay for them six nights		3	6
	For cleansing a room to put hay and oats in at Crediton			6
	For paper there			
	For sending out warrants for cheese			
	For paper at Tiverton			
			2	6
	For charges of 60 bags of biscuit and 20cwt of cheese		5	0
	from Lyme to Nutwell House:		2	8
	For two men to fetch teams from their quarters		3	4
	Paid for loading the provisions		4	0
	For shoeing waggon horses		10	0
	For mending of a waggon		6	0
	For watching the provisions two nights			
	For hay for the waggon horses			
	For six carters to go with the provisions			

		£	s.	d.
18/12/45- 21/12/45	**For charges of 20cwt of cheese from Lyme to Nutwell House:** For a man to watch the carts one night at Culliford For one night's hay for 10 horses there For hay to [feed] the horses at Sidford For a man to watch one night at Newton Poppleford For hay for the horses there For a new axletree and grease at Newton Poppleford For hay for the horses at Sidford one night Paid four carters For charges of John Searby's horse to go with the provisions to Nutwell and back		 1 2 1 1 1 2 5 2 4 7	 0 6 4 0 4 6 5 6 0 0
At the magazine in Lyme				
18/12/45	For mending the wall of one of the store chambers			8
5/1/46	Paid 2 men to help weigh and load cheese		2	0
5/1/46	Paid 2 men to load shoes and stockings		2	0
7/1/46	For 2lbs of packthread and 1 quire of paper		1	10
7/1/46	Paid 2 men for 2 days to bag up biscuit		4	0
7/1/46	Paid 2 men that brought in horses to carry biscuit to Tiverton		1	0
7/1/46	Paid 2 men that mended bags and for loading biscuit		1	0
10/1/46	Paid 1 man for loading biscuit		1	0
10/1/46	For removing of 300 cheeses of Mr Carridge's cellar (Mr Mayor having use for it) and for storing them in Mr Bragg's cellar		5	8
12/1/46	For 1 man for loading biscuit			6
12/1/46	For a paper book		1	4
12/1/46	Paid 1 man for turning cheeses and cutting biscuit 5 days		5	0
12/1/46	Paid 1 man the like for 2 days		2	0
28/12/45	Paid a messenger that came from Weymouth who brought word of the clothes		4	0
	For charges of shoes and stockings from Lyme to Tiverton, being 8 wain loads:			
1/1/46	For sending warrants into the country for ploughs [carts?]		3	0
2/1/46	Paid 4 men that came with carriages from Bridport		4	0
3/1/46	For hay for 16 oxen 1 night		4	0
6/1/46	For hay for 30 oxen 1 night Paid Henry Lush and his partner, carters for 4 days Paid Andrew Benford and his partner for 4 days Paid Thomas Collington and his partner for 4 days Paid William Foulkes and his partner for 4 days Paid Roger Pearsly and his partner for 4 days Paid Thomas Gunn and his partner for 4 days Paid William Orchard and his partner for 4 days Paid John Cozens and his partner for 4 days For hay for the cattle, being 60 at 15s. per night for 3 nights For watching the carriages	 2	10 8 8 8 8 8 8 8 8 5 7	0 0 0 0 0 0 0 0 0 0 0

		£	s.	d.
	For charges of fitting a magazine at Tiverton:			
7/1/46	For 200½ feet of board For 3 planks For 2 piggons For a lock For nails and spikes For 4 men's labour for 2 days For 2 nights' hay for the cattle, which brought the shoes and stockings in their return from Tiverton to Lyme	1 1	5 3 1 4 3 9 10	0 0 4 0 0 4 0
	For charges of 247 bags of biscuit brought from Lyme to Tiverton on horseback:			
8/1/46	Paid Roger Royle and Trevor North for 3 horses for 2½ days Paid Timothy Bland and William Wood for 5 horses for 2½ days Paid Thomas Bond for 2 horses for 2 days Paid Morgan Leighton for 1 horse for 2 days Paid Augustine Harvey and Richard Harris for 3 horses for 2 days Paid Robert Perry for 1 horse for 2 days For cleaning and shoeing waggon horses		7 11 4 2 6 2 6	0 8 0 0 0 0 0
9/1/46	For nails and spikes to use in the magazine For timber to repair the stairs For making of them		1 2 2	8 0 6
10/1/46	Payments to 42 men and women for horse hire			
11/1/46	Payments to 31 men and women for horse hire			
12/1/46	Payments to 12 men and women for horse hire Paid a messenger for bringing 2 letters from the headquarters about provisions Paid 3 men to help stow the biscuit and for cleansing the magazine at Tiverton Paid 8 men for horse hire Paid for paper and ink For bringing the coats, breeches, shirts, shoes and stockings into the magazine at Tiverton For 2 messengers sent to Lyme several ways to give notice that no more provisions should be sent to Tiverton, being the General's command, and for horse hire and horse meat [provender], and for mending the boards in the magazine	 2	 2 16 8 1 16 1	 0 0 0 4 0 0
	For charges for 17 wain loads of clothes from Weymouth to Tiverton:			
8/1/46	For 14 men and 7 teams, 5 horses in each team, one day at Weymouth	1	12	6
9/1/46	For 9 men and 5 teams, 5 horses in each team, one day at Weymouth	1	2	6
10/1/46	For 40 men and 100 horses one day at Weymouth	4	10	0
11/1/46	For 40 men and 100 horses one day at Borton	4	10	0
12/1/46	For 40 men and 100 horses one day at Whitchurch	3	13	4
13/1/46	For 40 men and 100 horses one day at Axminister	3	5	0

		£	s.	d.
14/1/46	For 40 men and 102 horses one day at Norcott	3	5	6
15/1/46	For 40 men and 99 horses one day at Cullampton	3	4	9
16/1/46	For 35 men 2 days at Tiverton For watching the carriages 7 nights For mending 2 bridges For loading the carriages For mending the carriages For 4 guides For sending warrants into the country	3 1	10 3 8 10 7 8 3	0 6 0 0 6 0 0
	For charges for 17 horse loads of clothes from Tiverton to Chard, containing 722 coats, 622 pair of breeches, 216 pair of stockings and 800 snapsacks:			
18/1/46	For carrying of pack cloths from Tiverton to Chard For 5 packboards Paid 5 men to take up horses Paid for making the packs For hay for 30 horses one night For 2 guides For 17 pack horses For five drivers 2 days Paid to John Pittfowles for himself and horse For carrying the clothes up into the magazine at Tiverton For 2 men to assist Jervis Kidd 2 days and for the charges of [his] horse For the charges of Jervis Kidd's horse for hire and his meat for 28 days	2 3 2	5 3 5 10 10 3 11 10 5 2 6 11	0 6 0 0 0 0 0 0 0 6 0 4
At Tiverton:				
23/1/46	For hay for 5 waggon horses 35 days, and one 21 days at 3d. per day For hay for 8 oxen 10 days and 5 days For 4lbs of copper to dress the waggon horses For 3 pecks of malt for mashes For 1 peck of barley to boil For 1 curry comb	2 1	9 2 1 3 1	0 0 0 0 8 2
26/1/46	For hay for 4 wagon horses for 10 days For charges of Fabian Mayhew's horse being employed in sending provisions from Lyme to Tiverton: For shoeing his horse For hay for 6 nights at Lyme For 2 pecks of oats For lying by the way 3 nights For nails and pin for the wagon		10 1 4 1	0 6 4 8 9 4
	For charges for bringing clothes from Tiverton to the headquarters at Chudleigh, [comprising] 2598 coats, 2952 pair of breeches 2082 shirts, being brought upon 100 State's horses:			
23/1/46	For cords, packthread and needles to pack them up Paid Mr Long for 14 days' labour For loading and unloading them 3 times For shoeing 1 of the waggon horses For cords, packthread and needles to pack them up	1	15 14 10 1 3	0 0 0 6 6

		£	s.	d.
23/1/46	Paid Mr Long for 14 days' labour For loading and unloading them 3 times For shoeing 1 of the waggon horses For hay for 4 waggon horses for 2 nights For guides at several times For watching them by the way several nights and at Chudleigh until the same delivered For bringing in 1 horse with the clothes which was gone out of the way For straw to lay under the clothes sent to several regiments For charges of Mr Gerrard's and Mr Blewitt's horses from Honiton to Tiverton, and back to Chudleigh, being 8 days For a bushel grains for the waggon horses at Chudleigh For 1 bushel of oats For 1 seam of hay For 2 shoes and nails Paid to Mr Bartholomew Garnett for himself and charges of his horse, being employed in the service 2 months	8	8 6 1 2 16 1 3 3 1 8	6 0 0 6 0 0 4 0 2 0
	For mending the magazine at Tiverton:			
3/2/46	For 1 post to prop up the loft For 1 joist, and spikes and nails For the carpenters' labour, being 3 men		2 2 6	0 4 0

Accounts approved by Thomas Herbert and Nicholas Potter, Commissaries of Parliament for the Army. Torrington, 17 February 1646

Free Quarter and Victuals

Some historians have asserted that the New Model Army (at least in the first months of its existence) was provisioned by quartering, in other words, the distribution of rations was administered locally by householders.[42] However, Sir Thomas Fairfax acknowledged that requisitioning from the countryside was not wholly effective during the army's march from Oxford towards Leicester. On 8 June 1645 he informed Sir Samuel Luke, the Parliamentarian Governor of Newport Pagnell that although he had demanded victuals from the Buckingham Committee, these had not been forthcoming. As Fairfax wrote, however, the failure of supplies to arrive as his regiments marched through, 'much discontents the soldiers and necessitates them to straggle abroad, which may prejudice the inhabitants in the county'. Instead, he asked him for supplies, since his garrison and that of Northampton had been

42 Gentles, *New Model Army*, chapter 2; James Scott Wheeler, 'Logistics and supply in Cromwell's conquest of Ireland', in Mark Fissel (ed.), *War and Government in Britain, 1598–1650* (Manchester: Manchester University Press, 1991), pp.38–56; Aryeh J. S. Nusbacher, 'Civil Supply in the Civil War: Supply of Victuals to the New Model Army on the Naseby Campaign, 1–14 June 1645', *EHR*, 115 (2000), pp.145–160.

supplied with cereals from Buckinghamshire and adjacent Bedfordshire in previous years.[43] Even so, there is evidence that although Luke was able to provide some victuals, his garrison was left critically short of supplies. He had been authorised on 1 June 1645 to 'call in a competent number of forces out of the adjacent counties for your assistance, and to fetch in provisions'.[44] During the Civil Wars, when not in garrison, troops were usually quartered in villages and hamlets, where civilians would be expected to accommodate several men and horses, in addition to feeding them. Preferably, this would be paid for by the soldiers out of their own pockets, but this was very rare in practice, mainly because pay was often far in arrears. More commonly, 'free quarter' – not free in the sense that no payment would be made but was so called because no immediate payment was necessary – was taken, whereby tickets or vouchers were left with individual householders, noting the number of men and animals they had quartered, and the total charge incurred by them. Once endorsed by a commissioned officer, tickets were to be presented to the relevant army's treasury (if possible), where the sum would be reimbursed.

Theoretically, regulations governed the requirements which troops could make of a householder, yet although bills for free quarter were sometimes honoured by the soldiers and officers themselves, they were sometimes left unpaid, the intention being that the petitioner would claim them later. In this regard, Turner described the general Continental practice:

> But they will be refreshed when I tell them of free quarter which Princes and their generals are many times forced for want of money to grant, where they can quarter their armies in towns and villages, and this often proves the destruction of a country. For though no exorbitance be committed, and that every man both officer and soldier demand no other entertainment than what is allowed by the Prince or State where they serve; yet when an army cannot be quartered but close and near together, to prevent infalls, assaults and surprisal of an enemy, it is an easy matter to imagine what a heavy burthen these places bear, whom in poor men's houses, six, seven, eight, it may be fourteen or fifteen soldiers are lodged, for in such cases it is ordinary to quarter two thousand foot, or a thousand horse in a little town, where perhaps there are not above three or four hundred houses. And withal it is very hard to get soldiers and horsemen kept within the limits of their duty in these quarters, after they have endured hunger, thirst, and other hardships in the field.[45]

The exception to the norm was the New Model Army. The strict prohibition on free quarter was related to the imparting of strict discipline among Sir Thomas Fairfax's troops, but more so, it was an indicator of regular pay being a high priory both of Parliament and his senior officers. At the end of April 1645, regiments received an

43 Tibbutt (ed.), *Letter Books*, pp.560 & 620.
44 *CSPD, 1644–45*, p.554.
45 Turner, *Pallas Armata*, pp.201–202.

additional fortnight's pay, an action that encouraged many unwilling recruits to come forward. Nevertheless, on 30 September Sprigge noted:

> the army marched towards Shaftsbury and were mustered in their march, the General continuing still at Warminster, choosing to do so, not only for the forementioned reason, but also till he might hear that the treasure for the army is at least on the way from London, the soldiers being so out of money, that they were all enforced to take free quarter, which they had not done till then.[46]

By late 1646, the New Model had begun to suffer from the same financial confines as its predecessors and opponents, which were intensified by severe pay arrears, thus forcing commanders to implement the unpopular custom of free quarter.[47] The Committee of Both Kingdoms formulated new procedures to govern the maintenance of the army on campaign. Hereafter, the Committee aimed to assuage the burden placed by troops upon the localities, while at the same time guaranteeing that quarter and provision would be readily available. It was able to ban officers from taking free quarter and provision, and when pay was delayed vouchers would be issued in return for quarter and rations.[48] Additionally, the Committee ordered that no individual resident should be necessitated to provide services or products beyond their own means. This order protected the local administration from carrying the responsibility of assigning quarters and provision for the army, in addition to safeguarding the Committee from excessive individual claims for reparation. Each of these orders were accompanied by strict penalties, including the cashiering of officers.[49]

On 16 May 1645 Parliament issued its 'Instructions to the Parliamentary Commissioners sent to reside with the Army', which included the observation of the following rules:

> For the ease of the country, the said Commissioners are to endeavour that no officer or soldier be quartered in any place but by the quartermaster, first showing his commission, if it be required, and by what authority he takes up such quarters; and giving a ticket of the names of every person which he shall quarter, expressing of what regiment, troop, or company the same person so quartered is; and the number of horses there quartered, and at whose house; together with the day of the month, and to subscribe his name thereunto. Saving whereby reason of the great numbers of them cannot be inserted, and then their numbers to be expressed in place of their names. That no quarter or provisions for man or horse in any quarters be taken without payment of ready money; but in case of necessity for want of pay; which the Parliament will use all means possible to prevent. And in

46 Sprigge, *Anglicana Rediviva*, pp.127–128.
47 Gentles, *New Model Army*, pp.48–52.
48 *CSPD 1644–45*, p.428.
49 Rushworth, *Historical Collections*, VII, 32–33, 838; *LJ*, VII, p.311.

> case any quarter or provision shall be taken without payment, the captain or quartermaster shall by writing under their or one of their hands, certify what provisions have been so had, within what time, by whom, and of what regiment, troop, and company, from whom and the value thereof. Provided, that where the Army shall be upon their march, not staying above 24 hours in a place, the rates shall be 4d. a night for hay, 3d. a night for grass, 4d. a peck for oats, 6d. a peck for peas and beans, and 7d. for a peck for barley and malt (which provision of barley and malt is not to be taken but where no other grain for horse-meat is to be had), 8d. a day is to be paid for the diet of every trooper or horseman, 7d. a day for every dragoon, and 6d. a day for every foot soldier, pioneer, waggoner, or carter, that shall not be officers by commission, or of the Life Guard troop. Provided also that no inhabitant whatsoever shall be compelled to furnish any provision but what he has in his house of his own. And that no officer or soldier shall compel him to do otherwise, upon pain of cashiering, or such other punishment as the commander-in-chief shall think fit.[50]

The householder William Bushell of Marston Trussell in Northamptonshire claimed that on 'the night after Naseby fight' he provided quarter to 46 men and 52 horses under the command of Colonel Rossiter to the value of £4, whereas the constable of Harleton in Wintersley hundred recorded that on 12 December 1645 'there was a company of foot soldiers, which went under Lieutenant Colonel Kempson [Weldon's regiment] which was one day and night, being 50 in number to the charges of £1 5s.'.[51] Throughout the western campaign of 1645–6, Sir Thomas Fairfax, the army's commander-in-chief maintained strict levels of discipline among the rank and file, and made every effort to refrain from free quarter because it alienated the local populace. One pro-Parliament newsbook reported for 17 May 1645:

> This day we are assured, that Sir Thomas Fairfax, whose honourable advance to, and return from the West, which the love of the people, as numerous as they went, as to the regiments, returned, paying for what he took, keeping the soldiery together, so as they straggled not, nor wronged any; and yet the party he had with better, such as had been a little wild, discipline civilizes as the hammer the roughest stones. The General himself making a speech to his officers, full of severity, yet mixed with love (which to avoid envy we here omit) did this day, after his necessary repose to Newbury march to Blewbury, intending to straighten Oxford until the intended supplies come.[52]

However, by clearing the West Country the New Model extended the tax base from which it could be supported, thus reducing the army's self-reliance and rendering

50 Rushworth, *Historical Collections*, VI, pp.32–33; *The Kingdomes Weekly Intelligencer*, 13–20 May 1645. TT, E284[23].

51 TNA, SP28/173/2, f. 343v.

52 *The Moderate Intelligencer*, 15–22 May 1645. TT, E285[7].

Military encampment during the siege of Breda, 1628, Jacques Callot. (Rijksmuseum)

the payment of troops more difficult. As the army reached Warminster on 27 September 1645, Sprigge sorrowfully reported, 'the soldiers being so out of money, that they were all enforced to take quarter, which they had not done till then'.[53] On 14 November 14 soldiers of Sergeant Major George Sedascue's troop of Ireton's regiment were accommodated for 16 days and nights at Harleton at a cost of £22 18s. Likewise, in May 1646 the Buckinghamshire township of Cuddington gave quarter for 240 horses and 60 dragoons of Captain Daniel Abbot's company belonging to Colonel Okey's regiment. In both the latter instances the inhabitants received immediate compensation.[54]

By comparison, when the Scots Covenanter Army commanded by Alexander Leslie, 1st Earl of Leven, left the North of England in 1645 to undertake long marches through the Midlands, its difficulties increased daily. Before setting out from Appleby in May 1645, Leven wrote to the Commissioners at York, to represent 'the great impediment we find through the want of draught and provisions'.[55] He was compelled to issue promissory tickets for the provisions he obtained, and the inhabitants were little disposed to furnish food with the indefinite prospect of repayment. During the siege of Hereford, in August 1645, the army for 10 days 'not seeing bread but one day, all the rest living upon beans, green corn, and fruit'.[56] In February 1646, before Newark, it was represented that for two weeks the infantry had not received 18d. worth of provisions weekly, and that there was not £10 worth of food in their magazines. Consequently, Leven resorted to what his ally condemned as 'free quarters and disorderly plunderings', taking upon credit the provisions he was unable to pay for.[57] For the Covenanting invasion of England in January 1644, the Committee of Both Kingdoms had proclaimed its desire 'to take the most orderly and reasonable way' for provisioning the army.[58] The districts through which it passed were ordered to furnish 'such provisions as shall be necessary' to the officers and men billeted upon them, the daily rates and allowances for all ranks (the maximum daily provisioning which could be demanded for them), or could be charged for their maintenance, being set out in a 'Schedule of Allowances' appended to the proclamation.

53 Sprigge, *Anglia Rediviva*, p.127.
54 TNA, SP28/173/2, f. 343v; SP28/149/1, f. 41v; SP28/149/4, unfol.
55 *CSPD 1644–45*, pp.537, 556, 596.
56 David Buchanan, *Truth Its Manifest* (London: 1645), pp.46–47.
57 *LJ*, VIII, pp.34 & 143.
58 Rushworth, *Historical Collections*, V, pp.612–613.

On 26 November 1649 Colonels Charles Fleetwood and Edward Whalley were ordered to send 1,000 infantry recruits, raised by them for the Commonwealth forces in Ireland, to Chester, although they were diverted to Bristol, a further 5 days' march away. To prevent the soldiers from 'the taking of free quarter and other disorders', the treasurers of deans and chapters' lands were to forward to Whalley, upon account, 8d. a day for each man for five days, to pay for their quarters. Likewise, Colonel Thomas Harrison was to pay, 'out of the assignations for his regiment', to Colonel Henry Cromwell's cavalry troop of 100 men, waiting at Chester, 'their entertainment during their stay for a wind, and until they are shipped for Ireland, and also one month's pay in advance, when they ship for Ireland'. Another officer, Colonel Francis Hacker, made the same payments to the three troops of his regiment crossing to Ireland.[59]

According to Gentles, between April and July 1645 the New Model Army's impact on the countryside was the same as any other civil war army. However, he based this conclusion solely upon the claims of local constables and householders in Northamptonshire, and thus, he asserted:

> At the time of Naseby, for example, the newly recruited army descended like clouds of locusts on the defenceless countryside of Northamptonshire and Warwickshire. For four months from April to July the army was being relatively well paid: thirteen out of seventeen weeks for the foot, and nine or ten out of seventeen for the horse. Yet, if the householders of both counties can be believed, Fairfax's men seized mammoth quantities of sheep, lambs, pigs, calves, butter, cheese, bacon, beer, wheat, barley, peas, oats, meal and malt. Bored with their Spartan diet of cheese and biscuit, the soldiers were ravenous for meat on the eve of battle. Their horses were no less hungry: between 7,000 and 8,000 of them consumed whole meadows and pastures, some freshly seeded. The loss of grass was a leading complaint, heard over and over again.

He further claimed that, except for bread and cheese, the New Model, like other forces of the period procured a good 90 per cent of [its] consumption locally.[60]

Similarly, Kishlansky suggested that 'in its composition and organization as much as in its material condition of pay and supply, the New Model Army exhibited few dissimilarities from the old armies', although his principle concern in his study was the political ascendancy of the army.[61] Such comments can be challenged, however, given the availability of a wider body of documentary material. Foard described Fairfax's Army in Northamptonshire as having been mostly supplied by the county committees from local resources, employing evidence from the Civil War Loss Accounts of local parishes, albeit from early weeks of the Naseby campaign, but accepts that some previous assumptions can be questioned, and 'when one analyses the information in detail on a countrywide basis

59 *CSPD 1649–50*, p.406.

60 Gentles, *New Model Army*, p.45.

61 Kishlansky, *Rise of the New Model Army*, p.70.

a different conclusion may perhaps be drawn. This is not of course to dispute that the impact of the army could still be seen as oppressive, the needs of any large army were bound to place pressure on the resources of an area, however carefully the provisioning was controlled'.[62]

Few of the Northamptonshire accounts have much to say for 1645 and 1646 (perhaps suggesting that the footprint of Fairfax's Army made little or no impact upon many areas). However, the constable of Boughton – which it seems did not offer quartering to soldiers, testified 'we find that at Naseby fight we were continually oppressed with foot and horse that did belong to Parliament, until we had neither horsemeat nor man's meat left us to our expense of £30. Also, at Collingtree on 11 June 1645 it was claimed that 'some men paid slenderly for their quarters'.[63] Even so, the evidence largely shows that the soldiers usually paid for their quartering. Luke, not a man who was overly benevolent towards the New Model Army, recounted that on 12 June 'the foot officers pay well and drink well', though he also complained that two days later the officers of Colonel Edward Rossiter's regiment of cavalry 'so far as I can hear pay no quarters, nor the horse'.[64] Any lack of payment for quarter and rations among the army would appear to have been uncommon, however. On 3 April Sir Thomas Fairfax had departed London for Windsor, and the following day £7,000 was conveyed to the town, while another £3,000, went to Reading 'towards the payment of 14 days' pay to such officers and soldiers as shall appear in the muster rolls, under the hands of such person or persons as shall be appointed to take the muster and listed under my command there.'[65] There was also an additional £10,000 at Windsor on 27 May for the soldiers, and this was ordered to be conveyed via St Albans and Newport Pagnell on 13 June.

Two days later, Cromwell instructed Luke to transport this 'treasure' from there to Northampton, where it would be collected.[66] Furthermore, pay warrants record various disbursements to military units. Amongst the foot, Fairfax's own regiment received £341 14s. 9d. on 7 June for 7 days' pay; two days later the officers and soldiers of Colonel Sir Hardress Waller's regiment were paid the sum of £153 4s. 10d., being 7 days' wages 'according to the muster of 23 May to 30 May'; similarly, on 10 June £91 11s. 8d. was paid to the companies commanded by Captains Dancer and Browne of Colonel Rainborowe's regiment. Among the New Model's dragoons, the sum of £35 18s. 8d. was received by the officers and soldiers of Captain Skirmager's company on 9 June, while on the same day £42 1s. 8d. went to Sergeant Major Moore's command. Some cavalry units benefitted from 7 days' pay also. For instance, on 7 July 1645 Colonel John Butler's own troop received £73 13s. 4d., whereas on 12th July Captain Walter Parry's troop was paid £54 14s. 2d.

Additionally, on 9 June the officers, artificers and firelock guards of the train of artillery had 7 days' wages amounting to £473 15s. 1d.[67] Thus, not only was the army

62 Foard, *Naseby*, pp.168–169.
63 TNA, SP28/171/4, f. 401v.
64 TNA, SP28/173/1, unfol.
65 TNA, SP28/29/1, ff. 4r, 23r, 168r.
66 *CSPD 1644–5*, pp.590–592.
67 TNA, SP28/30/5, ff. 450r–454r, 463r, 467r, 474r–476v.

adequately paid, but Sir Thomas Fairfax also seems to have made every effort to ensure that the rules were adhered to. It can be seen from numerous events during his command of the army that he cared about the condition of his soldiers, but that he would stand no indiscipline, which he punished severely. In May 1645 two soldiers were hanged for disorder and desertion on the march into the Southwest, and on the return journey another had been executed, making it clear 'that it should be death for any man to plunder'.[68] Moreover, with the New Model Army in the vicinity of Blandford *The Moderate Intelligencer* reported for 4 July, 'there is an excellent harmony in the Army, instead of drinking and gambling, plundering, etc., they pray, and discourse. When one speaks the rest are silent, much like expounding. Exercise arms, and labour for skill how to offend their enemy, defend themselves', thus attesting to the highly developed sense of brotherhood, training and motivation amongst the soldiers.[69]

To ensure that the New Model Army was efficiently provisioned with as little impact on the local population as possible, before it marched from Oxford on 5 June 1645 – Sir Thomas Fairfax having received orders to engage the King and recapture Leicester instead – warrants were sent to the County Committees of Northamptonshire, Bedfordshire and Buckinghamshire ordering them to bring supplies to the army. When his troops reached Buckinghamshire, Fairfax made every effort to supply the army through the local administrative system, and to control his forces to stop them from ranging widely to take provisions. That he was only partially unsuccessful was a reflection as much on the state of the county as the discipline of the army. Supplies had, however, been sent to the army from the Eastern Association and, unlike the soldiers who should have joined Fairfax from East Anglia, most of these supplies arrived before 12 June 1645.[70] Similar orders to the Deputy Lieutenants of various English counties to bring in whatever provisions they could for the supply of Sir Thomas Fairfax's Army in expectation of future reimbursement were issued on 16 June, following the Battle of Naseby.[71] It does not appear from the sources that there was a particular difficulty in victualling the troops, and Rushworth's comment that the night before the engagement the soldiers 'had not a bit of bread to a regiment for their refreshment' sounds like they had consumed all their victuals during the rapid march and had temporarily outstripped their logistical support.[72] According to the author of *Bellum Civile*, before the Battle of Stratton in 1643 Cornish Royalist troops had only 'a dry biscuit apiece, for want of other provisions'.[73] Equally, the soldiers of the Earl of Essex's Army marching to the relief of Gloucester in 1643 were described as carrying 3 days' rations in their snapsacks, whereas amongst the Parliamentarian infantry at the Second Battle of Newbury in October 1644 'most of them had 3 days' provision prepared by command in his snapsack'.[74]

68 Sprigg, *Anglia Rediviva*, p.15.
69 *The Moderate Intelligencer*, 3–10 July 1645. TT, E292[21].
70 *CSPD 1644–5*, p.589.
71 Bod. Lib., Ms Tanner 60/1, f. 171r.
72 *An Ordinance of the Lords and Commons*. TT, E288[26].
73 Charles Chadwick-Healey (ed.), *Bellum Civile: Hopton's Narrative of His Campaigns in the West Country, 1642–44* (Somerset Record Society, 1902), p.41.
74 *A True and Exact Relation of the...Red and Blue Regiments ... Who Marched Forth For the Relief of the City of Gloucester, Oct 2 1643* (London: 1643). TT, E69[15]; John Vicars,

Amongst the New Model Army neither provision nor quarter was to be taken without payment of ready cash. However, in the event of lack of pay these were to be itemised by the captain or quartermaster of individual troops and companies. When on the march and not stopping for more than one night then disbursements amounted to:

> 4d. a night for hay, 3d. a night for grass, 4d. a peck for oats, 6d. a peck for peas and beans, and 7d. for a peck for barley and malt (which provision of barley and malt is not to be taken but where no other grain for horse-meat is to be had), 8d. a day is to be paid for the diet of every trooper or horseman, 7d. a day for every dragoon, and 6d. a day for every foot soldier, pioneer, waggoner, or carter.[75]

As Fairfax's regiments passed into Northamptonshire in mid-1645 the local administrative system was utilised with far greater success, probably because the county had been largely hostile to the King's Army, which employed methods of gathering victuals more akin to plundering. As a result, Fairfax's forces could be concentrated in a few villages close together, with the infantry at the headquarters and, where necessary, in one or two adjacent villages. However, as Sprigge reported, 'The Army being come to Wootton [on 11 June 1645], they found there none of the best accommodation for quarter; only, what was wanting that day, was kindly and respectfully endeavoured to be supplied by the mayor and magistrates of Northampton, who the same night came to the general at headquarter, upon the errand of a congratulatory and present'.[76] Moreover, the concentration of New Model units in this part of the county indicates that the soldiers did not all stay in buildings, but probably, as they did on 11 June near Piddington, 'lying in the fields'.[77]

In Northamptonshire the New Model's Commissary of Victuals and the Deputy Lieutenants of the county appear to have compelled the constables of individual parishes, via warrants, to furnish money or provisions. This method was fundamental to the mobilisation of a supply chain involving the transportation and storage of supplies ahead of the army as it advanced. Hence, on 10 June the villagers of Grafton Regis sent foodstuffs to Stony Stratford, some 5 miles to the southeast to the value of £2 7s. 8d. for three troops of horse, and the following day they forwarded more victuals, costing £3 6s. 4d. to the same town to supply Captain Thomas Nevell's troop of Colonel Rich's regiment. Likewise, 10 dozen loaves and 20lbs of bacon were transported from Whiston for onward movement to Hardingstone, near to the army's headquarters at Wootton, whereas Cogenhoe sent 10 dozen loaves of bread, 40lbs of cheese, and a load of firewood along the same route for the use of the soldiers.[78] In similar fashion, the accounts of the small village of Harleton

Magnalia Dei Anglicana (London: 1646), p.58.

75 Rushworth, *Historical Collections*, VI, pp.32–33; *The Kingdomes Weekly Intelligencer*, 13–20 May 1645. TT, E284[23].

76 Sprigge, *Anglia Rediviva*, p.30.

77 TNA, SP28/173, unfol.

78 TNA, SP28/171, ff. 31r & 581r.

record that on 12 June 1645, '7 sheep taken away by the officers and soldiers under the command of Sir Thomas Fairfax, the same night that they came for provision, having no satisfaction at all for the sheep to the value of £2 16s.'

On the same day Samuel Hearne received £2 10s. from commissaries 'for provision brought up into Northampton', while on 14 June:

> There came some officers and soldiers in the night time and came into men's houses, and took away provision to be carried away to Sir Thomas Fairfax's Army lying in the fields, they took away great store of meale and caused it to be baked, and besides took bread, butter, sheep, bacon, beer, and what provisions they could find, giving no satisfaction at all for it, and causing the provision to be carried away instant to Kislingsby and from thence to Gilsborough, being the day before Naseby fight to the value of £8.[79]

Such provisions appear to have been removed from civilians as part of the victualling system involving the issuing of warrants, and transportation of foodstuffs to collection points ahead of the advancing army, a system that continued throughout the New Model Army's march into the West Country. Few instances of stealing by Fairfax's soldiers were reported by local people.[80] Although the inhabitants of Kislingbury mentioned that 'Sir Thomas Fairfax quartered with us one night with great part of his horse and all his foot, which did eat and feed in the town and fields to the value of £100', they only reported the theft of 19 sheep, 1 calf, and a strike of malt following the lodging of over 10,000 troops there on the night of 13 June 1645.[81]

The logistical operations employed in the assembling and transportation of these supplies are recorded in some detail in the extensive accounts of the constable of Great Houghton. A small detachment of troopers and commissaries arrived there on 11 or 12 June 1645 to oversee the delivery of victuals to the army. William Denton, constable of village, had to provide 'for 8 soldiers quartering when they come for provision for the army to Kislingbury and 8 horses [at a cost of 6s.]'. Similar arrangements also occurred at Cogenhoe, which gave free quarter for 16 horses and 5 men from the train of artillery during the gathering of supplies, and the constable of Welford, situated 15 miles north-west of Northampton noted that Commissary General Orpin had valued the victuals provided by that village on 16 June.[82] On 11 June Fairfax ordered Sergeant Major Skippon to draw the bulk of the New Model Army into battle order, he dividing it into 'several brigades of horse and foot, in order to their being better disposed of for an engagement'.[83] The wider dispersal of cavalry and dragoon units had been necessary because of the need for grass for their horses. On 12 June, 2,000 New Model cavalry were situated in the meadows of Harpole. The constable of Rothersthorpe later claimed payment 'for quartering Colonel Fiennes' regiment one day and one night [and] one day before Naseby fight',

79 TNA, SP173/2, ff. 342r–343v.
80 Nusbacher, 'Civil Supply', p.151.
81 TNA, SP28/173/5, unfol.
82 TNA, SP28/173/2, unfol.; NRO, 175P/38, unfol.
83 Sprigge, *Anglia Rediviva*, p.29; Rushworth, *Historical Collections*, VI, p.40.

while 200–300 of the draught and riding horses belonging to the train, in addition to those of the officers were around the village of Collingtree.[84]

Edward Orpin first received pay for himself, along with a clerk and two deputies on 25 April 1645. On 15 October he had £29 19s. 3d., 'being 21 days' pay for himself as Commissary General of Victuals, and his two deputies and two clerks.' The following day, two further amounts were made over to Orpin, the first being £7 15s. for 24 days' pay for Nicholas Cowling, being 'one man being upon special service entertained as assistants [to him] during the siege before Bristol from 25 August to 18 September', and a second imbursement of £12 14s. 7½d., 'being 21 days' pay for several officers belonging to the said commissary who have no established pay, but are allowed (according to an Ordinance of Parliament to the Commissioners of Parliament in the army the same to remain 11 August last)'.[85] Orpin had acted as Commissary of Victuals in the Earl of Manchester's forces in 1644, but during May and June 1645 he was responsible for overseeing the victualling of the New Model Army, which included the procurement of transportation of food supplied from local sources, in addition to making payments for both the victuals, horse teams and waggons. He also established a magazine at Lyme, supplied by sea from London and supplemented by local rations, initially to victual the relief of the siege of Taunton by a New Model infantry brigade and cavalry units, although a portion of the train of artillery was also sent by road to provide logistical support to that force.

During autumn 1645 Sir Thomas Fairfax pushed on into the Southwest with the intention of destroying the Royalist forces there. Following an unsuccessful encounter with Goring at Axminster in early October, he advanced to Chard and Tiverton, which was speedily captured as a cannon shot broke the chain supporting the drawbridge. With pay for the soldiery running out, it was difficult for Fairfax to maintain discipline during such circumstances, yet he moved his regiments to Crediton and deployed it about Exeter. With oncoming winter rains made further campaigning difficult, compelling him on 8 October to report to his father, 'the extreme coldness of the weather, and want of clothes, make us act slower'. The army was blighted by sickness and Sir Thomas himself was 'exceedingly troubled with rheumatism and a benumbing coldness in my head, legs, and arms, especially on that side I had my hurts'.[86] By late 1645, if not earlier, Commissary Orpin's remit became a much wider one and included the storage, transportation, and distribution of stores – including clothing, arms and victuals – by land and sea via ports such as Portsmouth, Lyme, and Weymouth, from magazines at Windsor, Reading and Chard to the New Model in the Southwest of England. As such, Orpin's role was fundamental, not only to its sustenance but also the high performance and morale of Sir Thomas Fairfax's troops throughout the campaign. The instructions issued to the commissary officers of the New Model by Parliament on 16 May 1645 provide some insight into the procedures they were meant to adhere to in undertaking their role.

Thus, care should be taken that:

84 TNA, SP28/173, unfol.

85 TNA, SP28/29/1, f. 5r; SP28/32/1, ff. 135r, 201r, 206r.

86 Robert Bell (ed.), *Memorials of the Civil War* (London: Richard Bentley, 1849), II, p.251.

> commissaries of the victual and provisions (who are hereby required thereunto) do take notice, and keep account, of all such victual and provisions, for horse and men, as are brought in, and freely given, for the supply of the armies; and where provisions are brought into the army by way of sale, and ready money cannot be paid, to give tickets, according to usual rates, whereby such persons as shall so bring in the same may have the like benefit as others in case of quarter without money as aforesaid, and give copies of such tickets to the commissioners, upon pain and fine of punishment, at discretion of the commander-in-chief; and the commissioners are hereby authorised to take care, that such provisions as are delivered by the commissaries to any officers or soldiers, for their supply, be brought to a just and true account, and certified to the treasurer, that he may defalk so much out of the several entertainments of such officers and soldiers, from time to time, as the provisions received by them as aforesaid shall amount unto.[87]

Armies of the Civil Wars depended greatly upon the existing civilian infrastructure, so the road transportation of stores and victuals from London to Portsmouth was especially important. On 15 July 1645 the Committee of Both Kingdoms ordered a Mr Fielder 'to convoy the provisions going to Portsmouth for the army; to meet them at Godalming and convoy them to Midhurst'. Likewise, Colonel Richard Norton, the Parliamentarian governor of Portsmouth was to rendezvous with the waggons at Midhurst 'and to escort the provisions going from hence to Portsmouth for Sir Thomas Fairfax', in addition to assisting Captain Potter (one of the New Model's commissaries) 'in the shipping and dispatching of the same away from thence to the army'.[88]

The establishment of the New Model Army's train of artillery, assented to on 5 March 1645, included a total of 132 waggons and carts – 59 close (enclosed) waggons, 19 open waggons, 18 open carts, and 36 tumbrels – in addition to 1,038 draught and riding horses. On the face of it there was no provision for either the Commissaries of Victuals, or their vehicles. However, 68 close waggons were constructed for the New Model in April and May 1645, 'according to contracts made with the Committee of the Army' and costing £13 apiece, and delivered by Thomas Bateman, the principal manufacturer of wheeled vehicles and gun carriages to the army. Of these, 43 were supplied directly to Thomas Phipps, Commissary to the Train, who subsequently assigned 7 close waggons and 4 close carts to Commissary Orpin. Another 3 close waggons and 1 close cart were received by Orpin's subordinate Nicholas Bond, a Commissary for the Victuals 'for the service of the army of Sir Thomas Fairfax'.[89] Moreover, on 23 May 1645 the Commons agreed that £10,000 was to await Sir Thomas Fairfax at Windsor, along with provisions for the siege of Oxford, including 20 close waggons for provisions.

These were accordingly delivered, 'according to the Establishment of the rest of the train, to the Commissary for the Provisions, to carry provisions for the use of the army', as part of a substantial issue of ordnance, ammunition, small arms and

87 *LJ*, VII, p.377.

88 *CSPD 1645–7*, p.19.

89 TNA, SP28/30/3, ff. 249r–250r; WO55/1647, unfol.; WSL, Ms Salt 463, unfol.

tools from the Ordnance Office for the siege of the city.[90] So there clearly was provision by the State for waggons for transportation of stores and provisions, including victuals (probably for centrally supplied loads of cheese and biscuit). According to Gerhold, a seventeenth century waggon with a team of six horses – drawn at length (i.e. with the animals in single file) – could transport about 2 tons.[91] A close or closed waggon was one with 'an enclosed waggon bed usually under supported canvas or a similar material, which was essential for keeping the contents of the waggon as dry as possible and were primarily used for materials that would be otherwise damaged, such as gunpowder which would be rendered useless if damp.'[92]

It is possible to agree with Nusbacher's general assertion that 'there is no record of a commissariat sufficient to victual the Army under Sir Thomas Fairfax. There is no record of personnel nor of supplies for such a train. And there is no mention of the organisation of a large commissariat as part of the Army. It can be inferred from these significant silences that the New Model Army did not transport is own food supplies', although there is evidence that measures were taken by the Committee for the Army to facilitate the supply of foodstuffs to the New Model Army in 1645–46, if only in the form of cheese and biscuit, and some beef.[93] In addition to the waggons provided to commissaries for the transportation of stores, four Commissioners of Parliament Residing in the Army were Colonel Martin Pindar, Thomas Herbert, Harcourt Leighton, and Captain John Potter. These seem to have been endowed with a wide range of authority, and their instructions were issued to them on 16 May 1645.[94] The army's commissary officers – Captain Hampden, Michael Herring, Humphrey Lower and Nicholas Cox – were also responsible for provisioning and victualling the troops they were assigned to. Nicholas Bond served under Orpin as Commissary of Victuals.

Moreover, William Jones was paid as Commissary General of Horse Provisions in 1645, with his four assistants, while there were commissary generals for ammunition and for draught horses among the establishment of the train of artillery. Similarly, 10 conductors of ammunition – each paid 2s. per day – were also on the strength of the army, presumably acting as assistants to commissaries and quartermasters, and intermediaries between the train and the regiments of the army. Thomas Phipps performed a key role in the logistical operation of Fairfax's Army as Commissary to the Train.[95] More than a few of these men had previously served in the same or similar roles in Essex's forces. It must be added, however, that the title of Commissary General in the New Model Army granted to Colonel Henry Ireton in spring 1645 was an honorific one – given command of a regiment of cavalry, this was to mark his role as second in command of the New Model horse under Lieutenant General Oliver Cromwell.

90 *CJ*, IV p.153.
91 Gerhold, *Carriers and Coachmasters*, p.52.
92 Price, *Soldiers and Civilians*, p.41.
93 Nusbacher, 'Civil Supply', p.150.
94 *LJ*, VII, p.377.
95 TNA, SP28/30/3, ff. 249r–250v; SP28/30/4, f. 343r; SP28/31/4, ff. 465v, 472r–473r, 491r; SP28/32/2, f. 202r.

The logistical deficiencies in supplying Essex's Army in 1644 were laid bare by the following letter sent by Pindar and Herbert to Speaker William Lenthall on 24 October from Reading. After outlining the army's motions 'about Reading and Newbury', they wrote:

> Touching the necessities of our own army, give us leave to represent some things to your consideration. The army most part of this march from Portsmouth has suffered in want of provision, partly through the indigency of the country through which we passed and partly due to want of commissioners whose continued absence is of extraordinary prejudice, it being an employment both of care and pains; and though a deputy may endeavour yet wanting the reputation the work fails much in the practice. Wherefore we beseech you to take some course, both to expedite the commissaries of provisions – both which are and have long been absent – to attend their charge, and if the House seem pleased to hasten some biscuit and cheese hither, the passage being safe, the way not bad, and the soldier thereby would be exceedingly cheered.[96]

Both during the Naseby campaign and the New Model Army's march into the Southwest, the use of parish teams to transport supplies (including victuals) seems to have been the normal practice. In June 1645 various Northamptonshire villages were obliged to provide teams of horses and men, some of which were also present with the train of artillery at Naseby, although there are no reports of teams being lost. As Fairfax's regiments advanced, some teams travelled considerable distances to supply them as they arrived at towns and villages on the way.[97]

Markets

Most European armies during the early modern period habitually suffered from difficulties in maintaining regular access to provisions to feed and clothe the soldiers. In recounting his sufferings while on campaign with the Swedish Army, Turner wrote, 'I was at the sieges of several towns and castles, and at many brushes, encounters and … all the time suffered exceeding great want of both meat and clothes, being necessitated to by constantly in the fields with little or no shelter, to march always a foot, and drink water.'[98] Geoffrey Parker mentions that during the 1590s a magazine was established in Milan to supply the Spanish troops in Lombardy with low-priced food.[99] Even so, Nusbacher, in his study of the victualling of the New Model Army suggested that Fairfax's force:

96 HMC, *Thirteenth Report, App. I*, pp.188–9.
97 TNA, SP28/171/1, f. 10r; SP28/171/3, f. 612r.
98 Sir James Turner, *Memoirs of His Own Life and Times* (Edinburgh: 1829), p.6.
99 Geoffrey Parker, *The Army of Flanders and the Spanish Road 1567–1659: The Logistics of Spanish Victory and Defeat in the Low Countries' Wars* (Cambridge: Cambridge University Press, 2004), p.79.

> was thus too big to subsist on the local economy, and no evidence can be found that it was capable of supplying its own food. It is known that a market followed the army, and in the absence of evidence that the Army was supplied in other ways, it must be inferred that it drew its supplies through the commercial market rather than relying on local resources or on a commissary system.[100]

Though little is known about markets accompanying armies in a British context, contemporary writers referred to markets either accompanying armies, or being set up at, or adjacent to, them on campaign. The Articles of War, both for Essex's and Sir Thomas Fairfax's armies established rules for the regulation of vintners and sutlers (private sellers of food, drink and other goods) who accompanied their forces, and augmented the provision of victuals to their soldiers. Moreover, Orrery, in describing the encampment of armies wrote:

> Behind the last huts of these 2 files of huts, there is a void space of 20 foot in length, and the breadth is that of the lane, and the two files of huts beyond which said void place, the sutlers, and victuallers, have their huts, which are 10 foot long; and their huts for their drink, and for their dressing their meat, is also 10 foot long; and this void space of 20 foot between the soldiers last huts, and the huts of the victuallers and sutlers, is left, because by continual dressing meat for the soldiers, the huts of the victuallers are apt to take fire, and this vacuity, in case they do take fire, is convenient for people to quench it, before it can take hold of the soldiers' huts; in none of which, on any pretence, fire is to be allowed.[101]

Whether any such measures were adhered to among the New Model Army is difficult to know.

Various narrative sources hint at the existence of a market which followed the New Model Army and serviced its personnel in 1645–1646. From this the soldiers might buy the mainstay of their provisions and other necessities if they had the money, of which Fairfax and his officers tried to maintain as much as possible. In early July 1645, for instance, convoys of money were sent to Portsmouth for onward movement to Lyme for the New Model Army, and were guarded by the cavalry regiments of Colonels Rich, Pye, and Fiennes.[102] It is conceivable that one of the causes of the widespread sickness among the ranks in the late autumn of 1645, apart from the poor accommodation and some lack of warm clothing, was the inability to pay for bread. Thus, on 12 November it was reported, 'We had from the West to this effect, that the cause of the sickness in our army was for want of money to buy good food, which put them upon fruit and roots, and often without bread'.[103] In early May 1645 the Royalist newsbook *Mercurius Civicus* reported, '[before Oxford] there is a daily

100 Nusbacher, 'Civil Supply', p.155.
101 Orrery, *Treatise*, p.84.
102 *CSPD 1645–7*, pp.4–7.
103 *The Moderate Intelligencer*, 6–13 November 1645. TT, E309[11].

market … where is not a soldier that offers to take anything but gives satisfaction for, whereas for 28 May 1645 as Sir Thomas Fairfax's Skippon's regiments of foot were before the city, another observer wrote 'provisions cheap, money wanting'.[104]

During the New Model's siege of Bristol in August-September 1645, it was reported:

> There are three markets kept for our army on Gloucestershire side, one at Barton hundred, one at the headquarter, the other at Burden near the great fort, the soldiers pay for what they have, and behave themselves so civilly and courteously that they have gained the affection of country; and on the contrary they are as much alienated from Prince Rupert and his soldiers.[105]

During the last siege of Oxford, which began in May 1646, Sprigge described how '[the Royalists] levelled their pieces, so as to shoot not the Leaguer on Headington Hill (and on that side Lieutenant Colonel Cotsworth was slain with a great shot) and likewise into the Leaguer on Colonel Rainborowe's side, where they killed with their shot a sutler and others in their tents'.[106] Furthermore, *The Weekly Account* stated on 1 June, 'butter is sold for 4d. at the Leaguer and all other sorts of provisions is brought thither so plentifully, that they are sold at as cheap a rate as in most markets in England. The soldiers give ready money for what they have and offer not the least violence to the country.'[107]

For 26 June 1645, being the day after a Parliamentary committee was constituted to consider the conditions for the surrender of the Royalist garrison, another reported:

> This day the citizens of Oxford opened their shops, and had the benefit of a full and quiet market from the country, without any disturbance of our soldiers, who took nothing but what they paid for, a favour they had seldom met with before the surrender, which makes the citizens exceeding glad that they have made so happy a change from penury to plenty, from thraldom to liberty.[108]

It is possible that the market accompanying the New Model Army may have been introduced specially for the campaign into the Southwest to ensure that the soldiers under the command of Sir Thomas Fairfax were not exposed to the logistical failings which had contributed to Essex's defeat the previous year. It could be, that owing to Fairfax's grievances in June 1645 that any reliance on foraging and quartering was having a negative impact upon his army's ability to obtain sufficient victuals, the commander-in-chief, with the support of Parliament, encouraged traders and

104 *Mercurius Civicus*, 7–14 May 1646. E337[21]; *The Moderate Intelligencer*, 22–29 May 1645. TT, E286[9].

105 *Mercurius Civicus*, 28 August–4 September 1645. TT, E229[7].

106 Sprigge, *Anglia Rediviva*, p.259.

107 *The Weekly Account*, 27 May–3 June 1646. TT, E339[14].

108 *Kingdomes Weekly Intelligencer*, 23–30 June 1646. E342[6].

sutlers selling provisions to follow the New Model Army wherever it marched. In maintaining strict levels of discipline, he prohibited his soldiers from plundering or making threats against merchants, which in turn created a safe environment in which sutlers and vendors felt safe in dealing with the troops. Consequently, Nusbacher contends that 'this mobile supply market was a major factor in the speed and prosecution of the campaign as Fairfax and his men gained mobility and strategic speed which was denied to their opponents.'[109]

Both cavalry and dragoon clothing, presumably including items such footwear, coats and perhaps even buff coats, appear to have been the responsibility of either the soldiers themselves or their officers, because no procurement of such items is discernible from contemporary documents. If they were purchased from traders, then this would be suggestive of the presence of vendors who could stock such items ready made up, or relevant craftspeople accompanying the market to meet this requirement. It seems likely also, that quite a few sutlers and attendants were female. According to Mary Ailes:

> Beyond caring for soldiers' domestic needs, women also carried out important functions in maintaining and enhancing the armies' supplies through their work as sutlers ... often women who were wives or widows of soldiers worked as sutlers, selling food and supplies to soldiers in order either to supplement their husbands' income or support themselves financially after their husband's deaths.[110]

Horse Victuals

As the soldiers of the New Model Army needed to be fed, so did their horses. As previously mentioned, William Jones acted as Commissary General of Horse Provisions in the army, a position he had previously held in Essex's forces, with four assistants under him. From April 1645 onwards he was paid 13s. per day, and his subordinates each received 9d. per day.[111] In addition to grazing, during the seventeenth century military horses were usually provided with fodder or provender (sometimes referred to as 'horse meat' in contemporary documents), comprising hay and oats on campaign, but this diet was sometimes supplemented with peas and barley.

The standard daily ration for cavalry mounts in the British Civil Wars seems to have been one peck of oats (usually about two gallons or eight quarts). However, measures were not fixed with the same exactness as today, and they inclined to fluctuate from location to location. As Robinson asserts, 'It also possible that measures which apparently had the same name were actually different for different commodities, and that in some places words had completely different meanings, so that under

109 Nusbacher, 'Civil Supply', pp.155–156.

110 Mary Elizabeth Ailes, 'Camp Followers, Sutlers, and Soldiers' Wives: Women in Early Modern Armies (*c.* 1450-*c.* 1650)', in *A Companion to Women's Military History* (Leiden: Brill, 2021), pp.61–92, (p. 69).

111 TNA, SP28/32/2, f. 202r.

certain circumstances, bushels were called pecks and pecks were called bushels'.[112] In July 1643 the daily allowance of some of the Earl of Denbigh's horses was 6d. worth of hay, one peck of oats, and a little peas or beans.[113] Likewise, in October 1644 the Royalist Richard Symonds noted that at Blandford there were six quarts to a peck and 24 quarts to the bushel.[114] That he found this extraordinary enough to record accentuates the broad variations in practice.

In May 1645 Parliament established a scale of charges to be paid by the New Model on the march. This amounted to 4d. a night for hay, 3d. for grass, 4d. for hay and a peck of oats, 6d. for a peck of peas and beans, and 7d. for a peck of barley and malt. Provision of barley and malt was 'not to be taken but in case of necessity, where no other grain for horse meat is to be had'.[115] Nevertheless, it was deemed that:

> every officer by commission, or person of the Lifeguards troop, shall pay the full value for his provisions of diet or horse meat; but, if he pay not present money to the full value, but leave a ticket or certificate in such manner as is aforesaid, shall content himself with such ordinary diet for himself and servants as the party with whom he quarters is provided of, without putting the said party to the trouble or charge of seeking abroad; otherwise, upon complaint thereof made to the commissioners, such officer to be fined and punished, at the discretion of the commander-in-chief.[116]

Documents relating to the financing and supply of Sir William Brereton's Parliamentarian army in Cheshire include various payments for horse provisions. In March and May 1644 Commissary John Miller received 240 measures of oats at 11d. per measure from the sequestrators of Bucklow hundred, whereas in late 1645 '120 measures of barley, ground into maize valued at £13 were transported to the Chester Leaguer at Chester'.[117] Some of Brereton's cavalry officers took measures into their own hands when faced by shortages of provisions and concentrated feed. While quartering in the Wirral in mid-1645 the Parliamentary officials at Hooton complained when Captain William Shepley's troopers commandeered land and harvested – among other commodities – 50 measures of oats 'without order' at 12d. per measure, and a further '46 measures of oats not paid for to the state'.[118] Equally, the sequestration accounts of Macclesfield hundred record that at some time in late 1644 three measures of oats worth 3s. 4d. were issued to Brereton's dragoons to be fed to their horses.[119] Commissary officers were active in appropriating fodder when the army was on the march or in quarters. One estimate of equine nutrition suggests that horses performing a moderate day's work require roughly 25,000

112 Gavin Robinson, 'Horse Supply in the English Civil War 1642–1646', PhD thesis (University of Reading, 2001), p.209.
113 TNA, SP28/34/2, f. 249r.
114 Symonds, *Diary*, p.127.
115 *LJ*, VII, p.377.
116 *LJ*, VII, p.378.
117 BL, Ms Harley 2166, f. 130r; Ms Harley 1943, ff. 7r–8v; Ms Harley 2137, ff. 55v, 105v.
118 BL, MS Harley 1999, ff. 17r, 69r, 71v.
119 BL, MS Harley 2130, f. 209v.

calories per day and 45 litres of water. Therefore, a 500-strong regiment of horse or dragoons needed 3,400–4,500kg of fodder and 5,000 gallons of water each day. All of this had to be purchased or requisitioned and distributed to mounted units by commissaries.[120]

Cruso recommended in 1632, that 'to lodge or encamp the cavalry, a special care must be had of the commodity of water, and where they may be under shelter: for one cold or rainy night might ruin the cavalry, nothing hurting a horse sooner than cold or wet'.[121] Thus, when on 4 August 1641 Sir John Conyers, Lieutenant General of the Horse, ordered Captain John Mennes of Commissary General Henry Wilmot's regiment to rendezvous with the King near Doncaster, he added:

> It will be requisite, when they do march, that every trooper carry behind him in his oat sack three or four baits of oats or bread for his horse, and provision for himself, for some of them will be more than 24 hours from their quarters; and in the meantime let them feed their horses as well as they can, and put their equipage in good order that they may not be ashamed to be seen. And when they march let them have ammunition delivered to them.[122]

Consequently, any dearth of foodstuffs for the feeding of cavalry and dragoon horses could seriously limit the effectiveness of mounted formations, as well as the general condition of the animals. On 27 November 1643 the newly appointed Royalist governor of Oxford, Sir Arthur Aston, appraised Prince Rupert of the military situation in Northamptonshire and Oxfordshire. While reporting that 'the fortifications at Towcester will be complete enough next week to be defensible against a surprise', he added that Royalist purveyors had arrived to thresh corn recently seized from Parliamentarian sources to supply Towcester and Oxford. With only three cavalry troops remaining at Northampton, Aston advised Rupert that the majority of the Royalist Horse in the area 'must withdraw to avoid ruin because of their bad losses already'. In a further dispatch Aston objected to the Prince's orders to use parties of horse to obtain provisions for a magazine at Towcester, which Rupert had made strong by constructing water filled ditches and using the remains of the Roman walls. He left a powerful mounted force in the town before returning to Oxford. Aston warned Rupert that covering the threshing and carrying in of corn was too dangerous and time-consuming, and thus refused to undertake it. His advice was that it was easier to remove the main cavalry force, 'preventing its ruin and removing the worst burden'.[123]

No lists of the purchase, storage and distribution of provender are known, but the accounts of Commissary Orpin provide an insight into the supply of foodstuffs for horses and oxen employed in the transportation of stores to the New Model Army.

---

120 Robin Higham, 'Some Thoughts on the Thirty Years War', *Bellum Tricannale* (Prague, 1997), p.340.

121 Cruso, *Militarie Instructions for the Cavalrie*, pp.66–67.

122 *CSPD 1641–43*, p.72.

123 WSL, Ms Salt 477/11–12.

Among the charges for carrying 2,240lbs of cheese 25 miles westwards from Lyme to Nutwell in December 1645 are the disbursement of 2s. 6d. for 1 night's hay for 10 draught horses at Culliford, 1s. 4d. for 'hay to feed the horses at Sidford', in addition to the same at Newton Poppleford. On 23 January 1646 the sum of £2 9s. was paid at Tiverton for hay for 5 waggon horses for 35 days and 1 for 21 days at 3d. per day; 3s. went on '3 pecks of malt for mashes', and another 8d. for '1 peck of barley to boil'. Sums were also paid earlier in the month for fodder for oxen to haul 8 wain loads of shoes and stockings from Lyme to Tiverton – 46 animals were provided with hay for 1 night at a cost of £4 on 3 January, while a further £10 was laid out 3 days later for hay for 30 oxen for a night. Seventeen wain loads of clothing were also sent from Weymouth to Tiverton on 12 January 1646, before continuing to Chard 4 days later. Although these vehicles are described as carrying 722 soldiers' coats, 622 pairs of breeches, 216 pairs of stockings, and 800 snapsacks between them, no details are given of any disbursements for provender for the animals which hauled them.[124]

Draught horses were preferred to oxen because of their power, speed and agility, even if they cost more to keep. During the Middle Ages oxen (or bullocks) had been capable of drawing larger loads than horses, yet by the seventeenth century the quality and size of draught horses had improved.[125] John Langdon, in his study of medieval draught animals, found that horses consumed considerably more oats per year than oxen, while cart horses on average consumed 20s. 9d. worth of oats, hay, straw and pasture per year, as opposed to 6s. 5d. for oxen.[126] Ox-drawn wains were recorded far more commonly than the sturdier, horse-drawn cart in probate inventories.[127] During the Civil Wars oxen appear to have been employed more often by Royalist armies, although in March 1644 a Council of War in the West Country realised that 53 oxen in the train of artillery were 'not to be so fit as useful ... as horses are', and ordered their sale and replacement with draught horses.[128] As the oxen in Orpin's accounts for the supply of the New Model Army are either associated with wain transport, or described as 'fat' or fattened, in addition to 'cattle', could mean that the latter were stock animals which were being driven to be butchered as fresh beef for the soldiers. Payments also included amounts for 'salt to powder the meat' at Chard, whereas men were engaged in 'weighing and loading beef into waggons' before transportation by sea from Lyme to Ireland.

124 TNA, SP28/147/2, ff. 352r–357r.

125 J. F. Willard, 'Inland transportation in England during the fourteenth century', *Speculum*, 1 (1926), pp.361–74.

126 John Langdon, *Horses, Oxen and Technological Innovation: The Use of Draught Animals in English Farming from 1066–1500* (New York: Cambridge University Press, 1986), pp.160 & 227–228.

127 Stuart, *Wagons, Carts, and Pack Animals*, p.3; Stephen Porter, 'Farm Transport in Huntingdonshire, 1610–1749', *Journal of Transport History*, 3 (1982), pp.35–45.

128 W. C. and C. E. Trevelyan (eds), *The Trevelyan Papers* (Camden Society, 1872), III, pp.15–16.

5

Horses, Saddlery and Harness

The procurement and retention of quality troop horses for the cavalry during the British Civil Wars was essential. Cruso stated, 'For the reforming of the cavalry, there is moreover required a singular care, that the companies be supplied with good horses: wherefore it will be necessary, that when the cavalry is retired from the field, the captains make sale of such horses as be unfit for service and buy better.'[1]

Mounts were a valuable investment, although they were expensive to maintain. On 4 February 1643 in a letter to John Pym, Sir William Brereton complained that two of his best horses with their saddles and pistols had been seized at Chester the previous August.[2] According to Peter Edwards, saddle horses for the cavalry, 'ideally had to be 15 hands high, nimble and capable of charging at pace.'[3] The Parliamentarian armies procured many of their mounts on the open market. London (especially Smithfield) met the heavy demands imposed on it, and a cavalry horse could sell for £10 or £12, a nag for under a pound, although for bulk purchases £6 to £8 was normal. Brereton and Sir Thomas Myddelton obtained horses in the capital in 1643 and 1644, as did the Eastern Association and New Model Army. Regional forces also turned to local suppliers – at Penkridge in Staffordshire the county kept one of the best horse fairs in England, especially for quality saddle mounts.

The research undertaken by Thomas Crawshaw into the finances of the Earl of Essex's Army, and Gavin Robinson on the supply of horses to the New Model Army, reveals that the majority of the new cavalry troops raised for Essex's forces in 1642 did not receive the £600 allowance to purchase 60 mounts, but instead received horses directly from London civilians through the Propositions system. Robinson found that in 1642 and 1643, 3,775 horses were listed for the cavalry, with another 2,489 dragoon mounts and draught horses.[4] A further 524 draught horses were delivered to the army between 9 November 1642 and 26 January 1643, representing half of the number of horses required by the train of artillery. The shortfall continued

1 Cruso, *Militarie Instructions*, p.24.
2 HMC, *Portland*, I, p.94.
3 Peter Edwards, 'Turning Ploughshares into Swords', p.68; 'The Supply of Horses to the Parliamentarian and Royalist Armies in the English Civil War', *HR*, 68 (1995), pp.49–66.
4 Tom Crawshaw, 'Military Finance and the Earl of Essex's Regular Army: 1642–1644', unpublished PhD thesis (York University, Toronto, 2013), pp.480–483; Gavin Robinson, 'Horse Supply and the Development of the New Model Army, 1642–1646', *War in History*, 15 (2008), pp.121–140, (pp.124–125).

to be made up by hiring and impressing draught animals.[5] Parliament's Ordinance of 10 May 1643, 'to redress the abuses in taking horses for the supply of the army', authorised the Deputy Lieutenants and Propositions Committees in each county to regulate the acquisition of mounts, while an amendment of 29 May approved the levying of horses by county quota.[6]

On 3 December 1642 Parliament ordered that Brereton should 'have liberty to raise 300 horses in the several counties where they shall be brought in voluntarily, upon Propositions'.[7] The accounts of another Cheshire officer, Colonel Robert Duckenfield include several payments for horses, equipment and clothing for his troop. Typically, an immediate burden was the provision of cavalry mounts. By May 1643 he disbursed £342 for 43 horses. The various entries illustrate the prices and quantities involved: £80 paid for 'six able horses I put into my troop, valued at £13 6s. 8d. apiece'; another nine mounts, valued at £70; £224 for 32 horses, valued at £7 apiece; and the sum of £48 laid out on 'six horses more put into my troop which I am engaged to pay for at £8 apiece'. Duckenfield later stated, 'All the horses to my knowledge that have served or have been used for my troop which has continued complete about 4 years has lost the state nothing but as before mentioned, excepting 15 horses that I had ordered from the deputy lieutenants for to raise in my neighbourhood about April 1643.'[8] Moreover, the certificate of service for Cornet Richard Brereton, who served in Duckenfield's troop from 27 November 1642 to 13 November 1643, mentions that he constantly mustered three horses of his own completely equipped.[9] Similarly, in early 1644 Duckenfield paid £3 6s. to William Davenport for horses from his Bramhall estate, yet going by this relatively low price they may have been smaller animals rather than expensive cavalry mounts.[10]

On 11 January 1645 the initial establishment of the New Model Army was revised to 22,000 men, composed of 6,600 horse, 14,400 foot and 1,000 dragoons.[11] There would, it was intended, be 11 regiments of cavalry (each with 6 troops of 100 troopers, plus commissioned and non-commissioned officers); 12 infantry regiments (each with 10 companies and nominal strength of 1,200), and one of dragoons (of 10 companies, each of 100 men, besides officers). Of these, three regiments of horse and four of foot came from Essex's Army, nine of horse and four of foot from the Eastern Association, and the remaining two regiments of foot from Sir William Waller's forces. It has been assumed that the cavalry regiments were already up to strength, however, the documents recording the addition of recruits, and the extensive supply of horses, saddles and weapons to the various regiments do not bear this out. Included in the establishment of the new army's cavalry was Sir Thomas Fairfax's Lifeguard. This was originally intended to form a troop in his regiment, but on paper it remained separate. The unit received 40 pairs pistols and holsters,

5 TNA, SP28/143, unfol.
6 *LJ*, VI, pp.39–40 & 68–69.
7 *CJ*, II, p.874.
8 TNA, SP28/128/10, ff. 8r–8v.
9 BL, MS Harley 2128, f. 73r.
10 TNA, SP28/128/10, f. 5r.
11 *CJ*, IV, pp.16–17; *CSPD 1644–1645*, p.205.

40 saddles and '40 able horses, geldings and mares at £9 apiece' in April 1645. On 19 March 1645 the Commons ordered that, 'a fortnight's pay be forthwith provided for the Lifeguard of my Lord General.'[12]

Similarly, the Committee for the Army was instructed on 14 April to consider, 'how the troop of gentlemen which were of the Lifeguard to the Earl of Essex may be taken into the New Model and maintained'. Consequently, Robert Scawen, the chairman of the Committee, drew up the following report on the composition and supply of Sir Thomas Fairfax's Lifeguard on 25 April:

> That the troop, late the Lord General's Lifeguard, shall have 3s. per day each more than an ordinary trooper. That this troop shall be one of the six troops that shall be of Sir Thomas Fairfax his own regiment, as to the ordinary entertainment. And Sir Thomas Fairfax is desired to take Captain Doyley to command those gentlemen, and to put another captain in his stead, in Colonel Graves his regiment. They shall have 40 horses, and 40 pair of pistols, to recruit [supply] them.
>
> Ordered by the Commons assembled in Parliament that the Committee for the Army do write to Sit Thomas Fairfax, to desire him speedily to appoint a rendezvous for the troop late the Lord General's Lifeguard, that they receive their fortnight pay, the horse and their arms.[13]

This was agreed upon by the Commons the same day.[14] Both Charles D'Oyley and his captain lieutenant, Henry Hall, had previously served in Essex's Lifeguard. On 20 July 1645 a warrant was issued:

> to pay Henry Hall, captain lieutenant of the Lifeguard the sum of £259 13s. 4d., being 10 days' pay for the officers and soldiers of that troop according to the muster of 5 May last, commencing the 19th of the same month. And also the sum of £12, being 24 days for two gentlemen who were absent at the said muster, but by the general's command were certified in the said roll to even them with the rest of the troop. And also the sum of £89 15s. 2d., being 11 days' pay for the said troop according to the muster of the 16th of June.[15]

At Naseby Sir Thomas Fairfax and his Lifeguard were in the thick of the fighting on the New Model Army's right wing, particularly during the destruction of Prince Rupert's infantry regiment of bluecoats. According to the Royalist, Bulstrode Whitelock:

> The General had his helmet beat off, and riding in the field bare headed up and down from one part of his Army to another, to see how they stood, and what advantage might be gained, and coming up to his own Lifeguard

12 TNA, SP28/29/2, f. 254r; SP28/140/7, f. 276v; WO47/1, f. 242v.
13 Bodl. Lib., Ms Tanner 60/1, f. 123r.
14 *CJ*, IV, pp.83, 110, 119, 123.
15 TNA, SP28/31/1, ff. 79r, 106r.

> commanded by Colonel [*sic.* – Captain] Charles D'Oyley, he was told by him that he exposed himself to too much danger, and the whole Army thereby, riding bare headed in the fields, and so many bullets flying about him, and D'Oyley offered his General his helmet, but he refused it, saying it is well enough Charles: and seeing a body of the King's foot stand, and not at all broken, he asked D'Oyley if he had charged that body, who answered, that he had twice charged them, but could not break them. With that Fairfax bid him to charge them once again in the front, and that he would take a commanded party, and charge them in the rear at the same time, and they might meet together in the middle, and bad him, when Fairfax gave the sign to begin the charge. D'Oyley pursued his General's orders, and both together charging that body put them into a confusion, and broke them, and Fairfax and D'Oyley met indeed in the middle of them, where Fairfax killed the ensign, and one of D'Oyley's troopers took the colours, bragging of the service he had done in killing the ensign and taking the chief colours. D'Oyley chide the trooper for his boasting and lying, telling him how many witnesses there were who saw the General do it with his own hand, but the General himself had D'Oyley to let the trooper alone, and said to him, I have honour enough, let him take that honour to himself.[16]

Such tactics accorded with Vernon's instructions in his cavalry manual:

> if the foot be drawn up into complete order, it will be very necessary for the cavalry to have some pretty stratagem, in the charging of the foot, or else it will be very difficult routing the foot, which may be performed after this manner or the like, you are to divide your troop or parties into three squadrons, each squadron having an able soldier to lead them, who are to charge in full career all at one instant upon the front, rear, and flank of the foot. The officer that leads on the squadron, that charges the front, is to charge as the others in full career, till he comes close unto the pikes' heads, and then suddenly stopping is suddenly to command with an elevated voice, close your file or the like, which sudden command being loud will sometimes cause those pikes that stand charged against the other two squadrons, either in the flank or rear, to extend their bodies towards the front, which will give a fit advantage unto one of the squadrons to slip in between, and so make way for the other two squadrons to charge in, and utterly rout the front, but you must always observe that this stratagem must always be performed suddenly and altogether as at one entire motion.[17]

The conduct of Sir Thomas Fairfax and his Lifeguard at Naseby against the dogged Royalist foot is unsurprising given his previous combat experience and wounds sustained. One observer wrote, 'Our General was in some danger, hazarding his own

16 Bulstrode Whitelock, *Memorials of the English Affairs* (London: 1682), p.145.
17 Vernon, *The Young Horse-man*, p.44.

person, but blessed to God came off well.'[18] Moreover, though by dint of seniority the Lifeguard was positioned on the extreme right of the Parliamentarian line during the battle, its direct presence amongst the fighting might partly be explained by the fact that on the evidence of pay warrants to Fairfax's own regiment in the days before Naseby, it mustered about 490 troopers, and was the third weakest cavalry unit in the army after Ireton's and Fleetwood's regiments.[19] Additionally, as Hopper suggests, Sir Thomas' 'attraction to danger was persistent and he paid for it', in other words, his numerous battlefield wounds were largely a result of his conviction to be at the centre of the action.[20]

The evolution of mobile, or manoeuvre, warfare involving the horse and dragoons has been seen as fundamental to the creation and transformation of the New Model Army in 1645. Much of the recognition for its success lies with Cromwell, though both Fairfax and he were successful and dynamic cavalry officers. Thus, one writer has described him as 'one of the most original and able commanders ever to lead English troops in battle.'[21] His use of manoeuvre tactics, that is, the delivery of a decisive mounted strike (the army's main fighting power) at a key point and time in the conflict, is evident at Naseby (where the King's Oxford Army was defeated in just two hours). During the Battle of Langport, which took place on 10 July 1645, the Royalist commander, General George Goring occupied a strong rearguard position to cover the withdrawal of his slow-moving artillery train, while his main force occupied a ridge running north to south. From a tactical perspective the ridge offered Goring a formidable position, but Fairfax and Cromwell quickly utilised their disciplined mounted formations. As Sprigge reported:

> Our foot [commanded by Colonel Thomas Rainborowe] advanced down the hill to the pass, and with admirable resolution charged the enemy from hedge to hedge, till they got the pass; the enemy's horse upon this drew down towards us, whereupon our horse advanced over the pass up the hill to the enemy. The forlorn hope of horse commanded by Major Bethell [Whalley's regiment], gave a valiant and brave charge indeed, broke that body that charged him, and the next reserve: our reserve of horse that was commanded by Major Desborough [of Fairfax's regiment], very resolutely charged the next standing bodies of the enemy so home, that instantly they put them to a disorderly retreat, and our musketeers came close up to our horse, firing upon the enemy, whereupon their regiments of white colours, and black colours of foot, before ever they engaged, marched away apace; the forlorn under Major Bethell [of Colonel Whalley's regiment], and those under Major Desborough, were going in pursuit of the chase, but receiving

18 *A glorious victory obtained by Sr. Thomas Fairfax, June, the 14. 1645* (London: 1645). TT, E288[21].

19 TNA, SP28/30/2, ff. 185r–195r.

20 Hopper, *'Black Tom'*, p.179.

21 Jonathan R. Moore, 'Oliver Cromwell and the English Experience of Manoeuvre Warfare 1645–1651, Part One', *Cromwelliana* (1993), pp.15–26; 'Part Two', *Cromwelliana* (1994), pp.24–36.

> orders to stay till more bodies of horse were come up, that the pursuit might be orderly, and with good reserves, in case the enemy should face about, and charge again, (which was not impossible) they obeyed their orders, as good soldiers will, though it check their sweetest pleasure (as to pursuing a flying enemy was no less).[22]

As such, Sir Thomas Fairfax regarded Langport as his greatest victory.

The entire strength of the New Model's horse in May and June 1645 has been estimated at around 7,200, but though useful, such computations are difficult to achieve because precise strengths of units are rarely found in contemporary documents. Moreover, there are chronological gaps in the records, and during the Naseby campaign a New Model brigade consisting of 3,000 infantry and the cavalry regiment under the command of Colonel Richard Graves was detached from the main army to aid the besieged garrison of Taunton. Blackmore's estimates of the strengths of regiments extrapolated from surviving pay warrants are most useful, in that they are based on the theoretical rates of pay for officers and soldiers, as well as the assumption – largely from the army's establishment – that each unit contained 10 commissioned and non-commissioned officers in its ranks. Hence, it is possible to compute to some degree of accuracy that at Naseby on 14 June 1645 there were present just over 5,200 troopers, in addition to around 1,000 commissioned and non-commissioned officers.[23] If an estimated strength for Graves' regiment of 500 is added, this would bring this to 5,700 troopers, some 1,500 below the prescribed establishment figure of 7,200. Moreover, the strength of Colonel John Okey's New Model dragoon regiment at Naseby was 676 men, besides commissioned officers and non-commissioned officers.[24]

Such statistics are partly corroborated by other sources. When Colonel Bartholomew Vermuyden was ordered by Cromwell, at the command of the Committee of Both Kingdoms to effect a link-up with the Scottish forces under the Earl of Leven in the Midlands in May 1645, he had with him 'a party of 2,000 horse and 500 dragoons' of his own, Colonels Nathaniel Rich's, John Fiennes', Robert Pye's and John Okey's regiments.[25] Such numbers tend to correspond with those in army pay warrants issued in the weeks immediately before Naseby. On 25 August 1645 Lieutenant General Cromwell received the sum of £212 4s. 4d. 'for 14 days' pay for the officers and soldiers of his troop according to the muster taken 11 August 1645'. Three days later, he had £47 5s. for the pay of 2 corporals, 1 trumpeter and 30 troopers belonging to his regiment, 'being wounded at the fight at Naseby and mustered by order of the Committee for the Army [on] 22 July and for the receiving pay upon all the musters taken of them since 16 June for 14 days' pay commencing the 16th of the said month'. Moreover, £218 10s. was disbursed to Cromwell, being

22 Sprigge, *Anglia Rediviva*, pp.64–65.

23 David Blackmore, 'Counting the New Model Army', *ECWT*, 58 (2004), pp.3–5.

24 TNA, SP28/29/1, ff. 13r-v, 59r-v, 107r, 187r; SP28/30/3, f. 293r; Stephen Ede-Borrett, 'Some Notes on the Raising and Origins of Colonel John Okey's Regiment of Dragoons, March to June, 1645', *JSAHR*, 87 (2009), pp.206–13.

25 *CSPD 1644–5*, pp.486, 504, 515.

the pay for 1 surgeon, 3 trumpeters, 2 corporals and 101 troopers 'mustered as recruits in his regiment [on] 22 July last for 20 days commencing muster day.'[26] In April 1645 his double regiment of horse from the Eastern Association was reorganised into the nascent New Model Army to form Sir Thomas Fairfax's and Colonel Edward Whalley's regiments, with single troops each joining Sir Robert Pye's and Colonel Nathaniel Rich's regiments.

On 8 June 1645 Vermuyden resigned his commission, and command of his regiment passed to Cromwell. In the field the unit was led by Sergeant Major Robert Huntington. According to 'The sick and wounded men that came into Northamptonshire the 14th June 1645 under command of the honourable General, Sir Thomas Fairfax'; the regiment suffered 2 officers, 1 corporal and 4 troopers killed at Naseby, and additionally 35 troopers were seriously wounded.[27]

These various figures are partly corroborated by a set of pay schedules for the New Model brigade of cavalry and dragoons operating in Oxfordshire in late December 1645. Broken down into individual troops, they record that the General's regiment mustered 78 commissioned and non-commissioned officers, and 611 troopers; Ireton's regiment contained 71 officers and 439 troopers; Fleetwood's regiment had 71 officers and 445 troopers; while Whalley's fielded 66 officers and 512 troopers; bringing the total strength of the brigade to 2,393 officers and men.[28] If these totals were extrapolated to calculate the overall numbers of the 11 cavalry regiments of the New Model, then the figure would be roughly 5,500 troopers – some 1,700 lower than the army's establishment. Such figures are important in the context of the present chapter because estimates of the effective strength of the mounted arm of Sir Thomas Fairfax's forces offer clues as to the scale of its demand for horses in 1645–1646. To this must be added the draught horses of the train of artillery, in addition to the haulage and pack animals requisitioned and hired by the army's commissaries.

The principal source for the supply of horses to Sir Thomas Fairfax's Army is the account book of the London Commissaries John Smith and Thomas Richardson.[29] This records all receipts from the Smithfield horse dealers and of horses distributed to the New Model between April 1645 and August 1646. Each entry usually stipulates how many animals were delivered, which dealers supplied them, how much they cost, the dates on which they were supplied, the officers who received them, and the total price. Nevertheless, the manuscript has limitations in that the level of detail varies, two folios are missing and much of the second section is damaged. Moreover, several mounts cannot be linked to any cavalry troop or dragoon company, while 1,200 troop horses were delivered to Thomas Cooke, Mark Master of the army, and there is no trace of where these went after he had taken delivery of them. Similarly, there are a further 427 horses whose recipients are unknown or cannot be identified with any certainty, whereas it is impossible to determine the exact dates of delivery for some of the entries. Such entries are complemented to some degree by

26 TNA, SP28/31/3, ff. 265r, 266r, 270r.
27 TNA, SP28/173/1, f. 10r.
28 TNA, SP28/34/4, ff. 490r–498v.
29 TNA, SP28/140/7, ff. 276v–291v.

warrants issued by the Committee for the Army for payments to suppliers upon the delivery of these horses. Contracts were agreed with the partners John Stiles, Harvey Conway, Richard Clough, Peter Everard, and Percival Stanley, in addition to the dealers Thomas Benion, William Booth, and Thomas Crosman, who on 4 April 1645 were granted a monopoly of the London horse trade. Moreover, Parliament barred any other trader, for the space of a month, 'to presume to buy any horses, fit for the service of war, to sell again'.[30]

Each of these animals was paid for by warrants issued by the Army Committee under Robert Scawen. A total of 5,206 horses were for the cavalry, 1,057 were for dragoons, and 460 were draught horses for the train of artillery. The initial contract was made jointly with Stiles, Conway, Clough, and Everard, for 1,200 troop horses at £7 10s. apiece. A corresponding warrant for deliveries dates from 25 March 1645 and is for the payment of £1,500 for 200 troop horses – this and four other warrants from March and April relate to the first five deliveries of 200 horses recorded in the account book.[31] Although some early warrants matching the provision of dragoon horses appear incomplete, during April and May 1645 Stiles, Conway, et al. provided 300 dragoon 'naggs and mares' at £4 apiece.[32] There were no significant changes in the prices paid by the Army Committee for the horses supplied by the dealers. Although cavalry mounts could fluctuate slightly in price – those animals purchased for £9, £7 10s. and £6 inferring differences in size and physical build – those meant for dragoons were consistently supplied at £4 each. Hence, dragoon horses were often regarded as 'inferior' to cavalry mounts in that rather being of a lesser quality, they were simply lighter beasts, unsuitable for carrying cuirassiers or harquebusiers on campaign.

Towards the end of 1645, the London Militia Committee sold 200 dragoon horses to the Committee for the Army for the use of Fairfax's forces. This was a very unusual arrangement, which was authorised by Parliament on 23 December.[33] The deal was made quickly, since on 12 January 1646 the Army Committee disbursed £410 10s. to the New Model's Mark Master, and the following day authorised Commissary Thomas Richardson 'to pay the quarters of 200 dragoon horses at Brentford and Hounslow bought by this Committee of the Militia of London.' These horses were then conducted to the army by Captain Christopher Mercer of Okey's regiment, with the assistance of 20 dragoons.[34] Given that there was only one regiment of dragoons in the New Model Army, there can be no doubts about which unit received the mounts. As Robinson found in his analysis of the supply of mounts to the army, there are no dragoon horses unaccounted for in the army commissaries' account, so the statistics for Okey's regiment are far more precise than those for the cavalry. Consequently, they had 667 horses from the commissaries, amounting to 67 percent of the establishment of 1,000 dragoons. Having received 200 new horses in July

30 *CJ*, IV, p.99.

31 TNA, SP28/28/3, f. 310r; SP28/29/1, ff. 164r, 199r, 236r; SP28/140/7, f. 276v.

32 TNA, SP28/29/1, ff. 166r–166v, 204r; SP28/29/2, f. 258v; SP28/31/5, f. 542r; SP28/140/7, f. 276v.

33 *CJ*, IV, p.383.

34 TNA, SP28/36/6, ff. 646r, 659r, 707v.

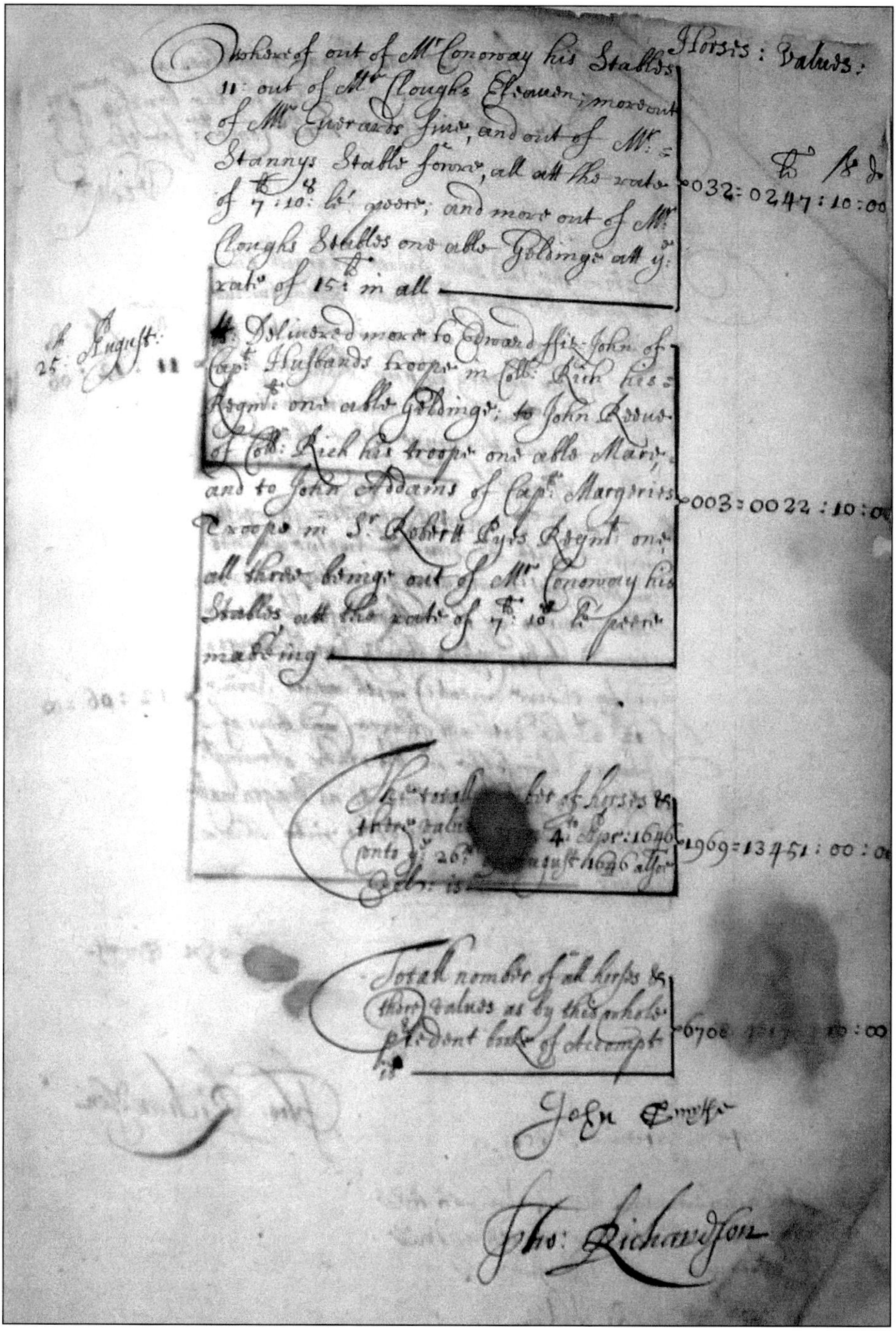

Whereof out of Mr Conoway his Stables 11: out of Mr Cloughs Eleaven; more out of Mr Gerrards Five, and out of Mr Stannys Stable Seven, all att the rate of 7li: 10s: ye peece; and more out of Mr Cloughs Stables one able Geldinge att ye rate of 15li in all — Horses : Values: li s d 032: 0247: 10: 00

25th August. Delivered more to Edward ffitz-John of Capt Husbands troope in Coll: Rich his Regmt one able Geldinge; to John Rodus of Coll: Rich his troope one able Mare; and to John Adams of Capt Margeritts troope in Sr Robert Pyes Regmt one; all three beinge out of Mr Conoway his Stables att the rate of 7li 10s ye peece making — 003: 0022: 10: 00

The totall [illegible] of horses & their values [illegible] 4 Apr: 1646 unto ye 26th August 1646 [illegible] — 1969: 13451: 00: 00

Totall nombre of all horses & their values as by this whole precedent booke of Accompt is — 6700 [illegible] 10: 00

John Smith

Tho: Richardson

Troop horses delivered, from the accounts of Commissaries John Smith and Thomas Richardson. (TNA, SP28/140/7)

1645, Okey's men received no more from the commissaries until November 1645. Moreover, between June 1645 and June 1646, the regiment was supplied with 572 horses, corresponding to 57 percent of the establishment.[35]

Given some discrepancies in totals and missing entries, it is possible to ascertain that between March 1645 and August 1646, Stiles and his partners supplied just over 6,700 horses for the New Model, costing over £46,000. These horses were delivered to John Smith and Thomas Richardson, the same commissaries who had dealt with the thousands of horses acquired by Essex's Army in 1642, who then issued them to army officers, keeping extremely detailed records. Each of the horses bought in April and May 1645 were delivered by the commissaries to the Mark Master, John Cooke, who branded them with the State's mark before distributing them to individual regiments. In November 1645 Sir Thomas Fairfax ordered the Committee for the Army to pay for remounts assigned to Captain John Grove's troop of Colonel Whalley's regiment and to have them branded.[36] This expedient helped the army to retrieve horses illegally sold to civilians, either by deserters or just soldiers hoping to gain some cash. By 19 August 1645 Cooke had been replaced by Francis Childs, who himself was superseded by Edward Cludd in January 1646.[37] It is likely that many of the horses purchased were needed to bring the cavalry and dragoons up to strength, and to replace unfit animals which had been brought from the old armies.

The earliest consignments of horses into the Mark Master's stables were '200 horses: 67 geldings and mares at the rate of £9 each, 66 more at £7 10s., and 67 more at £6 each' received on 3 April 1645 at a cost of £1,500; and '100 dragoon naggs and mares at £4 each', for which the sum of £400 was paid two days later. By the end of May some 1,200 troop horses for the cavalry, 390 dragoon horses, and 40 horses for Fairfax's Lifeguard were purchased. From 7 June 1645 onwards, horses are recorded as being supplied directly from stables to military units. Hence, Cornet James Jennings of Captain William Cecil's troop of Ireton's regiment received '30 able horses geldings and mares out of Mr Richard Clough's stables, 10 at £9, 10 at £7 10s. and 10 at £6'; on 10 June '30 horses geldings and mares out of Mr Clough's stables, 30 more out of Mr Conway's and 40 out of Mr Gerrard's stables at £9, £7 10s. and £6', worth an overall £750 were issued to Colonel Fleetwood's regiment; while '100 horses geldings and mares out of Mr Everard's stables 33 at £9, 134 at £7 10s. and 33 at £6' went to Sergeant Major Richard Cooke of Sir Thomas Fairfax's regiment on 1 July.[38] It appears that these horses were much-needed, especially as some cavalry units remained understrength, although it is difficult to know whether in some cases this was due to a lack of recruits or mounts, or both. The 3 different prices paid for these animals might be reflective of their differing sizes, ages, and quality.

There is evidence that when they were reduced into the New Model some troopers brought horses with them, but most of these probably needed to be replaced since they were weakened by previous campaigns. On 8 April 1645 Colonel Charles Fleetwood reported to the Committee for the Army that the 14 horses conveyed

35 Robinson, 'Horse Supply', p.138.
36 TNA, SP28/64, f. 781r; SP28/177, unfol.
37 TNA, SP28/31/3, f. 225r; SP28/36/6, f. 659r.
38 TNA, SP28/140/7, ff. 276v–277v.

into his regiment from Sergeant Major Ingoldsby's troop were 'very poor and weak, as we might expect from their great duty'. Moreover, it was reported the following day that among the Earl of Essex's cavalry 'divers troopers have lost their horses in the service'.[39] Parliament had resolved on 5 April that an additional 1s. a day, over and above the pay assigned to ordinary troopers, should be awarded to each of the 100 troopers of Captain Knight's troop, for bringing in their own horse and arms, whereas on 23 April the Surrey Committee was ordered to 'secure the horses and arms of Captain Savile's troop', which had mutinied, and forward them to Reading for the New Model Army's use.[40]

Table 11: Horses Purchased from Smithfield Horse Dealers and Delivered to the New Model Army, June 1645-August 1646 by Commissaries John Smith and Thomas Richardson (TNA, SP28/140/7)

Cavalry regiments			
Fairfax's	270	Rich's	384
Butler's	322	Pye's	424
Sheffield's	290	Whalley's	246
Fleetwood's	453	Graves'	257
Rossiter's	0	Ireton's	494
Vermuyden's/Cromwell's	399	Unknown	527
Totals	4,066		
Okey's dragoon regiment	667		
Total	4,733		

Colonel Edward Rossiter's regiment was included in the establishment in April 1645, but it normally operated in Lincolnshire, where it originated, although it did participate at Rowton Heath in September. When Rossiter's arrived at Naseby on 14 June 1645 it reportedly contained about 500 troopers – 100 below its nominal strength – and when it quartered at Marston Trussell on the night of the battle the regiment had 493 in its ranks. Only 1 man was recorded as seriously wounded during the Battle of Naseby.[41] Smith and Richardson's accounts show that Rossiter's was not supplied with horses like the rest of the New Model, nevertheless it did receive saddles. On 5 June 1645, however, the Commons granted the Committee for the Army the power to deliver '100 horses to recruit [supply] Colonel Rossiter's regiment; the horses to be paid for out of the monies appointed to come in out of Lincolnshire, upon Sir Thomas Fairfax his ordinance.'[42]

Quantities of cavalry and dragoon horses were supplied from central sources as replacements in July and August especially, probably due to losses at Naseby and the military operations around it. On 15 August, for instance, Fairfax signed a warrant for 'an able horse to be forthwith provided to Henry Barton, trumpeter to Sergeant

39 *CSPD 1644–5*, pp.394–395.
40 *CJ*, IV, p.101; *CSPD 1644–5*, pp.427–428.
41 TNA, SP28/173/2, unfol.; SP28/173/1, f. 16r.
42 *CJ*, IV, p.163.

Major Fincher's troop, he having lately lost his own in the service.'[43] Remounts were also obtained from local sources, particularly in the West Country. On 19 May 1645, Parliament ordered the Committee of the Army to issue warrants to the treasurers at war to pay £200 a week for 6 months for the buying of horses for the New Model, and further instructed 'that the horses so bought shall be disposed, by order of Sir Thomas Fairfax, to such soldiers, as the Commissioners, upon examination how the soldier came to lose his horses, shall think fit to be supplied.' Equally, on 23 October it was agreed that they should be paid £500 immediately, with an additional £200 per month for buying horses 'for the supplying and filling up, from time to time, such troops as are or shall be defective or broken troops.'[44] An essential source for the acquisition of horses by direct purchase is the notebook of the treasurer to Thomas Herbert and Vincent Potter, commissaries of the army, comprising receipted issues, copy letters and instructions for the acquisition of animals and other items in several counties along the army's line of march between 10 October 1645 and 5 January 1646. In February 1646 various mounts were bought at Ottery St Mary in Devon, although in other cases, horses were obtained directly from troopers or officers.[45]

However, the procedures followed in these transactions were often complex and the way in which some of these remounts are documented can be misleading, particularly because in most cases animals already acquired were brought into state ownership and the receipts endorsed on the warrants did not necessarily indicate the actual receipt of a horse. On 3 July 1645 Trumpeter Jonathan Waite of Fairfax's Lifeguard received a replacement horse, 'his being unserviceable'. Another warrant was issued on 24 July for the delivery of a black mare, along with a saddle and furniture, 'to Mr Thomas Barratt of the Lifeguard', which on paper he obtained on 15 August. Likewise, on 12 November 1645 Sir Thomas Fairfax instructed the Commissioners of Parliament residing in the army to supply Captain John Bushell of Sheffield's regiment with 'an able horse fit for service, he having his own killed under him at Bristol'.[46]

Draught horses were normally larger than saddle horses, and strength was more imperative than speed or agility when drawing heavy loads. In March 1645, the establishment of the New Model Army's train of artillery was set at 30 guns and 132 horse-drawn vehicles of various types, necessitating 234 draught horses to haul the ordnance, 792 for the waggons, carts and tumbrels, with 12 horses for the conductors to ride, giving a total of 1,038 horses.[47] The Earl of Essex's train had been of a similar size. In May 1644, its accounts show that it had 613 state-owned draught horses, 179 hired from contractors, and 50 teams (usually 5 to 6 animals to a team) temporarily impressed.[48] It is clear, then, that until the autumn of 1645, when they were purchased directly from London traders, a significant number of these were

43 TNA, SP28/31/1, f. 137r.
44 *CJ*, IV, pp.148 & 318.
45 TNA, SP28/129/10, ff. 10r–13v.
46 TNA, SP28/33/2, f. 117r.
47 TNA, SP28/145, ff. 60r–63v; *CJ*, IV, p.71; *A&O*, I, pp.653–655.
48 TNA, SP28/146, ff. 183r–183v.

enrolled into the New Model. On 14 March 1645 Parliament assigned a quota of 1,056 impressed draught horses on the City of London, 17 eastern and southern counties, and the Isle of Ely.[49] The reasons for this are unclear, though it might have been that the Committee for the Army was less inclined to purchase large quantities of such animals outright at this point, in order to direct money towards the provision of other much-needed items such as ammunition, firearms, and clothing. This measure was more successful than in 1644 because payment was allowed to be deducted from the monthly assessment. This was a temporary measure, however, and by September 1645 the Smithfield dealers were in the process of supplying most the army's draught horses. Thus, on 1 September we find an entry in the accounts of Commissaries Smith and Richardson for the receipt of 20 draught horses out of Conway's stables, 20 from Clough's, 6 from Everard's and 6 from Stanley's stables at £7 the pair for the train of artillery, at a cost of £420.[50]

Nevertheless, on 19 April 1645 40 animals were provided by the Lord Mayor and Committee of London for the New Model's train, 'according to an Ordinance of Parliament, dated 14 March 1645'. These were received by Commissary Thomas Robinson the following day. One week later Robinson took charge of another 52 'able draught horses for the service of the State in drawing the train of artillery under the command of His Excellency Sir Thomas Fairfax'. Similarly, a warrant date 30 April records the following:

> Bought and delivered to the commissary for draught horses for Sir Thomas Fairfax's Army as by certificates from the said commissaries appears according to an agreement made with the Committee appointed for London by Ordinance of Parliament dated 15 February 1645 by us, William Booth and Thomas Bonion [horse dealers and conductors for the City], 116 draught horses, being their proportion of 161 horses appointed to be provided by the City of London and the County of Middlesex by Ordinance of 14 March 1645, which 116 horses at £6. The cost of such horses amounts to the sum of £696.[51]

During its military operations in 1645 and 1646 the New Model Army captured significant amounts of horses from the King's forces. Although like prisoners, such numbers were sometimes rounded up in reports, 200 draught horses belonging to the Royalist train of artillery were taken at Naseby on 14 June 1645.[52] Moreover, the use of requisitioned parish teams to transport supplies seems to have been the normal practice.

However, the commissary officers were ordered in May 1645 that:

> no teams, horses, or carts, shall be impressed, or taken, but by warrant under the hand of the commander-in-chief, the lieutenant general of the

49 *A&O*, I, pp.653–635; *CSPD 1644–5*, p.345.
50 TNA, SP28/140/7, f. 278r.
51 TNA, SP28/30/3, ff. 255r & 259r.
52 Sprigge, *Anglia Rediviva*, p.40.

> ordnance, or such commissary respectively as shall be authorised so to do, which warrant is to be produced upon such impressed or taking; and that the same teams, horses, or carts, be not compelled to go further than present necessity shall require, always discharging those first that shall have gone farthest; and that there shall be present payment for every team, horse, cart, or driver, so taken, according to such allowances as are or shall be established by order of Parliament, or, in want thereof, according to such rates as the commissioners shall think fit, by the consent of the commander-in-chief; and, in case of necessity such present payment cannot be made, that the officer by whose warrants the teams and carts are impressed, or such other under officers as he shall employ for that purpose, till the superior officer's certificate can be made, shall certify and leave a ticket what is due for such horses, carts, and drivers, and to whom, according to such establishment or rates which shall be set as aforesaid: Provided, that no commissary of waggons, or other officer whatsoever, shall take any carts, waggons, or horses, that are bringing provisions to the City of London and Westminster.[53]

In early June 1645 the Northamptonshire village of Cogenhoe had to provide 'a team and men seven days for carrying carriages after the army' at a cost of £3 10s. Hence, they were also present with the train of artillery at Naseby, although there is no report of the team being lost. Moreover, as Fairfax's troops advanced, some teams were required to travel long distances to provision it. The constable of Burton Latimer paid out £3 'for provision sent to Sir Thomas Fairfax's Army at Leicester presently after the fight at Naseby', while Denton parish submitted a claim 'for going to Leicester to sue for team and cart 4s.', in addition to 'a further two days seeking for our team and cart 3s. 6d.'. They were unsuccessful, because an assessment was made on 20 October 'for the easing of money after one month's tax and a half to pay for the arrears for the horses and cart, which was lost when the General went by and provision sent for him to Kislingbury.'[54] The activities of Thomas Richardson, Waggon Master General to Essex's forces and subsequently the New Model, was critical to this operation in terms of the transportation of matériel, and the organisation of waggoners, carters, and vehicles. On 8 December 1645 the Committee of Both Kingdoms ordered that 'a warrant be issued for pressing carts to transport the clothes for the army from Reading to Portsmouth', and throughout the winter of 1645 to 1646 Commissary Orpin paid considerable sums for the hiring of waggons, draught horses and packhorses for the carrying of loads if victuals, arms, ammunition and clothing for the supply of the New Model during its operations in the Southwest of England.[55]

According to Markham, the Waggon Master or Carriage Master of an army 'ought to be a man of exceeding good consideration and trust; well stayed in manners and

53 *LJ*, VII, p.377.
54 TNA, SP28/171/1, f. 10r; SP28/171/3, ff. 612r.
55 *CSPD 1645–7*, p.253.

discreet in all his actions, for to his charge is delivered the conduct and guard of all the baggage and necessaries belonging to the whole army'. Likewise, he should have:

> the charge and commandment of all horses, mules, garrons, waggons, carts, sleds and other implements whatsoever, to carry and convey all the needful baggage either of meat, drink, or apparel which any way depends upon the army: and not only appoints under him all such ministers as shall see the same mounted and laden out of every several quarter, but also being so furnished, places them in array and ranks as he purposes they shall march, designing every man to his place and order, which no man shall dare or presume to break, upon pain of either having so much money defaulted and taken from his wages, or else some other bodily punishment at the discretion of the waggon-master … Lastly it is the office of the waggon-master to look to the goodness and sufficiency of all the waggons and other carriages which he has in his charge, to see that the bodies be whole and tight, the wheels strong and well bound, the axletrees unstrained and well clouted, and all the harness and implements belonging to the cattle for draught that it be firm, new and untattered; and to this end he shall ever have near and about him men of these trades, as coddlers, or knackers, cartwrights, Smiths and the like, with whatsoever is needful for their use (which he shall receive by appointment from the master of the ordnance,) and so he shall keep everything perfect and in good order, both to the General's good, the soldiers' profit, and his own reputation, for howsoever some other smaller things depend upon his knowledge; yet these I have already shewed, are the main substance of his cares, and the full duties which are expected in his office.[56]

The impressment accounts of the Surrey Committee (which was liable for 40 animals) from 1645 and 1646 contain various references to the employment of draught horses for the use of the New Model Army. Hence, on 7 April 1645 a horse and harness were delivered to the *White Hart* at Guildford 'at the price of £6 for Sir Thomas Fairfax's use by the appointment of the Committee'. An acquittance for payment 'out of the first month, pay which was out of the said parish funds' is dated 17 May. Two days later the Deputy Lieutenants issued a warrant 'for the payment of charges of the impressing of soldiers for Sir Thomas Fairfax in the West Division, and for conducting them to Staines, also for conveying the draught horses charged upon this division for the said army to Kingston, amounting to £19 7s. 5d.'.

Further sums were laid out by various local constables and officials for the provision of such horses from the West Division of Surrey during May and June 1645, for onward water transport to the army's headquarters at Reading. On 20 November 1645 the high collector for Reigate hundred recorded that he had disbursed £7 1s. 'for impressing, coating and conducting soldiers, and buying draught horses and other charges thereunto incident according to an Ordinance of Parliament dated 14

56 Markham, *Five Decades of Epistles of Warre*, pp.94–96.

March 1645, which is to be allowed by the treasurers by warrant according to the said ordinance'.[57] The same accounts show that such sums of money were usually reimbursed by the county committee within a few weeks. In late June 1645, as the victorious New Model passed through Warwickshire the parish of Leamington Hastings had various teams impressed 'for the General's army after Naseby fight', for which it claimed the sum of £7 2s. Similarly, Milverton had 'one team sent from the said town, being charged by warrant to carry ammunition for Sir Thomas Fairfax his Army about the beginning of June 1645', while 'about the later end of June' another team hauled another load 'being set forth upon that service two days', at a cost of 10s.[58]

The establishment for the New Model's train of artillery included a master farrier, who received 4s. per day, and 6 other farriers, each paid 1s. 6d. per day. Likewise, 1 close waggon driven by 6 horses was allocated to 'farriers, their tools and physic for horses', whereas 1,000 spare horseshoes and nails were transported in the same fashion.[59] Contracts made with suppliers to the New Model Army include those made on 1 February 1645 for 3,000 horseshoes costing 4d. each and 30,000 horseshoe nails at 9d. the pound.[60] Pay schedules for Fairfax's, Ireton's, Fleetwood's, and Whalley's regiments of horse, and Okey's dragoons made out on 23 December 1645 confirm that each cavalry troop was meant to have its own farrier, although evidence of their prevalence among dragoon units remains unclear.[61] In 1645 the farrier to Captain Hanson's company of London dragoons received 2s. per day, the same as the corporals and drummers.[62] In November 1642 Colonel Richard Browne's newly formed Parliamentarian regiment profited from the payment of £6 14s. 3d. to 'the farrier for shoeing horses', 5s. 6d. to a farrier for two days, £7 8d. 0d. 'to Garfield Wilman and others for shoeing dragoons' horses', another disbursement of £1 7s. 9d. for shoeing mounts, in addition to £1 7s. 9d. for 6 dozen horseshoes and 5s. 7d. for 750 horseshoe nails.[63] Similarly, the sum of £1 5s. 6d. was paid 'for shoeing dragoons' horses' for Sir Anthony Irby's regiment in early 1643.[64] Even though shoeing horses was the main work done by farriers in the early modern period, many of them were skilled medical practitioners. Their work with horseshoes and metal also associated them with blacksmiths.

Farriers' bills during the Civil Wars include charges for 'curing horses' and other treatments. For example, Captain Richard Grenville disbursed in April 1643 the sum of £2 10s. 'for keeping and curing a lame troop horse, which I left with him, for thirteen or fourteen weeks', and a further £1 9s. 4d. to a Mr Hussey of Henley for the same thing, the mount being left in his care for about five weeks.[65] On 8 August 1644 Corporal George Day of Colonel Purefoy's Parliamentarian regiment of Horse in

57 TNA, E179/187/468B, ff. 50r, 52r–54r, 56r, 58r, 61r; SP28/244/1, f. 472r.
58 TNA, SP28/185, f. 1v; SP28/183/35, f. 5v.
59 TNA, SP28/145. ff. 60r–63v.
60 TNA, SP30/37/1, f. 25r.
61 TNA, SP28/34/4, ff. 490r–498v.
62 TNA, SP28/131/8, f. 1r.
63 TNA, SP28/144/2, ff. 29r–34r.
64 TNA, SP28/313/4, unfol.
65 TNA, SP28/149, f. 159v; Wilson, *Buckinghamshire Contributions*, p.125.

Warwickshire paid the sum of 2s. 4d. to a farrier 'for bleeding, dressing and shoeing' a troop horse, while further disbursements were made for dressing mounts.[66] In 1610, Gervase Markham wrote the first book exclusively concerned with farriery and equine medicine. Aimed at horsemen, his treatise on horse care was considered authoritative and thus came out in dozens of editions. Markham followed the prevailing philosophy about health and illness in this period for humans and other large animals: the humoural theory of disease and wellness, whereby the four humours of the body (blood, phlegm, bile, and black bile) needed to be kept in balance, and illness was a result of a lack of balance in these substances.[67] One of the troopers of Sergeant Major John Desborough's troop of the Eastern Association Army paid 10s. for curing his horse of farcy in February 1644.[68] This was described by Markham as a highly infectious and fatal disease, characterised by ulcers or pustules along the horse's veins.[69] In July 1649 John Williams, 'master farrier for the Train' received the sum of £24 3s. 9d. for drugs and farriers' tools for Ireland.[70]

Cavalry Saddles

The procurement of quality troop saddles was vital to all armies of the Civil Wars. In November 1642, the Ordnance Office supplied saddles to several troops of Essex's Army by warrant of the Committee of Safety. Captain Francis Russell's troop received 100 saddles in February 1643, in addition to armour, pistols and carbines, although no other instances of issues from this source are known before 1645, and they may have been 'great saddles' left over from the Bishops' Wars.[71] In Cheshire, Sergeant Major Philip Mainwaring's troop was raised over the winter of 1642–1643, with funds being issued in London to purchase saddles.[72] An inventory of the goods of Edmund Jodrell of Yeardsley, taken by the captain lieutenant of Brereton's own troop on 28 April 1643 includes two great saddles (valued at £1 15s. apiece), four hackney saddles (at 6s. 8d. each), 'bridles with bits and snaffles', various saddle-cloths, three pairs of 'great brass stirrups' and two pistol barrels.[73] From their independent magazine in London John Bradley and Owen Rowe delivered fewer than 300 saddles to Essex's Army, 100 of which were supplied at 20s. apiece to his own regiment in early 1644. These must have been troop saddles because another batch of '60 great saddles at 50s. each' was paid for around the same time.[74]

66 TNA, SP28/136/26, ff. 1r, 7r–8r.

67 Gervase Markham, *Markham's Maister Peece, Containing all Knowledge Belonging to Smith, Farrier, or Horse-Leech, Touching on Curing All Diseases in Horses* (London: 1610), preface.

68 TNA, SP28/28/4, f. 358v.

69 Markham, *Markham's Maister Peece*, pp.457–458.

70 *CSPD Interregnum 1649–50*, p.577.

71 TNA, WO55/387, ff. 38r, 42v, 78r.

72 TNA, SP28/225/3, f. 725v; SP28/263, f. 154r.

73 JRL, JOD/62c; James Hall (ed.), *Memorials of the Civil War in Cheshire and the adjacent counties by Thomas Malbon, of Nantwich, Gent., and Providence improved by Edward Burghall*, Lancashire and Cheshire Record Society, 19 (1889), pp.245–247.

74 TNA, SP28/264 f. 11v; SP28/147/3, f. 593r.

The Committee for the Army began agreeing contracts for the supply of saddles to the New Model in March 1645, while warrants were issued for payments for deliveries by contractors the following month.[75] Between April 1645 and April 1646 the Ordnance Office took delivery of an estimated 9,379 saddles, of which 759 were for dragoons. Additionally, 500 unserviceable dragoon saddles were repaired at 5s. 6d. apiece by the London saddlers George Langley and Nathaniel Rawlinson. These were paid for and returned to the Ordnance Office within a remarkably short space of time, before being issued to Fairfax's Army.[76] The large volume of saddlery manufactured during this period reflects both the increased capacity of the London manufacturers, and the significant expansion of the army, and its mounted capability especially. London saddlers continued their dominance of the trade in 1645, but the Army Committee employed a new procedure for purchasing saddles, whereby it made indentures with saddlers and approved payment after the items had been delivered into the Ordnance Office. Hence, most contracts were fulfilled within one week of being agreed. Saddles were generally supplied to the New Model in multiples of 10, often with corresponding quantities of pistols and holsters for the horse, and snaphaunce muskets for the dragoons. Thus, on 7 April 1645 '20 saddles furnished and 20 pairs of pistols with holsters' were received by Captain William Rainborowe for his troop in Colonel Sheffield's regiment, while 10 days later Captain Christopher Mercer took delivery of 100 dragoon saddles and 100 snaphaunce dragoon muskets for furnishing his company'.[77]

Although the purchase, receipt and issue of saddles are recorded in various kinds of documents, it is possible to trace the process of their supply to the New Model Army in 1645 and 1646. Even so, some books containing copies of contracts for saddles cover different periods, which do not necessarily overlap. Correspondingly, some differences between the dates on which indentures were notified to the Officers of Ordnance exist – for instance, four contracts given in ML, Ms 46 78/708 as 5 June 1645 are listed in TNA, WO47/1 under 1 June, whereas those appearing under 28 June in the former are dated 27 June in the latter. The reasons for such discrepancies are unclear, though the decision by the present author has been taken to prefer those provided in WO47/1 as it is a more complete record. Among the earliest contracts for the supply of saddles to Fairfax's Army is that agreed with William Pearce of the Saddlers' Company for 600 troop saddles 'furnished with stran bitts, large trees, well-plated with iron, and 3 girths at 18s. apiece according to the pattern in the Tower'. Having been notified to the Ordnance Officers on 1 April 1645, the delivery was made in full on 5 April and payment of £540 was made two days later.[78]

Other contracts notified on 1 April were the one agreed with Thomas Webb and Nathaniel Rawlinson of Fleet Street for 500 troop saddles at 17s. apiece; these were brought into the Ordnance Office stores 4 days later. These saddlers also produced quantities of dragoon saddles for the New Model. Similarly, Elizabeth Betts delivered 100 troop saddles at 18s. apiece on 5 April, for which she received £45. Each of

75 TNA, WO55/1646, f. 135v; WO55/1662, f. 54r; WO55/1663, unfol.; WO55/1664, f. 24r.
76 TNA, WO47/1, f. 109r; WO55/1663, f. 40r; SP28/29/1, ff. 212r, 240r.
77 TNA, WO55/1647, unfol.; WSL, Ms Salt 463, unfol.
78 TNA, WO47/1, f. 167v; WO55/1663, unfol.; SP28/29/1, f. 188r; ML, Ms 46 78/708, f. 114r.

these contracts appears to have been notified to the Ordnance Officers and fulfilled on 5 April. Thomas Capper also supplied 100 troop saddles at 18s. apiece on 7 April, while on 26 April Elizabeth Worrall fulfilled her contract for 100 saddles at the same price; the reason for the relative delay to her delivery is unknown, however.[79]

Later indentures and warrants indicate that by mid-1645 the price paid by the Committee for the Army for troop saddles had decreased. For example, in June three saddlers – George Langley, Joseph Hitson, and Jane Gower – supplied them for 16s. 6d. each, whereas on 5 July Stephen Harmer delivered 100 troop saddles, at a rate of 16s. each, for which he received £80 on 10 July.[80] On 29 April 1645 Parliament had ordered the immediate dispatch of 1,000 saddles, bridles, and furniture, 1,000 pair of pistols and holsters, and 500 pair of spare holsters to Windsor, 'to be disposed of by the Committee of Both Kingdoms now residing in the Army, or by Sir Thomas Fairfax, for this present expedition [the New Model's impending march to relive Taunton], as they shall think most convenient.'[81] This is but one indicator that some of Fairfax's cavalry units were in urgent need of equipment at this time.

Two New Model regiments of horse were supplied with spare saddles. On 30 June 1645 Sir Robert Pye's and Colonel Nathaniel Rich's each received '90 saddles with furniture and 90 spare saddles with furniture.'[82] No specific reason for this is apparent, and no other issues of saddles are specified as spare, rather than for ready use, although there is a possibility that some larger batches included spares. Pye's and Rich's commands were among the first to receive equipment, with five troops belonging to the former receiving 100 pairs of pistols, holsters, saddles, backs, breasts, and pots on 3 April 1645, and the latter being supplied with like quantities of pistols, holsters, and saddles at the same time.[83] Pye's and Rich's regiments received 424 horses and 384 horses respectively in 1645 and 1646, whereas pay warrants for both regiments suggest that on the eve of the Battle of Naseby on 14 June 1645, Pye's mustered close to their establishment figure of troopers, while Rich's was 545 troopers, which was about average for the New Model Army's horse. Besides, a corporal and 24 troopers were added to the strength of Captain William Baugh's troop on 30 May 1645, and on 21 July 10 officers, 72 troopers, in addition to 13 wounded soldiers mustered in Captain Edward Dendy's troop.[84] Quantities of both pistols, holsters, and spare holsters were supplied to Fairfax's cavalry from the Ordnance Office. On 29 April 1645, 500 cases of pistols with holsters, and 500 pairs of spare holsters were delivered to Commissary Phipps of the Train of Artillery, whereas in June and July more than 400 spare holsters were distributed among the troops and regiments of the New Model Army.[85]

---

79 TNA, WO47/1, ff. 211r, 219r; SP28/29/1, ff. 174r, 183r, 185r, 186r, 188r, 190r, 220r; SP28/29/2, f. 257r; ML, Ms 46 78/708, f. 114r.

80 TNA, WO55/1663 unfol.; SP28/30/4, ff. 370r–372r, 377r; SP28/31/5, f. 507r; ML, Ms 46 78/708, f. 92r.

81 *CJ*, IV, p.126.

82 TNA, WO55/1646, ff. 132r, 133r; WSL, Ms Salt 463, unfol.

83 TNA, WO55/1647, unfol.; WSL, Ms Salt 463, unfol.

84 TNA, SP28/30/4, f. 400r; SP28/31/1, f. 82r.

85 TNA, WO55/1647, unfol.; WSL, Ms Salt 463, unfol.

Cantle Pad Saddles

In addition to the troop saddles issued to the cavalry, quantities of cantle pad saddles were supplied to the New Model Army. Derivative of the oldest form of saddle, by the seventeenth century they had separate pads on either side of the horse's back, rather like a modern riding saddle.[86] Cantle pad saddles are first explicitly mentioned in contracts in July 1645, although it is possible that some of the saddles described as 'pad saddles' in the earlier contracts might have been of this type. One agreement from 2 April 1645 describes the 250 saddles ordered from the saddler William Kettle as 'pad saddles with good iron plates and stran bitts with good furniture complete' at 17s. each, whereas another contract from later in the month was for 'pad saddles with two loops behind and no great buckles for the crupper' at 18s.[87] On 28 June 40 cantle pad saddles were received from Francis Joiner, while another consignment of 100 saddles costing 18s. apiece were brought into the Ordnance Office by William Deacon on 5 July in full settlement of his contract.[88] In July a cantle pad saddle cost 17s. or 18s., as opposed to 16s. or 16s. 6d. for troop saddles. The receipts and delivery books of the Ordnance Office record that out of a total of 9,379 new saddles of all types, 220 cantle pad saddles were delivered between April 1645 and April 1646. All such items were issued to Sir Thomas Fairfax's horse between September and December 1645.[89] In considering how these saddles were used, it could that in any cavalry troop, several treeless pad saddles would be of use for fitting to the backs of the proportion of remounts that the fixed tree of the standard issue saddle would not work with, in other words, horses with particularly broad or narrow backs would benefit from the greater flexibility of the pad saddle.[90] Furthermore, no sizes for troop or dragoon saddles for the New Model are given in the sources, just quantities and prices.

Consequently, on 2 September 1645 '10 cantle pad saddles furnished' were delivered along with 20 troop saddles and 40 pairs of pistols with holsters to Captain John Blackwell's troop of Lieutenant General Cromwell's regiment. Four pad saddles were received with 4 troop saddles by Sergeant Major Matthew Tomlinson of Sir Robert Pye's regiment for his troop on 20 September, whereas on 4 October 7 troopers from Butler's regiment were each furnished with a cantle pad saddle, and a pair of pistols with holsters. Additionally, on 21 October 1645 10 cantle pad saddles with furniture were delivered to Commissary George Hall, while 2 days later, Trooper John Fuller of Sir Thomas Fairfax's own troop received 1 for himself. Moreover, on 31 October Ralph Knowles, clerk to Sergeant Major Horton's troop in Colonel Butler's regiment took delivery of 18 cantle pad saddles with furniture – 5 were for Troopers John Smith, John Shuster, James Mills, Samuel Weston, and

86 G. Tylden, *Horses and Saddlery: An Account of the Animals Used by the British and Commonwealth Armies from the Seventeenth Century to the Present Day* (London: J. A. Allen, 1965), pp.112–13.

87 TNA, WO47/1, f. 211r; ML, Ms 46 78/708, f. 112r.

88 TNA, SP28/31/5, ff. 496r, 499r; Bodl. Lib., Ms Eng. hist. C14, ff. 31v, 32v.

89 Robinson, *Horse Supply*, pp.180–181.

90 Thanks to Rosie Sales and Alan Larsen for this suggestion.

Thomas Russell of Butler's own troop; 8 for Troopers Richard Jones, William Jones, Ralph Knowles, Benjamin Arundel, Giles Cooke, Edward Blanco, Jeremy Newton, and Edward Gylie of Horton's troop; with a further 5 for Troopers James Moore, Robert Hopday, John Welsby, John Jacob, and Andrew Vanstone of Captain Foley's troop of the same regiment.

On the same day, Lieutenant Edmund Challender of Captain Evanson's troop in Colonel Whalley's regiment was supplied with 10 saddles of the same kind. Eight were for the use of Evanson's troop; 1 for the colonel's own troop, and another for Thomas Moore, trooper in Captain Coleman's troop. Likewise, John Caldwell and George Brown, troopers under Sergeant Major Tomlinson, were issued a cantle pad saddle apiece. In each of the above cases, the saddles were supplied with an equivalent quantity of pairs of pistols and holsters.[91] By comparison, among the quantities of saddles and tack obtained in London for Sir Thomas Myddelton's Parliamentarian forces in 1644 were 70 pad saddles, bridles and other equipment, costing £65 10s., in addition to two (probably local) purchases 'for 39 pad saddles with their furniture at 20s. a piece'.[92]

Dragoon Saddles

In describing the arms and equipment of dragoons, Monck observed that they 'ought to have a good ordinary horse, saddle, snaffle, reins, stirrups, and stirrup-leathers, a halter, and two girts.'[93] Dragoon saddles were both lighter and far more inexpensive than cavalry saddles. As dragoons used their horses simply for transport and did not usually fight mounted, they required much less support from their saddles. The earliest known contract for saddles for the New Model Army's dragoon regiment – notified to the Ordnance Office on 4 April 1645 – was with the saddlers George Langley and Nathaniel Rawlinson of Fleet Street for '300 dragoon saddles at the price of 5s. 6d. per saddle with their furniture, 100 to be delivered by the 1st of this month and 200 the next.' The initial 100 saddles were delivered on 5 April and the second batch 13 days later. Both the warrants issued for their payment and two receipts books describe these items as 'old dragoon saddles repaired and made serviceable', while the reduced price compared to the new items suggests the same.[94] Various contracts were placed for the army with Elizabeth Betts – a major producer of troop and dragoon saddles, and saddle furniture in London. On 5 June 1645 she consented to supply 140 'new dragoon saddles with furniture at 7s. 6d. per saddle'. One hundred of these were received on 22 June, while another 100 new dragoon saddles at the same price were ordered on 6 August.

91 TNA, WO55/1646, ff. 194r, 207r; WO55/1647, unfol.; WSL, Ms Salt 463
92 TNA, SP28/346/1, unfol.; SP28/346/2, unfol.
93 Monck, *Observations*, p.28.
94 TNA, SP28/29/1, ff. 213r; 240r; WO47/1, f. 211r; WO55/1662, f. 18v; Bodl. Lib., Ms Eng. hist. C14, ff. 4v, 13v; ML, Ms 46 78/708, f. 112v. The latter gives the overall figure as 500.

Dragoon horse with reproduction saddle, made by Tomáš Filip-Leatherwork. (Courtesy of Graham Webb)

On 14 July Nicholas Rechford agreed to supply 50 dragoon saddles at 7s. 10d. the saddle, with furniture.[95] Likewise, 100 dragoon saddles were received from Percival Shergold on 9 March 1646, although no record of any contract for this order is known.[96] Nonetheless, such items were somewhat cheaper than cavalry saddles, which were procured for between 16s. and 18s.[97] In all, the Ordnance Office took receipt of 738 dragoon saddles between April and December 1645, and another 299 between June and July 1646, giving a total of 1,037. The analysis of sources pertaining to the Committee for the Army and the Ordnance Office, comprising Treasury warrants, commissaries' accounts, and receipts and disbursements books provides a clear picture of the military equipment, and horses supplied to Colonel John Okey's regiment between April 1645 and July 1646. There seems little reason to think that most, if not all, of the quantities of dragoon saddles received by the Ordnance Office were supplied directly to the regiment. The accuracy of the sources

95 TNA, SP28/31/5, f. 539r; SP30/37, ff. 21v, 45r, 51r; Bodl. Lib., Ms Eng. hist. C14, f. 29v; ML, Ms 46 78/708, ff. 45r, 51r.

96 TNA, SP28/140/3, unfol.; Bodl. Lib., Ms Eng. hist. C244, f. 1r.

97 TNA, PRO30/37, ff. 91v, 109r–112v; ML, Ms 46 78/708, ff. 21r, 54r, 93r, 109r.

allows us, as with snaphaunce muskets and cartridge boxes, to calculate both how many dragoon saddles were issued and in some instances to which sub-units.

On 7 April 1645 Captain John Farmer received 100 saddles and 100 snaphaunce dragoon muskets; Captain Christopher Mercer had 100 saddles and firearms 'for his company of dragoons' a week later. On 22 April he further obtained '100 dragoon saddles with furniture and 100 muskets out of the stores provided for Sir Thomas Fairfax his Army, for the recruiting [suppling] of Colonel Okey's, Sergeant Major Gwilliam's and the said Captain Mercer's troops'. While at the relief of Taunton on 14 July 1645 Farmer was issued with a further 200 snaphaunce muskets, 200 dragoon saddles and 200 cartridge boxes, 'being for the recruiting of Colonel Okey's regiment'.[98] Furthermore, a warrant from the Committee for the Army, dated 8 November 1645, ordered the supply of saddles 'by indenture' to Cornet Christopher Purslow of Captain Farr's company of dragoon saddles and snaphaunces to Corporal Thomas Holmes, and Dragoons Mark Frost, William Egle, Henry Bunce, John Bailey, William Bailey, William Pinsey, William Cole, John Lawrence, Richard Soale, Edward Bartholomew, William Hithe, Gideon Blythe, Walter James, John Cogger, Charity Cogger, William Walker, Thomas Croft, William Carlyn, William Jenkins, Edward Davies and Samuel Heath, 'the said persons being of the same troop and regiment, out of the stores provided for Sir Thomas Fairfax his Army'.

These items were delivered two days later, during a period when Farr's and other companies were on reconnaissance duties in the Taunton area.[99] Moreover, on 15 June 1646 Cornet Purslow took delivery of a further 11 dragoon saddles and snaphaunce muskets for 1 corporal and 10 soldiers (each being named); 9 of each were received by Cornet Roger Farr on 16 June; 31 by Cornet William Tinge on 21 June; 20 by Captain Bridge for his company on 16 July; and 5 by Lieutenant Francis Bolton of Captain Abbot's company the following day. Hence, by July 1646 a total of 775 saddles for dragoons had been supplied to Okey's regiment by the Ordnance Office.[100] This figure tends to correspond with numbers of horses supplied, in addition to the known strength of the unit in 1645–1646. There are no dragoon horses unaccounted for in the army commissaries' account, so the statistics for Okey's regiment are far more precise than those for the New Model's cavalry. Therefore, they received 672 horses from this method (amounting to 67 percent of the establishment of 1,000 dragoons), although on 23 December 1645 Parliament authorised the purchase of 200 dragoon naggs from the London Militia Committee for the use of Fairfax's Army.[101] Similarly, contemporary eye-witness accounts describe substantially lower numbers under Okey's command in April and May 1645 as '400 and odd', and '500 dragoons', whereas calculations of the regiment's pay warrants on the eve of the Battle of Naseby arrive at an all-ranks strength of 676 men.[102]

98 TNA, WO55/1647, unfol.; Bodl. Lib., Ms Add. C247, ff. 2r, 6v; WSL, Ms Salt 463, unfol.

99 TNA, WO55/1646, f. 237v; Sprigge, *Anglia Rediviva*, p.157.

100 BL, Ms Add. 35332, ff. 9r–11r, 21r, 24v; TNA, WO55/1646, ff. 234r, 249v.

101 TNA, SP28/140/7, ff. 276v–289v; *CJ*, IV, p.383; Robinson, 'Horse Supply', pp.138–139.

102 TNA, SP28/29/1, ff. 13r–13v, 59r–59v, 107r, 187r; SP28/30/3, f. 293r; *Mercurius Civicus*, 24 April–1 May 1645. TT, E284[1]; *CSPD 1644-5*, p.504; David Blackmore, 'Counting the New Model Army', *ECWT*, 58 (2004), pp.3–5; Andrew Abram, *Dragoons and Dragoon Operations in the British Civil Wars, 1638–1653* (Solihull: Helion & Co., 2023), p.284.

Table 12: Troop, Pad and Dragoon Saddles Received by the Ordnance Office from Contractors for the NMA, April-December 1645 (Bodl. Lib., Ms Eng. hist. C14; TNA, SP28/29/1-34/3)

f. 1r	1/4/45	Ordered that the Officers of the Ordnance shall receive the particulars above contracted for and give certificates to the parties for what they received, and the officers are to view the arms. Robert Scawen	
Receipts of consignments brought into his Majesty's Stores from the several artificers hereafter mentioned, being for the supply and furnishing of the Army under the command of Sir Thomas Fairfax by virtue of the abovesaid order:			
f. 2v	2/4/45	300 saddles furnished	Nathaniel Rawlinson
f. 3r	2/4/45	200 saddles furnished	Thomas Webb
f. 3r	2/4/45	200 saddles furnished	Elizabeth Betts
f. 3v	5/4/45	600 saddles furnished	Mr Warden and Co. of Saddlers
f. 3v	5/4/45	100 saddles furnished	Thomas Capper
f. 4r	5/4/45	100 saddles furnished	William Deacon
f. 4v	5/4/45	100 old dragoon saddles furnished	Nath. Rawlinson & George Langley
f. 8r	11/4/45	250 saddles furnished	Thomas Kyte
f. 8r	11/4/45	250 saddles furnished	William Kettle
f. 9r	12/4/45	200 old dragoon saddles	Nath. Rawlinson & George Langley
f.13v	18/4/45	200 old dragoon saddles furnished	Nath. Rawlinson & George Langley
f. 16r	24/4/45	100 saddles furnished	Elizabeth Worrall
f. 25v	6/6/45	100 saddles furnished	Elizabeth Betts
f. 26r	8/6/45	100 saddles furnished	George Langley
f. 26r	8/6/45	50 saddles furnished	Jane Gower
f. 26v	10/6/45	50 saddles furnished	Richard Brayne
f. 27r	12/6/45	50 saddles furnished	Jane Gower
f. 27v	14/6/45	100 saddles furnished	Joseph Hitson
f. 29v	22/6/45	100 new dragoon saddles furnished	Elizabeth Betts
f. 30r	23/6/45	100 troop saddles with furniture	Thomas Webb
f. 30v	27/6/45	50 saddles furnished	Joseph Hitson
f. 30v	27/6/45	100 saddles furnished	George Langley
f. 31r	2/7/45	50 saddles furnished	Richard Brayne
f. 31v	3/7/45	40 cantle pad saddles furnished	Francis Joiner
f. 32r	4/7/45	100 saddles furnished	Thomas Webb
f. 32r	5/7/45	100 saddles furnished	Nath. Rawlinson
f. 32v	5/7/45	250 saddles furnished	John Hawton & Nicholas Retchford
f. 32v	5/7/45	100 cantle pad saddles furnished 100 saddles furnished	William Deacon
f. 33r	20/6/45 & 5/7/45	50 saddles furnished	William Platt

f. 33r	5/7/45	100 saddles furnished	Henry Woodley
f. 33v	5/7/45	100 saddles furnished	Stephen Harmer
f. 33v	5/7/45	100 saddles furnished	William Hussey
f. 34r	5/7/45	50 saddles furnished	Merrick Spender
f. 35v	8/7/45	100 saddles furnished	Thomas Kyte
f. 36v	11/7/45	100 saddles furnished	John Hitson
f. 36v	12/7/45	60 saddles furnished	George Langley
f. 39v	21/6/45 & 16/7/45	100 saddles furnished	Elizabeth Betts
f. 39v	16/7/45	100 saddles furnished	Elizabeth Worrall
f. 40r	16/7/45	50 dragoon saddles furnished	Nich. Retchford

Table 13: Troop, Pad and Dragoon Saddles Delivered by the Ordnance Office to the NMA, April-August 1645 (TNA, WO47/1, WO55/1662, WO55/1664, WO55/1646, WO55/1647 and WSL, Ms Salt 463)

4/4/45	80 saddles furnished	20 to Nathaniel Waterhouse, cornet to Sir Robert Pye; 20 to Sgt Major Nathaniel Rich; 20 to Captain Matthew Tomlinson & Captain Charles Holcroft (Pye's regt)
4/4/45	20 saddles furnished	William, Lord Caulfield for his troop (Graves' regt)
5/4/45	40 saddles furnished	Paul Bunting for the supplying of two troops in Middleton's/Butler's regt
5/4/45	80 saddles furnished	Captain John Bush for Vermuyden's regt
5/4/45	50 saddles furnished	Captain James Berry for Fairfax's regt
7/4/45	20 saddles furnished	Captain William Rainborowe for his troop in Sheffield's regt
7/4/45	20 saddles furnished	Lieutenant Watson to furnish himself and his troop (possibly Captain Thomas Ireton's troop of Sidney's/Rich's regt)
7/4/45	100 dragoon saddles	Captain John Farmer (Okey's regt)
10/4/45	50 saddles furnished	Sgt Major George Sedascue for his troop, and the troops of Captain John Hoskins and Captain Robert Gibbons (Ireton's regt)
12/4/45	20 saddles furnished	Roger Hopkins, lieutenant for the furnishing of Sgt Major John Alford's troop (Sidney's/Rich's regt)
14/4/45	20 saddles furnished	Captain Thomas Neville's troop in Sidney's/Rich's regt
14/4/45	20 saddles furnished	Captain James Berry for Whalley's regt (though Berry was in Fairfax's regt)
15/4/45	60 saddles furnished	Cornet Paul Bunting, 20 for Captain Walter Perry's troop; 20 for Sgt Major Horton's troop (Middleton's/Butler's regt); 20 for Captain Thomas Pennyfather's troop (Livesey's/Ireton's regt)
15/4/45	20 saddles furnished	Captain Lieutenant Roger Hopkins in Sidney's/Rich's own troop
17/4/45	100 dragoon saddles	Captain Christopher Mercer's dragoon company
18/4/45	20 saddles furnished	Sergeant Major John Desborough's troop (Fairfax's regt)
18/4/45	20 saddles furnished	Captain Arthur Evelyn's troop (Sheffield's regt)
19/4/45	120 saddles furnished	Sergeant Major Thomas Harrison for Fleetwood's regt

20/4/45	20 saddles furnished	Edward Johnson, cornet to Captain Henry Middleton for his troop (Vermuyden's regt)
21/4/45	120 saddles furnished	Captain Rands for the 6 troops of Rossiter's regt
21/4/45	20 saddles furnished	Captain Ralph Knight for his troop in Pye's regt
22/4/45	8 saddles furnished	John Holmstead, Provost Marshal General of the horse
22/4/45	100 dragoon saddles	Captain Mercer for Okey's, Gwilliam's and Mercer's companies
22/4/45	20 saddles furnished	Captain Edward Dendy for his troop (Sidney's/Rich's regt)
22/4/45	20 saddles furnished	Captain Thomas Ireton for his troop (Sidney's/Rich's regt)
22/4/45	20 saddles furnished	Thomas Wicks, Provost Marshal General of the foot for the furnishing of his servants
22/4/45	20 saddles furnished	Captain Thomas Ireton for his troop (Sidney's/Rich's regt)
23/4/45	20 saddles furnished	Michael Thompson, cornet to Sgt Major Christopher Bethell of Whalley's regt for his troop
23/4/45	20 saddles furnished	James Wilson, Quartermaster to Ireton's troop
1/5/45	20 saddles furnished	Cornet Bunting for Captain William Bough's troop (Rich's regt)
1/5/45	20 saddles furnished	John Everard, cornet to Captain Christopher Fleming of Grave's regt for the supply of 6 troops
2/5/45	20 saddles furnished	Benjamin Pett, clerk to Captain Ralph Margery (Pye's regt)
6/5/45	120 saddles furnished	60 for Captain Adam Lawrence's troop; 60 for Captain William Packer's troop (Fairfax's regt)
6/5/45	20 saddles furnished	Captain John Reynolds's troop (Vermuyden's/ Cromwell's regt)
7/5/45	60 saddles furnished	Captain William Gwilliam's troop (Ireton's regt)
13/5/45	40 saddles furnished	Henry Ward for 2 troops of Ireton's regt
21/5/45	1 saddle furnished	Trooper Thomas Browne of Captain Margery's troop (Pye's regt)
21/5/45	4 saddles furnished	Troopers John Smith, John Collier, Abraham Morris and William Blanch in Butler's regt
23/5/45	3 saddles furnished	Troopers Francis Feast, Ralph Penny and John Jones in Butler's regt
29/5/45	1 saddle furnished	Trooper Samuel Longbottom in Fairfax's troop
6/6/45	100 saddles furnished	Captain William Coleman of Fleetwood's regt for his troop
6/6/45	100 saddles furnished	Sergeant Major Thomas Harrison for Fleetwood's regt
9/6/45	40 saddles furnished	James Jennings, cornet to Captain William Cecil of Ireton's regt for said troop
10/6/45	20 saddles furnished	Gilman Taylor, lieutenant to Captain Thomas Howard of Fleetwood's regt for said troop
30/6/45	90 saddles furnished and 90 spare saddles furnished	Lawrence Farr, servant to Colonel Pye for his regt

30/6/45	90 saddles furnished and 90 spare saddles furnished	Captain Lieutenant Edmund Hamden for Rich's regt
1/7/45	60 saddles furnished	30 for Captain Hoskins' troop; 30 for Captain Gibbon's troops (Ireton's regt)
1/7/45	90 saddles furnished	Richard Sparlin, 45 for Sgt Major Thomas Horton's troop; 45 for Captain Walter Perry's troop (Butler's regt)
2/7/45	1 saddle furnished	Trooper Benjamin Waller of Sergeant Major Robert Huntington's troop (Cromwell's regt)
7/7/45	180 saddles furnished	Quartermaster David Thompson to Captain William Rainborowe for Sheffield's regt
10/7/45	90 saddles furnished	Butler's regt
11/7/45	1 saddle furnished	Trooper Robert Warren of Captain Robert Swallow's troop of Whalley's regt
17/7/45	180 saddles furnished	Sergeant Major Huntington for Cromwell's regt
23/7/45	195 saddles furnished	Fairfax's regt
24/7/45	40 saddles furnished	Sir Robert Pye for the supplying of his wounded men come from Northampton
25/7/45	120 saddles furnished	Ireton's regt
25/7/45	36 saddles furnished	Whalley's regt
25/7/45	30 saddles furnished	John Everard for Captain Fleming's troop in Graves' regt
6/8/45	270 saddles furnished	Captain John Browne for the General's and Colonel Whalley's regts
11/8/45	3 saddles furnished	Troopers John Scudamore, Thomas Farmer and Robert Clarke of Butler's regt
13/8/45	72 saddles furnished	John Davies for Graves' regt
16/8/45	1 saddle furnished	John Wenham of Captain Perry's troop in Butler's regt
19/8/45	35 saddles furnished	Captain Ralph Margery for his troop
2/9/45	10 cantle pad saddles furnished 20 troop saddles furnished	Captain John Blackwell's troop of Cromwell's regt
10/9/45	16 saddles furnished	Corporal William Cartledge for Captain Edward Foley's troop in Butler's regt
13/9/45	5 cantle saddles furnished	Captain Ralph Margery for his troop in Pye's regt
4/10/45	7 cantle pad saddles furnished 7 pairs pistols with holsters	John Webster, Benjamin Perry, Thomas Ward, James Pearson, Thomas Bucknell, Randall Holmes, and Robert Stratford for Butler's regt

Horse Harness

Draught harness makers were meant to be members of the Saddlers' Company, although in practice they operated independently to saddlers. Trace harness and thill harness were both used together within a team, every fifth one to be for a 'thiller', being the horse ridden by the carter at the front of the team, which shows that teams of five horses were the norm. Even though 'great harness' was more expensive than ordinary harness (at 14s. per set, as opposed to 12s.), these were still purchased for the New Model Army in late 1645. Contracts for the supply of harness were agreed between the Committee for the Army and London-based manufacturers in large quantities, including that agreed with John Munnings, Richard Blisset, Peter Andrews, and the partners John Pitchford and Thomas Skinner on 17 July 1645 for 50 sets apiece. One group of indentures notified to the Ordnance Officers on 22 December contains some details of the items themselves and the contractual conditions to which they had agreed:

> Contracted with William Simons for 20 great harnesses at 14s. a harness and 12 thill harnesses of the same goodness and weight according to the former contract, to be brought into the Tower of London by equal proportions as above, for which it is to be contracted, he shall be paid as he brings them in.
>
> Then also contracted Thomas Skinner of Southwark and John Pitchford of the same for 30 horse harnesses according to the former contracts, to be brought into the Tower of London as aforesaid, and then contracted for 22 great harnesses at 14s. a harness, of which these must be 2 thillers' harnesses, the body traces 12lbs weight, the rest suitable to them at 9s., every harness to be also brought into the Tower and paid for as aforesaid for performance, whereof he has put his hand.
>
> Contracted with John Munnings of Whitechapel for 55 great harnesses, of which there must be 5 thillers' harnesses, the body traces 12lbs weight, the next 11lbs, the next 10lbs, the next 9lbs, the next 8lbs at 9s. apiece, to be brought into the Tower of London at the times in the former contract mentioned, for which he is to be paid as he brings them in.

Thus, Skinner and Pitchford's consignment was received on 14 March 1646; Munnings' on 26 March 1646; and Simons' on 28 March 1646. In each case, they were inspected and paid for on the same day they came in.[103] Between April 1645 and March 1646, a total of 1,680 trace and 390 thill harness, with an additional 50 'harness complete' were received into the Ordnance Office for the use of Fairfax's Army and paid for.[104] All deliveries of harness by the Ordnance Office to the army were made directly to the train of artillery. Hence, between 18 April and 1 May 1645 a total of 1,050 'sets' of harness, in addition to '120 trace and 30 thill harness' were issued to Commissary Thomas Phipps. A further 200 sets were delivered to his assistants, Richard Fenner and Henry Jarman.[105] These, it would seem, were more than adequate to equip the establishment figure of 792 draught horses for the waggons, and 234 draught horses for hauling the ordnance belonging to the New Model's train.

103 TNA, WO47/1, *passim*; WO49/82, f. 317v; ML, Ms 46 78/708, ff. 64v, 88r–88v, 106r, 112v, 116r.
104 TNA, SP28/29/1, ff. 125r–135r; TNA, SP28/31/5, ff. 444r–447r; TNA, SP28/30/4, ff. 342r, 354r; Bodl. Lib., Ms Eng. hist. C14, *passim*; Bodl. Lib., Ms Eng. hist. C244, ff. 2r–9v.
105 TNA, WO55/1647, unfol.; WSL, Ms Salt 463, unfol.

6

Arms and Accoutrements I

One of the main aims of the Committee for the Army in spring 1645 was to fully equip the New Model Army's regiments of foot, and almost entirely from scratch. The mainstay of the weaponry of the infantry during the Civil Wars was the pike and the musket. Of these the pike was considered by military writers to be the more honourable weapon, because it was the more ancient and gentlemen who enlisted in the ranks preferred to 'trail the pike'. Writing in 1590 Sir Roger Williams asserted that 'the pike is the strength of all battles', while 60 years later Richard Elton provided a chapter entitled 'Several reasons why the pike is the more honourable arms'.[1] According to *Directions for Musters*, a set of drill instructions published in 1638:

> The pikeman must be armed with a pike seventeen foot long head and all (the diameter of the staff to be one inch ¾) the head to be well-steeled, 8 inches long, broad, strong, and sword-pointed; the cheeks 2 foot long, well riveted; the butt-end bound with a ring of iron.[2]

Pikemen provided the main defensive arm of the infantry, especially against mounted troops, though they also possessed a formidable offensive capacity. The latter was witnessed by Parliamentarian commander Sir John Meldrum in October 1643, when leading a sally from the besieged garrison of Hull. He wrote later, 'The violence of our soldiers was abated by 100 pikes of the enemy, who charged the van of our foot, scattered and in disorder did drive us backward again and enforced us all to a shameful retreat'.[3] The 'push of pike' technique is described by Sir John Smythe, who in 1595 wrote:

> [When the pikes are] ready to encounter with another … letting fall the points of their pikes and carry them close breast high with both hands

1 Sir Roger Williams, *A Briefe Discourse of Warre* (London: Thomas Orwin, 1590), p.39; Richard Elton, *The Complete Body of the Art Military* (London: Robert Leybourn, 1650), pp.1–2.

2 *Directions for Musters Wherein is shewed the order of drilling for the musket and pike* (Cambridge: Thomas Buck and Roger Daniel, 1638), unpaginated.

3 *A True and Exact Relation of the Great Victories Obtained by the Earl of Manchester and the Lord Fairfax Against the Earl of Newcastle's Army in the North* (London, 19 October 1643). TT, E71[5].

> steadily and firmly, the points full in the face of their enemies. And the second rank likewise straightening and closing themselves by rank and front, and joining themselves to the back of the first rank, and following them step with step carrying their pikes above hand over the shoulders of the first rank, the points of their pikes likewise towards the face of the enemy's.[4]

Following the Battle of Montgomery on 18 September 1644 Sir William Brereton related, 'it came to push of pike, wherein they [the Royalists] were much too hard for us, having many more pikes.'[5] It was reported that during the fighting at Bristol in September 1645 Lieutenant Colonel Bowen and other officers, leading Colonel Thomas Rainborowe's regiment 'were two hours at push of pike, standing upon the palisades, but could not enter'. Furthermore, Sir Thomas Fairfax described that during the New Model Army's storming of Torrington, in heavy rain on the night of 16 February 1646, three infantry regiments, including Colonel Hammond's and his own, 'went up for reserves, till at last they fell on in earnest; after very hot firings our men coming up to the barricadoes and line, the dispute continued long at push of pike, and with butt-ends of muskets, till at last it pleased God to make the enemy fly from their works, and give our men the entrance.'[6] In 1661 William Booth of Nantwich petitioned that while serving in Ireland he had received various wounds, including being 'run through the breast with a pike'.[7] At Naseby on 14 June 1645 Commissary General Henry Ireton, whose left wing of New Model horse had been initially mauled by Prince Rupert's cavalry, brought his remaining squadrons to the assistance of the infantry being hard pressed by a brigade of the King's foot. As Sprigge recounted, Ireton 'commanded the division that was with him to charge that body of foot, and for their better encouragement he himself with great resolution fell in amongst the musketeers, where his horse being shot under him, and himself run through the thigh with a pike and into the face with a halberd, was taken prisoner by the enemy.'[8]

Between March 1645 and spring 1646 the Committee for the Army contracted with London suppliers for pikes of 'good ash 16 foot with steel heads' for the New Model Army at between 3s. 10d. and 4s. 2d. apiece – rather cheaper than the 5s. and 5s. 6d. paid by some regional armies, and those sent to Ireland in January 1643 and October 1646.[9] They were often supplied by contractors in consignments of 100 or 200, and distributed to the army in batches between 500 and 3,000. As with other items of equipment, the gradual reduction in prices doubtless reflects the increase in the organisation and output of the London arms industry, as well as a more discounted rate for larger orders. The prices paid by the Committee for the Army for pikes compare favourably with those purchased for other Parliamentarian forces. A

4 Sir John Smythe, *Instructions, Observations and Orders Mylitare* (London: 1595), pp.25–26.
5 *LJ, VI*, p.715.
6 *Rushworth, Historical Collections*, VI, pp.88, 98.
7 CRO, QJF/89/2, f. 206r.
8 Sprigge, *Anglia Rediviva*, p.37.
9 Bodl. Lib., Ms Rawlinson A110, f. 26v; *CJ*, IV, p.698.

total of 200 pikes were supplied to Sir Thomas Myddelton's forces by London manufacturers on 6 June 1643 at a cost of 5s. 6d. each.[10] Likewise, on 20 September one of the Earl of Manchester's agents in London informed the Essex Committee, 'I have got from Mr Edwards in Philip Lane 42 pikes; he could not supply more and could only promise as many a week hence. So I have procured good pikes and sent an account: 58 pikes at 6s., 250 pikes at 5s. 10d., 42 pikes at 5s. 9d.; total £102 7s. 10d'.[11]

A total of 8,400 pikes were received into the Ordnance Office stores from various sources between April 1645 and December 1646. This included 7,025 obtained via contracts and a further 1,375 that were procured and paid for, but not contracted for, and recorded in the Ordnance Office receipt books.[12] Included in these totals were 550 Spanish pikes supplied by the pike maker Robert Hammond costing 4s. apiece, for which he received payment on 9 October, in addition to 200 Dutch pikes from Francis Webb at the same price.[13] Like Dutch sword blades, significant quantities of pikes were imported into Britain from the Low Countries, especially via the ports of Dunkirk and Ostend in Flanders, and Amsterdam in The United Provinces. In autumn 1642, for instance, the Committee of Safety authorised the purchase of 12,000 muskets with rests, 1,500 pairs of pistols 1,200 carbines, 6,000 pikes, 600 sets of cavalry armour and 6,000 corselets through Thomas Andrews and Stephen Estwick, who in turn, 'asked their factors in Holland and France to obtain the weapons and by 4 October 2,690 muskets and 3,956 rests, 246 carbines, 66 dragoons, 980 pairs of pistols with cases, 401 suits of harquebusier armour and 2,331 corslets had been received.'[14] Though the Spanish and Dutch pikes procured for the New Model in 1645 were relatively modest in terms of quantity, there may have been further consignments received that do not appear in the Ordnance Office books.

Table 14: Notification of Contracts to the Ordnance Office for the Supply of Pikes for the NMA (TNA, WO47/1; Bodl. Lib., Ms Eng. hist. C14; ML, Ms 46 78/708)

Date	Quantity and type	Price each	Contractor
1 or 4/4/45	600 pikes	4s. 2d.	John Edwards
9/4/45	1000 long pikes well-headed and footed	4s.	Owen Rowe
10/4/45	500 long pikes	4s. 2d.	Elizabeth Thacker, widow
15/5/45	100 pikes	4s. 2d.	Bartholomew Wray
15/5/45	200 long pikes	4s. 2d.	John Edwards
9/6/45	100 long pikes at 16 foot	4s. 2d.	Thomas Bayman
2/7/45	200 long pikes	4s. 2d.	John Edwards

10 TNA, SP28/346/1, unfol.
11 BL, Ms Egerton 2647, f. 139v; HMC, *Seventh Report*, pp.563–564.
12 TNA, SP28/29-36, *passim*; SP28/352/1, unfol.
13 TNA, SP28/352/1, unfol.; ML, Ms 46 78/708, f. 103r.
14 TNA, SP28/161/3, f. 284r.

Date	Quantity and type	Price each	Contractor
11/7/45	200 long pikes to be delivered 160 on Saturday next and 40 more on Monday next	4s. 2d.	John Thacker
11/7/45	200 long pikes to be delivered on Saturday	4s. 2d.	Bartholomew Wray
11/7/45	100 long pikes for 50 on Saturday and the other 50 on Monday next	4s. 2d.	Thomas Bayman
12/9/45	600 pikes	4s. 2d.	John Edwards
18/9/45	400 Spanish pikes of 15 foot	4s. 0d.	Robert Hamond
19/9/45	150 Spanish pikes	4s. 0d.	Robert Hamond
19/9/45	250 English pikes	4s. 2d.	Bartholomew Wray
19/9/45	200 pikes	4s. 0d.	Francis Webber
22/12/45	500 pikes of good ash 16 foot with steel heads, a fourth part of them to be brought in monthly to the Tower of London: one fourth part upon the last day of this instant December, another fourth part on the last of January, another fourth part on the last of February & the other fourth part on the last of March next ensuing. The pikes are to be all marked thus (105)	3s. 10d.	John Edwards
22/12/45	500 pikes of good ash of the same length with steel heads at the same price to be brought in and paid for according to the former contracts. The pikes to be marked thus (106)	3s. 10d.	Thomas Bayman
22/12/45	600 pikes according to the former contracts. The pikes to be marked thus (107)	3s. 10d.	Anthony Webster
22/12/45	500 pikes according to the former contracts to be brought in at the times before mentioned by equal proportions (108)	3s. 10d.	Susanna White
22/12/45	600 pikes according to the former contracts to be brought in at the times before mentioned by equal proportions (109)	3s. 10d.	Edward Touch
22/12/45	650 pikes according to the former contract to be brought into the Tower of London before the last day [of] March for which they are to be paid as they bring them in. 200 to be marked thus (122) 225 to be marked thus (123) 225 to be marked thus (124)	3s. 10d.	Anthony Webster, Susanna White & Thomas Bayman
22/12/45	250 pikes according to the former contract to be brought into the Tower of London at the time beforementioned for which it is contracted, he shall be paid as he brings them in, for performance whereof has put his hand to be marked thus (125)	3s. 10d.	John Edwards

Date	Quantity and type	Price each	Contractor
23/12/45	400 pikes of good ash and 16 foot long with steel heads at 3s. 10d. apiece to be brought into the Tower of London as follows: 100 of them the last of this instant December, 100 more the last day of January, 100 more the last of February & the other 100 the last of March next following, for which it is contracted that he shall be paid as he brings them in for performance whereof he has set his hand. The pikes are to be marked thus (1)	3s. 10d.	John Thacker
8/12/46	500 pikes of good ash and 16 foot long with steel heads at 3s. 10d. apiece to be brought into the Tower of London, for which it is contracted, for he shall be paid upon certificate of the Ordnance Office, the receipt of the said pikes for performance whereof he has set his hand. The pikes are to be marked thus AW 500 Robert Thacker, marked R 200 Susanna White, marked S 300 John Edwards, marked E 200 Bartholomew Wray, marked BS 200 Thomas Bayman, marked TB 250 Silvester Keen, marked BK 250 Ralph Boulter, marked BK (Partners) Total 2,400	3s. 10d.	Anthony Webster, et al
	At the Committee for the Army 8/12/45 The Committee approves these contracts, and desires that the Officers of the Ordnance will take notice thereof and carefully see that the provisions be answerable to the agreements and for as many of the provisions as they shall receive in and allow to certify the same unto this Committee. Robert Scawen		

Table 15: Warrants for Payments to Contractors for the Delivery of Pikes to the Ordnance Office for the NMA (TNA, SP28/352/1; Bodl. Lib., Ms Eng. hist. C14; Ms Eng. hist. C244)

Date	Quantity and type	Price each	Contractor
24/3/45	200 long pikes in full of his contract	4s. 2d.	John Edwards
3/4/45	200 long pikes in part of his contract	4s. 2d.	John Edwards
19/4/45	1000 long pikes in part of his contract	4s. 2d.	Owen Rowe
23/4/45	200 long pikes in full of his contract	4s. 2d.	John Edwards
26/4/45	500 long pikes in full of his contract	4s. 2d.	Elizabeth Thacker
28/4/45	1000 long pikes in part of his contract	4s. 2d.	Owen Rowe
15/5/45	200 long pikes in full of his contract	4s. 2d.	John Edwards
2/6/45	100 long pikes in full of his contract	4s. 2d.	John Bayman
5/6/45	200 long pikes in full of his contract	4s. 2d.	John Edwards

Although there are a few instances of 15-foot-long Spanish pikes being issued to troops during the Civil Wars, the idea that the New Model Army was considering a general reduction in the length of pikes at this time, given the relatively small quantities involved, is difficult to substantiate. One report of the siege of Drogheda by Catholic forces under Féilim Ó Néill during the Irish Rebellion of 1641 noted that in the course of an assault on a breach in the town wall the defenders, 'finding the rebels' pikes to be shorter than theirs by a yard, charged them home, and the Lord Moor (coming in with some horse) and Sir John Borlace hastened to the breach, and kept out any more from entering, and most of those that came in were cut off'.[15] Likewise, complains made about Scotch troops at Benburb in 1646 who cut off a foot or two from their pikes should be regarded in the context of longer (18 foot) Irish-made weapons and the characteristics of handling pikes in windy conditions.[16] Henry Hexham, an English writer who had served in the Low Countries, illustrated a lozenge-shaped pike head in his military manual, while the same style is depicted by Jacob de Gheyn in his military manual of 1607.[17] In the 1670s the British professional soldier, Roger Boyle, Earl of Orrery stated that he was 'very desirous, that all our pikes may be sixteen foot and a half long, the staves to be of seasoned ash, which are strong, and light; and that from the iron heads of the pikes, there may be thin iron plates for four foot deep. Lozenge heads I like well, both because they are sharp to enter, and when entered, broad to wound with'. He also recommended:

> The pikes armed at the points with lozenge heads, if the cheeks, or sides of the pikes are not armed with thin plates of iron four foot deep, are very apt to be broken off near the heads, if the push be vigorous, and the resistance considerable. Nor is this all, for unless the pikes be armed with those thin iron plates, they are easily cut off with sharp swords, for the pike, especially toward the end, is carried tapering, to poise it the better, and thereby renders it the more flippant for those who use it; so that the slenderer part of the pike, if unarmed, is the more liable to be cut off, it being there nearest the enemy; whereas if the pikes were armed with those thin plates, and four foot deep, no cutting swords (which are always of the shortest) could destroy the pikes, since that part of the staff of the pike which is unarmed, would be out of the reach of the horseman's sharp cutting sword.[18]

15 Rushworth, *Historical Collections*, V, p.506.

16 E. H. (ed.), *The History of the War in Ireland, from 1641–1652, by a British officer of the regiment of Sir John Clotworthy* (Dublin: McGlashan & Gill, 1873), p.49. The entire quote reads: 'Withal to my knowledge, the soldiers, some were not strong [enough] in the British Army for his pike in a windy day, would cut off a foot, and some two, of their pikes, which is a damned thing to be suffered'.

17 Henry Hexham, *The First Part of the Principles of the Art Military practiced in the Warres of the United Netherlands* (Delft: 1642); Jacob de Gheyn, *Wapenhandelinghe van Roers Musquetten ende Spiessen* (The Hague: 1607).

18 Roger Boyle, Earl of Orrery, *A Treatise of the Art of War dedicated to the King's Most Excellent Majesty* (1677), pp.27–28.

Orrery's 'plates of iron four foot deep' are also referred to as cheeks, bars or languets in contemporary documents. Though none of the descriptions of pikes issued to the New Model Army in 1645–1646 mention these, one contract made on 12 January 1654 for 5,000 pikes specifies 'the bars to be strong and serviceable, in length 2 feet or two and twenty inches'. Equally, on 20 October 1657 an agreement was made for 3,500 pikes that were 'to be furnished at 3s. 4d. apiece, to be made of good ash, 16 feet long, bars to be strong and serviceable, the length to be 2 feet or 22 inches, the staves to be coloured with *aqua fortis*'.[19] The frequently held view is that languets were fitted to prevent the socketed pike heads from being cut off, but it is possible that they were also there to protect the shaft of the pike as it tapered towards the point, and as such might have distributed the force of impact over a larger area.

The most common form of pike head in the British Isles seems to have been the 'small steel head' recommended by George Monck, which sounds comparable to the 'well-steeled, 8 inches long, broad, strong, and sword-pointed' head stipulated in *Directions for Musters.* At Benburb the Irish pikes, according to one of the defeated officers, possessed heads that were 'far better to pierce, being four square and small', while the Scottish pike heads were 'broad-headed, which are the worst in the world'.[20] As previously noted, one contract for the supply of pikes to the New Model – that for 1,000 agreed with Rowe on 9 April 1645 and delivered in full 19 days later – specified that they were to be 'well-headed and footed'.[21] The latter probably refers to butt rings or ferrules, as specified by 1638 manual – 'the butt-end bound with a ring of iron' – a ring of flattened iron with possibly a retaining cross rivet attached to the butt of the pike. These are mentioned nowhere else in the abbreviated contracts, which either means that it was omitted, or it was regarded as a standard feature of pike staves and there was no requirement to state it. In June 1649 Captain Edward Tomlins was paid in full on his contract for £79 for 'staves and putting on 790 pike-heads for Ireland', in addition to delivering 1,600 backs, breasts, and pots, and 1,600 muskets.

Nonetheless, on 3 April 1651 the Council of State ordered the payment of £100 15s. to Edward Tench 'for 1,990 pike heads and feet, and 10 cases to pack them in for Ireland', while a further £50 12s. was to be given to the same contractor 19 days later for supplying '1,000 pike heads and 1,000 pike feet for the forces in the North of Ireland'.[22] Correspondingly, 6,000 heads and sockets for pikes, along with 500 barrels of powder, 300 cases of pistols and holsters, 500 snaphaunce locks for muskets, and 1,000 barrels of shot were sent to Ireland.[23] Hence, during this period at least, both heads and butt rings were regarded standard components of pikes. Such items must have been shipped to Ireland with the expectation that they would be fitted to staves produced by local craftsmen, possibly to reduce the cost of transportation. Some of the pikes issued to Irish Confederate troops in September 1642

19 TNA, WO55/1753, unfol.

20 George Monck, *Observations upon Military and Political Affairs* (London: 1671), p.26.; *History of the War in Ireland*, p.49.

21 TNA, SP28/352/1, unfol.; WO47/1, f. 235r; ML, Ms 46 78/708, fol. 110v.

22 *CSPD: Interregnum 1649–50*, p.573; *CSPD: Interregnum 1651*, pp.556 & 559.

23 *CSPI 1647–1660*, p.691.

had heads imported from France and Spain. Likewise, in February 1643 70 pike staves and 70 heads were sent from the Royalist magazine at Oxford 'to be headed', while on 22 April 1,040 pike heads were received into the stores there.[24] Pike heads with longer, four-sided diamond-shaped blades were excavated at the Jamestown Fort, while the image of pike shafts and loose heads in the Book of Armaments of Emperor Maximilian I (1459–1519) show both types of the latter, stored in barrels.[25]

The Committee for the Army also provided quantities of weapons to other Parliamentarian forces other than the New Model during the period 1645–1646. One warrant, dated 26 June 1645, was for the payment of £33 6s. 8d. for 160 pikes bought by the Committee of the Militia of London from William Thacker 'toward the furnishing of the regiment under the command of Colonel Bradley at 4s 2d apiece.'[26] On 24 March 1645 the first batch of 200 'long pikes' (possibly a synonym for English pikes) specifically for the use of Fairfax's Army was delivered by the pike maker John Edwards, for which he received payment 'in part of his contract' on 4 April. Edwards provided a further 200 pikes at 4s. 2d. apiece soon afterwards, for which on 15 April he was paid 'in full of his contract'.[27] The clear implication is that a previous arrangement for 400 pikes was fulfilled, although this does not appear in any of the notifications of contracts. The Committee for the Army agreed a further contract with Edwards on 1 April, this time for '600 long pikes'; these were duly received into the Ordnance Office stores in consignments of 200, on 22 April, 13 May and 2 June 1645 respectively.[28] Likewise, on 10 April 'Elizabeth Thacker, widow' agreed with the Committee to provide 500 pikes costing 4s. 2d. each. These were duly delivered 11 days later, and she was paid in full on 26 April.[29] It was on 9 June that Sir Thomas Fairfax reportedly marched to Sherington, two miles northeast of Newport Pagnell, 'and appointed a general rendezvous Tuesday of the whole forces near his present headquarters. As to the state of his Army, some refreshing being had for the foot, some more arms, 2,000 of which this day came to them, and some other necessaries for the horse, as pistols, etc., they are ready to engage when the Royalist army please'.[30]

A quantity of pikes was procured, however, from Colonel Owen Rowe. With 1,000 pikemen's backs, breasts and helmets these had formerly been in the possession of the Earl of Essex's Army and returned to the stores. Hence, on 9 April 1645 Rowe was contracted to supply the New Model with '1000 long pikes well-headed and footed at 4s., half in ready money the rest at three months'. The initial batch

24 BL, Ms Add. 34325, f. 30r; TNA, WO55/1661, f. 18r; James Hogan (ed.), *Letters and Papers Relating to the Irish Rebellion between 1642–46* (Dublin: Irish Manuscripts Commission, 1936), p.133; *ROP*, I, pp.77 & 202.

25 Bayerische Staatsbibliothek, Zeugbuch Kaiser Maximilians I – BSB Cod. icon. 222, f. 71r; https://historicjamestowne.org/collections/artifacts/pike – Object numbers 00271-JR, 00272-JR.

26 TNA, SP28/30/7, fol. 757r.

27 TNA, SP28/352/1, unfol.; Bodl. Lib., Ms Eng, C14, f. 2r.

28 TNA, WO47/1, f. 209r; Bodl. Lib., Ms Eng, C14, ff. 15r, 21v, 25r; ML, Ms 46 78/708, f. 114r. WO47/1 gives the date of the indenture as 1 April, though Ms 46 78/708 dates it to 4 April. Given the relative haphazard nature of the latter source, 1 April 1645 has been adhered to here.

29 TNA, SP28/352, unfol.; Bodl. Lib., Ms Eng, C14, f. 14v; ML, Ms 46 78/708, f. 44r.

30 *The Moderate Intelligencer*, 5–12 June 1645. TT, E288[7].

of 500 pikes was delivered (or transferred in this instance) on 19 April, while the outstanding quantity was received nine days later.[31] The phrase 'ready money' should not be interpreted too exactingly. During the early modern period it could be taken to mean payment within a period of up to 6 months.[32] Rowe and his colleague, John Bradley – the chief purchasing agent for arms and munitions on behalf of the Committee of Safety – had supplied various Parliamentarian forces, including the Earl of Essex's Army, from September 1642 onwards. During the following year they procured around 2,500 pikes, in addition to large amounts of other equipment. Likewise, in March 1645 Rowe delivered 200 pikes to the Aylesbury garrison.[33] It must be realised, however, that Bradley and Rowe operated a separate magazine in London that was independent of the Ordnance Office. This was established by order of the Commons on 1 July 1642, and going by Bradley and Rowe's account book it held relatively limited stocks of military stores.[34] Between 1644 and 1646 the English Parliament provided the Scottish Covenanter Army campaigning in the Midlands with 4,679 pikes, while on 21 June 1648 the Commons ordered that 6,000 muskets with bandoliers; 1,500 cases of pistols with holsters and spanners; 1,500 saddles; and 4,000 pikes be provided for the counties of the Northern Association.[35] The level of stocks in the Ordnance Office stores at this time is unknown, though only 2,040 pikes were received into the stores during the entire year, and most of those were issued to Sir Thomas Fairfax's regiments in London and the southeast of England.[36]

Because of the nature of the logistics employed by the New Model Army, whereby large quantities of supplies of arms, ammunition and clothing quantities were issued to the train of artillery, to be held as 'front line' stocks, or more usually, distributed through commissaries directly to the army's supply bases; direct deliveries of pikes to individual regiments appear rarely in the documents. The only clue to the items carried by the train of artillery itself for individual regiments of foot is contained in its establishment of March 1645, which designated 1 close waggon 'to carry the surgery chest, spare arms and ammunition of every regiment', each vehicle to be drawn by 6 draught horses. Given that close waggons might carry around 2 tons apiece, it seems unlikely that anything more than a small quantity of regimental spare weapons could be transported in them.[37] A total of 1,200 pikes were supplied to the train by the Office of the Ordnance for distribution to the New Model on 14 April 1645; 1,900 on 1 May; 500 on 12 May; 500 on 25 May; 200 on 29 May; 1,000 on 14 July; 1,000 on 18 September; and 500 Spanish pikes on 27 September.[38] Those issued on 14 July were transported as part of a larger consignment of arms by Francis Carter, who seven days later was paid the sum of £70 15s. 0d. 'for the carriage of the arms from London to Reading, being 3,000 muskets, 1,000 pikes, 3,000 bandoliers,

31 TNA, SP28/352/1, unfol.; WO47/1, f. 235r; ML, Ms 46 78/708, fol. 110r.
32 William Beveridge, *Prices and wages in England from the Twelfth to the Nineteenth Century* (London: Longmans, 1939), I, p.623.
33 *CSPD 1644–5*, p.348.
34 *CJ*, II, p.648; TNA, SP28/147/3, unfol.
35 *CJ*, V, p.609.
36 TNA, WO49/82 *passim*; SP28/140/3, *passim*.
37 TNA, SP28/145, ff. 60r–63v.
38 TNA, SP28/352/1, unfol.; WO47/1, f. 215r; WO55/1646, *passim*; WO55/1647, *passim*.

3,000 several and both powder, bullet and match'.[39] By the end of September 1645 4,300 pikes had been issued from the London stores, although there could have been further quantities procured from local sources that remain unrecorded in central sources. The purchasing of arms from regional suppliers appears to have been more common among local Parliamentarian forces and some Royalist armies. In supplying Sir William Brereton's army in Cheshire, in 1643 the sequestrators of Macclesfield hundred disbursed £2 10s. 'for making pikes for the public service', while the Manchester manufacturer William Duncalfe received £1 4s. for 24 pike-heads at 12d. each. On 20 May 1645 Nicholas Higginbottom provided drums and pikes for the foot companies in the Wirral garrisons.[40] Similarly, the accounts of the Royalist garrison of Lichfield include payments for the cutting down of wood to make pike shafts and their manufacture, including locally made pike heads.[41]

Though the warrants concerned with the supply of weapons, ammunition and other stores for the New Model Army deal mainly with road transportation from London to its principal magazine and distribution centre at Reading, consignments were also sent by flat-bottomed barges (lighters) on the River Thames. Between April and June 1645 about 75 tons of biscuit and 44.9 tons of cheese were purchased and brought by river from London to Reading and Windsor for Sir Thomas Fairfax's troops, while from April onwards drafts of recruits, and large quantities of munitions and arms were transported upriver and delivered to the New Model.[42] On 21 July Francis Carter transported by barge 1,000 pikes, 3,000 muskets and bandoliers, 4,000 swords and belts, with 2 tons of powder, match, and shot.[43] The Council of Sate ordered in December 1651 'the governor or officer-in-chief at Wallingford to deliver to Commissary John Phipps all the powder, match, bullet, and so forth, with certain exceptions, and bring away the said stores in a barge to the Tower, by which means the 300 barrels of powder for Ireland, and 100 grenadoe shells for the mortar pieces at Jersey, may be forthwith had, while the ships are lading'. However, on 29 January 1652 it was reported that one of the barges bringing ammunition from Wallingford Castle sank at a lock near Streatley, and 'of the powder, 200 barrels, and of the match, 12 tons, half is missing, and the rest it is feared unserviceable. Most of the bullet, 12 tons, is saved, if they can weigh up the barge'.[44] Colonel John Venn's newly raised Parliamentarian regiment which occupied Windsor Castle was transported from London in October 1642 with all its personnel, arms, horses, ammunition, and supplies in 'boats and barges', while various sums were paid to bargemen for carriage.[45]

39 TNA, SP28/126/1, f. 1r.

40 BL, Ms Harley 2130, ff. 88r & 91v.

41 Lichfield Record Office, Ms Lichfield 24, unf.

42 TNA, SP28/29/1, ff. 244r–245r; SP28/30/4, ff. 363r–364v, 371r; Aryeh J. S. Nusbacher, 'Civil Supply in the Civil War: Supply of Victuals to the New Model Army on the Naseby Campaign, 1–14 June 1645', *EHR*, 115 (2000), pp.145–160, (p. 152).

43 TNA, SP28/31/1, f. 75r.

44 *CSPD 1651–2*, pp.71, 122.

45 TNA, SP28/16/2, ff. 171r–171v; SP28/34/2, ff. 171r; SP28/126/1, ff. 8r–22v; SP28/263, ff. 76r–79r.

In 1644 various loads of clothing, arms, cannon and ammunition were transported to both Reading and Windsor for the Parliamentarian forces from Thames wharfs in London.[46] Moreover, accurate and detailed intelligence reports of the movement of weapons and ordnance to Royalist-held Reading, were fed to Sir Samuel Luke, Essex's Scoutmaster in March 1644. Consequently, on 7 March a scout from Oxford reported, 'on Sunday night last [3 March] there were 6 brass pieces of ordnance and a great number of pikes, muskets, and ammunition conveyed from thence to Reading by water', while on 6 March he observed '2 great iron pieces and as much ammunition as a barge could carry loaded for Reading, which (as he hears) were afterwards to be sent to Greenland Howse.' Two days later another spy coming from Oxford reported in similar terms of '8 or 9 pieces of ordnance and great store of ammunition' sent to Reading on Monday 4 March, in addition to '2 great iron pieces and a whole barge full of ammunition two days later.'[47] Additionally, with the disbandment of parts of Sir Thomas Fairfax's Army in May 1645, following the cessation of hostilities in England, it was proposed that:

> all the Train and provisions belonging to it which are at Oxford or Wallingford to be brought to London and put into the stores in the Tower. The Train to come from Oxford to Wallingford by land and thence the whole to come by water to London. The horse belonging to the Train to come by land with such other things as the Comptroller thinks best to send in that way.[48]

Included in the 'Inventory of armaments issued by the Master General of the Ordnance to Peregrine Pelham for the defence of Hull according to an order of the House of Commons', taken on 4 July 1643 were 940 pikes, in addition to other arms, including 2,656 infantry corselets and helmets; 5,570 collars of bandoliers; 1,216 muskets; 390 swords; 236 partizans; 280 bills; and 32 carbines.[49] On 19 March 1644 102 muskets with the like number of bandoliers and 50 pikes were issued from Charles I's magazine at Oxford 'for the arming of the new raised men of the Queen's Lifeguard', while one consignment delivered to Royalist-held Reading on 24 October were 60 muskets, 60 powder bags with girdles and hangers, and 200 long pikes.[50] Warrants issued by the Committee for the Army to the Ordnance Office and others for the delivery and transportation of pikes – mainly amongst consignments of clothing, ammunition and other weapons – to Sir Thomas Fairfax's foot during the remainder of the New Model's campaign in the Southwest of England in 1646 indicate that large quantities of stores were involved. Accordingly, on 16 January 1646 Waggon master General Thomas Richardson was ordered to transport 1,200 pikes 'out of the stores … to be sent to Portsmouth for Sir Thomas Fairfax's Army', which were delivered six days later; 50 pikes were sent with clothing to Sergeant

46 TNA, SP28/140/4, f. 40v; SP28/262, ff. 217r & 219r.
47 Tibbutt (ed.), *Letters*, pp.261–262.
48 *CSP Ireland 1647–1660*, p.752.
49 Hull History Centre, BRS/7/139.
50 TNA, WO55/459, f. 66r; WO55/1661, fol. 54v; *ROP*, I, pp.116; II, p.338.

Major John Browne 'to clothe and arm the old soldiers of [Rainborowe's] regiment' on 9 January, while on 13 January the unit received a second batch of 150 from Commissary Thomas Futter. On the same day Richardson conveyed 700 pikes, 1,700 coats and breeches, 1,500 shirts, 1,700 pairs of shoes, 1,700 pairs of stockings, 1,000 muskets with bandoliers, and 1,700 snapsacks to the army's new recruits waiting at Reading.

Richardson delivered a similar-sized batch (including 650 long pikes) on 14 February 1646 to equip recruits at Newport Pagnell, and on 26 February Browne's company of Rainborowe's regiment was supplied with 50 pikes, 100 matchlock muskets, 250 bandoliers, 100 coats, 100 pairs of breeches, 100 pairs of shoes, 100 shirts, 150 snapsacks and 2 drums. Likewise, on 26 March 1646 Richardson shipped 2,189 coats, 2,179 breeches, 2,184 pairs of stockings, 2,180 pairs of shoes, 1,200 shirts, 1,770 matchlocks, 1,775 bandoliers, 168 pikes, 36 drums furnished with cords, 1 ton of match, 10cwt of powder, and 10cwt musket shot to Northampton 'for the use of the new recruits there, being for the supply of Sir Thomas Fairfax's Army.'[51] Therefore, within the space of 10 weeks a total 2,968 pikes were issued directly to troops in the field from the Ordnance Office stores in London via the army's principal magazine at Reading, by commissaries and other logisticians. This equates to just under three-quarters of the 4,000 pikes estimated to resupply the New Model Army (amongst other clothing and arms) by Parliament on 29 December 1645.[52]

Like other military equipment, some batches of pikes received from suppliers into the Ordnance Office stores 'for the use of Sir Thomas Fairfax his Army' were identified either by recognisable maker's devices or numbers. Thus, on 23 December 1645, John Thacker of Fenchurch Street was contracted to deliver 400 pikes, '100 of them the last of this instant December, 100 more the last day of January, 100 more the last of February and the other 100 the last of March next following, for which it is contracted that he shall be paid as he brings them in for performance whereof he has set his hand. The pikes are to be marked thus (1)'.[53] These conditions were successfully met.[54] Something of methods employed by the Committee for the Army in administrating such indentures, in addition to those for other weapons and military equipment in December 1645 may be gleaned from the appended comments of its leader, Robert Scawen. He added, 'This Committee does approve of these contracts, and do desire that the Officers of the Ordnance will take notice thereof and carefully see that the provisions be answerable to their agreements. And for as many of the provisions as they shall receive in and allowed to certify the same unto this Committee'.[55]

Another supplier, Anthony Webster was obligated to deliver on 8 December 1646, '500 pikes of good ash and 16 foot long with steel heads at 3s. 10d. apiece to be brought into the Tower of London, for which it is contracted, for he shall be paid upon certificate of the Ordnance Office, the receipt of the said pikes for performance

51 TNA, WO55/1646, *passim*.
52 *CJ*, IV, p.388.
53 TNA, SP28/352/1, unfol.; WO47/1, f. 272v; ML, Ms 46 78/708, f. 16r.
54 TNA, WO55/1663, ff. 61r, 78v; Bod. Lib., MS Eng. hist. C14, ff. 2r & 70r.
55 TNA, WO47/1, f. 272v; ML, Ms 46 78/708, f. 16r.

whereof he has set his hand'.[56] Webster's pikes were to be marked AW. At the same time, seven other suppliers agreed to provide the following quantities:

> Robert Thacker, 500 pikes marked R
> Susanna White, 200 pikes marked S
> John Edwards, 300 pikes marked E
> Bartholomew Wray, 200 pikes marked BS
> Thomas Bayman, 200 pikes marked TB
> Silvester Keen, 250 pikes marked BK
> Ralph Boulter and partners, 250 pikes marked RB

Webster's consignment arrived in the stores on 24 December 1646; those of Thacker, White, Edwards, Wray and Bayman on 31 December; whereas Keen's and Boulter's were received on 23 February 1647.[57] Further quantities of pikes were procured for the Commonwealth forces during 1647–1648, which continued throughout the 1650s. In mid-1648 6,000 muskets, 1,500 saddles and 4,000 pikes were ordered for the supply of the regiments in Northern England.[58] In his letter to the Speaker on 22 August Lieutenant General Oliver Cromwell described that at the recent fight at Preston:

> the enemy was put into disorder; many men slain, many prisoners taken; the Duke, with most of the Scots horse and foot, retreated over the bridge, where, after a very hot dispute betwixt the Lancashire regiments, part of my Lord General's, and them, being often at push of pike, they were beaten from the bridge; and our horse and foot, following them, killed many and took divers prisoners.

Additionally, he reported that at Winwick two days later,

> We held them [the Engager foot regiments] in some dispute till our army came up; they maintaining the pass with resolution for many hours; ours and theirs coming to push of pike and very close charges.[59]

Between July 1649 and February 1650 five pike makers supplied the Ordnance Office with a total of 14,750 pikes to be transported to Ireland, with Anthony Webster, who had provided large quantities to the New Model Army, bringing in 11,700 alone.[60] During the late 1650s quantities of pikes were supplied to the English forces in Flanders. According to its commander, Major General Thomas Morgan, at the Battle of the Dunes on 14 June 1658 the English contingent, drawn up in advance of the

56 TNA, PRO/37/4, unfol.
57 TNA, SP28/140/3, unfol.; SP28/352/1, unfol.
58 *CJ*, V, p.609.
59 Andrew Barclay, Tim Wales, John Morrill (eds), *The Letters, Writings, and Speeches of Oliver Cromwell* (Oxford: OUP, 2022), I, p.200.
60 *CSPD 1649–50*, pp.571–600.

Anglo-French army, 'on hands and knees crept up the hill, and gave the enemy's foot two good volleys, and with our pikes forced them to retreat'.[61] On 15 July the Ordnance Officers at the Tower of London were ordered to supply, 'in addition to former consignments', 1,000 pikes, with 500 corslets and headpieces; 700 backs, breasts and pots; 700 pairs of pistols and holsters; 700 carbines; and 1,000 muskets. Additionally, an order was issued on 2 September that '700 pikes and muskets be removed from Dover Castle to Mardyke, left there in May 1657 by Sir Thomas Reynolds' forces'.[62]

Matchlock Muskets

Musketeers during the British Civil Wars were commonly issued with the smoothbore, muzzle-loading matchlock musket (often supplied early in the war with a rest), bandolier and sword, and this was no different in the New Model Army. Instructions issued in 1636 for arming the English and Welsh militia declared that muskets were meant to be of one standard bore (12 bullets to the pound 'rolled in', resulting in a barrel bore roughly matching the diameter of a 10 bore bullet) and that each musketeer 'shall be furnished with a sufficient whole musket, the barrel thereof shall be four feet in length and no more', the total length of the weapon being five feet two inches. Furthermore,

> every such person appointed to serve with a full musket shall be further furnished and armed with a good bandolier, and with fifteen good and serviceable charges of turned wood, covered with leather and fastened there unto. Also with a good primer, worm and scourer, and a bullet bag annexed unto it, with a mould to cast such bullets as aforesaid.[63]

On 10 March 1645 the Commons resolved 'that 500 muskets, furnished now in the Magazine, which were of those which Mr Hill and Mr Pennoyer did furnish to the State, be delivered to Colonel White', for the supply of Fairfax's new army.[64] During spring 1645 matchlock muskets costing 10s., 11s. and 11s. 6d. were purchased for the New Model, while in 1646 Parliament contracted for '*English* matchlock muskets and bandoliers, at 14*s. apiece* for its forces in Ireland.'[65] Although minor variations in the price of muskets during the period of the Civil Wars are evident, it is worth noting that there was no general upward trend in the amounts paid by the Committee for the Army to gunsmiths and contractors. Moreover, the predominant position of the Committee in the business of procurement from 1645 onwards may have enabled it to hold down prices by bargaining more effectively, contracting for larger quantities

---

61 *Clarke Papers*, III, p.158.

62 *CSPD Interregnum 1658–9*, pp.94, 128.

63 Wrye, *State Papers Relating to Musters*, p.89; David R. Lawrence, *The Complete Soldier: Military Books and Military Culture in Early Stuart England, 1603–1645* (Brill: Leiden, 2008), p.189.

64 *CJ*, IV, p.74.

65 TNA, SP28/29/2, f. 249r; ML, Ms 46 78/708, ff. 81r–81v, 87r.

and offering suppliers a better opportunity for prompt payment. Allowing for a small number of inconsistencies in the records – some batches of weapons appear in receipts books without corresponding warrants for payment, and there are disparities in some of the dates – between spring 1645 and June 1646 a total of 16,250 matchlock muskets were obtained and paid for by the Army Committee for the use of Fairfax's Army. Large quantities of bastard musket shot, costing £17 per ton were supplied to both Essex's forces in December 1642 and the New Model in 1645 by plumbers and shot casters such as Daniel Judd.[66]

Nine London gunsmiths – John Norcott, John Tucker, Richard Jones, William Fell, Edward Barker, Edward Burrows and a consortium made up of William Greaves, William Watson, and George Day – initially supplied the Ordnance Office with matchlocks 'English full bore and proof' costing 11s. 6d. each. The earliest known delivery was that of '250 new muskets and 100 dragoon muskets' brought in by Norcott on 7 April 1645. The following day Tucker delivered 100 matchlocks (in addition to 252 pairs of pistols with holsters), and Jones supplied a further 300 muskets. Likewise, a total of 880 muskets were delivered by Greaves and his partners on 12 April, before delivering another 600 a week later.[67] Such quantities may have been specifically intended for the replenishment of the Tower stores, because on 10 April 1645 2,391 muskets, along with 5,000 bandoliers, 25 snaphaunces, 1,200 pikes, match and artillery ammunition had been delivered to Commissary Phipps of the New Model's train of artillery 'for the supply and furnishing of the said army'. Similarly, 1,986 matchlocks were transferred from the Earl of Manchester's former train on 17 April and supplied to Fairfax's troops eight days later, while a further 2,000 weapons were issued directly out of the stores on 18 April.[68]

Warrants ordering payments to Norcott and the other three suppliers in full of their contracts – following the receipt and inspection of the items – show that Tucker and Jones obtained remuneration on 9 April, with Greaves et al receiving theirs on 14 and 23 April respectively. The subsequent production capacity of this consortium is no better illustrated than by its delivery of 3,060 matchlock muskets on 16 July 1646 at a price of 11s. 6d. apiece.[69] A discrepancy exists, however, with the muskets delivered by Norcott on 7 April 1645, in that no warrant exists for the receipt of this order, the earliest being that issued on 15 April for '310 matchlock muskets in full of his contract'.[70] Norcott continued to supply large quantities of firearms to the New Model, though, delivering a total of 1,070 muskets of this type between 7 April and 2 May 1645. In addition to the quantities received from suppliers, during the same month the Committee for the Army requested 600 matchlock muskets at 10s. apiece from Lieutenant Colonel Hammond, the commander of the train of artillery, probably from existing stocks in the Tower stores, although it seems that only 491 'old muskets' were delivered.[71]

66 TNA, SP28/145, unfol.; SP28/31/4, f. 441r; SP30/37, f. 13r; SP28/32/3, f. 352r.
67 TNA, SP28/352/1, unfol.; Bodl. Lib., Ms Eng. hist. C14, ff. 5r, 6v, 9v, 14r.
68 TNA, SP28/29/1, f. 172r; WO55/1647, unfol.; WSL, Ms Salt 463, unfol.
69 TNA, SP28/29/1, ff. 205r–206v, 218r; SP28/31/5, f. 527r; SP28/352/1, unfol.
70 TNA, SP28/29/1, f. 219r; Bodl. Lib., Ms Eng. hist. C14, f. 10r.
71 TNA, SP28/352/1, unfol.; WO47/1, f. 391r; ML, Ms 46 78/708, f. 109r.

Table 16: Notification of Contracts to the Ordnance Office for the Supply of Matchlock Muskets for the NMA (TNA, WO47/1; WO55/1646; ML, Ms 46 78/708)

Date	Quantity and type	Price each	Contractor
3/4/45	3000 muskets	11s. 6d.	Richard Jones, John Norcott & William Fell
3/4/45	2000 muskets	11s. 6d.	John Watson, William Watson & their partners
10/4/45	600 matchlock muskets	10s. 0d.	Lt General Thomas Hammond
5/7/45	1000 muskets	11s. 0d.	Edward Barker
11/7/45	2000 muskets English full bore and proof	11s. 0d.	William & John Watson, Edward Burrows, Thomas Smith, William Greaves & George Day
11/7/45	100 matchlock muskets English full bore and proof	11s. 0d.	William Fell
26/7/45	300 muskets	11s. 0d.	Edward Burrows
1/8/45	You [Officers of the Ordnance] are to amend the certificate of Edwards Burrows [above] for 300 muskets at 11s. 0d., which is in the certificate at 11s. 6d. a musket		
22/12/45	200 matchlock muskets full bore and proof to be brought into the Tower of London as follows: 50 of them the last of this instant December, 50 the last day of January, 50 more the last of February & 50 more the last of March, for which it is contracted he shall be paid as he brings them in for performance whereof, he has set his hand. The muskets are to be marked thus (74)	10s. 0d.	John Silk
22/12/45	300 matchlock muskets according to the former contracts to be brought into the Tower of London at the times beforementioned by equal proportions. The muskets are to be marked thus (75)	10s. 0d.	John Silk
22/12/45	100 matchlock muskets according to the former contracts to be brought into the Tower of London at the times beforementioned by equal proportions. The muskets are to be marked thus (76)	10s. 0d.	William Gardner
22/12/45	500 matchlock muskets according to the former contracts to be brought into the Tower of London at the times beforementioned by equal proportions. 125 of them to be marked thus (77) 125 more marked thus (78) 125 more marked thus (79) The other 125 marked thus (80)	10s. 0d.	Robert Marden, Miles Knight, William Judge & Andrew Tyer

Date	Quantity and type	Price each	Contractor
22/12/45	100 matchlock muskets according to the former contracts to be brought into the Tower of London at the times beforementioned by equal proportions and marked with a swan	10s. 0d.	John Wheelwright
22/12/45	100 matchlock muskets according to the former contracts to be brought into the Tower of London at the times beforementioned by equal proportions and marked thus (81)	10s. 0d.	John Eales
22/12/45	100 matchlock muskets according to the former contracts to be brought into the Tower of London at the times beforementioned by equal proportions and marked thus (82)	10s. 0d.	Walter Benge
22/12/45	100 matchlock muskets according to the former contracts to be brought into the Tower of London at the times beforementioned by equal proportions and marked thus (83)	10s. 0d.	Henry Cox
22/12/45	100 matchlock muskets according to the former contracts to be brought into the Tower of London at the times beforementioned by equal proportions and marked thus [blank]	10s. 0d.	Richard Staples
22/12/45	100 matchlock muskets according to the former contracts to be brought into the Tower of London at the times beforementioned by equal proportions and marked thus (84)	10s. 0d.	Henry Charsley
22/12/45	200 matchlock muskets according to the former contracts to be brought into the Tower of London at the times beforementioned by equal proportions and marked thus (85)	10s. 0d.	William Wallys
22/12/45	100 matchlock muskets according to the former contracts to be brought into the Tower of London at the times beforementioned by equal proportions and marked thus (86)	10s. 0d.	Richard Nunneley
22/12/45	100 matchlock muskets according to the former contracts to be brought into the Tower of London at the times beforementioned by equal proportions and marked thus (87)	10s. 0d.	Richard Jones
22/12/45	2000 matchlock muskets according to the former contracts to be brought into the Tower of London at the times beforementioned by equal proportions and marked thus (88)	10s. 0d.	William Watson
22/12/45	600 matchlock muskets according to the former contracts to be brought into the Tower of London at the times beforementioned by equal proportions and marked thus (89)	10s. 0d.	William Fell
22/12/45	1000 matchlock muskets according to the former contracts to be brought into the Tower of London at the times beforementioned by equal proportions and marked thus (90)	10s. 0d.	Edward Burrows

Date	Quantity and type	Price each	Contractor
22/12/45	1000 matchlock muskets according to the former contracts to be brought into the Tower of London at the times beforementioned by equal proportions and marked thus (91)	10s. 0d.	Edward Barker
22/12/45	250 matchlock muskets according to the former contracts to be brought into the Tower of London at the times beforementioned by equal proportions and marked thus [blank]	10s. 0d.	Robert Hamond
22/12/45	100 matchlock muskets full bore and proof according to the former contracts to be brought into the Tower of London at the times beforementioned by equal proportions for which they shall be paid as they bring them in for performance, whereof they have put their hands. 40 marked thus (119) 30 marked thus (120) 30 marked thus (121)	10s. 0d.	William Burton, William Bates & George Fisher

Table 17: Warrants for Payments to Contractors for the Delivery of Matchlock Muskets to the Ordnance Office for the NMA (TNA, SP28/29/1-2; SP28/30/4; SP28/30/4)

Date	Quantity and type	Price each	Contractor
9/4/45	100 matchlock muskets in full of his contract	11s. 6d.	John Tucker
9/4/45	350 matchlock muskets in full of his contract	11s. 6d.	Richard Jones
14/4/45	880 matchlock muskets	11s. 6d.	William Greaves, William Watson & George Day
15/4/45	310 matchlock muskets in full of his contract	11s. 6d.	John Norcott
15/4/45	750 matchlock muskets in full of his contract	11s. 6d.	Richard Jones
23/4/45	320 matchlock muskets in full of his contract	11s. 6d.	John Norcott
25/4/45	600 matchlock muskets in full of their contract	11s. 6d.	Wm Greaves, Wm Watson & Geo. Day
12/5/45	120 matchlock muskets in full of his contract	11s. 6d.	John Norcott
16/5/46	208 matchlock muskets in full of his contract	11s. 6d.	John Tucker
16/5/46	191 matchlock muskets in full of his contract	11s. 6d.	Richard Jones
23/5/46	520 matchlock muskets in full of his contract	11s. 6d.	Wm Greaves, Wm Watson & Geo. Day
16/7/46	3060 muskets	11s. 6d.	Wm Greaves, Wm Watson, Geo. Day & Thos Smith

On 29 December 1645 the Commons assented to a proposal from the Committee for the Army for the cost of supplying the New Model with arms, munitions, clothing, horses, and saddlery for its winter campaign in the West Country and at the siege of Oxford. This included the provision of 7,000 matchlocks.[72] Hence, 19 separate

72 *CJ*, IV, p.388.

contracts had been agreed with an additional 17 London gunsmiths to produce such quantities, this time at a cost of 10s. per item. Although these indentures do not survive, the Committee notified the Officers of the Ordnance on 22 December that accordingly the consignments would, 'according to the former contracts to be brought into the Tower of London at the times beforementioned by equal proportions and marked.'[73] A survey of the relevant receipts books and warrants indicates that all 7,000 muskets were subsequently delivered and paid for, the first batches (being 125 from Robert Murden, Miles Knight, William Judge and Andrew Ewer; and 50 muskets from William Gardner) coming in on 20 January 1646 and the final consignment of 100 received from William Fell on 27 April.[74] In all, a total of 16,480 matchlock muskets were issued to the New Model Army by the Ordnance Office in 1645 and 1646. On 14 July 1645 3,000 matchlock muskets were delivered to Reading magazine. These were transported with other arms, including 1,000 pikes, 3,000 bandoliers, with proportional powder, bullet, and match'.[75] In February 1646 Colonel Rainborowe's regiment of foot was equipped with 450 muskets and bandoliers, in addition to 200 pikes. Similarly, on 26 March 1,770 muskets were transported with other stores to Northampton to be issued to new recruits.[76]

There is some evidence of anxiety over the quality of muskets, pistols and pistol holsters supplied to the Ordnance Office. Apart from the recorded instances of sub-standard weapons being delivered to the stores, the Court of the Gunmakers' Company discussed measures for proving firearms on various occasions during the Civil Wars.[77] Before muskets, pistols and other small arms were paid for and accepted into the Ordnance Office, they required testing. This job technically belonged to the Proof Master of the Ordnance, who was responsible for testing each weapon, however, the gunmakers themselves often were issued gunpowder to proof their own firearms and certify that they were well-made. It took approximately two ounces of powder to proof each one, and since muskets normally used only one ounce of powder per shot, probably two rounds were fired from each weapon to test if it would burst or crack. Such arrangements could provide an opportunity for collusion between the Ordnance Officers and manufacturers, or at least a conflict of interests. In 1646 William Watson, who also provided firearms to the New Model Army, was described as 'Proof Master at the Tower Armoury', where he was engaged in proving small arms which had been brought to the stores. He was simultaneously Warden of the Gunmakers' Company.[78] Thus, contracts were made both with the furbishers employed at the Ordnance Office, and with gunsmiths and cutlers in the City.[79]

73 TNA, WO47/1, unfol.; ML, Ms 46 78/708, ff. 81r–87r.
74 TNA, SP28/140/3, ff. 69r–71v; Bodl. Lib., Ms Eng. hist. C14, ff. 65r–83v; Ms Eng. hist. C244, ff. 2r 15r–16r.
75 TNA, SP28/126/1, f. 1r.
76 TNA, WO55/1646, unfol.; WO55/1647, unfol.
77 TNA, WO47/1, ff. 230v, 233r.
78 TNA, WO55/1646, ff. 366r, 379v; W. M. Stern, 'Gunmaking in seventeenth century London', *JAAS*, I (1954) pp.55–100.
79 TNA, WO47/1, ff. 1r, 20r, 177r; 219v; WSL, Ms Salt 463, unfol.

On 17 April 1645 the gunsmith George Fisher was employed by the Officers of the Ordnance to overhaul 104 muskets. Of these, 52 were to be 'made clean and repaired'; 5 to be 'made clean and repaired, and new locks'; 25 'made clean and repaired, and new stocked'; and 22 'made clean and repaired, and new stocked and locked'. These weapons might have been some of the 1,986 muskets received into the Tower armoury from the Earl of Manchester's train the same day, while a further 1,500 arrived on 2 May 1645. Similarly, on 23 July George Tibbut was paid the sum of £30 for fixing 340 muskets belonging to the New Model Army at Windsor, and a further £111 5s. on 10 October 'for new stocking and locking of 470 muskets at 4s. 6d. apiece, and for fixing 110 muskets at Windsor at 1s. per piece'.[80] It is worth postulating that whereas 'repairing' such firearms would be obvious, the references to them being 'remade' or 'restocked' might have meant a method of reducing the weight of the stock from the older heavy type of musket that needed a rest, to the newer type that did not.[81] Although no references to the repair or restocking of cavalry pistols for the New Model Army are known, the detailed accounts of the Parliamentarian garrisons of Malmesbury and Great Chalfield include payments in 1645 for 'stocking the troopers' pistols per bill', and to 'the gunsmith for mending their arms per bill' and 'the joiner for stocking the troopers pistols, upon his bill'.[82]

One of the Ordnance Office receipts books includes entries relating to weapons 'received into the stores within the Office of the Small Guns at the Tower of London'. This was responsible for maintaining all muskets and other firearms purchased by the government, although its staff consisted of only one officer and two furbishers, meaning that it could only do minor maintenance on the weapons which were almost exclusively made by craftsmen in London. On 5 February 1648 Commissary Phipps delivered 1,002 matchlock muskets 'new stocked, locked, and fixed'; 1,339 muskets 'new stocked, locked, fixed and new proofed, including 159 bastard-bore' to the army.[83] Furthermore, in 1645 the reliability and quality of pistols, and pistol holsters was something of a concern to the Ordnance Office. The time taken to fulfil a contract might be extended if there were delays in proving the firearms, or if they were found to be unsatisfactory. Occasionally supplies were delivered without having first been proved – or test fired. On 3 April 1645 the Committee for the Army contracted with 'Mr Bartlett at the Excise Office' for 200 pairs of Dutch snaphaunce pistols full bore and 200 pair of holsters at a price of 28s. per set. Upon inspection 187 pairs were found to have been delivered without proof marks, while out of these 117 pairs were under bore. There is no record of any payment for these, however, which might be explained by the following warrant, issued by Robert Scawen, chairman of the Committee, on 2 May:

80 TNA, SP28/31/4, f. 546r; SP28/32/1, f. 9r.

81 Thanks to Stephen Ede-Borrett for this suggestion.

82 John Pafford (ed.), *Accounts of the Parliamentary Garrisons of Great Chalfield and Malmesbury, 1645–1646* (Wiltshire Archaeological and Natural History Society, 2 (1940), pp.75–78.

83 TNA, SP28/140/3, f. 140r.

> Whereas this Committee agreed and contracted with Samuel Bartlett for 200 pair of pistols for the service of the State, which he says are delivered into the storehouse in the Tower accordingly, which pistols some of them are not yet proved whether serviceable for the State. These are to require you to deliver back to the said Mr Bartlett the said 200 pair of pistols, to be carried by him to the gunsmiths to be proved, and after proof to receive them of him again, and certify the receipt and proof of the same pistols to this Committee.[84]

The previous day, the Army Committee instructed that these weapons be returned to Bartlett, who was to take them to the gunsmiths 'to be proved, and after proof to receive them of him again, and certify the receipt and proof of the same pistols to this Committee.'[85] Similarly, the gunsmith John Tucker was contracted for 1,200 pairs of pistols and holsters before 3 April, 200 at £1 7s. and 1,000 at £1 8s. per pair.[86] In reply, the officers declared that they had only obtained 910 pairs of pistols from him, 300 of which they had yet to inspect. A further 590 pairs were delivered by Tucker during May 1645, though it is unclear if they were proved either. Hence, the Committee ordered the Officers of the Ordnance on 25 April 1645 not to accept any more pistols from Tucker or his agents.[87]

Some of the holsters, specified in one contract agreed in December 1645 as being constructed of calfskins, 'inside and out well-sewed and lacquered', and costing 2s. 6d. a pair, were also found to be faulty. On 6 June 1645 the Committee of Both Kingdoms resolved 'that Captain Middleton be ordered to speak with the Committee of the Army to explain the defect of the holsters, that enquiry may be made as to who served them in order to punish for deceit'.[88] Indentures for the supply of holsters often took longer than most to complete, up to two months on some occasions. This may reflect the complexity of the manufacturing process, the length of time required to prepare the leather, and possibly a shortage of raw materials. Hence, the 500 'calfskin holsters' contracted for on 28 June 1645 were delivered in semi-weekly batches of 100 between 7 August and 3 September.[89] According to Ordnance Office records, in 1645–6 a total of 7,740 pairs of pistols – mostly described as 'snaphaunce pistols', although there is evidence that a few of those issued came with spanners, thus denoting wheellocks – with holsters were ordered for the use of Sir Thomas Fairfax's Army, whereas 6,121 were delivered to cavalry units.

During April 1645 alone, over 1,500 pairs of pistols and the same quantity of holsters were issued to the fledgling cavalry of the New Model Army. The first units to receive them were 5 troops of Sir Robert Pye's regiment as part of a consignment of 100 pairs of pistols, holsters, saddles, backs, breasts, and pots on 3 April

84 TNA, WO47/1, f. 233r.
85 TNA, WO47/1, f. 233r; WO55/1663 ff. 11r, 17r–18v.
86 TNA, WO47/1, ff. 209r; ML, Ms 46 78/708, f. 114r.
87 TNA, SP28/29/1, ff. 205r, 213r; Bodl. Lib., Ms Eng. hist. C14, ff. 6v, 11v–13r, 19v, 21r.
88 *CSPD 1644–5*, p.570.
89 TNA, SP28/31/5, ff. 463r, 466r; SP28/32/3, fol. 339r; Bodl. Lib., Ms Eng. hist. C14, ff. 44r–45v.

1645. The following day 20 pairs of pistols, holsters and saddles were delivered to Captain William, Lord Caulfield's troop of Colonel Graves' regiment; on 5 April two (unnamed) troops of Colonel Butler's regiment received 40 sets of each, Captain John Bash's troop of Vermuyden's regiment had 80 sets, while 50 sets of each were issued to Captain James Berry's troop of Sir Thomas Fairfax's regiment.[90] On 29 April 500 cases of pistols with holsters, in addition to 500 pairs of spare holsters were delivered to Commissary Phipps of the Train out of the stores, presumably to be held as first-line stocks for the supply of New Model cavalry units.[91] A total of 1,500 sets of spare holsters, costing 2s. 6d. each, were brought in by William Welsh, Ambrose Sandford, Thomas Gill, and Christopher Townsend, but although further quantities of pistols may have been procured from other sources, including imported foreign models, it appears that all the holsters were produced by London craftsmen.[92] Two comprehensive Ordnance Office books – WO55/1647 and Ms Salt 463 – containing warrants for the issue of arms and equipment to the New Model Army record that between 3 April and 10 June 1645, the latter being four days before the Battle of Naseby, a total of 1,083 pairs of new pistols with holsters were distributed among its regiments of horse and other mounted commands.

Table 18: Notification of Contracts to the Ordnance Office for Pistols and Holsters for the NMA (TNA, WO55/1647; WSL, Ms Salt 463; ML, Ms 46 78/708)

Date	Quantity and type	Price pair	Contractor
3/4/45	50 pair of pistols with holsters full bore and proof	27s.	John Pembury
3/4/45	1200 pair of pistols and holsters	200 at 27s. 1000 at 28s.	John Tucker
3/4/45	200 pair of pistols and holsters	28s.	Mr Bartlett at the Excise Office
3/4/45	500 pair of pistols with the best holsters, English full bore and proof	26s.	John Watkins
1/5/45	To receive into the stores in the Tower 300 pair of pistols with holsters	26s.	Edward Burrows
1/5/45	Also 50 pair of pistols with holsters	26s.	Robert Murden
20/5/45	40 pair of pistols English full bore and proof	26s.	Robert Murden
5/6/45	50 pair of pistols with good holsters, English full bore and proof	26s.	William Fell
10/6/45	60 pair of pistols with good holsters, English full bore and proof	26s.	Robert Murden
10/6/45	200 pair of pistols with good holsters, English full bore and proof	26s.	Edward Burrows
10/6/45	50 pair of pistols with good holsters, English full bore and proof	26s.	William Fell

90 WSL, Ms Salt 463, unfol.
91 TNA, WO55/1647, unfol.; WSL, Ms Salt 463, unfol.
92 TNA, SP28/29/1, ff. 213r, 218r; SP28/29/2, ff. 241r, 251r, 256r; SP28/30/4, ff. 350r, 356.; SP28/31/5, ff. 450r, 502r, 511r; SP28/352/1, unfol.; Bodl. Lib., Ms Eng. hist. C14, ff. 6v, 11v–13r, 19v, 21r; ML, Ms 46 78/708, ff. 83v, 92v, 104r–105r, 112r, 114r.

Date	Quantity and type	Price pair	Contractor
20/6/45	300 pair of pistols with good holsters, English full bore and proof	26s.	Edward Burrows
20/6/45	80 pair of pistols with good holsters, English full bore and proof	26s.	Robert Murden
26/6/45	200 pair of pistols with holsters. All English full bore and proof	26s.	William Fell
26/6/45	750 pair of pistols with good holsters English full bore and proof	26s.	William Watson, John Watson, William Greaves, George Day & Thomas Smith
26/6/45	100 pair of pistols English full bore and proof with holsters of calfskins	26s.	Robert Murden
26/6/45	150 pair of pistols English full bore and proof with holsters of calfskins	26s.	George Fisher
26/6/45	150 pair of pistols English full bore and proof with holsters of calfskins	26s.	Edward Burrows
11/7/45	100 pair of pistols with good calfskin holsters	26s.	William Fell
22/12/45	200 pair of snaphaunce pistols full bore and proof with holsters of calfskins, inside and out well-sewed and lacquered to be brought into the Tower of London as follows: 50 of them the last day of this instant December, 50 more the last of January, another 50 the last of February and the other 50 the last day of March next ensuing, for which it is contracted that the said William Garner and Geoffrey Petty shall be paid monthly for the same as they bring them in for performance, whereof they have set their hands. 100 marked thus (92) the other marked thus (93)	20s. 4d.	William Garner & Geoffrey Petty
22/12/45	550 pair of snaphaunce pistols and holsters according to the former contract, to be brought in and paid for as aforesaid. 220 marked thus (94) 215 marked thus (95) 215 marked thus (96)	20s. 4d.	Robert Murden, Miles Knight & William Judge
22/12/45	200 pair of snaphaunce pistols and holsters of the same goodness and at the same price, to be brought in and paid for as aforesaid. 100 of the pistols marked thus (97) the other 100 marked thus (98)	20s. 4d.	Andrew Tyer & John Pope
22/12/45	200 pair of snaphaunce pistols and holsters of the same goodness, and at the same price, to be brought in and paid for as aforesaid. The pistols to be marked thus (99)	20s. 4d.	Walter Benge
22/12/45	30 pair of snaphaunce pistols and holsters of the same goodness, and at the same price, to be brought in and paid for as aforesaid	20s. 4d.	Henry Cox

Date	Quantity and type	Price pair	Contractor
22/12/45	500 pair of snaphaunce pistols and holsters of the same goodness, and at the same price, to be brought in and paid for as aforesaid. The pistols to be marked thus (101)	20s. 4d.	George Drew
22/12/45	500 pair of snaphaunce pistols and holsters of the same goodness, and at the same price, to be brought in and paid for as aforesaid. The pistols to be marked thus (101)	20s. 4d.	George Drew
22/12/45	100 pair of snaphaunce pistols and holsters, according to the former contracts, to be brought in and paid for as aforesaid. The pistols to be marked thus [blank]	20s. 4d.	Richard Nunnerley
22/12/45	1000 pair of snaphaunce pistols and holsters, according to the former contracts, to be brought in and paid for as aforesaid. The pistols to be marked thus (102)	20s. 4d.	William Watson
22/12/45	400 pair of snaphaunce pistols and holsters, according to the former contracts, to be brought in and paid for as aforesaid. The pistols to be marked thus (103)	20s. 4d.	William Fell
22/12/45	500 pair of snaphaunce pistols and holsters, according to the former contracts, to be brought in and paid for as aforesaid. The pistols to be marked thus (104)	20s. 4d.	Edward Burrows
22/12/45	220 pair of snaphaunce pistols and holsters, according to the former contracts and marked thus [blank]	20s. 4d.	Robert Hamond

Table 19: Warrants for Payments to Contractors for the Delivery of Pistols and Holsters to the Ordnance Office for the New Model Army (TNA, SP28/29/1-31/5)

Date	Quantity and type	Price pair	Contractor
9/4/45	250 pair of pistols and holsters	28s.	John Tucker
14/4/45	100 pair of pistols and holsters	28s.	John Tucker
14/4/45	100 pair of pistols and holsters	28s.	William Fell
14/4/45	286 pair of pistols with holsters	28s.	Wm Greaves, Wm Watson & George Day
24/4/45	50 pair of pistols with holsters in full of their contract	27s.	Robert Jeffery, subcontracted to John Tucker
24/4/45	80 pair of pistols with holsters in full of their contract	27s.	Robert Jeffery, subcontracted to John Tucker
25/4/45	170 pair of pistols with holsters	28s.	Wm Greaves, Wm Watson & George Day
29/4/45	100 pair of pistols with holsters in full of their contract	27s.	Robert Jeffery, subcontracted to John Tucker

Date	Quantity and type	Price pair	Contractor
29/4/45	50 pair of pistols with holsters in full of their contract	28s.	Robert Murden
12/5/45	50 pair of pistols with holsters in full of their contract	28s.	John Norcott
16/5/45	148 pair of pistols with holsters in full of their contract	28s.	John Tucker
8/7/45	80 pair of pistols with holsters	30d.	Robert Murden
9/7/45	750 pair of pistols with holsters in full of their contract	30d.	Wm Watson, Geo. Day & Thos Smith
9/8/45	100 pair of pistols with holsters	30d.	Robert Murden

Table 20: Notification of Contracts to the Ordnance Office for Holsters for the NMA (TNA, WO47/1; Bodl. Lib., Ms Eng. hist. C14; ML, Ms 46 78/708)

Date	Quantity and type	Price pair	Contractor
26/6/45	500 pair of holsters of calfskin	30d.	William Welsh & Ambrose Sandford
28/6/45	500 pair of calfskin holsters in 14 days, 300 in a week and 200 in 14 days	30d.	Thomas Gill
28/6/45	500 pair of calfskin holsters	30d.	Christopher Townsend

Table 22: Warrants for Payments to Contractors for the Delivery of Holsters to the Ordnance Office for the service of the New Model Army (TNA, SP28/31/4-32/3)

Date	Quantity and type	Price each	Contractor
31/7/45	500 pair of holsters for pistols	30d.	Ambrose Sandford & William Welsh
18/8/45	100 pair of holsters for pistols	30d.	Christopher Townsend
20/8/45	100 pair of holsters	30d.	Christopher Nicholson
3/9/45	100 pair of holsters for pistols	30d.	Christopher Townsend

Thus, Sir Thomas Fairfax's regiment received 191 pairs of pistols and holsters; Pye's 100; Butler's 62; Vermuyden's, then Cromwell's 122; Sheffield's 20; Ireton's 410; Rich's 100; Fleetwood's 280; Whalley's 20; Graves' 40; and Rossiter's 20. An additional 40 pairs of pistols with holsters were issued to Fairfax's Lifeguard; 8 to John Holstead, Provost Marshal General of the horse; and 20 to Thomas Wicks, the Marshal General of the foot. Though such quantities might be reflective of the levels of recruitment amongst the New Model's regiments of horse since April, it also suggests (when compared to the corresponding numbers of saddles distributed to the same units) that in mid-1645 some of these regiments lacked a substantial portion of their necessary equipment. Hence, any notion that a significant percentage of the already existing cavalry units absorbed into the New Model appeared 'kitted out' lacks evidence. On 5 June the Commons granted the Committee for the Army the authority to provide Fleetwood's, Ireton's, and Rossiter's regiments with 100 horses, 100 pairs of pistols, and 100 saddles, with furniture.[93] On the same day it was resolved that an extra 1s. a day, over and above the pay assigned to ordinary troopers, 'shall be allowed to each of the 100 troopers of Captain Knight's troop, they furnishing their own horse and arms'.[94] That they received this amount as an incentive for bringing in their own mounts and equipment suggests that such a practice was uncommon. Knight had previously acted as lieutenant to Captain John Okey, and then commander of a troop described as Manchester's Lifeguard, and later served in the New Model Army regiment of Sir Robert Pye. This unit was particularly under-equipped, his five other troops having received between them 100 pairs of pistols, holsters, saddles, backs, breasts, and pots on 3 April.[95]

Cavalry horses and weapons were also received from other sources. On 23 April the Committee of Both Kingdoms ordered the Deputy Lieutenants of Surrey to 'secure the horses and arms of Captain Savile's troop [which had mutinied], and send them to Sir Thomas Fairfax'. Moreover, the troopers were redeployed in the New Model Army, 'as Sir Thomas shall see cause'.[96] The documents recording the supply of pistols to Fairfax's cavalry also record that in June and July 1645 over 400 spare holsters were distributed among the troops and regiments of the New Model directly by the Ordnance Office. This included 100 pairs given to Sergeant Major Thomas Harrison 'for the recruiting [supplying] of Colonel Fleetwood's regiment', along with 40 saddles, and 40 pairs of pistols with holsters. On 1 July 30 pairs of extra holsters went to Captain Hoskins' and Captain Gibbon's troops of Ireton's regiment, while 45 more were supplied to Colonel Butler's own troop, in addition to the troops in his regiment commanded by Sergeant Major Thomas Horton and Captain Walter Perry. Similarly, on 7 July Quartermaster David Thompson of Captain William Rainborowe's troop received 90 pairs, to be distributed among Sheffield's regiment, whereas a week later the same quantity was delivered to Sergeant Major Robert Huntington for Lieutenant General Cromwell's regiment, which had previously been under the command of Colonel Vermuyden.[97]

Snaphaunce Muskets

Specifications given in the notification of contracts for snaphaunces supplied to the New Model Army between April and December 1645, indicate that they were to be 'full bore and proof, and four feet long'. Additionally, entries in receipts and disbursements books refer to these as either 'snaphaunce muskets English full bore and proof' or 'snaphaunce muskets full bore and proof, and four feet long'. Whether in these cases the term 'English' equated to 'English' or dog-lock mechanisms, or if such descriptions were synonymous with each other is open to question, however. In May 1645 William Fell furnished Sir Richard Browne, the governor of Abingdon,

93 *CJ*, IV, p.163; *The Moderate Intelligencer*, 5–12 June 1645. TT, E288[7].
94 *CJ*, IV, pp.101, 365.
95 TNA, E121/4/2/73, entry 179; WSL, Ms Salt 463, unfol.
96 *CSPD 1644–5*, pp.427–8.
97 TNA, WO55/1647, unfol.; WSL, Ms Salt 463, unfol.

with 100 snaphaunce muskets costing 17s. 0d. apiece, during a period when he and others were supplying them to the Ordnance Office magazine for 15s. 6d.[98] In terms of the New Model Army, in April 1645 a group of London gunsmiths – including John Norcott, William Watson and partners, and Richard Jones – were contracted to provide 1,000 'snaphaunce muskets English full bore and proof', at 15s. 6d. each. An additional 50 were to be provided by Lieutenant General Thomas Hammond at a cost of 14s. 0d. apiece, although these were probably older weapons belonging to Essex's former firelock guard.[99] A small batch of 24 snaphaunce muskets were purchased at the lower rate of 13s. 4d. from the gunmaker Peter Gregor on 27 December 1645, though generally the price of standard (as opposed to dragoon models, costing 15s. 6d.) snaphaunces was reduced by late 1645 to 12s. 4d., probably due to bulk ordering. However, in October 1646, 17s. 0d. was paid for these items for service in Ireland.[100]

On 22 December 1645 the purchase of a further 300 snaphaunces, described as 'full-bore and proof, and four foot long at 15s. 4d. apiece' was agreed with three contractors, although there are some discrepancies amongst the records of the receipt and distribution to Fairfax's Army by the Ordnance Office of these and earlier consignments. In a broader sense, this is mainly because the officers were required to maintain records in duplicate, and minor discrepancies between different copies of the same document might contain variations in names, dates and quantities. Moreover, entries in the ledger books were composed from the original records after transactions had occurred, occasionally months later, and there is some evidence of faulty transcription. Tracing the whereabouts of the 1,000 snaphaunces contracted on 3 April 1645 with Norcott (200); Watson, William Greaves, George Day and Thomas Smith (500 between them); and Jones (300) presents considerable difficulties because they do not appear in any treasurers' warrants, nor records of receipts into the Ordnance Office and subsequent distribution to military units.

Whatever the existing stocks of these weapons were, on 2 May 1645 120 snaphaunce muskets were delivered to Commissary Phipps of the Train of Artillery, while 12 days later a further 25 were received by him.[101] It seems likely that these firearms were supplied to the New Model Army's firelock guard. The fulfilment of four contracts notified to the Ordnance Office on 22 December 1645 is more possible to pin down. The 100 snaphaunce muskets produced by Walter Benge were delivered into the Ordnance Office on 13 February 1646. William Fell – who was to supply at 14s. 4d. apiece '100 snaphaunce muskets full bore and proof, and four feet long according to the former contracts, to be brought into the Tower of London at the times before mentioned by equal proportions, for which he is to be paid as he brings them in for performance whereof, he has set his hand' – brought in 20 to the Small Arms Office on 27 April, while the outstanding 80 were received on 13 March. Likewise, Edward Burrows' indenture for 200 snaphaunces was fulfilled in two

98 TNA, WO47/1, ff. 208v, 210r; SP28/30/1, f. 18r.
99 TNA, WO47/1, ff. 209v, 235v; ML, Ms 46 78/708, ff. 109r.
100 *CJ*, IV, p.698; ML, Ms 46 78/708, ff. 78r–79r, 98r, 110r, 114r.
101 TNA, WO47/1, f. 235r; WO55/1646, unfol.; WO55/1647, unfol.; WSL, Ms Salt 463, unfol.; Bodl. Lib., Ms Eng. C247, f. 10v.

consignments of 100 each, one on 28 February and the other on 6 March 1646. By comparison, the 600 weapons agreed with William Watson and his partners on 22 December 1645 were delivered on 16 March 1646 as part of a consignment including 1,000 matchlock muskets and 595 pairs of pistols with holsters.[102]

Allowing for some discrepancies, the contract books and warrants for 1645–1646 record orders for 16,250 matchlock muskets and 3,045 snaphaunces of all types. Nevertheless, the actual quantity of these weapons delivered by the Ordnance Office land stores to Sir Thomas Fairfax's Army between April and December equates to 10,010 matchlocks and 894 snaphaunces, whereas 6,470 and 199 respectively were supplied in 1646.[103] Given such figures, a small number of snaphaunces were issued to the New Model's dragoons and probably the firelock guard. There is no direct evidence of any of these weapons being supplied to infantry units as they were during the Commonwealth period, although a number could have been issued to every company in the army for the purpose of sentry duty.[104] On 12 June 1650, 600 matchlocks, 200 snaphaunces, 800 collars of bandoliers, 400 pikes, 20 drums and 24 halberds were distributed to Colonel Robert Gibbon's newly raised regiment; similarly, 100 snaphaunce muskets, along with 700 matchlocks, 800 bandoliers, 400 pikes, 20 drums and 20 halberds were supplied to the Lord General's regiment of foot (Colonel George Monck's) at Berwick in August 1650. In June 1642 the Lords Justices of Ireland had requested that '1,000 firelock pieces fixed may be also sent us, which will be of singular use and advantage to us in the services here as we find by the experience we have of the 400 firelocks lately sent us, many of which are not fixed'.[105]

Snaphaunces had clear advantages over matchlocks in terms of safety because they reduced the danger of accidental powder explosions, and the firearm was also more economical, avoiding the need for large quantities of match. On 1 February 1648 it was agreed to send 1,000 snaphaunces to Dublin, 'if they are in store, both for the sparing of match and for the better carrying on of the many services for which they are more proper.'[106] Because of the safety aspect, firelocks (infantry soldiers armed with the firearm, as opposed to dragoons carrying them) were frequently utilised to guard artillery trains. In this fashion, in October 1642 Captain William Legge's company of firelocks had acted independently at Edgehill in guarding the King's train of artillery, while both the Earl of Essex's and Sir William Waller's Parliamentarian armies contained firelock guards. With the snaphaunce there was no damp match to consider during wet weather, while glowing matches could be seen in the dark, and were thus less preferable for night-time operations. Turner contended, 'It is impossible to hide burning matches so well in the night-time, especially if there is any wind,

102 TNA, SP28/140/3, ff. 80r, 86r, 113r, 116r; Bodl. Lib., Ms Eng. C244, ff. 2v, 16r, 18v.

103 TNA, WO55/1646, *passim*; WO55/1647, *passim*; SP28/140/3, ff. 80r, 86r, 113r, 116r; SP28/352, *passim*.

104 BL, Ms Add. 35332, ff. 147v, 180v.

105 *Calendar of the Manuscripts of the Marquess of Ormonde, K. P., preserved at Kilkenny Castle* (London: HMSO, 1902), II, pp.137 & 142–143.

106 *CSPI 1647–1660*, p.772.

(though there be covers made of white iron, like extinguishers purposely for that end) but that some of them will be seen by a vigilant enemy, and thereby many secret enterprises are lost'.[107]

As alluded to previously, the vast majority of the snaphaunce muskets procured by the Committee for the Army and issued by the Ordnance Office for the New Model Army were supplied to Colonel John Okey's regiment of dragoons. When the Civil Wars began dragoons were predominantly issued with matchlock muskets, although some units were issued with snaphaunces from the beginning or replaced their matchlocks over time. On 18 November 1642 Colonel Richard Browne, the commander of a regiment of Parliamentarian dragoons raised in London, paid a carrier the sum of 6s. 3d. 'for bringing two loads of powder, and one load of bullets and match'. Similarly, in spring 1643 Sir Anthony Irby expended 6s. 8d. on 84 yards of match for his dragoons.[108] However, in August 1642 Colonel John Browne's regiment of the Earl of Essex's forces had 600 short muskets delivered to it.[109] Similarly, on 16 November a warrant was issued to supply Colonel Wardlaw's dragoons of the same army with 600 muskets, 600 bandoliers, 600 swords with belts, 2,000lbs of gunpowder and shot proportional from the Tower stores.[110] That no match was supplied infers that the firearms received on 19 September, and referred to as 'bastard muskets', were snaphaunces.[111] Sir William Brereton's dragoons in Cheshire were often referred to by contemporaries as 'firelocks', owing to their association with these weapons, and from late 1642 all the soldiers were armed with them. Despite having been provided with both matchlock and snaphaunce muskets on 21 November 1642, a year later Brereton petitioned Parliament to send by sea 100 pairs of pistols, 300 muskets and 200 or 300 firelocks, adding 'These are not to be procured upon any terms in this country [the county of Cheshire] wherein I could raise good store of men if I could arm them'.[112]

The Dutch writer, Johann von Nassau recommended Scottish snaphaunce muskets for dragoons, although matchlocks and wheellock carbines were also commonly used on the Continent.[113] But it was Vernon, who suggested in 1644:

> The dragoon's arming is only offensive, having a good fire and cock musket something, a wider bore, then ordinary hanging in a belt by a swivel at his side, with a good sword and ordinary horse, it being only to expedite his march, for he must perform his service on foot, the ordinary marching is usually ten abreast, and when they come in service, nine of them alight casting the bridle over the next sideman's horse's neck, and for one in ten serves to keep their horses, the rest perform the service; it is a good and

107 Turner, *Pallas Armata*, p.176.

108 TNA, SP28/144/2, f. 29r; SP28/313/4, unfol.

109 TNA, WO55/1937, unfol.; WO55/1754, unfol.

110 TNA, WO55/1754, unfol.

111 TNA, WO55/1937, unfol.

112 BL, MS Harley 2128, ff. 25r, 34r; HMC, *Thirteenth Report, App. I*, p.157.

113 Werner Hahlweg, *Die Heeresreform der Oranier, Das Kriegsbuch des Grafen Johann von Nassau-Siegen* (Wiesbeden: Selbstverlag der Historischen Kommission, 1973), p.315.

> special principle, to have our soldiers both horse and foot well chosen, well-armed, and well disciplined.[114]

Likewise, Monck suggested that the offensive arms of the dragoon were:

> A musket, or a good snaphaunce to a musket barrel; the which I hold much better for dragoon-service, being upon occasion they may be able to make use of their snaphaunces on horseback, and upon any service in the night they may go undiscovered. He must have also a belt to hang his musket in, with a pair of bandoliers, and a good long tuck, with a belt. And all your dragoons ought to have swine-feathers.[115]

Military garrisons during the British Civil Wars habitually consumed large quantities of match, even if at times it was only issued to sentries. On 30 May 1643 Sir William Savile, the Royalist governor of Sheffield advised his deputy, 'For the match you write for, I shall send you some, but I put you in mind once more to use your snaphaunce pieces to keep sentry with. They will save our match'.[116] Similarly, every 20 musketeers were issued a snaphaunce musket at Stafford in December 1644, 'for want of muskets with firelocks upon the guards in this garrison there has been much match spent'. The governor, Colonel Simon Rugeley was still requesting these weapons two months later, 'in regard the garrison is short of match be pleased to lend the snaphaunces [from the Earl of Denbigh's magazine] to save the said match'.[117] Another significant benefit of snaphaunces over matchlocks was the ability to carry a weapon ready to fire.

But although snaphaunces held certain advantages over matchlocks, they were more expensive. In early 1645 matchlock muskets costing between 10s. and 11s. 6d. were purchased for the New Model Army, and in 1646 Parliament contracted for 'English matchlock muskets and bandoliers', at 14s. apiece for its forces in Ireland.[118] In April 1645 two London gunsmiths, William Watson and Edward Burrows provided the New Model with 200 'snaphaunce muskets English full bore and proof', at 15s. 6d. each, while in October 1646, 17s. was paid for similar items. On 22 December 1645 another consignment of snaphaunces 'full-bore and proof, and 4 foot long at 15s. 4d. apiece' were brought from the Tower. Similarly, 24 of them were purchased at the lower rate of 13s. 4d. apiece from the gunmaker Peter Gregor on 27 December 1645. On 10 January 1646 John Silke senior of Whitechapel was contracted to supply to the New Model 200 'snaphaunce dragoons full-bore and proof' at the same price, 'to be forthwith brought into the Tower of London'.[119] Except for the latter example, it seems likely, however, that most of the full bore

114 Vernon, *The Young Horse-man*, pp.8–9.
115 Monck, *Observations*, p.27.
116 W. D. Macray (ed.), *Beaumont Papers: Letters Relating to the Family of Beaumont of Whitley, Yorkshire* (London: Nichols, 1884), p.70.
117 D. H. Pennington and I. A. Roots (eds and intro.), *The Committee at Stafford, 1643–1645* (Manchester: Manchester University Press, 1957), pp.230, 256, 296.
118 TNA, SP28/29/2, f. 249r; TNA, SP30/37, ff. 81r–81v, 87r.
119 *CJ*, IV, p.698; TNA, SP30/37, ff. 73r, 78r–79r, 98r, 110r, 114r.

firelocks supplied to the army were not meant for Colonel Okey's dragoon regiment. Various contracts and warrants ordering their delivery specify 'dragoon muskets', 'dragoon muskets with snaphaunce locks' and 'snaphaunce dragoons'. These were shorter barrelled than standard snaphaunces, and cost 20 to 30 percent more than matchlock muskets issued to the foot. In August 1642 Colonel John Browne's regiment of dragoons in the Earl of Essex's Army had 600 short muskets delivered to it, whereas the dragoons under the command Sir William Brereton in Cheshire command, were issued with snaphaunces from the beginning and the dragoons were referred to as 'firelocks' throughout the First Civil War.[120]

In April 1645, during the initial arming of Sir Thomas Fairfax's nascent army, the sum of £77 was disbursed 'unto John Norcott in full of his contract for 100 dragoon muskets with snaphaunce locks at 15s. 6d. apiece'; Norcott later supplied a further 105 of the same firearms. Likewise, on 14 April the London gunmakers John Watson, William Travis and George Day were paid for 100 snaphaunce muskets for dragoons at 15s. 6d. each.[121] Perhaps like some of those purchased for the Earl of Essex's forces, and possibly units of the Royalist Army in 1642, these weapons were shorter (36 inch, rather than 48-inch barrels) and lighter models that those supplied to the foot and firelock guard of the New Model's train of artillery. Evidence in support of this contention derives from the contractors' warrants. One, dated 1 August 1645, to pay Daniel Judd, plumber and shot caster the sum of £119 'for 7 ton of bastard musket shot at £17 0s. 0d. per ton'. Moreover, on 22 October Judd also received a contract for '10 ton of bastard musket shot and 1 ton of pistol shot at £17 0s. 0d. each ton weight, to be delivered into the stores in the Tower of London before 1 January next for the use of Sir Thomas Fairfax's Army'.[122] Writing in 1672, Venn recommended that dragoons' muskets 'are to be somewhat wider in the bore than the field musket, and about two foot and nine inches in length'.[123]

Table 23: Notification of Contracts to the Ordnance Office for the Supply of Snaphaunce Muskets for the NMA (TNA, WO47/1; Bodl. Lib., Ms Eng. hist. C14; SP28/352; ML, Ms 46 78/708)

Date	Quantity and type	Price each	Contractor
3/4/45	200 snaphaunce muskets English full bore and proof	15s. 6d.	John Norcott of the Minories, gunsmith
3/4/45	500 snaphaunce muskets English full bore and proof to be delivered in 14 days	15s. 6d.	William Watson, William Greaves, George Day & Thomas Smith
3/4/45	300 snaphaunce muskets English full bore and proof	15s. 6d.	Richard Jones of East Smithfield
10/4/45	50 snaphaunce muskets	14s. 0d.	Lt General Thomas Hammond

120 TNA, WO55/1937, unfol.; WO55/1754, unfol.; BL, Ms Harley 2128, ff. 25r, 34r.
121 TNA, SP28/29/1, ff. 198r, 218r–219r; SP28/29/2, f. 249r.
122 TNA, SP28/31/4, f. 441r; SP30/37, f. 13r.
123 Venn, *Military and Maritine [sic] Discipline*, pp.8–9.

Date	Quantity and type	Price each	Contractor
11/7/45	200 snaphaunce muskets English full bore and proof	15s. 6d.	William Watson and Edward Burrows
22/12/45	100 snaphaunce muskets full bore and proof, and four feet long to be brought into the Tower of London 25 of them every month till the 100 be brought in for which it is contracted, he shall be paid as he brings them in for performance whereof, he has set his hand. The muskets to be marked thus (70)	14s. 4d.	Walter Benge
22/12/45	600 snaphaunce muskets full bore and proof, and four feet long according to the former contracts, to be brought into the Tower of London at the times before mentioned by equal proportions, for which he is to be paid as he brings them in for performance whereof, he has set his hand. The muskets to be marked thus (71)	14s. 4d.	William Watson & partners
22/12/45	100 snaphaunce muskets full bore and proof, and four feet long according to the former contracts, to be brought into the Tower of London at the times before mentioned by equal proportions, for which he is to be paid as he brings them in for performance whereof, he has set his hand. The muskets to be marked thus (72)	14s. 4d.	William Fell
22/12/45	200 snaphaunce muskets full bore and proof, and four feet long according to the former contracts, to be brought into the Tower of London at the times before mentioned by equal proportions, for which he is to be paid as he brings them in. The muskets to be marked thus (73)	14s. 4d.	Edward Burrows

Table 24: Notification of Contracts to the Ordnance Office for the Supply of Dragoon Snaphaunces for the NMA (TNA, WO47/1; ML, Ms 46 78/708)

Date	Quantity and type	Price each	Contractor
27/12/45	24 dragoon muskets	13s. 4d.	Peter Gregor
10/1/46	200 snaphaunce dragoons full bore and proof to be forthwith brought into the Tower of London, for which it is contracted they shall be paid when they bring them in for performance, whereof they have set their hands. 100 of them marked thus (40) (41) 40 of them marked thus (42) 30 of them thus (43) and the other 30 thus (44)	12s. 4d.	John Silk

Table 25: Treasury Warrants for Payments to Contractors for the Delivery of Dragoon Snaphaunces to the Ordnance Office for the NMA (TNA, SP28/29/1-2; SP28/30/4; SP28/31/5; SP28/352)

Date	Quantity and type	Price each	Contractor
9/4/45	100 dragoon muskets with snaphaunce locks in full of his contract	15s. 6d.	John Norcott
14/4/45	110 dragoon muskets with snaphaunce locks	15s. 6d.	William Greaves, William Watson & George Day
15/4/45	70 dragoon muskets with snaphaunce locks in full of his contract	15s. 6d.	John Norcott
23/4/45	30 dragoon muskets with snaphaunce locks in full of his contract	15s. 6d.	John Norcott
25/4/45	192 dragoon muskets with snaphaunce locks	15s. 6d.	William Greaves, William Watson & George Day
28/5/45	35 dragoon muskets with snaphaunce locks	15s. 6d.	Lieutenant General Hammond
6/5/45	100 dragoon muskets with snaphaunce locks in full of his contract	15s. 6d.	Richard Jones
23/5/45	198 dragoon muskets with snaphaunce locks	15s. 6d.	Wm Greaves, Wm Watson & Geo. Day
26/7/45	200 dragoon muskets with snaphaunce locks	15s. 6d.	Wm Watson & Edward Burrows
1/6/45	50 dragoon muskets with snaphaunce locks	15s. 6d.	William Fell
19/2/46	100 dragoon muskets with snaphaunce locks	15s. 6d.	Walter Benge

Various contracts specified 'dragoon muskets', 'dragoon muskets with snaphaunce locks' and 'snaphaunce dragoons', but they also mentioned swivels and slings.

Although Royalist examples are difficult to locate, while at Romford on 16 August 1643 the Parliamentarian Committee for Essex issued a warrant for the payment of £30 0s. 0d. to Thomas Jupe in full 'for 360 bandoliers at 20d. a pair delivered to Captain Holcroft, Captain Harbottle and Captain Miller.' Moreover, the sum of £342 0s. 0d. was disbursed to John Watson, a London gunsmith for '360 muskets with ringnails, belts and swivels'. These items, which were 'furnished for dragoons', were to be delivered to the same captains. On the same occasion, the Committee ordered Lieutenant Colonel Edward Birkhead, an officer in the Essex Trained Band and agent for the procurement of arms to the Eastern Association Army 'to deliver and direct you to pay unto Captain Holcroft, Captain Harbottle [and] Captain Miller, or any one of them, the sum of £9, for and towards three colours and six drums for their several companies of dragoons under the command of the Earl of Manchester.'[124]

While at Farnham on 28 August 1644 Sir William Waller benefitted from the supply of '5,000 belts for their muskets' for the conversion of his foot into dragoon

124 TNA, SP28/227/1, f. 4r.

regiments.[125] Moreover, upon the formation of Sir Richard Browne's London-raised and equipped dragoon regiment in November 1642 the sum of £30 0s. 0d. was paid to 'Mr Leighton and his partners in full for belts', and £88 19s. 0d. 'to Mr Coward for slings and belts', while a carrier received 10d. for the delivery of belts.[126] On 31 March 1646, 200 snaphaunce dragoon muskets were delivered to the Ordnance Office from the contractors William and John Watson, and on the same day '200 belts and swivels for dragoons' were received from William Watson and Henry Thrall, contractors who regularly supplied considerable quantities of arms and accoutrements to the army.[127] Such items continued to be utilised, since in March 1648 Colonel John Okey's regiment was issued '200 serviceable firelocks dragoons, 200 swivels and belts' by the Ordnance Office.[128] Moreover, warrants for the supply of arms and equipment to the Commonwealth Army in Ireland in August 1649 included one for the payment of £2,988 1s. 8d. to Roger Carlisle and three other gunsmiths for 2,000 matchlocks, 474 snaphaunce muskets, and '1,000 dragoons' arms with swivels'.[129]

Bandoliers

During the Civil Wars musketeers and some dragoons were commonly issued with the smoothbore, muzzle-loading matchlock musket (though various dragoon units, including Okey's New Model regiment, possessed snaphaunces), bandolier and sword. Instructions issued in 1636 for arming the English and Welsh militia declared that muskets were meant to be of 1 standard bore (12 bullets to the pound) and that each musketeer, 'shall be furnished with a sufficient whole musket, the barrel thereof shall be four feet in length and no more', the total length of the weapon being 5 feet 2 inches.[130] Besides, 'every such person appointed to serve with a full musket shall be further furnished and armed with a good bandolier, and with fifteen good and serviceable charges of turned wood, covered with leather and fastened there unto. Also with a good primer, worm and scourer, and a bullet bag annexed unto it, with a mould to cast such bullets as aforesaid'. A list for 'provision of arms and other necessaries for his Majesty's store [in Ireland]', dated 20 September 1642, mentions 'Boxes according to 15 to the pound for decayed bandoliers for musketeers, 90,000; and primers for every fifteen boxes of that number, 6,000; and girdles to supply decayed bandoliers, 6,000.'[131]

According to Francis Markham, writing in 1626:

125 *CSPD 1644*, p.460.
126 TNA, SP28/144/2, ff. 30r–31r.
127 TNA, SP28/140/3, unfol.
128 BL, Ms Add. 35332, f. 76r.
129 *CSPD 1649*, p.586.
130 Wrye (ed.), *State Papers Relating to Musters*, p.89; Lawrence, *Complete Soldier*, p. 189
131 James Hogan (ed.), *Letters and Papers Relating to the Irish Rebellion Between 1642–46* (Dublin: The Stationery Office, 1936), p.134; *CJ*, II, pp.576, 793, 807.

> About their bodies baldrickwise from the left shoulder under the right arm, he shall carry bandoliers of broad leather ... and to this bandolier shall be fastened by long double stings (at least a quarter of a yard in length a piece, that they may with more ease be brought to the mouth of the musket) one large priming charge ... and at least twelve other charges of wood, all made of some tough light wood or else of horn, and covered with leather.[132]

Similarly, Turner recommended in his *Pallas Armata*:

> To a musketeer belongs also a bandolier of leather, at which he should have hanging eleven or twelve shot of powder, and bag for his ball, a primer, and a cleanser. But it is 30 years ago since I saw these laid aside in some German armies; for it is impossible for soldiers, especially wanting cloaks (and more want cloaks than have any) to keep these flasks (though well and strongly made) from snow and rain, which soon spoils them, and so makes the powder altogether useless. Besides, the noise of them betray those who carry them in all surprisals, onslaughts, and sudden enterprises. Instead of those let patrons [cartridges] be made, such as horsemen use, whereof each musketeer should be provided of a dozen; these should be kept in a bag of strong leather, or the skin of some beast well sowed, that it be proof against rain, this bag he may carry about his neck in a bandolier, or if the weather be extremely rainy, in one of his pockets, and in the other a horn with priming powder, and his cleanser tied to it. By this a musketeer hath these advantages, he shall be sure to charge with dry powder, and that is no small advantage; next, it is a more ready way to charge than the other, for he hath no more to do but to bite off a little of the paper of his patron, and put his charge of powder and ball in at once, and then ram both home.[133]

At Romford on 16 August 1643 the Parliamentarian Committee for Essex issued a warrant for the payment of £30 to Thomas Jupe in full 'for 360 bandoliers at 20d. a pair delivered to Captain Holcroft, Captain Harbottle and Captain Miller'. Moreover, the sum of £342 0s. 0d. was disbursed to John Watson, a London gunsmith for '360 muskets with ringnails, belts and swivels'. On 13 September 1642 Birkhead had been instructed to pay the sum of £73 6s. 8d. to Watson for 800 bandoliers at 22d. per pair, while eight days later he was to authorise the manufacturer 'to provide forthwith 200 muskets, full-bore with rests, at the rate of 17s. 6d. the musket and rest, and so many bandoliers at 22d. the pair'.[134] The reason why the bandoliers issued to Manchester's dragoons the month previously were fractionally cheaper is unclear, although prices were known to fluctuate among army suppliers depending on availability. In February 1644 1,500 bandoliers were purchased from London suppliers for Sir William Brereton's army in Cheshire.[135] It seems likely that some of these

132 Markham, *Five Decades of Epistles of Warre*, p.34.
133 Turner, *Pallas Armata*, p.176.
134 TNA, SP28/227/1, ff. 6r–9r.
135 *CSPD 1644*, p.26; *LJ*, VI, p.446; JRL, TW/287.

were supplied to the dragoons as no mention is made in sources of these troops being issued powder bags. Captain John Kynaston's company of foot in Sir William Myddelton's regiment of Sir Thomas Myddelton's brigade, received 60 swords and belts, 60 collars of bandoliers and 24 muskets on 2 September 1644.[136] Similarly, Sir Thomas purchased 300 sets at 1s. 2d. each in October 1644.[137] The price of these bandoliers compares with those supplied to Fairfax's Army in early 1645, which were got for 1s. 6d. each, although one consignment cost 1s. apiece.[138]

The earliest contracts for the supply of bandoliers 'for the furnishing of the army under Sir Thomas Fairfax' were agreed in spring 1645. Hence, on 3 April the Officers of the Ordnance were notified of the following quantities to be supplied, all at a cost of 1s. 2d. apiece: 1,000 bandoliers from Richard Bradley; 2,000 from John Gace; 1,000 from Henry Thrall; 1,000 bandoliers from Thomas Roach; and another 1,000 from Nathaniel Humphries. Moreover, the partners Bradley and Thrall were contracted on 7 April to bring in 2,000 bandoliers; the following day Humphries and Roach agreed to deliver 2,000; while Gace was contracted on 10 April for 1,000 collars and the same number four days later.[139] Treasury warrants for the payment of contractors upon the delivery of stores show that each of these indentures were delivered in full, and within a remarkably short space of time. Consequently, Bradley's and Thrall's consignments arrived by 8 April 1645; those from Roach and Humphries before 9 April; whereas the collars brought into the stores by Gace were in two batches, 2,000 on 15 April and 1,000 on 2 June.[140] These were issued out of the Ordnance Office stores to the New Model just as swiftly, because on 10 April 1645 5,000 collars were distributed 'by indenture to John Phipps, Commissary to the Train of Artillery under the command of Sir Thomas Fairfax' as part of 'the several parcels of munitions hereafter mentioned for the supply and furnishing of the said Army'. A further 2,000 were supplied on 18 April, 500 on 9 May and another 1,000 three days later. The largest single quantity of bandoliers issued to the New Model was 5,500 collars, received by the commissaries of the train at Reading on 1 May 1645 as part of a major issue of arms, munitions, and ordnance.[141]

By 21 June more than 12,000 collars of bandoliers had been contracted for by the Committee for the Army with manufacturers. Whether there was a quantity of bandoliers already in the stores (some of which might conceivably have been reconditioned), or other deliveries remain unrecorded, but by 24 May 14,500 sets had been supplied to the New Model Army, a figure corresponding with 100 more than the establishment of the foot agreed on 11 January 1645. We might assume at least a third of these were held by the train and commissaries as 'first-line stocks', given that the musket to pike ratio in the New Model Army and Commonwealth forces was 2:1, and estimates by some historians of the strength of the infantry deployed

136 TNA, SP28/45/1, f. 130v; SP28/346, f. 283r.
137 TNA, SP28/346/2, unfol.
138 TNA, SP30/37, ff. 72r, 89r.
139 TNA, WO47/1, f. 208v; Bodl. Lib., Ms Eng hist C14, ff. 5r, 6r–7v; ML, Ms 46 78/708, f. 114v.
140 TNA, SP28/29/1, ff. 193r, 196r, 202r–203r, 223r; SP28/30/4, fol. 367r; Bodl. Lib., Ms Eng hist C14, ff. 5r–7v.
141 TNA, WO55/1646, unfol.; WSL, Ms Salt 463, unfol.

at Naseby being under 9,000.[142] The proportion of two musketeers to one pikeman in Fairfax's Army is confirmed by Richard Elton, who served among its ranks. He recommended, 'I should rather advise all captains that have occasion to raise their companies to have two thirds' musketeers, and but one of pikes'.[143] A list of Sergeant Major Thomas Smith's company belonging to Colonel Sir Hardress Waller's regiment, compiled on 1 August 1645, names two commissioned officers, one sergeant, two drummers and 105 private sentinels. In the first division of shot are 39 soldiers, 36 in the second, and 28 in the pike division, thus representing a ratio of one pike to 2.6 musketeers, although at company level the variance in minor numbers between musters was not uncommon.[144]

At least eight London contractors supplied the Ordnance Office for the use of the New Model Army with bandoliers between April 1645 and July 1646, and where known, their backgrounds reflect the range of trades associated with the construction of such items. John Gace of Eastcheap was a wood turner and former Master of the Turner's Company, who had supplied bandoliers to the Massachusetts Bay Company in 1628 and also 3,200 bandoliers; 1,700 shovels and spades, in addition to '50 Flemish spades' to Sir Thomas Fairfax's forces.[145] Nathaniel Humphries, who lived 'next to the Boar's Head in Candlewick Street', was a Member of the Iron Mongers' Company, while Thomas Roach of the 'Black Boy on the east side of St Michael's Lane', was of the Haberdashers' Company. Probably due to the nature of the written documents, most references to the purchase and receipt of bandoliers for the New Model lack any specific details. Such bare descriptions could cover a range of types, and especially wooden bottles with wooden tops. Thus, the terms 'bandoliers' and 'bandoliers with wooden chargers' are included, for instance, in the 2,000 collars received at 1s. 2d. each from John Gace and Richard Newbury on 15 April 1646; 2,000 from Henry Thall, Richard Ramsey and Thomas Bostock on 7 May 1646; and the 500 from Richard Newbury on 10 July 1646.[146] Interestingly, none of these consignments appear among the previous notifications of contracts to the Ordnance Office.

Another typical, yet slightly cheaper order is that of 22 December 1645, wherein Edward Barker was to provide '1,000 bandoliers with good belts to be forthwith brought to the Tower of London for which it is contracted he shall be paid when he brings them in for performance, whereof he has set his hand 1s.'; these were brought into the stores on 22 January 1646.[147] It could be that most of the wooden chargers were simply oiled to prevent the black powder contained within becoming damp, and to protect the wood itself, although there is a possibility that some were covered in leather. A contract agreed between John Gace and the Massachusetts Bay Company Colony, an English settlement on the east coast of North America,

142 See, for instance, Peter Young, *Naseby 1645* (London, 1985), p.245 (6,400); Maurice Ashley, *The Battle of Naseby* (Stroud, 1992), p.72 (8,000); Glenn Foard, *Naseby*, pp.199–203 (8,720).
143 Richard Elton, *The Complete Body of the Art Military* (London: Robert Leybourn, 1650), p.2.
144 TNA SP28/122, f. 50r. Thanks to Charles Singleton for alerting me to this source.
145 TNA, SP28/29/1, f. 123r; SP28/140/3, f. 115v; WO47/1, f. 211r; WO55/1662, ff. 6r, 31v.
146 TNA, SP28/140/3, ff. 111v, 114r, 120r.
147 TNA, SP28/140/3, f. 69r; ML, Ms 46 78/708, fol. 114v.

dated 1628 contains considerable detail covering the construction and appearance of the bandoliers supplied by him. The 40 collars or sets were to be 'of neates leather, broad girdles, each with 12 chargers, with one of a priming box of wood, covered with black leather, at 2s. apiece, to be delivered next [week], the boxes to be for bastard musket size, excepting 10 for full muskets, and these to be marked 'M', the others for bastard muskets 'B'.'[148] It appears that both the bandolier bottles and priming boxes were similar in construction, in that they were made of wood and covered with black leather. On 15 March 1648 2,200 new bandoliers, 'including 200 covered with leather' were got for the Commonwealth forces from Richard Newbury. Similarly, in February 1649 Newbury, Thrall and Bostock supplied 1,500 bandoliers 'covered with neates leather, stringed and ringed', with a further 2,000 of the same on 23 April.[149]

Before 7 January 1646 Thomas Jupe, Thomas Roach and Nathaniel Humphries were contracted to supply 4,000 collars of bandoliers, 'the boxes of strong double plate, the heads of the same with whipcord strings and good belts according to the pattern to be brought into the Tower of London monthly by equal proportions for which it is contracted, they shall be paid as they bring them in for performance, whereof they have set their hands'. This was fulfilled, because on 7 February '1,500 bandoliers of double plate' at 1s. 8d. apiece came in from them (although Jupe's name does not appear in the documentation and he may have no longer been part of the consortium, as he is not mentioned in connection with other agreements), along with 1,200 cartridge boxes for carbines at 10d. apiece, arrived on 17 February. The final 2,500 sets were received on 3 March, but with no accompanying specifications.[150] These 5,500 bandoliers may have been part of the estimate of the quantities of clothing and equipment to supply the New Model Army for its winter campaign, presented to Parliament in December 1645, which includes '8,000 bandoliers of tin covered', in other words, tin-plate.[151] During the 1990s, 25 complete, semi-complete or fragmentary bandolier bottles were recovered from an Elizabethan shipwreck off Alderney. These were all cut from copper alloy sheeting and joined along their seams with lead/tin solder, while their bodies are of a truncated form. Eyes were attached to the caps and bodies to take the strings from which they were suspended.[152] Similarly, various bandolier bottles and caps made of copper alloy, iron and lead were found by the Jamestown Rediscovery Project dating from around 1610, although as with other sites, any wooden chargers and caps would not survive, except in specific circumstances, hence the preponderance of metal items.[153]

In January 1646 Gace was engaged to supply '2,000 bandoliers of boxes of wood with whole bottoms to be turned within and not bored, the heads to be of wood

148 Nathaniel Shurtleff (ed.), *Records of the Governor and Company of the Massachusetts Bay in New England* (Boston: W. White, 1853), I, p.31.

149 TNA, SP28/140/3, ff. 143v, 150r, 153v.

150 TNA, SP28/36/2, f. 248r; SP28/140/3, ff. 78v, 88v; Bodl. Lib., Ms Eng. hist. C14, ff. 76r, 86r; ML, Ms 46 78/708, f. 72r.

151 *CJ*, IV, p.388.

152 Jason Monaghan and Mensur Bound, *A Ship Cast Away About Alderney* (Alderney Maritime Trust, 1997), pp.95–8.

153 historicjamestowne.org/collections/artifacts/bandolier/

and to be laid in oil three times over, and to be coloured blue, with blue and white strings of strong thread twist, and good belts to be brought into the Tower monthly by equal proportions for which it is contracted, they shall be paid as they bring them in for performance, whereof they have set their hands'. These powder bottles or charges held about nine drams of black powder, since the inner dimensions were 'turned' and not simply bored, so that the capacity was significantly increased. Gace provided a further 1,000 collars of identical specification on 17 March.[154] There appears to be no direct record of the receipt of the first consignment into the Ordnance Office, although there is a combined receipt, dated 4 March 1646, from Gace and Richard Newbury for 2,000 collars, though any further details of these is not given. However, the second batch of 1,000 bandoliers was brought in by Gace on 15 April.[155] A further 1,000 bandoliers were delivered by Newbury on the same day; 2,000 by Thrall, Ramsey and Thomas Bostock on 30 April, another 1,500 of the same by them on 10 July; and 500 of the same specification on 11 July, bringing the total of blue-painted bandoliers to 8,000.[156] Although the evidence is slight for the later supply of such items to the Ordnance Office, on 9 February 1649 1,500 bandoliers 'with whole bottoms blue-painted in oil with neates leather collars, stringed and ringed' were received from the partners Newbury, Thrall and Bostock, while Thomas Jupe, Thomas Roach and Nathaniel Humphreys brought in 2,000 of the same on 23 April.[157]

How common such items were among the New Model Army is difficult to know, given that more than 25,200 bandoliers were received from Ordnance Office sources between April and 1645 and July 1646, and of these 22,100 are recorded as being delivered during a corresponding period. The question of why at least 8,000 bandoliers had coloured strings, and their charges painted blue is difficult to answer. Such strings could have been used before but were not mentioned in previous orders. Also, blue-painted charges – seemingly less than a third of the total quantities of bandoliers purchased for the foot regiments under the command of Sir Thomas Fairfax – may have been more common, though this seems unlikely. Hence, the 'blue-painted' bandoliers contracts were for something out of the ordinary, as so many more details are specified. It may be the case then, that the colouring of such items was meant to indicate that they belonged to the new national army and not one of the local units.

Besides, various quantities of weapons and accoutrements, including bandoliers, were provided to other Parliamentarian forces during this time. The Committee for the Army agreed on 2 December 1645 to supply 400 swords and belts, 100 muskets and 400 collars of bandoliers for the garrison of King's Lynn, with a further 200 bandoliers sent to troops at Boston.[158] The account books of Charles Bowles, Parliamentarian receiver-general for Kent, include a payment made on 7 August 1647 of £66 13s. 4d. to James Steane of London for '800 collars of bandoliers of

154 TNA, WO55/1662, ff. 6v, 31v. ML, Ms 46 78/708, ff. 69r, 72r.
155 TNA, SP28/140/3, unfol.; PRO/30/37/4, unfol.; Bodl. Lib., Ms Eng. hist. C244, f. 15r.
156 TNA, SP28/140/3, unfol.; Bodl. Lib., Ms Eng. hist. C244, ff. 17r, 21v, 114r, 120r.
157 TNA, SP28/140/3, ff. 150v, 153v.
158 *CJ*, IV, pp.274, 363.

him had for the use of this county at 20d. per collar'. Likewise, on 21 June 1648 the Commons ordered that 6,000 muskets, 6,000 bandoliers, 1,500 cases of pistols with holsters and spanners, 1,500 saddles, and 4,000 pikes be provided for the counties of the Northern Association.[159]

Table 26: Notification of Contracts to the Ordnance Office for the Supply of Bandoliers to the NMA (TNA, WO47/1; WO55/1662; PRO/30/37/4; Bodl. Lib., Ms Eng hist 14; ML, Ms 46 78/708)

Date	Quantity and type	Price each	Contractor
3/4/45	1000 bandoliers	14d.	Richard Bradley
3/4/45	2000 bandoliers	14d.	John Gace
3/4/45	1000 bandoliers	14d.	Henry Thrall
3/4/45	1000 bandoliers	14d.	Thomas Roach
3/4/45	1000 bandoliers	14d.	Nathaniel Humphries
7/4/45	2000 bandoliers	14d.	Bradley &Thrall
8/4/45	2000 bandoliers	14d.	Humphries and Roach
10/4/45	2000 bandoliers (1,000 on 10/4; 1,000 on 14/4)	14d.	John Gace
21/6/45	200 bandoliers at the former rate	14d.	John Gace
5/7/45	1000 bandoliers	14d.	Edward Barker
11/7/45	500 bandoliers	14d.	Richard Bradley
11/7/45	1000 bandoliers	14d.	John Gace
11/7/45	500 bandoliers	14d.	Henry Thrall
18/9/45	1000 bandoliers	14d.	John Gace
18/9/45	1000 bandoliers	14d.	Richard Bradley
18/9/45	1000 bandoliers	14d.	Henry Thrall
18/9/45	500 bandoliers	14d.	Nath. Humphreys
18/9/45	500 bandoliers	14d.	Thos Roach
19/9/45	500 bandoliers	14d.	Nath. Humphreys
19/9/45	500 bandoliers	14d.	Thomas Roach
22/12/45	1000 bandoliers with good belts to be forthwith brought to the Tower of London for which it is contracted he shall be paid when he brings them in for performance, whereof he has set his hand	12d.	Edward Barker

159 TNA, SP28/130/4, f. 34v; *CJ*, V, p.609.

Date	Quantity and type	Price each	Contractor
7/1/46	2000 bandoliers of boxes of wood with whole bottoms to be turned within and not bored, the heads to be of wood and to be laid in oil three times over, and to be coloured blue with blue and white strings of strong thread twist, and good belts to be brought into the Tower monthly by equal proportions for which it is contracted, they shall be paid as they bring them in for performance, whereof they have set their hands. 1000 of the belts to be marked thus (38) The other 1000 thus (39)	20d.	John Gace
7/1/46	4000 bandoliers the boxes of strong double plate, the heads of the same with whipcord strings and good belts according to the pattern to be brought into the Tower of London monthly by equal proportions for which it is contracted, they shall be paid as they bring them in for performance, whereof they have set their hands.	20d.	Thomas Jupe, Thomas Roach & Nathaniel Humphreys
17/3/46	1000 bandoliers of boxes of wood with whole bottoms to be turned within and not bored, the heads to be of wood and to be laid in oil three times over, and to be coloured blue with blue and white strings of strong thread twist, and good belts to be brought into the Tower of London and received within two months next after the date hereof, by which it is contracted, they shall be paid as they bring them in for performance, whereof they have set their hands.	20d.	John Gace
17/3/46	1000 bandoliers of boxes of wood with whole bottoms to be turned within and not bored, the heads to be of wood and to be laid in oil three times over, and to be coloured blue with blue and white strings of strong thread twist, and good belts to be brought into the Tower of London and received within two months next after the date hereof, by which it is contracted, they shall be paid as they bring them in for performance, whereof they have set their hands.	20d.	Richard Newbury
30/4/46	2000 bandoliers of boxes of wood with whole bottoms to be turned within and not bored, the heads to be of wood and to be laid in oil three times over, and to be coloured blue with blue and white strings of strong thread twist, and good belts to be brought into the Tower of London and be received immediately, for which it is concluded and contracted, they shall be paid as they bring them in for performance, whereof they have set their hands.	20d.	Henry Thrall, Richard Ramsey & Thos Bostock
11/6/46	1500 bandoliers of boxes of wood with whole bottoms to be turned within and not bored, the heads to be of wood and to be laid in oil three times over, and to be coloured blue with blue and white strings of strong thread twist, and good belts to be brought into the Tower of London to be viewed within 10 days after the aforesaid day, forthwith concluded and contracted, they shall be paid as they bring them in for performance, whereof they have set their hands.	20d.	Henry Thrall, Richard Ramsey &Thos Bostock

Date	Quantity and type	Price each	Contractor
11/6/46	500 bandoliers of boxes of wood with whole bottoms to be turned within and not bored, the heads to be of wood and to be laid in oil three times over, and to be coloured blue with blue and white strings of strong thread twist, and good belts to be brought into the Tower of London to be viewed within a month after the aforesaid day, forthwith concluded and contracted, they shall be paid as they bring them in for performance, whereof they have set their hands.	20d.	Richard Newbury

Table 27: Warrants for Payments to Contractors for the Delivery of Bandoliers to the Ordnance Office for the NMA (TNA, SP28/29/1-32/1; SP28/140/3)

Date	Quantity and type	Price each	Contractor
8/4/45	1000 pair of bandoliers in full of his contract	14d.	Richard Bradley
8/4/45	1000 pair of bandoliers in full of his contract	14d.	Henry Thrall
9/4/45	1000 pair of bandoliers in full of his contract	14d.	Nathaniel Humphreys
9/4/45	1000 pair of bandoliers in full of his contract	14d.	Thomas Roach
15/4/45	2000 collars of bandoliers in full of his contract	14d.	John Gace
2/6/45	1000 bandoliers in full of his contract	14d.	John Gace
8/6/45	200 bandoliers in full of his contract	14d.	John Gace
16/7/45	1000 collars of bandoliers	14d.	John Gace
16/7/45	500 collars of bandoliers	14d.	Richard Bradley
26/7/45	Acquittance for 200 pair of bandoliers for the new regiment	14d.	John Gace
26/7/45	500 collars of bandoliers	14d.	Henry Thrall
22/9/45	1000 collars of bandoliers	14d.	Henry Thrall
22/9/45	1000 collars of bandoliers	14d.	John Gace
4/10/45	500 collars of bandoliers	14d.	Nathaniel Humphreys
4/10/45	500 collars of bandoliers	14d.	Nathaniel Humphreys
4/10/45	500 collars of bandoliers	14d.	Thos Roach
9/10/45	1000 collars of bandoliers	14d.	Richard Bradley
7/2/46	Received 1500 collars of bandoliers	14d.	Thos Roach
3/3/46	Received 1500 collars of bandoliers	14d.	Roach & Humphries
4/3/46	Received 2000 collars of bandoliers	14d.	Gace & Newbury
15/4/46	Received 2000 collars of bandoliers	14d.	Gace & Newbury
7/5/46	Received 2000 collars of bandoliers	14d.	Thrall, Ramsey & Bostock

Surviving documents, including warrants for the issue of arms and equipment to military units, clearly establish that the proportion of 2 shot to 1 pike was retained among Parliamentarian regiments during the Commonwealth period. The quantities concerned also scotch any notion that the use of pikes during the latter part of the First Civil War and Commonwealth period decreased. On 16 February 1647 the Committee for the Affairs of Ireland reported that 'Lieutenant Colonel William Wetton will raise and transport a regiment of foot for Colonel Monck, himself to be lieutenant colonel, and the rest of his officers to be of his own election; and to be approved by both Houses; and to consist of 1,200 men, besides officers, in 10 companies'. Before marching, the unit was to be supplied with 800 muskets, 800 bandoliers, and 800 swords, in addition to 400 pikes and 400 swords.[160] A total of 60 matchlocks, 12 snaphaunces, 72 collars of bandoliers, 30 pikes, 2 drums and 2 halberds were received by Captain Foulis' company of Colonel Robert Overton's regiment on 21 May 1650; likewise on 1 July 700 matchlocks, 100 snaphaunces, 800 bandoliers, 400 pikes, 20 drums and 20 halberds were delivered to Colonel Robert Bennett's regiment of foot.[161]

Monck suggested that musketeers marching at the vanguard of an army 'ought to have 2 pairs of bandoliers furnished with powder and bullet, and in case you have no bandoliers, let there be provided for each musketeer … 12 cartridges, which they ought to carry in their righthand pocket, and 12 bullets apiece in their pockets besides'.[162] As to the practicality of bandoliers and cartridge boxes among dragoons, Orrery observed:

> I am also on long experience an enemy to the use of bandoliers, but a great approver of boxes of cartridges; for then, but by biting off the bottom of the cartridge, you charge your musket for service with one ramming. I would have these cartridge boxes of tin, as the carbines use them, because they are not so apt to break as the wooden ones are, and do not in wet weather, or lying in the tents, relax.[163]

Quantities of bandoliers were also captured by both sides. Following the Parliamentarian victory at Marston Moor in July 1644 the Eastern Association Army's stores were augmented by 4,550 muskets, 800 pikes and 40 barrels of powder, also ordnance, shot, swords and bandoliers, while the garrisons that surrendered to these forces in the weeks following the battle, delivered up lesser amounts of weapons and ammunition.[164]

Some examples survive of a different design of bandolier, considered rare by historians – although, it seems, on little or no evidence – which may have been issued to civil war soldiers. Fragments of two items in Barnstable Museum and a complete set at Haddon Hall, Derbyshire, dated to the seventeenth century, contain a leather flap to protect the bottles from rain, and a system to retract the bottles within the flap. This could also protect them from tangling or spilling powder when not in use or on horseback. The Haddon example has twelve wooden charges with wooden caps,

160 *CJ*, V, p.465.
161 BL, Ms Add. 35332, ff. 169r, 179v.
162 Monck, *Observations*, p.150.
163 Orrery, *Treatise*, p.31.
164 John Lilburne, *Innocency and Truth Justified* (London: 1646), pp.25 & 70.

and appears to be complete. An archaeological survey of the area of the Cheriton battlefield, known today as Dark Copse Field, undertaken in 2007 revealed the presence of 47 pewter powder bottle caps belonging to bandoliers and tops from powder flasks.[165] Finds made at various locations on the Naseby site by Mike Westaway and Peter Burton and then used by Glenn Foard, include both lead musket shot and bandolier caps.[166] A contract with the London manufacturers Thomas Jupe (who also furnished Essex's forces), Thomas Roche and Nathaniel Humphries, dated 7 January 1645, was for the supply of 4,000 bandoliers, 'the boxes of strong double plate, the heads of the same with whipcord strings, and with good belts according to the pattern at 1s. 8d. apiece'.[167] During the excavations of the Jamestown Rediscovery Project of the English settlement in Virginia in 1994 over 400 bottles and caps made from copper alloy, iron and lead were found, dating to *c.* 1607–1624, although any wooden ones may not have survived.[168]

165 James Bonsall, 'The Study of Small Finds at the 1644 Battle of Cheriton', *JCA*, 3 (2007), pp.29–52, (pp.34–5); Kevin M. Claxton, 'The Battle of Cheriton: The analysis of artefacts from an English Civil War Battlefield', *JCA*, 13 (2018), pp.80–96, (p.85).

166 Foard, *Naseby*, pp.247–248.

167 TNA, SP30/37, f. 72r.

168 https://historicjamestowne.org/collections/artifacts/bandolier – various object numbers.

7

Arms and Accoutrements II

Colonel John Okey's dragoon regiment of the New Model Army was issued with cartridge boxes from the outset. On 9 April 1645 Ordnance Office was notified of a contract with Nathaniel Humphries of Crooked Lane, in the parish of St Michael, to supply '500 cartridge boxes for dragoon muskets at 10d. apiece'. These were delivered on 11 April, and a week later a warrant was issued for the payment of £20 16s. 8d. to Humphries 'in full for his contract'. A further 500 cartridge boxes for the dragoons were received from Richard Bradley on 23 April 1645.[1] It has been suggested that these 1,000 *cartouches* were cartridges for artillery use – pre-measured amounts of gunpowder contained within a cylindrical canvas or paper case.[2] However, except for the brief entries in Ms 46 78/708, other records specifically state that such items were 'for the dragoons', and thus must in fact be cartridge boxes. Humphries and Bradley were both major suppliers of bandoliers and leather goods to the New Model Army, while Humphries provided 1,200 cartridge boxes for cavalry use in January 1646. Additionally, in August 1642 747½ ells of canvas were purchased for Essex's Army along with wooden formers used for shaping cartridges, while large quantities of canvas were procured by the Committee for the Army and issued to the New Model Army's train of artillery. Some of this must have been used for making up gun cartridges.[3] One of the officers of the train, a close waggon and 6 draught horses were apportioned to the Master Gunner, Francis Furin, and his mates 'to put cartridges in'.[4]

Given the size of the regiment during the Naseby campaign, it can be assumed that around 700 of the cartridge boxes supplied by Humphries and Bradley in April 1645 were distributed to Okey's dragoons by commissaries almost immediately. Nevertheless, during the relief of Taunton on 14 July Captain John Farmer took charge of 200 snaphaunce muskets, 200 dragoon saddles and 200 cartridge boxes, 'being for the recruiting [supplying] of Colonel Okey's regiment'.[5] The exact design of the latter remains unknown as any specifications are missing from the contracts

1 TNA, WO47/1, f. 235r; SP28/29/1, fol. 233r; Bodl. Lib., Ms Eng. C14, ff. 8v, 15v.
2 Stephen Bull, *The Furie of the Ordnance: Artillery in the English Civil Wars* (Woodbridge: Boydell, 2008), pp.22–3.
3 TNA, SP28/131/2, f. 11r; WO49/82, f. 317v; WO49/82, unfol.; Bodl. Lib., Ms Eng. C14, f. 26r; ML, Ms 46 78/708, f. 60r.
4 TNA, SP28/145, f. 62v.
5 TNA, WO55/1646, f. 146r; WSL, Ms Salt 463, unfol.

– other than that they cost 10d. apiece – while extant examples are incredibly scarce. Two boxes on display in the Heeresgeschichtliches Museum, Vienna are made of buff leather, with double flaps and a rough-hewn wooden block for holding cartridges, though admittedly these could date from the late seventeenth century. No waist belts appear to have been issued to go with the boxes purchased from Humphries and Bradley the previous April, although there is the possibility that they were sourced from more local suppliers. There is no record in the various Ordnance Office books, nor in other documents, of any cartridge boxes or belts being allocated to the fire-lock guard of the New Model, although if they did indeed have them, these items may not have been procured via regular methods. One hint that musketeers issued with snaphaunces may have, in some instances at least, been supplied with cartridge boxes rather than bandoliers comes from a warrant to the Officers of the Ordnance in June 1645 to distribute 60 matchlock muskets, 60 snaphaunces and 60 swords to Herbert's regiment of foot.[6]

Various glovers in Oxford and the surrounding areas produced powder boxes or bags, as well as girdles and hangers for Charles I's main field army. On 6 June 1643, the King's stores in New College took possession of 401 powder bags from them, and 200 girdles, hangers and bags from Thomas Jones, a leading manufacturer.[7] In June and July, he sent in 2,000 girdles and hangers.[8] Among the smaller consignments delivered into the magazine at Reading from Oxford on 24 October 1644 were '60 muskets, 60 powder bags with girdles and hangers, [and] 200 long pikes'.[9] The exact design of the powder bags or boxes remains unknown since none are known to have survived. However, one illustration in the early sixteen-century armaments book of Maximilian I depicts two lots of items: one appears to be small leather powder bags with drawcords, which may have accommodated a waist belt; the others have the appearance of square-shaped leather pouches with flaps, in addition to loops designed for belts or girdles.[10]

On 10 January 1646 a contract agreed with Nathaniel Humphries – who had previously delivered 500 boxes for the dragoons of the New Model Army – was notified for 1,200 cartridge boxes of 'strong plate covered with black leather, 700 of them half-round and the other 500 double at 10s. a piece.' He was obliged to bring them into the Ordnance Office, 'for which it is contracted, he shall be paid when he brings them in for performance, whereof he has set his hand'. Humphries duly delivered them on 7 February as part of a consignment with 1,500 collars of bandoliers, produced by him and his sometime partner Thomas Roach.[11] The likelihood is that the 1,200 cartridge boxes were intended for the cavalry, because they appear among various accoutrements associated with carbines notified to the Ordnance Officers on 10 January 1646 and delivered later that month by other craftsmen. Henry Thrall

6 TNA, WO49/82, f. 271v; WO55/460, unfol.

7 TNA, WO55/1661, f. 5r; *ROP*, I, p.103.

8 TNA, WO55/1661, f. 91r, 96r, 99v, 109v, 111r; BL, MS Add. 34352, f. 49r; *ROP*, I, p.103.

9 TNA, WO55/1661, f. 54v; *ROP*, I, p.116.

10 Bayerische Staatsbibliothek, Zeugbuch Kaiser Maximilians I – BSB Cod. icon. 222 Cod. icon. 222, f. 23r.

11 TNA, SP30/37/1, f. 73r; SP28/140/3, unfol.; Bodl. Lib., Ms Eng. C14, f. 76r; ML, Ms 46 78/708, f. 73v.

agreed to deliver '820 cartridge belts of good leather and strong buckles according to the pattern at 8d. apiece, and for 500 cartridge girdles at 2s. 8d. a dozen.' He was to mark these belts and girdles '(45)'. Under another arrangement Thrall was obligated to supply a further 200 carbine belts and 200 cartridge girdles 'according to the former contract, to be brought and paid for as aforesaid and marked thus (46)'.

In connection with what was probably a third contract, a warrant was issued on 9 February 1646 to pay him the sum of £14 6s. 8d. for 500 belts at 7d. per belt. Richard Rumsey was contracted to supply 200 carbine belts, to be marked '(47)', although an aquittance for £29 3s. 4d., signed on 4 February by Rumsey relates (like Thrall's above) to an earlier settlement to deliver 1,000 belts at 7d. apiece. Moreover, '200 belts for carbines according to a previous order' were obtained from Thomas Bostock, 'citizen and girdler of London' on 2 January 1646, while another supplier, John Mundy received payment of £7 5s. 10d. on 14 February for '250 belts at 7d. a belt'.[12] Hence, the latter payments made to Bostock and Mundy relate to earlier debentures agreed with the Committee for the Army, of which no notifications of contracts exist. During the Commonwealth period, on 25 August 1649, the Treasurers at War paid 'Henry Thrall and Thomas Bostock, belt-makers' £83 6s. 8d. for 2,000 carbine belts for Ireland. Similarly, the following October the Council of State expended a total of £30 for 400 carbine belts and swivels for the army in Scotland.[13] The prices for each belt represented here are 1s. 6d. and 10d. respectively. It is unlikely that the costs were linked into those for carriage, however, because various civil war accounts show that freight was customarily charged separately.

The figures provided in the Ordnance Office books and Treasury warrants point to a total of 1,520 cartridge belts, 700 cartridge girdles and 1,650 carbine belts being brought into the stores in January and February 1646. While there is the suggestion that the cartridge 'belts' and 'girdles' were different items (or at least of differing quality), given that the former are described as 'of good leather and strong buckles' costing 8d. each, and the latter at 2s. 8d. a dozen or 2½d. apiece, this is difficult to quantify. On 6 July 1644 Colonel John Fiennes paid the sum of £8 'for colours and standards' for his regiment, while the following month 1s. 1½d. was disbursed for carbine belts for his command, in addition to between 10s. 8d. and 14s. for carbines, and 5s. 6d. for six 'keys and swivels for carbines'.[14] Following his defeat while besieging Banbury Castle in October 1644 Colonel Fiennes' troopers lost 200 pair of pistols, and 200 backs, breasts, and pots. It was duly ordered 'that he will undertake to furnish them himself, so as he may have an assessment for the payment of it within three months, upon the moneys that were appointed by Ordinance of Parliament to Sir Walter Erle, out of the arrears of the assessments of London and Middlesex, for the providing of arms'.[15] The pistols, however, were not delivered to the regiment until 2 May 1645. Although Fiennes' regiment was not part of the establishment of the New Model, and was paid and supplied separately to it, such

12 TNA, SP28/36/2, unfol.; SP28/140/3, unfol.; ML, Ms 46 78/708, f. 73r.
13 *CSPD Interregnum 1649–50*, p.574; *CSPD Interregnum 1650*, p.368.
14 TNA, SP28/139/19, ff. 207r–207v.
15 TNA, WO55/460, unfol.; *CSPD 1644–5*, pp.188 & 447.

comparisons are highly valid because Fiennes and his troopers fought at Naseby and participated in the army's operations in Oxfordshire in 1645.

Moreover, on 7 July 1645 the Committee of Both Kingdoms wrote to Sir Thomas Fairfax, informing him that having selected Fiennes' regiment to deliver money to Portsmouth for the New Model, and subsequently rejoin the army, currently in Somerset:

> This regiment having lost many horses, both by their long marches with that army and in the fight at Naseby Field, where we are informed, they did very good service, we recommend it to you for some recruits [supplies] out of those horses which by the late Ordinance you are enabled to take for that purpose out of the enemy's quarters. By this means the enemy will be weakened, and that regiment fitted for future service. The horses were raised without charge to the State, and they have not hitherto had any recruits, we therefore desire that they may be supplied in this way.[16]

The quantities of cartridge box belts and carbine belts purchased for the New Model horse in early 1646 appear to have represented more than enough for the recently secured 1,202 carbines, though the 'extra' items raise the possibility that other stocks were already in the stores, and or previously issued out. On 22 January 1646 1,000 carbines with swivels and belts, and 1,000 cartridge boxes for carbines with girdles were delivered as part of a consignment of arms to the magazine at Portsmouth to be issued to Sir Thomas Fairfax's troops.[17]

During the seventeenth century, cartridges consisted of a sealed paper tube, containing a measure of black powder and a bullet at one end. Writing in 1616, Wallhausen maintained that harquebusiers should either use powder flasks and bullets from a bag or, alternatively, cartridges.[18] Likewise, the cavalry practitioners Cruso and Vernon agreed that only paper cartridges were to be used as ammunition for both cuirassiers and harquebusiers.[19] The latter wrote in his manual of 1644:

> if you use cartridges, you shall find in your cartridge case a turned wooden pin which you must take, having cut lengths of white paper something broader than the pin is in length, and roll the paper on the pin, then twist one end of the paper, and fill it almost full of powder, then put the bullet on top of the powder, twisting that end also, then put it into your cartridge case, now when you come to load your carbine or pistol with these cartridges, you must bite off that end of the paper where the powder is, pouring it into your carbine or pistol, then put in that bullet, and some of that paper will serve as a wad after it, and ram home, but always observe that your bullet be not too big, but that it may roll home to the powder, for if there be any distance between the bullet and powder, it is like to break the barrel of your carbine or pistol. But if you use a flask, which in my judgement is far better than cartridge,

16 *CSPD 1645–7*, p.7.
17 TNA, WO55/1646, unfol.
18 Wallhausen, *Kriegskunst*, p.35.
19 Cruso, *Militarie Instructions*, pp.37–42; Vernon, *Young Horse-man*, p.8.

> because that many times the trotting of your horse in long march, shakes out all the powder of your cartridges and thereby causes you to be unprovided for the sudden charge of the enemy, you must gauge your flask and so load your carbine and pistol with powder and bullet as before, but never prime before you have spanned. Now the quantity of the powder usually required for the loading of either carbine or pistol is half the weight of the bullet.[20]

In a similar fashion, Monck suggested that musketeers marching at the vanguard of an army 'ought to have two pairs of bandoliers furnished with powder and bullet, and in case you have no bandoliers, let there be provided for each musketeer ... twelve cartridges, which they ought to carry in their righthand pocket, and twelve bullets apiece in their pockets besides'.[21] As to the practicality of bandoliers and cartridge boxes among dragoons, Orrery observed:

> I am also on long experience an enemy to the use of bandoliers, but a great approver of boxes of cartridges; for then, but by biting off the bottom of the cartridge, you charge your musket for service with one ramming. I would have these cartridge boxes of tin, as the carbines use them, because they are not so apt to break as the wooden ones are, and do not in wet weather, or lying in the tents, relax.[22]

Swords

The sword was the principal weapon of the cavalry during the British Civil Wars, but it was also used by every other type of soldier. Surviving records and existing examples show that there were different patterns for the horse and foot, at least among swords supplied to Parliament. Among the notifications of contracts for the New Model Army While only 200 are mentioned as being specifically for the cavalry, it is impossible to be certain that the remaining weapons were intended for the foot. There is no noticeable explanation of the infrequent appearance of swords in the Ordnance Office receipts books. Only 300 swords are recorded as having been delivered to the land forces of Parliament between April 1645 and June 1646, even though during a corresponding period a total of 31,800 of these weapons were procured by the Army Committee and paid for. However, various quantities of swords are recorded as being delivered into the Ordnance Office stores and subsequently distributed to the New Model Army during this time. These include the 2,500 swords and belts at 4s. 6d. per set accepted from Benjamin Hawkins on 10 April 1645; 1,500 swords and belts from Richard Tredwell six days later; and 500 swords with Dutch blades and belts delivered by Richard Jones on 19 July 1645.[23]

20 Vernon, *Young Horse-Man*, p.10.
21 Monck, *Observations*, p.150.
22 Orrery, *Treatise*, p.31.
23 TNA, SP28/29/1, ff. 207r, 226r; SP28/31/5, f. 535r; WO55/1646, unfol.; WSL, Ms Salt 463, unfol.

At least 11,600 swords and belts were distributed by the Ordnance Office to the New Model foot. Of these, 4,826 swords and 4,908 belts were included among consignments of weapons packed at the Reading magazine on 11 December 1645 for transportation to Portsmouth for Sir Thomas Fairfax's troops in the West Country.[24] In the absence of definite information, and assuming that the records themselves are not defective, it must be accepted that these deliveries (in addition to backs, breasts and helmets) were made directly to the army, perhaps because they were not proved at the Tower. This assumption that these stores did not pass through the Ordnance Office is enhanced by an order made to its officers on 16 January 1646 for supplying the New Model Army with 2,200 swords which was not complied with.[25]

The modern term 'mortuary sword' is now applied to a particular type of straight, double-edged broadsword of the mid-seventeenth century and used principally by the cavalry. Other categories of broadswords are the so-called proto-mortuary sword and the basket-hilted sword.[26] In 1622 Francis Markham endorsed the use of 'a basket hilt of a nimble and round proportion after the Irish, strong scabbards of lacquered or well-rosend leather, chapes of iron, and girdles and hangers suitable to the same'.[27] Similarly, in his *Military Instructions for the Cavalry*, published ten years later, John Cruso recommended 'a good sword, which was to be very stiff, cutting, and sharp-pointed', while John Vernon mentioned 'a good stiff sword sharp-pointed'.[28] In July 1650 William Arthur provided the Parliamentarian forces in Ireland with 81 swords with Irish hilts, 60 ammunition swords, and 150 sword belts.[29] In 1629, the Lieutenant of Ordnance, Sir John Heyden, was sent to Rotterdam where he met German swordsmiths from Solingen in the Ruhr Valley, possibly refugees from the Thirty Years' War. *Klingenschmieldes* (forgers), *Schwertschleifer* (grinders), *Schwertharters* (hardeners), and *Schwertfegers* (polishers) were persuaded to come to Hounslow in England and set up sword-blade manufactories. Peter Munsten (the younger), Johann Kindt, Caspar Carnis (anglicised from Fleisch), Clemens Meigen and Clemens Horn (the younger) came, while Johannes Hoppie (the elder) relocated from the Royal Armouries at Greenwich to the new site. One of his surviving swords is signed *IOHANNES HOPPE 1634 ME FECIT GRENEWICH IN ANGLIA*.[30]

This is possibly why many documents of the period referred to the Solingen Germans who emigrated to England as Dutch and why they called their blades 'Dutch' blades. Nevertheless, this could also be a corruption of 'Deutsche' for German, or an indication that blades of various nationalities had been exported to England via Dutch merchants, who were known to order swords and other weapons specifically for resale. Many of these smiths signed their blades *ME FECIT HOUNSLO* (spellings vary) meaning, 'I was made in Hounslow', in the early years of

24 TNA, SP28/126/1, ff. 1r–5r.
25 TNA, WO/55/1646, f. 319v.
26 Blackmore, *Arms and Armour*, pp.24–31; Stuart C. Mowbray, *British Military Swords* (Mowbray Publishing, 2013), I, pp.178–225.
27 Markham, *Five Decades*, p.34.
28 Cruso, *Military Instructions*, p.29; Vernon, *The Young Horse-man*, p.8.
29 *CSPD Interregnum 1649–50*, p.581.
30 Thanks to Simon Frame for the information contained in this and the following section, and for allowing the use of photographs from his extensive collection of seventeenth century swords.

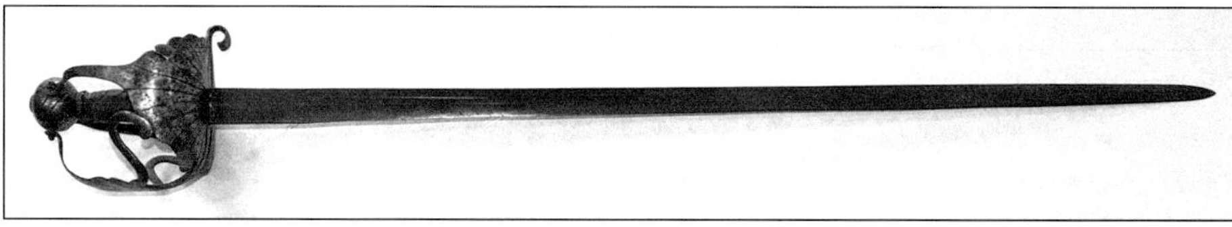

Proto mortuary sword with back sword-blade. (Courtesy of Simon Frame)

operation adding their names and often the Passau Running Wolf of Solingen. They remain famous for a sword-style known as the 'Hounslow Hangar', named from a few examples which survive where 'Hounslow' is prominently engraved or stamped on the blades.

Benjamin Stone, a freeman of the London Cutlers' Company, established a water-powered sword mill at Hounslow in 1630 for the grinding and polishing of blades. It initially employed immigrant German bladesmiths and was founded specifically to address the English reliance on imported weapons. Stone was already supplying the Ordnance Office with swords fitted with imported blades, and hence 'Hounslow' marks can be found on the blades of basket-hilted swords, hangers and rapiers of the period. Stone continued in business until 1642, when he and some of the craftsmen fled to Oxford, where a sword mill was set up at Wolvercote to supply the King's forces.[31]

On 20 November 1643, William Legge was given £100 'to be employed in building a mill at Wolvercote, for grinding of swords and for building forges, providing tools and other necessaries for sword-blade makers to be employed to make swords for our service'.[32] Similarly, a sum 'not exceeding £2,000' was ordered to be paid to Legge on 26 February 1644 'for providing swords and belts in the office of armouries, the same to be made at the usual price and according to the patterns by us appointed: also to provide tools and other necessaries for sword-blade makers employed by the said Master of the Armouries'. Such weapons were to cost '7s. 6d. for every sword and 2s. for each belt'.[33] By comparison, the Cutlers Company, which supplied the New Model Army with most of its swords, was not capable of making blades as there was no provision for running water, forging, grinding and polishing mills, and therefore the manufacture of steel inside the capital was impractical. However, most of the procured swords contained blades imported primarily from Solingen in Germany, through merchants in Amsterdam and elsewhere, and were fitted with hilts in London. Various complete swords were also imported and supplied to the army.

Infantrymen (and possibly dragoons) used munition quality thrusting swords, being cheaper and lighter versions of cavalry weapons. Instructions issued to the English and Welsh trained bands in 1626 referred to 'a good strong and serviceable sword, the blade thereof not to be above three foot in length, in a good scabbard

31 Stone, Benjamin (*fl.* 1605–1643), revised John Tofts White – *ODNB* (2004); Leslie Southwick, 'The London Cutler Benjamin Stone, and the Hounslow Sword and Blade Manufactories', *Arms and Armour*, 6 (2009), pp.12–61.

32 *CSPD 1641–3*, p.501.

33 *ROP*, I, p.176.

with belt or girdle and hangers fitted thereunto'. Similarly, in 1635 they were to be issued with 'a good sword of three foot long, cutting, stiff-pointed, with girdle and hangers'.[34] Monck recommended for musketeers, pikemen and dragoons 'a good long tuck, with a belt', while the Royalist Richard Atkins described his sword at Roundway Down in 1643 as a tuck and a colleague as wearing a hanger, although Atkins himself was an officer in Prince Maurice's regiment of horse.[35] As with armours and firearms, control over the specifications and quality of swords supplied by members of the London Cutlers' Company was achieved by their own appointed proof masters. On 29 July 1645 the Officers of Ordnance Office certified that William Roberts was 'a fit and able man to execute the Proof Master's place, now void'.[36] Likewise, the services of master craftsmen were engaged to inspect batches as they were delivered in accordance with the conditions of individual contracts. In July 1649 the Treasurers at War were ordered to pay the sum of £12 9s. to Samuel Laws, cutler, for inspecting swords for Ireland, while the following November he was to have a further £20 'for his pains in cleansing and proving swords in the Tower, in execution of the office conferred on him by the regulators'.[37]

On 4 May 1642, 1,000 arms were sent by the Ordnance Office to Minehead for transportation to Munster, Ireland. These 'complete arms [were] provided fitted and sent away by those respective officers for 1,000 men to Minehead. The swords belonging to those arms being in number 1,764 or thereabouts, to be Hounslow blades.' These swords were part of a larger consignment, comprising 347 corslets; 1,367 bandoliers; 354 pikes; 1,367 muskets; 3,367 musket rests; 32 drums; 56 partizans; 27 halberds; in addition to the 1,764 swords and belts.[38]

In September 1642 Colonel James Wardlaw's Parliamentarian dragoons received 600 swords with belts.[39] When Colonel Richard Browne's regiment was formed in November 1642 the sum of £265 7s. was disbursed to five London craftsmen for swords. One of these, Lawrence Bromfield, a member of London's Cutlers' Company and a captain in the Red Regiment of the London Trained Bands, also provided Browne's regiment with quantities of 'swords and belts' at a cost of £253 and also sold nearly 3,000 swords to the Committee of Safety in the first eighteen months of the war.[40] On 21 September 1643 Bromfield entered into an agreement to supply 300 swords for dragoons (possibly those in the Eastern Association Army), for which he was paid £105, or 7s. apiece.[41] Similarly, on 6 May 1644 '200 swords and belts at 7s. each' were procured by the Earl of Denbigh's commissary from an unnamed supplier, though his troop of horse had been equipped with arms and armour produced in London by Thomas Stevens.[42]

34 W. Wrye (ed.), *State Papers Relating to Musters, Beacons, Ship-money, &c. in Norfolk from 1626 chiefly to the beginning of the Civil War* (Norwich, 1907), pp.90, 200.
35 Monck, *Observations*, pp.26–27; Young and Tucker (eds), *Military Memoirs*, p.51.
36 TNA, WO/49/82, f. 323v.
37 *CSPD Interregnum 1649–50*, pp.579–80; *CSPD Interregnum 1650*, pp.601–602.
38 *LJ*, V, p.38; *Private Journals*, pp.433–434.
39 TNA, WO55/1754, unfol.
40 TNA, SP28/144/2, ff. 29r–34r.
41 TNA, SP/28/227/1, unfol.
42 WA, CR2017/C9/91; CR 2017/C10/68.

'Type 91' sword hilt. (Courtesy of Simon Frame)

The Committee for the Army contracted with the Company of Cutlers in London in March 1645 for swords and belts. Thus, items manufactured by over a dozen different London craftsmen for Fairfax's Army are recorded in various quantities, usually priced at 4s. 6d. a set. Some contracts, such as that agreed on 11 July 1645 with Thomas Freeman, Warden of the Cutlers for 2,000 swords and belts stipulate that the swords were to have Dutch blades.[43] There are receipts of similar items, as indicated by the '500 swords and belts with Dutch blades' delivered by Richard Jones by 19 July 1645 when a warrant for his payment was issued.[44] In both cases these weapons were priced at 4s. 6d. each, the same as those manufactured in London, and possibly containing the previously discussed imported German blades. Substantial quantities of foreign sword blades for English-made hilts to be added were imported into Britain between 1642 and 1646, mainly from Amsterdam. In October 1642 Parliament contracted with the agent Thomas Cunningham for the delivery at Leith of 6,000 muskets and bandoliers, 4,000 pikes and 10,000 swords with belts.[45] The arms were purchased in the Low Countries for the Scottish army in Ireland.

In October 1646 the cutler John Davies was engaged to supply Parliament's forces in Ireland with 'footmen's swords, Dutch blades, with belts, at 5s. 3d. per sword.'[46] However, among the charges brought against Davies the previous year was that in sending 600 swords to Ireland 'he was to have 6s. 6d. per sword of the State, and might have bought good German swords for 4s. and 4s. 6d. per sword, the swords which were provided by Mr Davies for that service were not worth 3s. 6d. per sword, being French blades and unserviceable.'[47] Few orders indicate whether such swords and belts were intended for the cavalry or foot, or indeed both, however. Nevertheless, on 7 April 1645 a payment of £800 was authorised to Robert Foulcer, 'one of the Company of Cutlers' for '3,000 footmen's swords and belts, and 200 horsemen's swords and belts at 5s. per sword and belt'.[48] However, the contract with Davies also

43 TNA, WO47/1, f. 209r; ML, Ms 46 78/708, f. 98r.
44 TNA, SP28/31/5, f. 535r.
45 *CJ*, II, p.793.
46 *CJ*, IV, p.698.
47 TNA, SP28/253/1/2, ff. 76v–77r, 96r–97r.
48 TNA, SP28/29/2, f. 314r.

involved cavalry weapons with belts costing 6s. 6d. apiece, whereas one tender to supply the British forces in Ireland in 1648 included the sum of £1,250 to be spent on '5,000 swords, with belts, at 5s. apiece' and a further £300 for '1,000 swords for horsemen, with belts, at 6s. each'.[49] In all, during the period 1645 to 1646 11,600 swords – of which only 200 are mentioned as being specifically for cavalry troopers – were procured by the Committee for the Army to be delivered to the Ordnance Office, though it is likely that more were acquired from other sources, possibly financed by enforced loans raised in London. Additionally, in February 1647 '2,000 footmen's swords and belts, Dutch blades, at 4s. 4d. apiece, and best English blades at 4s. apiece' were sent to Ireland for the use of troops under Colonel Michael Jones, while a report to the Committee at Star Chamber, dated 30 November 1647, recommended 'sending saddles and swords for cavalry and dragoons to [Colonel] Monck. If he has these, he will be able to organise raids and, according to reports from Ulster, to do great service'.[50] It could be, as the source does not distinguish between neither the types of saddles, nor swords, in this instance at least that troopers and dragoons were issued the same kind of both items.

Table 28: Notification of Contracts to the Ordnance Office for the Supply of Swords and Belts for the NMA (TNA, WO49/82; ML, Ms 46 78/708)

Date	Quantity and type	Price per set	Contractor
3/4/45	3200 swords and belts, whereof 200 are horsemen's swords	5s.	Warden and Company of Cutlers
3/4/45	1000 swords and belts	4s. 8d.	Hugh Hicks & John Varnan
3/4/45	1000 swords and belts	4s. 8d.	Robert Jeffrey
3/4/45	2500 swords and belts	4s. 8d.	Benjamin Hawkins
3/4/45	1500 swords and belts	4s. 8d.	Richard Tredwell
11/7/45	2000 swords and belts Dutch blades	4s. 6d.	Thomas Freeman, Warden of the Cutlers
11/7/45	400 swords and belts Dutch blades	4s. 6d.	Daniel Judd
3/8/45	1000 swords and belts	4s. 6d.	Robert Gilbert & Richard Rumsey

Table 29: Warrants for Payments to Contractors for the Delivery of Swords and Belts to the Ordnance Office for the NMA (TNA, SP28/29/1-32/3)

Date	Quantity and type	Price per set	Contractor
7/4/45	3000 footmen's swords and belts, and 200 horsemen's swords and belts	5s.	Robert Foulcer
10/4/45	2500 swords and belts in full of his contract	4s. 6d.	Benjamin Hawkins
10/4/45	1000 swords and belts in full of his contract	4s. 6d.	Robert Jeffrey

49 *CJ*, IV, p.698; *LJ*, X, pp.158–159.
50 BL, Ms Add. 35332, f. 51r; *CSPD 1645–47*, pp.593–594.

Date	Quantity and type	Price per set	Contractor
16/4/45	1000 swords and belts in full of their contract	4s. 6d.	John Varnan & Hugh Hicks
16/4/45	1500 swords and belts in full of their contract	4s. 6d.	Richard Tredwell
8/6/45	1000 swords and belts in full of his contract	4s. 6d.	Colonel Lawrence Bromfield
19/7/45	500 swords and belts Dutch blades	4s. 6d.	Richard Jones
31/7/45	400 swords and belts	4s. 6d.	Daniell Judd
31/7/45	3100 swords and belts	4s. 6d.	Thomas Freeman
23/9/45	500 swords and belts	4s. 6d.	Robert Jefferies
23/9/45	500 swords and belts	4s. 6d.	John Jackson
23/9/45	500 swords and belts	4s. 6d.	Richard Jones
23/9/45	500 swords and belts	4s. 6d.	Robert Gilbert
29/9/45	1000 swords and belts	4s. 6d.	Robert Tredwell
29/9/45	500 swords and belts	4s. 6d.	James Wright
6/10/45	500 swords and belts	4s. 6d.	Thomas Freeman
21/10/45	500 swords and belts	4s. 6d.	Robert Hammond

During the period 1642 to 1644 the London Militia Committee purchased sets of armours for the City Horse, while in May 1644 500 pairs of pistols, 500 saddles, 500 backs and breasts and 500 cavalry helmets were acquired from London suppliers for Sir William Brereton's regiment of horse.[51] Likewise, on 15 June the Commons ordered the issue of 400 swords and 400 pairs of pistols to Colonel Edwin Sandys' regiment of horse in Yorkshire. These arms were to be 'furnished out of the public stores and sent to the magazine at Hull'. The Commons ordered the delivery of 300 pairs of pistols with holsters, with 100 backs, breasts and pots to Cromwell, 'to arm his regiment' on 4 October 1644, while in February 1645 300 cavalry swords were ordered for Colonel John Fiennes' regiment, presumably from London cutlers.[52] By the time of the Battle of Naseby on 14 June 1645 over 10,000 swords and belts had been delivered to the Ordnance Office for the use of the New Model Army, while between July and October a further 8,500 were received from contractors.[53] In terms of their distribution among the army, on 18 September 3,000 infantry swords and belts were delivered by the Ordnance Office 'to Commissary Thomas Futter to be sent to Reading for Sir Thomas Fairfax his Army', among a consignment which also included 1,400 matchlock muskets, 3,000 bandoliers, 1,000 pikes, 5,000 snapsacks, 5,000 coats and breeches, 5,000 shirts, 5,000 pairs of shoes and 5,000 pairs of stockings.[54] Similarly, a warrant was issued on 16 January 1646 'to deliver to Thomas

51 TNA, SP28/14, ff. 47r, 55v; SP28/131/1, f. 2r; *LJ*, VI, pp.446, 551.

52 *CJ*, III, pp.531, 652; *CSPD 1644–5*, p.290.

53 TNA, SP28/29/1, ff. 207r, 208r, 224r, 226r; SP28/29/2, f. 314r; SP28/30/4, f. 374r; SP28/31/3, f. 436r; SP28/31/5, ff. 531r, 535r; SP28/32/1, ff. 5r 102r; SP28/32/3, ff. 368r, 369r, 370r, 372r, 377r, 383r.

54 TNA, WO55/1647, unfol.; WSL, Ms Salt 463, unfol.

Richardson out of the stores ... to be sent to Portsmouth for Sir Thomas Fairfax his Army' 500 pairs pistols with holsters, 1,000 matchlock muskets, 1,000 bandoliers, 1,000 carbines with swivels and belts, 1,000 cartouches for carbines with girdles, 1,200 pikes, 2,200 swords with belts, and 2,200 snapsacks. These were duly delivered six days later.[55]

Considerable quantities of swords were also purchased on behalf of the Committee of Safety with loans raised by the Committee for the Advance of Money for the Service of the Parliament, sitting at Haberdashers Hall, which do not appear in the Ordnance Office receipts books. For instance, on 14 January 1645 the Commons ordered that '300 pairs of pistols and holsters, and 700 swords, be provided upon the credit of Haberdashers Hall, to be repaid at three months end', to be conducted to Montgomeryshire to encourage the recruitment (presumably of cavalry) there. In September 3,000 swords, along with 5,000 muskets, 2,000 pikes, and 200 barrels of powder with a double proportion of match were supplied to the Scots Covenanter Army out of the Ordnance Office stores. Moreover, the Committee of Goldsmiths Hall agreed on 2 December 1645 to furnish the Parliamentarian forces in Lincolnshire with substantial military stores, including 400 swords and belts, 100 muskets and 400 collars of bandoliers for the garrison of King's Lynn; and 200 swords and belts, and 200 bandoliers for the foot at Boston.[56]

Cavalry and Pikeman's Armours

On 14 March 1645 the Commons ordered that £12,300 was to be 'forthwith provided and furnished out of the £80,000 borrowed of the City, for the 1,200 horse, with arms, pistols, and saddles.'[57] As far as arms and equipment were concerned, harquebusiers were meant to be issued with defensive armour in the form of a helmet, and back and breast plates. It has been suggested that some civil war cavalrymen wore metal bridle gauntlets or leather gauntlet cuffs to protect their left hands and wrists – as known from a few museum examples – but there is no evidence for any purchases of such items for the New Model Army. If worn, they must have been privately acquired. Harquebusier armours (described often as 'suits') comprised 'backs, breasts and pots', and cost about 20s. apiece. What appears to be the first batch, was for 1,000 sets from Colonel Owen Rowe, 500 delivered to the New Model on 3 April 1645 and 500 on 27 May 1645. Similarly, the armourer, Silvester Keen was contracted to supply '100 arms for horsemen, backs, breasts and pots' to the Ordnance Office at the same price on 5 April, which he delivered on 20 June.[58] Armours were supplied to some New Model cavalry regiments, especially during their initial formation, though most of these do not appear in the various warrants and issue books. It could be the case that various stocks either remained for some time in the Ordnance Office stores, or several cavalry troopers brought them with

55 TNA, WO55/1646, unfol.
56 *CJ*, IV, pp.19, 274, 363; *LJ*, VII, p.152.
57 *CJ*, IV, p.77.
58 TNA, SP28/352, unfol.; WO49/82, f. 146v.

them when they re-enlisted into Fairfax's Army, although the substantial quantities of pistols and saddles issued to the regiments of horse in April-May 1645 might suggest that this was not the case. On 14 March the Committee of Both Kingdoms informed Colonel Richard Graves that upon the reduction of the troops of the two regiments of the Lord General and Sir William Balfour into his own, they would be provided with a fortnight's pay, 'and order will shortly be given for their employment, and the remounting of such of them as are on foot and providing all with arms fitting them for service.'[59]

Subsequently, on 14 April Sergeant Major General Skippon wrote to the Speaker from Beaconsfield:

> Yesterday and this day, by God's continued help and blessing, all his Excellency's horse are reduced and settled into Colonel Graves', Sir Robert Pye's, and Colonel Sheffield's regiments, except Colonel Dalbier's and Behre's regiments, which are commanded to Gloucester. All the officers that are laid aside, did with all readiness and submissive obedience observe the commands of the inferior officers, having listed themselves again as private troopers; so that hitherto (blessed be God) this great, and I hope useful work for the public has been carried beyond our expectation that have been employed about it. Tomorrow, if the Lord will, I shall reduce and settle Colonel Weldon's, and Colonel Holborne's regiments of foot, which were with Sir William Waller, and now quartered at Ockingham. And I shall further endeavor with all diligence and faithfulness, whatsoever shall advance the public service. Those regiments of horse which were his Excellency's and Sir William Balfore's, do most humbly crave (as I do on their behalf) that they may have that which Colonel Graves says was promised to them. I have not else to trouble you with now, but begging pardon for my being so often troublesome to you (the conjunction of things now forcing the same) and humbly crave to be esteemed.[60]

In 1649 George Murray, a trooper in Captain Fleming's troop of Graves' regiment, petitioned that he had served between 15 September 1645 and 29 December 1646, and 'he brought in his horse and arms into the said regiment, which horse was killed at the last siege before Oxford, where he himself was wounded and maimed.'[61] Various quantities of defensive armour and helmets were procured for the New Model Army in 1645–1646 (1,640 sets by early June 1645), and there appears little reason why this equipment should have languished in the stores, rather than being distributed. However, the only recorded issue is that of 100 sets supplied to Colonel Robert Pye's regiment on 4 April 1645 along with an equivalent quantity of pistols, holsters and saddles.[62]

---

59 *CSPD 1644–5*, p.347.
60 Vicars, *Burning-Bush*, pp.133–134.
61 TNA, SP28/59, ff. 182v–183r.
62 TNA, SP28/352, unfol.; WO49/82, ff. 146v–148r; WSL, Ms Salt 463, unfol.

Table 30: Notification of Contracts to the Ordnance Office for the Supply of Cavalry Armour to the NMA (TNA, WO47/1; ML, Ms 46 78/708)

Date	Quantity and type	Price per suit	Contractor
3/4/45	200 backs, breasts and pots	20s.	Colonel Rowe
3/4/45	1000 backs, breasts and pots	20s.	Colonel Rowe
3/4/45	200 backs, breasts and pots	20s.	Sylvester Keen
3/4/45	100 backs, breasts and pots for horsemen	20s.	Sylvester Keen
20/6/45	100 backs, breasts and pots	20s.	Anthony Newman
20/6/45	100 backs, breasts and pots	20s.	Sylvester Keen
26/6/45	200 backs, breasts and pots	20s.	Thomas Stevens & Nicholas Marshall
26/6/45	200 backs, breasts and pots	20s.	Sylvester Keen
26/6/45	100 backs, breasts and pots	20s.	Anthony Newman
26/6/45	400 backs, breasts and pots	20s.	Peter Newton, Richard Wellman, Edward Bunion & John Wright
2/7/45	200 pots with three bars English	7s.	Edward Barker

Table 31: Receipts of Cavalry Armour to the Ordnance Office for the NMA (TNA, SP28/140/3; SP28/352/1)

Date	Quantity and type	Price per suit	Contractor
14/4/45	1000 backs, breasts and pots at three months beginning this date	20s.	Colonel Rowe
5/4/45	In full for 100 arms for horsemen, backs, breasts and pots	20s.	Silvester Keen
7/5/45	120 backs, breasts and pots	20s.	Silvester Keen
18/5/45	100 backs, breasts and pots	20s.	Silvester Keen
19/5/45	70 backs, breasts and pots	20s.	Silvester Keen
28/5/45	100 backs, breasts and pots	20s.	Silvester Keen
30/5/45	100 backs, breasts and pots	20s.	Anthony Newman
30/5/45	150 backs, breasts and pots	20s.	Nich. Marshall, Thos Stevens & John Wright
7/6/45	100 backs, breasts and pots, and 100 more pots at 7s. a pot	20s.	Ant. Newman
5/7/45	100 backs, breasts and pots	20s.	Peter Newton
5/7/45	100 backs, breasts and pots	20s.	Nicholas Marshall
8/7/45	100 backs, breasts and pots	20s.	John Wright
9/7/45	200 pots	7s.	Edward Barker
18/7/45	200 backs, breasts and pots, and 100 more pots		Silvester Keen & Ralph Boulter
23/7/45	100 backs, breasts and pots	20s.	Thomas Stevens
30/7/45	100 backs, breasts and pots, and 100 spare pots at 7s. a pot	20s.	Edward Bunnion
9/2/46	Received 200 backs, breasts and pots		John Berisford

Date	Quantity and type	Price per suit	Contractor
30/7/45	200 pots	7s.	Anthony Newman
4/8/45	100 pots	7s.	Nicholas Marshall
13/8/45	100 pots	7s.	Silvester Keen
15/8/45	100 backs, breasts and pots, and 100 spare pots	20s.	Richard Wellman
23/8/45	100 pots	7s.	Thomas Stevens
29/8/45	200 pots	7s.	John Wright & Peter Newton
18/4/45	50 backs, breasts and pot headpieces	17s.	William Fosbrooke
23/1/46	163 backs, breasts and pot headpieces	17s.	Silvester Keen
26/1/46	25 backs, breasts and pot headpieces	17s.	Samuel Aston
26/1/46	60 backs, breasts and pot headpieces	17s.	Wm Cox & George Gurden
26/1/46	50 backs, breasts and pot headpieces	17s.	William Fosbrooke
26/1/46	75 backs, breasts and pot headpieces	17s.	Richard Knight
26/146	125 backs, breasts and pot headpieces	17s.	Peter Newton
26/1/46	63 backs, breasts and pot headpieces	17s.	Anthony Newman
26/1/46	8 backs, breasts and pot headpieces	17s.	Thomas Manney
26/1/46	75 backs, breasts and pot headpieces	17s.	Thomas Rowe
26/1/46	25 backs, breasts and pot headpieces	17s.	Richard Ray
26/1/46	20 backs, breasts and pot headpieces	17s.	Solomon Chipchase
26/1/46	87 backs, breasts and pot headpieces	17s.	Rich. Wellman
29/1/46	62 backs, breasts and pot headpieces	17s.	Anthony Newman
31/1/46	50 backs, breasts and pot headpieces	17s.	Thos Stevens
6/2/46	150 backs, breasts and pot headpieces	17s.	Nicholas Marshall
9/2/46	25 backs, breasts and pot headpieces	17s.	John Holloway
10/2/46	100 backs, breasts and pot headpieces	17s.	Edward Ansley
20/2/46	75 backs, breasts and pot headpieces	17s.	Thomas Rowe
20/2/46	82 backs, breasts and pot headpieces	17s.	Richard Wellman
20/2/46	163 backs, breasts and pot headpieces	17s.	Robert Thurleby
20/2/46	163 backs, breasts and pot headpieces	17s.	Silvester Keen
21/2/46	20 backs, breasts and pot headpieces	17s.	Solomon Chipchase
21/2/46	125 backs, breasts and pot headpieces	17s.	Peter Newton
24/2/46	25 backs, breasts and pot headpieces	17s.	Richard Ray
24/2/46	50 backs, breasts and pot headpieces	17s.	William Fosbrooke
24/2/46	30 backs, breasts and pot headpieces	17s.	William Harrison
24/2/46	75 backs, breasts and pot headpieces	17s.	Richard Knight
24/2/46	50 backs, breasts and pot headpieces	17s.	Thomas Stevens
2/3/46	25 backs, breasts and pot headpieces	17s.	Samuel Aston
10/3/46	75 backs, breasts and pot headpieces	17s.	Nicholas Marshall
10/3/46	22 backs, breasts and pot headpieces	17s.	Thomas Manney
18/4/46	113 backs, breasts and pot headpieces	17s.	Peter Newton

Date	Quantity and type	Price per suit	Contractor
18/4/46	50 backs, breasts and pot headpieces	17s.	Thomas Stevens
19/3/46	25 backs, breasts and pot headpieces	17s.	John Holloway
24/3/46	163 backs, breasts and pot headpieces	17s.	Silvester Keen
24/3/46	25 backs, breasts and pot headpieces	17s.	Richard Ray
23/4/46	163 backs, breasts and pot headpieces	17s.	Silvester Keen
24/4/46	163 backs, breasts and pot headpieces	17s.	Samuel Aston
24/4/46	65 backs, breasts and pot headpieces	17s.	Richard Knight
24/4/46	75 backs, breasts and pot headpieces	17s.	Nicholas Marshall
24/4/46	25 backs, breasts and pot headpieces	17s.	Richard Ray
28/4/46	75 backs, breasts and pot headpieces	17s.	Thomas Rowe
30/4/46	88 backs, breasts and pot headpieces	17s.	Richard Wellman

Table 33: Notification of Contracts to the Ordnance Office for the Supply of Foot Headpieces to the NMA (TNA, WO47/1; ML, Ms 46 78/708)

Date	Quantity and type	Price each	Contractor
26/6/45	200 headpieces	7s.	Silvester Keen
26/6/45	200 headpieces	7s.	Anthony Newman
26/6/45	200 headpieces	7s.	Thomas Stevens & Nicholas Marshall
26/6/45	400 headpieces	7s.	Peter Newton, Richard Wellman, Edward Bunion & John Wright

The question of whether pikemen's armour was issued to the New Model Army is an important one. It can be interpreted that two types of armours were described in the Ordnance Office warrants and receipts books. This was first identified by Peter Edwards in *Dealing in Death*.[63] Seventeenth century military manuals generally maintained that pikemen ought to be larger and sturdier than musketeers, but how this worked in practice is difficult to know. In 1671 Turner complained about contemporary officers 'who take no notice to make a difference of those who are to carry muskets and pikes, distributing them promiscuously to the stronger and the weaker, whereas about all question, the tallest, biggest, and strongest should be ordered to carry pikes, that they may the better endure the weight of their defensive arms'.[64] The defensive value of pike armour is alluded to by a request from Colonel William Lockhart to Secretary John Thurloe in 1658, that 'if his Highness [Cromwell] could spare 1,2[00 or] 1,500 corselets for our pikemen, I would accustom them to wear them, when they mount their guards, and at all other reviews. A stand of 500 pikes well-armed, with headpiece and corselet, will be a very terrible thing to see in these countries.'[65] Arms and fighting equipment were also purchased and supplied to the foot in significant quantities. Three sets of accounts (SP28/29–32 and

63 Edwards, *Dealing in Death*, pp.150–151.

64 Turner, *Pallas Armata*, p.169.

65 Thomas Birch (ed.), *A Collection of State Papers of John Thurloe, Esq; Secretary to the Council of State* (London: 1742), VII, p.215.

SP28/352) – each containing warrants for payments to army contractors; and WSL, Ms Salt 463 Warrant Book of the Ordnance Office (deliveries) record that – bar duplications – between April and June 1645 the following was issued to Fairfax's Army (excluding dragoon muskets and cartridge boxes):

2,616 foot armours – backs, breasts and head pieces (by April 1646)
3,400 pikes
4,500 matchlock muskets
1,050 snaphaunce muskets English full bore and proof
7,800 bandoliers
10,000 swords
10,000 belts

How many sets of each were held in the Tower stores during the early months of 1645 is difficult to calculate, but stored there on 24 May were 500 muskets, 500 pikes and 500 bandoliers. It seems increasingly large amounts were issued to John Phipps, Commissary to the Train for immediate supply to individual regiments. Hence, on 1 May he received 4,791 matchlocks, 5,500 bandoliers and 1,900 pikes for issue to the New Model Army.

Continuingly hefty consignments were also sent by the Tower, via army commissaries and carriers to the New Model's foremost magazine at Reading, there to be distributed to the army in the field through a series of supply centres including Lyme, Weymouth and Chard. Though (unlike for the cavalry) few direct issues to foot regiments of arms and equipment are mentioned, some are. For instance, before 6 July 1645, when Colonel Weldon's regiment was encamped with the rest of the New Model at Crewkerne in Somerset, it received 200 muskets and 200 collars of bandoliers courtesy of the Parliamentarian committee at Lyme. This appears to have been an expedient arrangement designed to fulfil the immediate needs of the unit because a note in the Ordnance Office books states, 'Delivered unto John Tucker [out of the Tower stores] the muskets and bandoliers hereafter mentioned, being for the use of the Committee of the West in lieu out of so many delivered by that committee at Lyme for the recruiting [supplying] of Colonel Ralph Weldon's regiment under Sir Thomas Fairfax'.[66]

Beginning in April 1645, over half of the total armours received into the Tower stores are described as 'backs, breasts and pot headpieces' costing 17s. apiece. On 26 January 1646, for instance, Peter Newton supplied '125 suits of arms (viz) backs, breasts and pot headpieces at 17s. per suit', for which he received the sum of £106 5s. Such transactions are highly consistent and suggestive of foot armours. Indeed, from the end of 1645 onwards these are the only receipts for this type of equipment into the Tower stores, though there may have been other cavalry armours received from other sources. Few records of these transactions survive, yet on 2 September 1645 Parliament ordered that:

66 TNA, WO55/1646, f. 142r; WO55/1647, unfol.; WSL, Ms Salt 463, unfol.

> £200 shall be paid out of the receipts of the Excise, by Ordinance of 11 September 1643, unto Colonel Whalley, Captain Lawrence, Captain Canon, Captain Browne, and Lieutenant Disher, for the furnishing them with horses, arms, and other necessary accommodations, for the present service they are now employed upon and designed unto; whose receipt, together with this ordinance, shall be a sufficient discharge to the Commissioners of Excise, and every of them, for payment of the said £200 accordingly.[67]

Payments to carriers made in May 1644 for transporting weapons and equipment for the supply of the Earl of Essex's reinforced army about Abingdon included sums given to Thomas Duck 'for his cart and 4 horses laden with 300 pikes', and an identical arrangement with Richard Miles for delivering 200 pikes. Two carriers each were laden with 160 backs, breasts and pot helmets.[68] Whether the latter were meant for pikemen or harquebusiers is uncertain however since pistols and saddles were also transported in the convoy.

It is possible to argue that there is a gap in the evidence and there may have been more infantry armours in use during the First Civil War than researchers are aware of. As Foard suggest, 'some soldiers may have brought such equipment from old armies' upon enlistment under Sir Thomas Fairfax, and there may (like the Hull garrison example) have been enough already in storage in the Tower stores.[69] In 1639 the English Government ordered 1,500 sets of pike armour, in addition to 700 cuirassier arms, 700 pairs of holsters, and 3,000 muskets, 'to the pattern already delivered', from two suppliers in Hamburg, while in autumn 1642 the Committee of Safety ordered 6,000 pikemen's corslets from the Low Countries, although only 2,331 were received. Moreover, 6,000 were brought from Denmark and landed at Newcastle in early 1643 for the King's armies.[70] In terms of the home-grown production of foot armours by 1645, Edwards mentions critically:

> By the time the New Model was being equipped, the native industry had finally developed to the extent that it could supply a large proportion of the armour required. In spring and summer 1645 contracts were given to a number of leading members of the craft such as Thomas Stevens, Nicholas Marshall, Anthony and Peter Newman, Richard Wellman and Silvester Keen. To prepare for the campaigning season of 1646 the circle was widened to include several other practitioners, including Edward Anslow. Between April and December 1645, the armourers delivered 2,140 suits of armour and 1,100 additional headpieces, and in the first four months of 1646 a further 3,482 suits.[71]

67 HL/PO/JO/10/1/192; *LJ*, VII, p.562.
68 TNA, SP28/140/4, f. 31v.
69 Foard, *Naseby*, p.61.
70 TNA, SP81/46, ff. 214v, 220r, 243r; *LJ*, V, p.126.
71 Edwards, *Dealing in Death*, p.150.

Foard contends that the 'lack' of purchases of corslets and helmets to the New Model Army in 1645 'supports the argument that armour was no longer issued to pikemen by this time in the war'. However, even the Museum of London material shows that 1,500 'backs, breasts and pots' were contracted for the New Model between April and June 1645; an additional '200 pots with three bars English at 7s. apiece' were ordered the following month – clearly cavalry helmets. Such items, made to English specifications, were also imported from the Low Countries. Examples among the Littlecote Collection at the Royal Armouries, dating to the 1640s, are foreign-made imports.[72] Whether the 1,500 sets purchased for the New Model Army mentioned previously were for pikemen or cavalry is hard to know, going by price, though Pye's regiment of horse was issued 100 sets on 4 April 1645. A further 1,000 helmets were also ordered. In mid-1644 the London armourers Thomas Stevens and Nicholas Marshall supplied Sir William Brereton's army in Cheshire with 540 sets of pikemen's armour and 350 additional helmets.[73] Similarly, the same forces received 75 'headpieces for footmen' as part of a larger consignment shipped from London to Liverpool in March 1645.[74] A consortium of armourers provided Manchester's army with 800 complete suits in 1644, while Edward Anslow individually furnished the Kent forces with hundreds (possibly 500) of armours, which may have been retained by Weldon's and Holborne's regiments when they were absorbed into the New Model Army from the Southern Association in April 1645.[75]

The oft-repeated statement that as the Civil Wars progressed pikemen abandoned their armour is unconvincing and lacks definite evidence. In discussing the use and neglect of the pike among the Swedish Army in Germany in the 1630s, Turner wrote:

> I saw such an universal contempt of the pike that I could not admire it enough; for though after Gustavus Adolphus, King of Sweden entered Germany, squadrons and battalions of pikes were to be seen in all regiments and brigades of both parties, and that pikemen were still accounted the body of the infantry, yet after his victory at Leipzig over the Imperial forces under Tilly, the King's marches were so quick in pursuance of his successes, which followed one on the heels of another, and the retreats also of other armies from him, were so speedy, that first the pikeman's defensive arms were cast away, and after them the pike itself, insomuch that all who hereafter were levied and enrolled, called for muskets. But notwithstanding this, when new regiments were levied after that great King's death, colonels and captains were ever ordered to levy and arm pikemen proportionably to the musketeers; yet after they had endured some fatigue, the pike was again cast away, and no soldiers but musketeers were to be seen. Whether this was done by the supine negligence of the officers, especially the colonels, or for the contempt they had of the pike, I know not. But I am sure that for some years together I have seen many weak regiments composed merely of

72 Blackmore, *Arms and Armour*, p.15, figs 10–11.
73 TNA, SP28/168/2, unfol.
74 CRO, DDX/428, f. 80r.
75 TNA, SP28/168/2, unfol.; SP28/300, ff. 63r, 532r, 534r; SP28/130/3, ff. 8r, 41r, 47v.

> musketeers, without one pikeman in any of them, and surely, they were so much the weaker for that. Nor did I find long after that, that the pike got better entertainment in other places than in Germany.[76]

The context of this quote is very specific, and Turner makes it clear that the actions of the pikemen were largely down to a lack of discipline and poor leadership from the commissioned officers. In October 1644 discipline amongst some of Sir William Waller's regiments had broken down, not only involving incidents of mutiny and theft, but forcing his Council of War to censure officers for not preventing cavalry and dragoon units from robbing civilians. Moreover, on 7 December complaints were received that 'many abuses and violences are daily offered, and practised upon countrymen both in their dwelling, and travelling on the road by soldiers in plundering their horses, cattle, sheep, and other provisions from them, some of which intended for the market'.[77] It was within this climate that, from Andover, Waller and Sir Arthur Haselrige informed the Committee of Both Kingdoms:

> Last night 500 of the King's horse came into Salisbury, but the foot were delayed by the wet weather. In the heat of summer many of our men were unable to carry their arms, their marches being great, but now the weather is cold they exceedingly desire them. If you would send us immediately 500 backs, breasts, and pots, which will not cost above £500; it would embolden our men, discourage our enemies, and it may be advantage the public very many thousands; had we money certainly we would not want them. If this be granted, we desire there may be no delay, not one hour, and for expedition it would be well to send them by horse in panniers, by way of Farnham to Alresford, for thereabouts we conceive our foot will join.[78]

As with swords, not all acquisitions of backs, breasts and helmets for New Model Army's foot appear in the Ordnance Office books, and it is possible that some were received by military units directly from suppliers; for example, Colonel Owen Rowe who had delivered quantities of munitions direct from his magazine. Following the disbandment of Essex's Army in April 1645, the stocks at the Tower of London were made use of by various forces, including both the New Model Army and the pro-government forces in Ireland.

Hence, in April and May 1645 1,000 backs, breasts and helmets, and 1,000 pikes were supplied by Rowe to Sir Thomas Fairfax's Army; in 1643 Rowe had been authorised to contract for arms to the value of £5,000 for the supply of Essex's forces.[79] Likewise, on 10 July 1646 the Committee for Irish Affairs reported that:

---

76 Turner, *Pallas Armata*, p.177.

77 John Adair, 'The Court-Martial Papers of Sir William Waller's Army, 1644', *JSAHR*, 44 (1966), pp.205–226, (pp. 219–20).

78 *CSPD 1644–5*, pp.46–7.

79 TNA, SP28/352 unfol.; WO55/1662, ff. 13v; 41v; *LJ*, VI, pp.207 & 622.

> Nicholas Marshall, Edmund Bunion, Anthony Newman, and Ralph Bolser, on behalf of themselves and other armourers of London, their partners, have offered to provide for service in Ireland 1,000 good defensive arms for harquebusiers, consisting of backs, breasts, and pots, headpieces of good English work, the breasts to be pistol-proof, and the pots headpieces to be with three bars. All of them to be approved by the Governors of the Company of Armourers, and marked with their hallmark and delivered to such as this Committee shall appoint to receive them within eight days hereof. They ask payment at the rate of 19s. for each back, breast, and pot headpiece, out of the assessments for Ireland, raised by the orders of the House of Commons of 15 August 1645 and 9 March 1646.[80]

These could be the same 500 armours for the horse that were ordered 'to be sent away at once to Ulster, the Lord Lieutenant to order £150 to be paid to [Commissary William] Dobbins for carriage' on 11 September 1646, or alternatively, the '1,000 defensive arms' delivered six days later, along with 200 swords, and 'certain saddles and pistols' by the Committee for Irish Affairs to Colonel Algernon Sidney – formerly lieutenant colonel of the Earl of Manchester's regiment of horse – and other cavalry officers in Ireland. In anticipation of deployment to Ireland, on 23 July it was ordered that Sidney's own troop (among others) 'shall also be given arms, bridles and saddles, and horse furniture, the charge of transportation, and a month's pay for his officers'.[81] A report sent to Parliament on 20 June 1647 concerning 'the forces ready may go to Ireland', recommended sending Colonel John Ponsonby's regiment of horse and paying him according to the contract. His regiment is of 700 horsemen, besides officers, and he should receive £6,105 14s. 4d. in money, with pistols, saddles and defensive arms'. Subsequently, on 5 July the sum of £7,230 14s. 4d. was sanctioned for transporting the regiment to Ireland.[82]

Further quantities of armours were procured for Irish service between 1649 and 1651 from London craftsmen. On 6 July 1649 the Officers of the Ordnance were compelled to deliver to Captain Edward Tomlins 1,600 backs, breasts, and pots, with 1,600 muskets for Ireland; on 7 October 1649 the London armourer Edward Barker brought in 1,000 'harquebusiers' armours' to the Ordnance Office stores, for which he received the sum of £800; on 5 December he delivered '2,500 breasts, backs, and pots, being full suits of armour', and a further 500 sets on 25 April 1650. Equally, on 5 December 1649 Robert Studd supplied 300 'harquebusiers' breasts, backs, and pots, being full suits of armour, delivered into the stores', and on the same date the consortium of Marshall, Bunion, Newman, and Bolser brought in 3,000 sets (of which only 500 are described as 'harquebusiers' armours', although the rest may have been, even though they are listed merely as 'breasts, backs, and pots, being full suits of armour'). Similarly, the master armourer Edward Anslow provided 1,500 backs, breasts, and pots on 15 January 1651, for which he was paid £1,275.[83] These 8,800 sets (10,400

80 *CSPI 1633–1647*, p.472.
81 *CSPI 1633–1647*, pp.477, 511, 515.
82 *CSPI 1633–1647*, p.515; *CSPI 1647–1660*, p.756; *LJ*, IX, p.315.
83 *CSPD Interregnum 1649–50*, pp.540 & 599; *CSPD Interregnum 1650*, pp.573, 575, 582.

if the delivery to Tomlins is included) represented a considerable increase in the procurement and supply of defensive armours, both for and to, the military forces of the Commonwealth serving or appointed to serve in Ireland and Scotland.

The Commons had resolved on 10 March 1645 'that 500 muskets, furnished now in the Magazine, which were of those which Mr Hill and Mr Pennoyer did furnish to the State, be delivered to Colonel White', for the supply of the fledgling New Model Army.[84] Two days later, '491 old matchlock muskets, and for 35 dragoon muskets with snaphaunce locks' were delivered, probably from stocks in the Tower stores, by Lieutenant General Thomas Hammond, while on 24 April the New Model benefitted from 1,986 matchlocks from the remaining stocks of the Earl of Manchester's train of artillery.[85] Given the rigorous nature of seventeenth century warfare, in addition to general wear and tear, armours – like other military hardware – suffered damaged and required repairing, cleaning or replacing. Moreover, some armours were received from merchants by the Ordnance Office, which upon inspection were either unmarked or defective (or both) and therefore returned. One warrant from the Committee for the Army, issued on 22 December 1645, ordered the payment 'for the use of Sir Thomas Fairfax's Army unto Mr John Clarke for making, cleaning, repairing and new colouring of 346 backs, breasts and pots at 1s. 6d. per suit, the sum of £25 19s.; and for making, cleaning, repairing and new colouring of 13 odd backs and breasts at 1s. per back and breast, the sum of £13'.[86] On 28 May 1646 the Committee for the Army recorded:

> We the Officers of the Ordnance called to our assistance Edward Ansley, Henry Crouch, and William Harrison to take a view of such armours as were brought into the stores of the Tower unmarked by some armourers upon contract made with this Committee, and accordingly viewed the same, the particulars thereof we do humbly certify as follows:
>
> Brought into the stores within the Tower by:
>
> Samuel Ashton – 25 armours unmarked; 2 headpieces and 1 breast defective.
> Richard Wray – 25 armours unmarked; 2 backs, 2 breasts and 2 headpieces defective; 2 breasts and 6 headpieces unserviceable.
> Silvester Keen and Ralph Boulter – 163 armours unmarked; 7 breasts, 5 backs and 27 headpieces defective; 1 back, 1 breast and 5 headpieces unserviceable.
> Officers of the Ordnance:
> George Payler
> John Falconer
> John White[87]

84 *CJ*, IV, p.74.

85 TNA, SP28/352, unfol.; WO55/47/1, f. 229r; Bodl. Lib., Ms Eng. hist. C14, f. 9v. The matchlock muskets were probably from the same contract agreed with Hammond on 12 April 1645 to supply 600 of them (TNA, WO55/47/1, f. 216v; ML, Ms 46 78/708, fol. 109r).

86 TNA, SP28/33/3, f. 220r.

87 TNA, PRO/30/27/4, unfol.

There is nothing in this document to indicate whether such armours were for the horse or the foot, although the helmets are referred to as 'headpieces' rather than 'pots'.

Carbines

In addition to their defensive amour, harquebusiers were characterised by their use of a form of carbine, called a harquebus, but their weaponry also included a long-bladed cutting sword and a pair of pistols (both wheel locks and snaphaunces) carried in holsters. Regarding the type and function of the arms and armour of the horse to be employed in the 1640s, John Vernon recommended:

> The harquebuses and carbines arming is chiefly offensive, his defensive arms, as only an open cask or headpiece, a back and breast with buff coat under his arms; his offensive arms are a good harquebus, a carbine hanging on his right side in a belt by a swivel, a flask and cartridge case … and good fire-lock pistols in holsters. At his saddle a good stiff sword sharp pointed.[88]

According to Orrery:

> I acknowledge I would have every private trooper have his sword, or long tuck, his case of pistols, and carbine; and for defence, his back, breast and pot; at least, I would have the front and flanks of every troop in such armour. For besides the terror it gives to an enemy in his doublet, to fight with men of iron, and the encouragement it gives our own men; none knows what proof the armour is of. And it is most certain, that in combat, as well as pursuit, the sword does most execution; and no armour is less than sword proof.[89]

The Register of Bishop Bridgeman of Chester records payments in January 1639 for the equipping of light horsemen or harquebusiers for service in the Bishop's War. This included 5s. 'Richard Warmingham for mending the saddle', 20s. 10d. to Thomas Malbon for 'a sword, cap, belt, dragoon, girdle, and a snapsack', in addition to £1 18s. to John Malbon for a buff coat. Similarly, on 25 March the Cheshire gentleman, John Leche, supplied similar items for another harquebusier. He appears to have been provided with a mixture of new, recycled and upgraded equipment, for which, in part Leche paid 'Thornley the smith for making me my black armour with eyes and hooks, 3s. 6d., and for making a dragoon of the old caliver, lock, iron and spring to hang it with, scourer, worm and socket 5s. 6d.'. A description of the soldier's dress and equipment is detailed below:

88 Vernon, *Young Horse-man*, p.8.
89 Orrery, *Treatise of the Art of War*, pp.32–3.

> The furniture for a light horse is a great saddle, peytral, crupper, bridle and bit, and for the man, a buff coat, a headpiece, a sword and belt, a dragoon with a bolt, a flask with a scourer, and worm and a knapsack. My gelding was worth £10, my buff coat with points cost 43s., my saddle and furniture £3, dragoon, flask, scourer, worm and belt 30s. The headpiece 10s., sword and belt 20s., and the knapsack 18d. I gave my cousin in his purse 42s. 6d.[90]

In July 1645 Parliament ordered the conveyance 'for the supply of several garrisons in the West' out of the land and sea stores 200 barrels powder with match and bullet proportionable, the latter consisting of '10 tons of bullet, whereof 7 ton of musket shot, and 3 tons carbine and pistol bullet proportionable to the 200 barrels powder'. These were accordingly delivered on 11 and 21 July.[91] Nevertheless, the use of carbines during by Civil Wars cavalrymen does not appear to have been universal. Some quantities are recorded as being issued to Royalist troops from the Oxford magazine in 1643 and 1644, but whether this was in addition to, or in lieu of pistols, is unclear.[92]

In June 1643 the Parliamentarian general, Sir Thomas Myddelton purchased 200 carbine belts, 200 swivels, 70 powder flasks and 12 pairs of pistols in London for his newly raised cavalry, while in the October the Committee of Safety recommended that '70 pair of pistols and 70 carbines, and the other things belonging to them' be delivered to Colonel Ralph Ashton, the Parliamentarian commander in Lancashire.[93] In November 1642 the Cheshire colonel, Robert Duckenfield, received 63 pairs of pistols, 25 carbines and '63 body armours for so many troopers', which had been manufactured in London, and a further 10 carbines were purchased in for his troop in January 1643.[94] Similarly, one of the first items in the accounts of the Royalist garrison of Lichfield during the first siege of the city in 1643 records costs related to the raising of three troops of horse and the provision of carbines, saddles, and bridles, costing £900.[95] No issues of cavalry carbines are known for the Eastern Association, although for various reasons they may not have been recorded in the documentation. However, various quantities are documented for the Earl of Essex's Army. Similarly, carbines were supplied to troops of the City Horse in 1643 and 1644 priced 22s. apiece, along with pistols, armours and saddles.[96]

The earliest verified procurement of carbines for the New Model comes from January 1646. This might either have been because some of the troopers brought such

90 CRO, ZBR/3/1, unfol.; DLE/89, unfol.

91 TNA, WO55/1647, unfol.; WSL, Ms Salt 463, unfol.

92 TNA, WO55/459, ff. 207v, 340r, 514v, 606r; WO55/1661, f. 19r; *ROP*, II, pp.255, 260, 298, 303.

93 TNA, SP28/346/1, unfol.; HMC, *Tenth Report, App. IV*, p.68.

94 TNA, SP28/128/10, f. 2r. The sum of £35 6s. 4d. was made over to William Davenport 'for his charges in several journeys to London and providing of arms for my troop', an additional £5 was paid to Captain John Whitworth 'for carrying down the arms and ammunition from London' (ff. 1r, 5r, 7v).

95 Ian Atherton, 'Royalist Finances in the English Civil War: the Case of Lichfield garrison, 1643–5', *MH*, 33 (2008), pp.43–67, (p. 52).

96 TNA, SP28/14, ff. 47r, 55v; SP28/131/1, f. 2r.

items with them when they re-enlisted into Fairfax's Army, or they were returned into the Tower stores and reissued (though there is no documentary evidence to support this). On 10 January 1646 the Ordnance Office received notice that a total of 1,202 carbines with swivels were contracted for with six London gunsmiths – William Burton, John Silk junior, Walter Benge, Robert Murden, Edward Burrows and William Watson – at a considerably lower cost of 12s. 9d. each.[97] The agreement with Burton, for instance, was typical of the contracts to which they agreed, though particularly detailed specifications are lacking from the documentary entries. He was to ensure that '59 carbines full bore and proof with swivels to be forthwith brought into the Tower of London, for which it is contracted, he shall be paid when he brings them in for performance, whereof he has set his hand, 25 of them marked thus (48), 15 marked thus (49) [and] 19 marked thus (50)'. Such quantities of carbines may represent the Committee for the Army's response to the 'estimate of the charge to resupply the New Model Army' presented to the Commons on 29 December 1645. This included 4,000 'horse arms' (possibly corselets and helmets, or indeed carbines), 4,000 pairs of pistols and holsters, and 4,000 saddles with furniture.[98]

Entries in the books of receipts exemplify the process of the receipt of, and payment for, the 1,202 carbines ordered in January 1646. Among the 'Warrants for payment to army contractors for stores received by the Ordnance Office' are those dated 9 February for 347 carbines with swivels delivered by Walter Benge, 10 February for 59 of the same by William Burton, and 11 February for the 183 carbines brought in by Edward Burrows.[99] Receipts of consignments officially accepted into the stores are recorded in a book, 'containing certificates by the Officers of the Ordnance for the receipt of certain materials of war contracted for and supplied for Fairfax's Army' from 24 March 1645 to 4 March 1646. This contains an order from Robert Scawen, Chairman of the Committee for the Army, dated 1 April 1645 'that the Officers of the Ordnance shall receive the particulars above contracted for and give certificates to the parties for what they received, and the officers are to view the arms'.[100] Thus recorded is the receipt on 21 January 1646 of the full consignments of carbines with swivels, comprising 173 from Murden, 347 from Benge, 204 from William Watson, 183 from Burrows, 236 from Silk, and 59 from Burton. Perhaps in anticipation of these deliveries the Ordnance Office was ordered on 16 January 1646 to deliver 'out of the stores' a load of weapons to be transported to Portsmouth for Sir Thomas Fairfax's Army, which included 1,000 carbines with swivels and belts, and 1,000 cartridge boxes for carbines with girdles. They reached their destination six days later.[101]

97 TNA, SP28/36/2, unfol.; SP28/352/1, unfol.; Bod. Lib., Ms Eng. hist. C14, f. 65r; ML, Ms 46 78/708, f. 76r.
98 *CJ*, IV, p.388.
99 TNA, SP28/352/1, unfol.
100 Bod. Lib., Ms Eng. hist. C14, ff. 65v–67r.
101 TNA, WO55/1646, unfol.

Table 34: Notification of Contracts to the Ordnance Office for Carbines for the NMA (TNA, SP28/352/1; Bodl. Lib., Ms Eng. hist. C14; ML, Ms 46 78/708)

Date	Quantity and type	Price	Contractor
10/1/46	59 carbines full bore and proof with swivels to be forthwith brought into the Tower of London, for which it is contracted, he shall be paid when he brings them in for performance, whereof he has set his hand 25 of them marked thus (48) 15 marked thus (49) 19 marked thus (50)	12s. 9d.	William Burton
10/1/46	236 carbines full bore and proof according to the former contract, to be brought into the Tower of London and paid for as aforesaid 46 marked thus (51) 115 marked thus (52) 75 marked thus (53)	12s. 9d.	John Silk junior
10/1/46	347 carbines full bore and proof according to the former contract, to be brought into the Tower of London and paid for as aforesaid 58 marked thus (54) 18 marked thus (55) 12 marked thus (56) 140 marked thus (57) 42 marked thus (58) 62 marked thus (59) 20 marked thus (60)	12s. 9d.	Walter Benge
10/1/46	173 carbines full bore and proof according to the former contract, to be brought into the Tower of London and paid for as aforesaid 111 marked thus (61) 34 marked thus (62) 28 marked thus (63)	12s. 9d.	Robert Murden
10/1/46	183 carbines full bore and proof according to the former contract, to be brought into the Tower of London and paid for as aforesaid 121 marked thus (64) 12 marked thus (65) 50 marked thus (66)	12s. 9d.	Edward Burrows
10/1/46	204 carbines full bore and proof according to the former contract, to be brought into the Tower of London and paid for as aforesaid 130 marked thus (67) 19 marked thus (68) 38 marked with a Dolphin 17 marked thus (69)	12s. 9d.	William Watson

Table 35: Notification of Contracts to the Ordnance Office for Carbine Belts, Cartridge Boxes and Girdles for the NMA (Bodl. Lib., Ms Eng. hist. C14, f. 13r; Ms Eng. hist. C244; ML, Ms 46 78/708)

Date	Quantity and type	Price each	Contractor
10/1/46	1200 cartouches, the boxes of strong plate covered with black leather, 700 of them half-round and the other 500 double, to be forthwith brought into the Tower of London, for which it is contracted, he shall be paid when he brings them in for performance, whereof he has set his hand	10d.	Nathaniel Humphries
10/1/46	820 cartridge belts [girdles] of good leather and strong buckles according to the pattern at 8d. apiece and for 500 cartridge girdles at 2s. 8d. a dozen, to be forthwith brought into the Tower of London, for which it is contracted, he shall be paid when he brings them in for performance, whereof he has set his hand The belts and girdles marked thus (45)		Henry Thrall
10/1/46	200 carbine belts and 200 cartridge girdles according to the former contract, to be brought and paid for as aforesaid and marked thus (46)		Richard Rumsey
10/1/46	200 carbine belts according to the former contract, to be brought and paid for as aforesaid and marked thus (47)		Thomas Bostock, 'citizen and girdler of London'

Table 36: Receipts into the Ordnance Office of Carbine Belts for the NMA (TNA, SP28/36/2)

Date	Quantity and type	Price each	Contractor
2/1/46	200 carbine belts	7d.	Thomas Bostock
4/2/46	1000 carbine belts	7d.	Richard Rumsey
9/2/46	500 carbine belts	7d.	Henry Thrall
14/2/46	250 carbine belts	7d.	John Mundy

Snapsacks

Sometimes referred to as 'knapsacks', these were sausage-shaped bags worn over the shoulder, with a drawstring either at one or both ends to close them. Chiefly made of leather, they were important pieces of equipment issued to soldiers of the British Civil Wars and other seventeenth century conflicts. Snapsacks were used for carrying rations, spare clothing, and any personal items the soldier may have possessed. One contemporary source mentions that they were supplied for 'the carriage of small provisions of victuals for their better accommodation in their journey'.[102] For the refitting of troops at Portsmouth in May 1627 the Ordnance Office paid 1s. 3d. apiece to George Hambleton, 'leather seller of London at for

102 Dyfnallt G. Owen, G. (ed.), *Calendar of the Cecil Papers in Hatfield House, 1612–1668* (London: University of London & History of Parliament Trust, 1971), XXII, p.299.

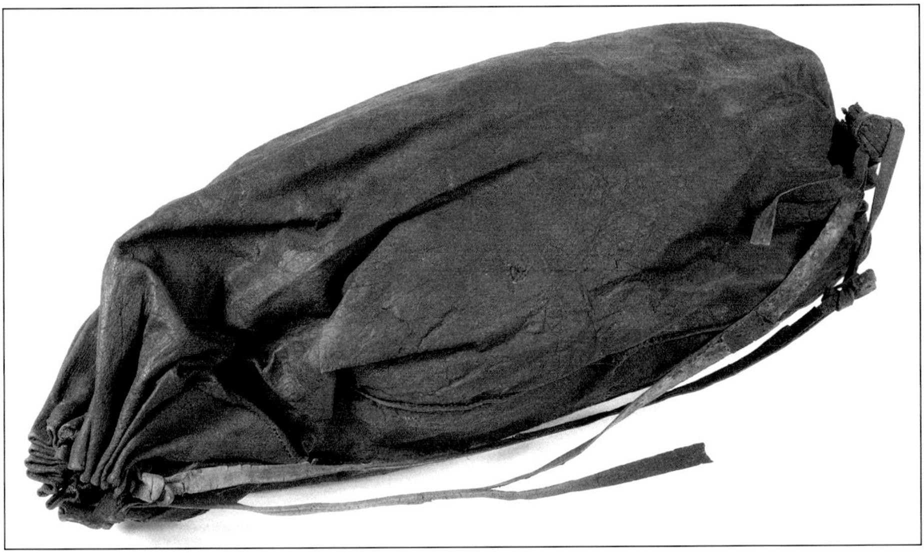

Seventeenth century snapsack. (Maritime Museum at Gordiaandreef in Lelystad)

knapsacks of black leather, by him, made and brought into his Majesty's store'.[103] Pro-government troops in Ireland in 1642-3 were issued with spare shoes, stockings, and shirts that may have been carried in their snapsacks alongside any rations. Surviving examples of snapsacks from the seventeenth century are extremely rare, though three such items were discovered in a shipwreck in the Ijsselmeer polders in the Netherlands and are now in the Maritime Museum at Gordiaandreef in Lelystad. These are made of leather, with corresponding carrying straps, and are dateable to 1620–1630. The largest is approximately 75cm in length and approximately 25cm in diameter.[104]

The suggestion that canvas was issued to soldiers in Ireland to make up snapsacks stems from a misreading of the sources. A proposed list of items to be supplied to the British forces there in 1648 includes '200 pieces of sackcloth, to pack up provisions here, and fit to make sacks in Ireland, to carry provisions for the soldiers upon their march, at 19s. per piece.' This follows an entry for '10,000 snapsacks, at 15d. per piece.'[105] Here the sackcloth or canvas was intended for the construction of packs for the transportation of supplies, probably by waggons and packhorses, to be disbursed to the troops, which also includes all kinds of military equipment as well as clothing. The use of canvas in this fashion is backed by evidence from contemporary documents. For instance, on 22 June 1642 Parliament disbursed to the Irish Adventurers for the delivery of clothing and 'for canvas, packing, and petty charges, £3 10s. more, by him delivered and paid for supply of the magazine for clothing the soldiers in Ireland'.[106] The financial accounts rendered by Edward

103 TNA WO49/55, f. 174r; WO49/59B, unfol.

104 https://beeldbank.cultureelerfgoed.nl/ accession number MA OB71-187.

105 *LJ*, X, pp.158–9.

106 Bod. Lib., Ms Rawlinson A110, f. 60v; *LJ*, V, p.155.

Orpin, Commissary General of Victuals, for the supply of Sir Thomas Fairfax's Army throughout the western campaign – via ship from London to Lyme and other ports, and by road to the army in the field – contain detailed lists of clothing packed at the Reading magazine for transportation to Portsmouth between December 1645 and February 1646. These include payments for canvas and packthread for the making up of packs to be transported on packhorses and waggons, such as 2s. paid on 10 September 1645 at the magazine in Lyme for 'ink and paper, 200 packs, thread and needles', and the sum of £1 15s. disbursed on 23 January 1646 in relation to the transportation of 2,598 coats, 2,952 pair of breeches, and 2,082 shirts, from Tiverton to Chudleigh by 100 packhorses for 'cords, packthread and needles to pack them up'. In addition the sum of 2s. 6d. was laid out for 'straw to lay under the clothes sent to several regiments'.[107]

Lyme, in Dorset, had been a strategically vital port as it could potentially control the sea route between Bristol and the English Channel. It was an important centre for the cloth trade and enjoyed some prosperity during the early modern period. In pointing out the strategic value of the port, the Lord High Admiral, Robert, Earl of Warwick wrote in June 1644, 'If Lyme be lost, it will have a very ill influence, the inclination of these parts depending on the success of that town, which the enemy values not so much for itself as for the men that are in it, who if at liberty, will quickly get a strength together, which the country will be well disposed to close withal'.[108]

One of the advantages which Lyme possessed was its ancient harbour or Cobb, which was protected by three forts. Designed originally to help the town withstand a sea attack, it was to prove its worth as an entry point for ships transporting supplies and manpower to the Parliamentarian garrison. According to one Royalist account of the siege, 'The town [is] befriended on the east side by the sea and fortified on the south part with a strong fort (called St Davies Fort) from whence was a line made extending itself to the sea on the north part'.[109] However, Prince Maurice was forced to abandon the siege of Lyme in June 1645.

Following the King's defeat at Naseby, the Southwest of England was the last region where Royalist strength, if united, could still present a serious challenge to Parliamentarian military power. Sir Thomas Fairfax recognised this and endeavoured to prevent any unification of Royalist forces. With the New Model's crushing defeat of Lord Goring's forces at Langport on 10 July 1645 and the retention of key ports by Parliament, such as Portsmouth, Lyme and Weymouth, various options for the supply of the army opened up, with convoys sent by either sea or by land. Thus, the New Model Army and its logistical tail possessed greater flexibility to respond to changing circumstances.

107 TNA, SP28/147/2, ff. 352r–7r; SP28/126/1, ff. 1r–5r.

108 *A letter from the Right Honourable Robert Earle of Warwicke, Lord High-admirall of England: to the Speaker of the House of Peeres. With an exact diurnall of all the most speciall and remarkable passages which have hapned during the siege of Lyme in Dorsetshire by Pr. Maurice his forces, from the 21 of February to this present* (London: 11 July 1644). TT, E50[25].

109 'Shipton's relation concerning the siege of Lyme', in A. R. Bayley, *The Civil War in Dorset, 1642–1660* (Taunton: 1910), p.138.

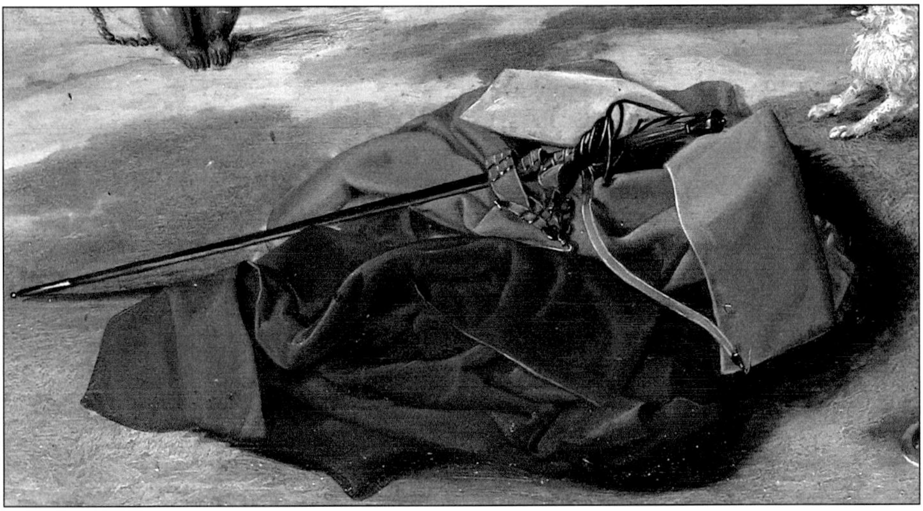

Snapsack shown in a detail from Dirck Hals' (1591–1656) painting *Fête Champêtre c.* 1627 (Dirck was the younger brother of the far better known Frans Hals). The central figure is a soldier who has cast off his equipment as he joins the party. This is an almost unique pictorial depiction of a snapsack, note its tubular pattern and the strap, showing that it was worn diagonally across the back. (Collection of the Rijksmuseum, Amsterdam)

Snapsacks, described as 'large and of good leather' were purchased in considerable quantities (and therefore as part of bulk orders) for the New Model in 1645 at 8s. per dozen (8d. each).[110] According to the records of the disbursement from the Tower stores, some of these went directly to foot regiments, such as Colonel Thomas Rainborowe's, which received 500 suits, 500 shirts, 500 pairs of stockings, 150 pikes, 350 muskets with bandoliers, 2 barrels powder, 4cwt match, and 500 snapsacks on 13 February 1646. However, most of the equipment was supplied to recruits. For instance, a warrant was issued on the same day to clothe and arm a draft for the New Model at Reading for the supply of 1,700 suits, 1,500 shirts, 1,700 pairs shoes, 1,700 pairs stockings, 700 pikes, 1,000 muskets with bandoliers, and 1,700 snapsacks. Similarly, on 26 March 2,189 coats, 2,179 pairs of breeches, 2,184 pairs of stockings, 2,180 pairs of shoes, 1,200 shirts, 1,770 matchlock muskets, 1,775 bandoliers, 168 pikes, 36 drums furnished with cords, 1 ton of match, 10cwt of powder, and 10cwt of musket shot was supplied to recruits in Northampton.[111] Moreover, a tender submitted to Parliament for supplying English forces in Ireland, dated 27 March 1648, included '10,000 snapsacks at 15d. per piece'.[112]

110 TNA, WO49/55, f. 174r; WO47/1, f. 209v; SP28/29/1, *passim*; ML, Ms 46 78/708, *passim*.
111 TNA, SP28/140/3, unf/; WO55/1646, unfol.
112 *LJ*, X, pp.158–9.

Table 37: Notification of Contracts to the Ordnance Office for Snapsacks for the NMA (TNA, WO47/1; ML, Ms 46 78/708)

Date	Quantity and type	Price each	Contractor
1/4/45	200 snapsacks	9d.	Michael Rayner
7/4/45	2000 snapsacks	9d.	Michael Rayner
2/7/45	The Committee for the Army do desire you to deliver into the Tower 200 snapsacks at the former rate they have been paid you 21 June 1645		Michael Byne
4/8/45	1000 snapsacks	9d.	Michael Rayner
6/9/45	500 snapsacks	9d.	Michael Rayner
22/12/45	3000 snapsacks large and of good leather at 8d. a dozen, to be delivered into the Tower of London by equal proportions: 500 the last of this instant December and the rest monthly until they be all delivered, for which the said Ralph Fairbank is to be paid as he brings them in. To be marked thus (126)	9d.	Ralph Fairbank
22/12/45	3000 snapsacks according to the former contract, to be brought into the Tower of London at the times beforementioned, by which it is contracted he shall be paid as he brings them in. To be marked thus (127)	9d.	Michael Rayner
22/12/45	2000 snapsacks according to the former contract, to be brought into the Tower of London at the times beforementioned, by which it is contracted he shall be paid as he brings them in. To be marked thus (128)	9d.	John Brown
22/12/45	3000 snapsacks at the same price and goodness as the former contract, to be brought into the Tower of London at the times beforementioned, by which it is contracted he shall be paid as he brings them in. To be marked thus [blank]	9d.	Matthew Appletree
22/12/45	1000 snapsacks at the same price and goodness as in the former contract, to be brought into the Tower of London at the times beforementioned by equal proportions, for which it is contracted he shall be paid as he brings them in. To be marked thus (129)	9d.	Joshua Primate

Table 38: Warrants for Payments to Contractors for the Delivery of Snapsacks to the Ordnance Office for the NMA (TNA, SP28/29/1-35/1)

Date	Quantity and type	Price each	Contractor
8/4/45	2000 snapsacks in full of his contract	9d.	Michael Rayner
18/4/45	2000 snapsacks in full of his contract	9d.	Michael Rayner
18/4/45	2000 snapsacks in full of his contract	9d.	Michael Rayner
8/7/45	200 snapsacks in full of his contract	9d.	Michael Rayner
18/8/45	1000 snapsacks in full of his contract	9d.	Michael Rayner
6/10/45	5000 snapsacks in full of his contract	9d.	Michael Rayner

On 11 December 1645 the clothing placed into packs and bundles by commissaries at the magazine at Reading 'to be sent to Portsmouth' for onward distribution to the New Model Army employed an alpha numeric system, being 'C' for coats, 'B' for breeches, 'St' for stockings, and 'S' for shoes.[113] Three packs of coats, each containing 50 bundles and weighing approximately 8cwt apiece, were marked 'C500'; five packs of breeches, each of 40 bundles and weighing each 8cwt apiece, were marked 'B400'; and one of the vats of shoes, about 6½cwt in weight contained 540 pairs and was marked 'S540'. Commonly, a pack of coats contained between 26 and 45 bundles, whereas 10 packs of breeches had 60 bundles, each bundle comprising either 10 coats or 10 breeches. Thus, the total items of clothing 'for the receipt of Sir Thomas Fairfax his Army by me [Commissary] Robert Emerson by the appointment of Mr Thomas Richardson, Waggon Master General' out of the Reading magazine on 15 December was 3,205 coats, 3,227 breeches, 3,512 shirts, 2,413 pairs of stockings, and 3,874½ pairs of shoes. Likewise, on 20 February 1646 Commissaries John West and William Humberson authorised the dispatch of 193 coats, 191 pairs of breeches, and 191 shirts, in addition to 761 pikes, 2,980 muskets, 4,826 swords, 4,908 sword belts, 790 bandoliers, and 2,600 snapsacks.

As soon as the clothing and weaponry had been examined, the items were placed into bundles and then packs or dry vats, depending on the type of clothing, until transportation by road bound convoys could be arranged. Convoys also had to be guarded during their journey. Commissary General Orpin made various payments to men in late 1645 and early 1646 for watching carts, oxen, and provisions brought along the New Model Army's line of march at Newton Poppleford, Chudleigh, and Tiverton. On 22 November 1645 a consignment of 165cwt of cheese, 180 bags of biscuit, and 20 hogsheads of beef was shipped from Lyme to the Parliamentarian garrison at Youghal in Ireland. Built-in to the costs were '200 yards of stuff to make bags to put the governor's biscuit in [and] 3lbs of packthread and making of them'. Orpin laid out the sum of £12 4s. 4d. on 18 January 1646 'for charges for 17 horse loads of clothes from Tiverton to Chard, containing 722 coats, 622 pair of breeches, 216 pair of stockings and 800 snapsacks'. This encompassed 5s. for carrying pack cloths from Tiverton to Chard, 3s. 6d. for 5 pack boards, 5s. for 5 men to take up horses, 10s. for making the packs, 10s. for hay for 30 horses one night, 3s. for 2 guides, £2 11s. for 17 pack horses, 10s. for five drivers 2 days, 5s. paid to John Pittfowles for himself and horse, 2s. for carrying the clothes up into the magazine at Tiverton, £3 6s. for 2 men to assist Jervis Kidd 2 days and for the charges of his horse, and £2 11s. 4d. for the charges of Kidd's horse for hire and his rations for 28 days.[114]

On 4 July 1645 Colonel John Fiennes' regiment of horse was given the task of protecting waggons used for the transportation of pay for the New Model Army from Reading, which was to go by land to Portsmouth and sent onwards to Lyme by sea. The regiments of Colonels Robert Pye and Nathaniel Rich were to accompany another convoy of money from Kent, and were ordered to 'go with it from London to Windsor, where joining with the convoy bringing the money from Reading, you are to convoy the whole to Portsmouth'. Moreover, on 24 July the treasurers

113 TNA, SP28/126/1, ff. 1r–4r.

114 TNA, SP28/147/2, ff. 352r–357r.

of the army were informed that 'being some money to be sent to [Fairfax's] army, which Sir Robert Pye is appointed to convoy, we desire that you would send it under that convoy to Portsmouth, and from thence to the army by the same way that the foot recruits shall go, whether by sea or land, which we leave to the decision of Sir Robert Pye to select as the soonest and safest way by which these provisions can be conveyed to the army'. Pye was also ordered 'with the horse you have in town [consisting of 40 troopers of his own regiment, 20 from Colonel Butler's regiment, 130 of Commissary General Ireton's regiment, Sergeant Major Thomas Harrison's troop of Colonel Fleetwood's regiment, and Sergeant Major Robert Huntington's troop of Cromwell's regiment] to convoy the money, provisions [and ammunition] for the army to Reading, where taking under your command the recruits, to march with the whole party to Portsmouth, and from thence to send the ammunition by sea to the army.'

The Committee of Both Kingdoms ordered the governor of Reading, Colonel John Barkstead on 15 July 1645 to send 20 musketeers to Windsor to safeguard a convoy of ammunition and arms on its passage to Reading, 'for the recruits which are to go to the army'.[115] Dragoons were also called upon for escort duties in support of the New Model. On 10 June 1645 Parliament ordered the provision of '100 dragoons to convey the money to be sent to Sir Thomas Fairfax's Army, and that they shall be paid for the same'. Additionally, parties of dragoons conveyed recruits and accompanied convoys of provisions, weapons and money from London, St Albans and Reading to its regiments in the West Country during the winter of 1645–1646.[116]

Drums, Colours, and Polearms

In infantry and dragoon regiments, commands were communicated by the beat of the drum. Additionally, drummers – like trumpeters in cavalry units – undertook special roles, such as acting as messengers and the dissemination of military intelligence. The English military writer William Barriffe stated in 1635, 'the drum is the voice of the commander, the spur of the valiant and the heart of the coward, and by it they must receive their directions, when the roaring cannon, the clashing of arms, the neighing of horses, and other confused noise causes than neither captain, nor other officer can be heard'.[117] Similarly, Elton stated:

> Every captain ought to have 2 good drummers, that knows how to beat all the several points of war before mentioned. It is likewise expedient that he should be a good linguist, in respect sometimes he may be sent unto an enemy for the ransoming of prisoners. His duty is, coming to the camp or garrison of an enemy, having his general's pass in his hat, to beat a call, till he is fetched in; and because he shall not discover the weakness of guards, works or trenches, he is led blindfold, and so carried to the commander,

115 *CSPD 1645–7*, pp.5, 19, 29–30.

116 *CSPD 1644–45*, pp.151, 196, 253, 267–8, 306, 359, 402, 434, 584.

117 William Barriffe, *Military Discipline: or, The young artillery man* (London, 1635), pp.11–12.

> and place where his prisoners are, with whom (after he hath ransomed them) he is to return to his own quarters, giving an account of such things he hath seen or heard, which may prove advantageous to his own party, or of any other thing he had opportunity by their neglect to take notice of.[118]

Soldiers during the Civil Wars were recruited by the 'beat of the drum'. Hence, for the raising of forces for Ireland on 30 May 1642 Parliament authorised various captains to 'have liberty to beat up drums in all places within the Kingdom of England, and Dominion of Wales; and thereby, or otherwise, to raise and levy so many soldiers volunteers, as shall suffice to make up unto every of the said captains, one complete company of 100 foot, besides officers, to be employed in the aforesaid service'.[119]

On 27 March 1645 60 new drums were received into the stores from Edward Tench, 'joiner'. With Giles Smart he provided a further 20 at the same price on 14 July 1645, and 20 more by himself on 17 February 1646, 50 drums with sticks on 17 March, and another 40 drums 'furnished'. Another supplier, Thomas Smith supplied the army with '50 drums with sticks' on 24 December, while Smart produced the same quantity eight days later.[120] There appears to be a lack of orders for and deliveries of drums between the latter date and early 1649, although the reason for this is obscure. On 14 February 1649 22 'new drums with walnut rims' were received from Daniel Hull, while on 19 February the equivalent number of 'new wainscot drums' came into the stores from Giles Smart.[121] In each of these cases the price paid was 24s. apiece. This is analogous with the £55 given to the drum-maker John Smart for 100 drums for Ireland in June 1649, and £58 10s. paid to Smith the following month for '100 drums, drumsticks, and spare drumheads, and 10 drums for dragoons for Ireland'.[122] Although the magazine belonging to the Ordnance Office was the most important source of military equipment and clothing for the New Model Army in 1645, it was not the only one.

As with Essex's forces, disbursements were made by the Army treasurers to regimental officers to permit them to purchase such items as drums and colours. Hence, in July 1645 Christopher Mercer, one of Colonel John Okey's dragoon captains, received funds to buy 10 drums for the regiment.[123] The treasurers also paid contractors, upon warrants from the Army Committee, for an array of stores which are mainly recorded in the warrants ordering payments to suppliers, in addition to the Ordnance Office receipts books. Assuming that the documents themselves are not faulty, it must be assumed that such deliveries were made straight to the Army. Some of these consignments are thus recorded in the various delivery books. Francis Markham wrote in 1622 that of the infantry lieutenant 'his only his weapon is a guilt partizan', while Monck remarked, 'lieutenants and sergeants ought to have

118 Elton, *Compleat Body*, p.178.

119 *CJ*, II, p.594.

120 TNA, SP28/140/3, ff. 62v, 97r, 114r, 122v, 123r; WO49/82, ff. 299v, 301v; Bod. Lib., Ms Eng. hist. C14, ff. 2v; 38v; 80v. Two books of debentures record that the Ordnance Office was notified of Tench's first contract on 1 April 1645 (TNA, WO47/1, f. 209v; MS 46 78/708, f. 114v).

121 TNA, SP28/140/3, f. 151r.

122 *CSPD Interregnum 1649–50*, pp.576–7.

123 TNA, SP28/31/5, f. 532r; SP28/36/1, f. 658v.

partizans and halberds of 11 foot in length.'[124] On 29 April 1648 the regiment in the Tower of London commanded by Colonel Robert Tichborne received 8 drums, 10 colours, 21 halberds, and 5 partizans from the Ordnance Office stores.[125]

Military standards, known by contemporaries as cornets for troops of horse, guidons for dragoons and ensigns for companies of foot soldiers, were carried while on the march and on the battlefield, but they were also used for rallying men during or after the chaos of battle. Also referred to as 'colours', they were made from lengths of silk (taffeta or the less expensive sarcenet) and made up by tailors (hence the appearance of cloth and trimmings in tailor's bills), while distinguishing marks in the form of emblematic images and mottos on cornets of horse, were applied by specialist painters.

During the Civil Wars standards were observed and recorded for the purpose of estimating the strengths of opposing forces. Soldiers were obligated to 'follow their colours', whereas 'to depart from the colours' (desertion), whether on the march or in battle, in theory meant the death penalty. Furthermore, 'articles of war' produced by both sides insisted that it was 'a disgrace worse than death' to abandon or lose the regiment's colours. Standards were also prized trophies of war. Ensigns carried by companies of foot were approximately 6½ feet square. According to Captain Thomas Venn each company of an infantry regiment would usually employ similar field colours and designs but would follow a system of differencing:

> The colonel's colour in the first place is of a pure and clean colour, without any mixture. The lieutenant colonel's only with a St George's arms in an upper corner next the staff; the major's the same, but in the lower or outer corner with a little stream *blazant*. And every captain with a St George's arms alone, but with so many spots or several devices as pertain to the dignity of their respective places.[126]

On 29 November 1644 Alexander Venner, ensign maker, was contracted by Parliament to provide 'drums, colours, halberds and partizans for the furnishing of Colonel Edward Aldridge's regiment, viz., for 8 new ensigns made of blue Florence sarcenet with distinctions of gold-coloured laurels with tassels to them ... at the rate of 45s. apiece'. Delivery was made into the Ordnance Office on 16 December 1644, the warrant drawn up for payment reading:

> There is due unto Alexander Venn, ensign maker, the sum of £18 to be paid out of such moneys as remain in the hands of Walter Earle, Knight, Lieutenant General of the Ordnance, received by him at Haberdashers Hall for the Lord General's Army (by order from the Commons House of Parliament, dated 28 November 1644) for the buying of drums, colours, halberds and partizans for the furnishing of Colonel Aldridge his regiment, viz: for eight new ensigns made of blue Florence sarcenet with distinctions

124 Markham, *Five Decades of Epistles of Warre*, p.78; Monck, *Observations*, p.58.
125 BL, Ms Add. 35332, f. 80v.
126 Thomas Venn, *Military Observations, Or the Tacticks Put into Practice* (London, 1672), p.181.

> of gold colour laurels and tassels to them. By this Alexander Venn provided and brought into his Majesty's Stores within the Office of the Ordnance for this service, which at the rate of 45s. apiece amounts to the sum of £18.[127]

Aldridge, however, refused to command this regiment of the Earl of Essex's Army when it was reformed in the New Model, and it passed to Colonel Walter Lloyd. Colonel Aldridge's regiment was not originally included in the refit at Portsmouth of the Earl of Essex's foot in November 1644, following the Parliamentary defeat at Lostwithiel.[128] The ensigns manufactured and supplied were:

> 7 orange colours with white mullets made of Florence sarsenet
> 8 crimson, in grain Florence with yellow mullets
> 8 crimson with white balls
> 8 green with yellow billets
> 8 green with yellow half-moons
> 8 green with white diamonds
> 8 white colours [there is no mention of any differencing device]
> And for repairing five existing ensigns[129]

Nevertheless, when these were received it was not noted which regiments obtained which colours. Chris Scott and Alan Turton have suggested, 'it would seem probable that the seven orange colours and the five repaired were for the 12 companies of the Lord General's Regiment'.[130] Money was made available to the Officers of the Ordnance by the Committee at Haberdashers' Hall for Essex's forces, in accordance with orders of 14 October and 28 November 1644. In all £207 4s. 6d. was paid out in settlement of contracts, with all recorded deliveries paid for.[131] Warrants recording payments to merchants for drums, colours, and polearms supplied to New Model Army's regiments of foot in spring 1645 show that some of the units formed from Essex's Army are likely to have brought their colours with them, whereas all other regiments received them as new. Hence, the New Model regiments under Skippon, Fortescue, Ingoldsby, and Harley might have carried either crimson or green ensigns. Besides, according to William Dugdale's diary, on 26 May 1645 during the second siege of Oxford, Sir Thomas Fairfax located 4 infantry regiments with 13 waggons by the newly erected river bridge at Marston. The following day, Dugdale recorded, '2 regiments of rebels, viz., the white and red, with 2 pieces of ordnance marched by Godstow [3 miles from Marston], and so to Hincksey'.[132] These might have been New Model units.

127 TNA, WO49/82, f. 58r; ML, Ms 46 78/708, f. 35r. See also NAM document: Receipt for colours, 6008-215.
128 TNA, SP28/21, f. 220v.
129 TNA, SP28/19/2, f. 174r.
130 Christopher L. Scott and Alan Turton, *Hey for Old Robin!: The Campaigns and Armies of The Earl of Essex During the First Civil War, 1642–44* (Solihull: Helion & Co., 2017), p.197.
131 TNA, WO49/82, ff. 58r–60r.
132 William Hamper (ed.), Sir William Dugdale, *The life, diary, and correspondence of Sir William Dugdale* (London: Harding, Lepard, and Co., 1827), pp.78–9.

Table 39: Drums, Colours, and Polearms Supplied to New Model Regiments of Foot, 1645

Regiment	Reference/notes
Sir Thomas Fairfax	Warrant dated 3 April 1645 authorising payment of £33 13s. for 2 colours, 10 partizans, 21 halberds and 21 drums.[133] Received 10 colours, 10 partizans and 23 halberds 23 April 1645. Delivered to Captain Richard Beaumont for Fairfax's regiment 20 drums furnished.[134] In May 1647 agitators in the regiment called themselves 'private soldiers of the green regiment of foot', very probably referring to the hue of their Colours.[135]
Sergeant-Major General Phillip Skippon	Warrant dated 21/4/45 authorising purchase of 2 colours.[136] Delivered to Lieutenant Arthur Helsam for Skippon's regiment 8 drums furnished 22/4/45.[137] The white colours issued to Essex's foot 11/44, may have been for this regiment.[138]
Colonel Sir Hardress Waller	Warrant dated 6/5/45 authorising payment to Colonel Waller for 10 colours, 10 partizans, 24 halberds and 21 drums.[139] Regiment described as having black ensigns at Basing on 11/10/45.[140]
Colonel Robert Hammond	Warrant dated 29/4/45 authorising payment to Colonel Crawford for 10 colours, 10 partizans and 23 halberds 23/4/45.[141] Warrant for 20 drums at 24s. apiece.[142]
Colonel Richard Fortescue	Warrant dated 24/4/45 authorising payment to Colonel Fortescue to furnish himself and his regiment with 2 colours, 3 partizans and 6 halberds.[143] Delivered 10 drums furnished.[144] Regiment probably carried crimson or green ensigns, issued to Essex's foot in November 1644.
Colonel Richard Ingoldsby	Delivered to Captain Charles Duckett for Colonel Ingoldsby's regiment 12 drums furnished 11/4/45.[145] Regiment probably carried crimson or green ensigns, issued to Essex's foot in November 1644.
Colonel Thomas Rainborowe	Warrant dated 5/4/45 authorising payment to Colonel Rainborowe's regiment the sum of £59 5s to furnish himself and his regiment with 10 colours, 10 partizans, 23 halberds and 22 drums.[146] Regiment had yellow colours at Worcester in July 1646.[147]
Colonel Ralph Weldon	Regiment received crimson ensigns on 22 December 1644 at a cost of £3 15s. apiece and probably retained them until the November 1645 reissue.[148] 27/11/45 payment of £57 19s. to Christopher Crisp to furnish Colonel Weldon's regiment with 10 colours at £20 15s.; 10 partizans at £6; 10 halberds at £7 4s. and 24 drums at £24.[149]

133 TNA, WO55/460, unfol., SP28/29/2, f. 248r.
134 WSL, Ms Salt 463, unfol.; Bodl. Lib., Ms Add. C247, f. 8r.
135 The copy of a letter sent to his Excellencie Sir Thomas Fairfax: With an account to the officers of the Generalls regiment, intended for satisfaction to their demands (London: 1647). TT, E390[3].
136 TNA, SP28/29/2, f. 237r.
137 WSL, Ms Salt 463, unfol.; Bodl. Lib., Ms Add. C247, f. 6v.
138 My thanks to Stephen Ede-Borrett for this suggestion.
139 TNA, SP28/30/4, fol. 339r.
140 The Kingdomes Weekly Intelligencer, 7–14 October 1645. TT, E304[24].
141 TNA, SP28/29/2, f. 247r.
142 SP28/29/2, f. 259r.
143 TNA, SP28/29/2, f. 227r 28/4/45.
144 WO55/460, unfol.; WSL, Ms Salt 463, unf.; Bodl. Lib., Ms Add. C247, f. 8v.
145 TNA, WO55/1646, unf.; WO55/1647, unfol.; WO55/460, unf.; Bodl. Lib., Ms Add. C247, f. 3r.
146 TNA, SP28/29/1, f. 180r.
147 Worcs Archives, BA 1714/899, f. 584r.
148 TNA, SP28/130/1, f. 61v.
149 SP28/33/2, f. 151r.

Colonel Edward Harley	No record of colours, partizans, halberds and drums received. Regiment probably carried crimson or green ensigns, issued to Essex's foot in November 1644.
Colonel Edward Montague	Warrant dated 2/4/45 authorising payment to Colonel Montague £59 5s to furnish himself and his regiment with 10 colours, 10 partizans, 23 halberds and 22 drums.[150] Regiment described as carrying blue ensigns at Basing on 11 October 1645.[151]
Colonel Walter Lloyd	Warrant dated 3/4/45 authorising payment of £41 13s. to Colonel Aldridge to furnish himself and his regiment with 2 colours at £4 3s. apiece, 10 partizans at £6, 21 halberds at £6 6s., and 21 drums at £25 4s.[152] Delivered to John Spooner, captain to Colonel Aldridge, for the furnishing of his troop [sic – regiment] 8 ensigns with staves, by order of the House of Commons 29/9/44.[153] On 29/11/44 Alexander Venner, ensign maker, was contracted by Parliament to provide 'drums, colours, halberds and partizans for the furnishing of Colonel Aldridge's regiment, viz., for eight new ensigns made of blue Florence sarcenet with distinctions of gold-coloured laurels with tassels to them .... at the rate of 45s. apiece'.
Colonel John Pickering	2/4/45 Colonel Pickering received £55 to furnish his regiment with 10 colours and £20 15s. for 10 partizans, 20 halberds, and 19 drums at £22 16s.[154] Regiment described as having blue ensigns at Basing on 11 October 1645.[155]
Firelocks	Warrant dated 11 April 1645 authorising payment for 2 colours, 2 partizans and 4 halberds.[156] Delivered 27/4/45 to Lieutenant General Hammond, or in his absence Commissary Phipps, 4 drums out of the stores provided for Sir Thomas Fairfax his army to furnish the firelocks of the Train of Artillery.[157] Based on Hammond's cavalry cornet being recorded as having a blue field, it is possible that the same hue was employed for the firelocks' ensigns.[158]

Cornets carried by troops of horse measured approximately two feet square, and usually contained emblematic devices and religious mottos.

As stated, many devices and mottos portrayed on cornets exemplified spiritual motivation for war. Parliamentarian examples often showed that their owners fought for the reformation of the Church of England and 'the true Protestant religion'. A bill or voucher for trumpet banners and cornets for Sir William Brereton's own troop, dated 30 May 1643 includes the following:[159]

150 TNA, SP28/29/2, f. 270r.
151 *The Kingdomes Weekly Intelligencer*, 7–14 October 1645. TT, E304[24].
152 TNA, SP28/29/1, f. 176r; WO55/460, unfol.
153 WSL, Ms Salt 463, unfol.; Bodl. Lib., Ms Add. C247, f. 4v.
154 TNA, SP28/29/1, f. 170r.
155 *The Kingdomes Weekly Intelligencer*, 7–14 October 1645. TT, E304[24].
156 TNA, SP28/29/2, f. 209r.
157 WO47/1, f. 227r.
158 Dr William's Library Ms Modern 12.7, f. 43r
159 TNA, SP28/225/1, f. 3r.

	£	s.	d.
For the two trumpet banners, black taffeta at £5 apiece	10	0	0
For two pairs of stirrups for the trumpeters at 15s. a pair	1	10	0
For the cornet staff	1	5	0
For the two cornets on black taffeta with silver and black fringe, and taffeta of the same at £5 apiece	10	0	0
Total	17	15	0

Similarly, one for a cornet belonging to Captain Lionel Copley's troop of the Earl of Essex's regiment of horse, produced on 18 December 1644 records:[160]

	£	s.	d.
For ¾ of orange damask	0	11	0
For 1½ ord of silk and silver fringe	0	8	6
For a pair of silk and silver cornet strings	0	16	0
For painting the cornet	0	15	0
For the cornet staff and case with belt, boot and swivel	1	8	0
For making the cornet	0	3	0
Total	4	2	6
The embroidering of your cornet cost	1	9	0

Even if very few of the troop cornets belonging to the New Model horse in 1645 and 1646 are known for certain, some level of extrapolation from the recorded devices of standards supplied to cavalry officers in Manchester's, Essex's and Waller's armies who transferred to Fairfax's Army is possible. Although Colonel Edward Whalley is recorded as having a new cornet of white figured damask, fringed in black and white.[161] Even so, more research into this topic would be highly valuable. Sir Thomas' Lifeguard carried his personal cornet of blue damask with blue and white fringe, probably the one noted when part of the army departed from Reading on 1 May 1645 that 'Sir Thomas Fairfax's colours are blue'.[162] Colonel George Fleetwood's cornet was blue with a blue and yellow fringe, depicting a hand holding a sword emerging from a cloud with the motto: *GOD IS MY STRENGTH*. That of Captain James Berry – later of Sir Thomas Fairfax's New Model regiment – was red with a red and white fringe, sporting the motto: *PRO REGE ET LEGE PARATI*. Similarly, the cornet ascribed to Sergeant Major George Sedascue of Ireton's regiment has a red field with a red and white fringe, representing a sun and rain cloud with the motto: *POST NVBILA PHAEBVS* on a white scroll.[163] Additionally, 3 cornet devices belonging to Colonel Richard Graves' New Model Army regiment of horse were described by

160 TNA, SP28/42/1, unfol.
161 Bl Sloane Ms 5247, f. 104v.
162 Dr Williams Library, MS Modern 12.7, f. 25r; *Perfect Passages*, 30 April–7 May 1645. TT, E260[32].
163 Dr Williams Library, MS Modern 12.7, ff. 36r, 45r, 90r; BL, Ms Sloane 5247, unfol.

Wood in September 1645. He recounted that when the unit was located at Thame, the Royalist governor of Oxford, Colonel William Legge, ordered it to be attacked, whereupon 'many arms were taken … besides 3 colours, 2 whereof had mottos. The one was *NON REOS RES*, and the other *PATRIA POSCENTE PARATUS*.[164]

When in mid-1647 the colonelcy of Rossiter's regiment passed to Philip Twistleton, who had served as captain in the unit previously, the regiment was given new cornets, each with a white field with black and white fringe and individual mottos on gold scrolls. The dating of the standards is confirmed by the names of the troop commanders provided by Turmile – Sergeant Major James Berry, and Captains Original Peart, Owen Cambridge, John Nelthorpe, and Hezekiah Haynes – and their various dates of service.[165] Likewise, in 1647, Thomas Horton, who had been sergeant major to Colonel Butler's regiment, took command when the latter resigned; on 20 April 1649 it was one of those chosen by lot to Ireland. Its officers and half of the troops subsequently refused to go, though on 26 August the regiment reportedly embarked.[166] Turmile therefore rendered 'Colonel Thomas Horton his regiment of horse for Ireland, July 1649' as 6 cornets with green fields, with green and fringes and individual devices therein.[167] Tentatively, we might postulate that the troop cornets carried by the New Model horse during the early years of its existence were of a familiar type, but it was not possible (nor perhaps desirable) to attempt a uniform hue for each regiment as there had been previously among some Parliamentarian and Royalist regiments, such as the Earl of Essex's, and those purchased for later Commonwealth units.

Surviving evidence for the design and hue of guidons for dragoon units during the British Civil Wars – carried, like in the Horse, by cornets, commissioned officers in each company – is comparatively slight, although some illustrations and descriptions appear in contemporary documents. Though the actual methods employed in the use of standards by dragoons are absent in contemporary manuals, some clues might be gleaned from those referring to the practices of cavalry units. Writing in the 1620s, Gervais Markham stated:

> The cornet shall be armed and horsed in all points both defensive and offensive, like the lieutenant, only instead of the truncheon, he shall carry charged on his right thigh, his captain's cornet [standard], which (being a private captain) should be compounded of colour and metal impaled, that is, the one half colour, the other metal. The substance of the cornet should be of damask [patterned textile], and the form must be almost square, only a little longer from the staff then on the staff and fringed about suitably. The staff shall be small like a foot ensign, and not so long as an ordinary lance; it must be headed with steel, and either guilt or silvered; with fair tassels suitable to the cornet. If the cornet belongs to a greater officer, it shall then

164 Clarke (ed.), *Life and Times*, pp.121–2.
165 Dr Williams Library, MS Modern 12.7, f. 114r; Wanklyn, *Reconstructing*, I, pp.83, 94, 106.
166 *The Moderate*, 28 August–4 September 1649. TT, E574[20].
167 Dr Williams Library, MS Modern 12.7, f. 116r.

> be of one entire colour, of less quantity and full square. And in this cornet, the captain may carry devise and word, or else none, at his own pleasure.

To this he added:

> The captain of dragoons shall be armed like the lieutenant of the harquebusiers; the lieutenant of dragoons like the cornet of harquebusiers (the cornet and pistols excepted for he shall carry the weapons of his own troop) and the guidon (for these shall not be led with a cornet) of the dragoons shall be armed like a private gentleman of harquebusiers. And here is to be noted, that the difference betwixt the cornet and the guidon is much; for the guidon is the first colours that any commander of horse can let fly in the field. This guidon is of damask fringed, and may be charged either with the crest of him that is the owner thereof, or with other devise at his pleasure; it is in proportion three foot at the least deep in the top next the staff, and upon the staff and so extended down narrower and narrower to the bottom where the end is sharp, but with a slit divided into two peaks a foot deep; the whole guidon is six foot long, and should be carried upon a lance staff. If the captain (owner of this guidon) shall do a good day's service, or produce from his virtue something worthy [of] advancement, so that he is called to a better command, as to lead harquebusiers, or cuirassiers, then the general or officer in chief, shall with a knife cut away the two peaks, and then it is made a cornet which is longer one way then another.[168]

Much in the same vein, his brother Francis (who equated the rank of cornet with the term guidon) instructed that:

> The cornet or guidon is the same that the ensign on foot is, and he ought ever to have two or three faithful and valiant friends in his range, which in all charges will have an extraordinary care of his colours, which is the captain's honour, and the company's safety. Now to speak a little of the guidon or colours themselves, howsoever in our latter times either by pride or ignorance they have been infinitely abused (every man taking upon him to carry what he pleases, and in what form he pleases) yet it is most certain that no man under the degree of a banneret may carry them square, but they must be of damask, either with device or without, three foot deep at the top, and so narrower to the nether end, which must be with two corners or peaks, which whensoever he is made a baron, or knight banneret, those corners are cut away, and the guidon is made square. These colours are carried upon a lance, and are in length full two yards or better. This gentleman which carries this cornet hath all the privileges which an ensign of foot has, and in his captain and lieutenant's absence commands the company, and by either of their deaths ought in right to be advanced into their places. In

168 Markham, *Soldier's Accidence*, pp.45–46.

> the quarter he is lodged as well as his captain, and in all marches has the leading of the middle file and follows next after his captain.[169]

On 26 September 1643, Sir William Waller's regiment of dragoons was observed by William Levett (and his manuscript was later copied by Richard Symonds) when it mustered alongside the London Trained Band and Auxiliary regiments in the Artillery Yard at Finsbury Fields. He described its Guidons as yellow and differenced by 1 to 5 black plates (or gunstones).[170] The six known Guidons of Colonel James Wardlaw's regiment of the Earl of Essex's Army were uniformly *azure* (blue), and fringed in blue and white, with all except colonel's own company guidon having a canton containing a St George's cross. The of the colonel's own company was plain blue, Lieutenant Colonel George Dundas's Guidon, bore the Latin slogan, in gold lettering: *BELLA BEATORVM BELLA*; the Guidon of Captain Alexander Nerne: *VINCIMVS AVSPICE CHRISTO*; the Guidon of Captain John Barne: *IN MONTE VIDIBITVR DEVS*; Captain James Stenchion: *PRO REGE RELIGIONE ET PRLIAMENTIO*; Captain Archibald Hambleton: *IUSTA TRIVMPHAT CAUSA*.[171] The Guidons carried by Okey's dragoon regiment are not recorded, although perhaps like the New Model horse, individual captains brought their own from their previous commands.

169 Markham, *Five Decades*, pp.83–84.

170 Levett's manuscript in National Army Museum 6807-52. Symonds' copy is BL, Ms Harley 986, ff. 111r–112v.

171 British Library Sloane Ms 5247, ff. 111–116. It should perhaps be noted that Dr Williams Library, MS Modern 12.7, f. 103r shows the same mottos for the Guidons of this regiment but allocates them to different officers. As the British Library manuscript is undoubtedly the earlier of the two, indeed the Dr Williams Library manuscript can definitely be dated to at least late 1647 and may even have been compiled in the 1650s, I have accepted the Sloane Ms 5247 allocations.

8

Clothing I

In its edition covering 27 November to 5 December 1645 the newsbook *The Scottish Dove* appealed to its readers thus:

> One thing more I am bound to remember you of and you are all bound to further it, and that is concerning the common soldiers in the General's (Sir Thomas Fairfax) Army. They went forth for us with their lives in their hands, and have adventured themselves in the high places of the field for the defence of our Religion, Laws and Lives; they have behaved themselves gallantly and God has prospered them, we and our prosperities shall reap the benefit, and are bound to relieve them. They are now in a want of clothes – woollen and linen, hose, shoes, and boots. The Parliament, in commiseration of their present necessity, have ordered that a collection be made for them. Their order was on the last Lord's Day read in all the churches within the Line, and by it they desire each man's charity in giving what they have, of old clothes, boots and hose, etc., and have appointed receivers to take them and to return you thanks for what you shall send. They desire you to send to Tallow Chandlers Hall; it is their desire and it is God's command. These men have been Champions for Christ, and what you do for them, you do for Christ. Remember that saying of our Saviour Christ – Matthew 25: 'When I was naked you clothed me not, etc. For what ye did it not to one of the least of these, ye did it not to me, verse 45'.[1]

There is no way of knowing how effective such initiatives were, and it seems unlikely that any great quantities of clothing would have been garnered in comparison with the enormous stocks produced for the army from suppliers and paid for in London with tax revenues. Nevertheless, it does reflect some popular concerns to clothe the soldiers of the New Model Army adequately, especially during its first winter campaign.

Following the receipt of his commission as commander-in-chief, on 1 April 1645 Sir Thomas Fairfax began the task of reducing the armies of Essex, Manchester and Waller, although his immediate priority was the formation of the New Model's regiments of foot and train of artillery. Significantly, on 10 March 1645 the Committee

1 *The Scottish Dove*, 27 November–5 December 1645. TT, E311[4].

for the Army provided an 'estimate of the arms to be provided for the magazines: That £31,989 be provided for furnishing a magazine of arms for horse and foot, and clothes for the foot'. An additional £4,406 was to be provided for the supply of the train.[2] Thus, a foremost responsibility of the Committee and Train was to procure and distribute clothing for and to the infantry. Therefore, this did not extend to the dressing of the mounted arm of the army, the horse and dragoons, nor the members of the train. Moreover, Sir Thomas Fairfax's Ordinance from the Commons of 13 March 1645 appointing him commander-in-chief of the New Model Army ordered, that he 'be enjoined forthwith to recruit, and put into pay, such regiments of horse and foot as are already passed, and agreed upon, by both Houses. That a fortnight's pay and clothes be forthwith provided for those companies that shall be recruited, to be paid and clothed as they come in upon the recruit'.[3]

Conscripts and Impressment

When the New Model was originally formed the responsibility for clothing conscripts was placed upon the county committees, who were to equip them before sending drafts of men to the army. On 19 March 1645 the Committee of Both Kingdoms issued a circular to the Deputy Lieutenants of a number of Counties setting out their individual quotas of levies, in addition to the clothing and condition of the recruits: London, Middlesex and Westminster (2,550), Suffolk (1,000), Norfolk (1,000), Norwich (60), Hertfordshire (400), Ely (150), Cambridgeshire (250), Huntingdonshire (150), Kent (1,000), Surrey (350), Sussex (600), Essex (1,000). On paper this would bring in 8,460 impressed men. Sadly, only the copy to the Committee of Essex has survived; it is here given in full:

> Whereas the Parliament have by their Ordinance of 17 February authorised you to raise, levy, and impress such number of soldiers for the defence of the King, Parliament, and Kingdom as shall be appointed by us the Committee of Both Kingdoms, we, finding it expedient that the army under Sir Thomas Fairfax should be forthwith completed to the full numbers, do by these presents appoint you to cause 1,000 able and serviceable men to be levied within Essex for that employment; and for your better performance of this service we have thought fit by way of direction to recommend the particulars following to your observation: That especial care be taken in the choice of able, full grown, and well clothed men meet for this employment; that the new recruits be brought from the place of their levying by their conductors unto the rendezvous at St Albans, there to be delivered to such officers as Sir Thomas shall appoint to receive them, by the 6 April; that care be taken in the choice of conductors and assistance afforded them to keep their men from straggling and pilfering the country as they go, or from departing from their colours; that the men so impressed be commodiously provided,

2 *CJ*, IV p.74.
3 *CJ*, IV, pp.75–6; *LJ*, VII, p.269.

as has formerly been the practice, with 1,000 red coats faced with blue; and that at the delivery of the men to the conductors their number and names shall be certified by indenture, a duplicate whereof to be sent to Sir Thomas Fairfax. The charge of all this service the Commons have thought fit to leave wholly to your management and good husbandry upon account, and have ordered you for the present to defray the same and to reimburse yourselves out of the first monthly assessment granted by the Ordinance for levying and maintaining the forces under Fairfax's command.[4]

As referred to above, conductors were officers responsible for the movement of soldiers, ammunition and other matériel. Within months, however, there were concerns in some quarters that the financial pressure of raising recruits and clothing them was becoming problematic. On 16 July the Deputy Lieutenants of Essex issued the following certificate:

> ...allowing the charges of John Fenning, of Romford, High Collector, for the first two months' assessment for Sir Thomas Fairfax's Army, within the hundreds of Becontree, Barstable, and Chafford. Whereas by Ordinance of 14 March 1645 it is ordained that the money for providing, buying, and conducting of the draught horses for transport and for the train of artillery, as also for levying, coating, and conducting of soldiers for the recruiting of Sir Thomas Fairfax's Army, shall be defrayed and borne by the several cities, counties, and places where the Committee of Both Kingdoms or Sir Thomas Fairfax shall appoint the same to be raised, and that such sums of money as shall be requisite for this service shall be disbursed, upon warrant of the said Committees, by the collectors of such places out of the first month's assessment as is before specified, and upon certificate thereof the respective collectors shall be allowed for so much money upon their accounts. We, being fully satisfied herein by sight of the bills and receipts produced by John Fenning of his advances for these services, amounting to £725 0s. 3d., do approve thereof, and direct that he be allowed the same by the Treasurers at Guildhall upon his account, as the Ordinance does direct.[5]

On 4 April 1645 the Suffolk Committee urged the Bailiffs and Deputy Lieutenants of Ipswich to send their recruits, who were at Stowmarket, to Bury St Edmunds, 'where clothing, pay and conduct money are provided'. Moreover, the chief constables of the various hundreds were ordered to 'issue warrants to the Petty Constables to levy their proportion of the 400 men charged on the county for Sir Thomas Fairfax's Army and send them fully equipped to Bury; Petty Constables are to bring with them 1s. impress money and 2s. conduct money for each soldier.'[6] However, in addition to clothing conscripts the counties were expected to equip deserters. On 5 April 1645, just prior to the re-enlistment of the soldiers of Pickering's regiment of

4 *CSPD 1644–5*, pp.358–9.
5 *CSPD 1645–7*, p.14.
6 Suffolk Record Office, HD36/A/137, HD36/A/142.

foot of the Eastern Association into the New Model Army, the Committee of Both Kingdoms informed the Committee of Suffolk that:

> Upon receipt of your letter concerning the disturbance made in your county by some old soldiers returned home, we have sent down to you Major Jubbes and Captain Axtell, two officers of Colonel Pickering's regiment [which had recently joined Major General Browne at Abingdon], to receive such soldiers as formerly belonged to that regiment, and to bring them to Reading. We desire you to furnish them with some clothes, as is expressed in your letter, and money for their supply, so that they may be brought thither without burdening the country. If any other soldiers will come along with them and serve in that regiment these officers will take charge of them.[7]

This would imply that Colonel John Pickering's regiment of foot was recruited in Suffolk and possibly Norfolk. Moreover, given that the soldiers were largely conscripted into Fairfax's Army, this is likely to have contributed to the high levels of desertion among the ranks in 1645. While in winter quarters at Abingdon in 1644–1645 the original regiment had experienced problems with retention, and when the regiment stood down on 5 April 1645 it mustered only 81 commissioned and non-commissioned officers, and 159 soldiers.[8] This somewhat large complement of officers was remedied, however, when on the same day Colonel Thomas Ayloffe's Eastern Association regiment was reduced into Pickering's New Model regiment to help bring it up to strength, its soldiers (according to a letter of Lieutenant Colonel John Hewson) were 'delivered' by their officers, none of whom themselves were retained.[9] Besides, it seems there was a particular amount of friction between Ayloffe's officers – who probably adhered to their colonel's Presbyterian beliefs, and Pickering's, who were Independents – whereas a similar conflict existed between the Newport Pagnell garrison and the latter regiment, perhaps aggravated by a competition for resources. Thus, on 19 May 1645 the Governor of Newport Pagnell, Sir Samuel Luke, reported, 'There is such an antipathy here between my men and the New Model that you will every day hear of new encounters. My party which encountered Colonel Pickering is returned with the loss of one man only, whom I intend to relieve so soon as I know where he is.'[10]

Rates of desertion among the New Model's infantry regiments were also exacerbated by lapses in organisation, and particularly the absence of conveying officers at some musters. On 31 May 1645 the Committee of Both Kingdoms wrote to Sir Thomas Fairfax:

> By the enclosed you will see that there has been some neglect in the officers' attendance at the place of rendezvous for receiving of recruits to come from

7 *CSPD 1644–5*, p.387.
8 TNA, SP28/267, ff. 95r, 133r.
9 TNA, SP28/35/4, f. 633r.
10 Tibbut (ed.), *Letter Books*, p.610, note 54.

> the several counties, and for want thereof many of the soldiers run away, whereby your numbers are still deficient. The charge the counties have been at in levying these recruits is [thus] lost, and new men are not raised without trouble and a new charge to the country. Give especial command to your officers to attend that charge, both for the more expeditious and effectual filling up of your numbers, and to avoid all unnecessary trouble and charge to the country.[11]

At the beginning of the First Bishops' War, on 19 March 1639 the Deputy Lieutenants of Suffolk had issued a warrant to the chief constables of the county's townships, requiring them to bring into Bury St Edmunds on 8 April next:

> ...your proportional part of 600 able men, that out of them may be selected such and so many for his Majesty's service as we are commanded, and also your proportion of £1,500 according to former and usual levies, with your proportion of coats, to be either blue lined with yellow, or grey lined with red, or red lined with white; the price not to exceed the sum of 10 or 11s.; all which charge shall be repaid you out of the general levy.

Likewise, 10 April 1640 the constables were ordered to 'provide coats at 10s. or 11s. each, better than they were last year; and for the colour, we would have them red lined with white for 600 men levied out of the county trained bands.'[12] In addition to Suffolk, documentary evidence for the clothing and equipping of conscripts for the New Model exists for other areas.

On 28 March 1646 Cambridgeshire Committee was instructed to provide the sum of £21 12s. for the transportation of clothing to the Ordnance Office stores, previously intended for the Eastern Association Army. Thus, on 28 February 16 soldiers' coats, 26 pairs of breeches, 26 snapsacks, and 90 shirts were received 'the day and year into the abovesaid stores within the Office of the Ordnance from the Committee for the County of Cambridge for the use of Sir Thomas Fairfax his Army.'[13] The County had already provided its recruits with clothing, since the Parliamentary collectors in Westminster had disbursed £61 14s. 8d. for coats and other garments for recruits for the New Model in 1645.[14]

Between 15 April and 30 May 1645, a total of 1,000 coats and 1,000 pairs of breeches were supplied to clothe the Norfolk recruits by that County Committee. A further 300 of each were brought into the Ordnance Office by two Norwich merchants on 13 June, whereas on 5 July another 300 coats and breeches arrived. Each suit cost 15s. 9d. – slightly cheaper than the 16s. and 17s. of those supplied by Richard Downes and others to the New Model Army during the same period. Similarly, from April to August 1645 a total of 1,469 pairs of stockings; 1,582 pairs of shoes; 1,212 shirts; and 1,432 snapsacks. In all, 24 merchants, including 10 cordwainers, were involved

11 *CSPD 1644–5*, p.548.
12 *HMC 13th Report, App. IV*, pp.393, 419.
13 TNA, SP 28/41, f. 376r.
14 TNA, SP28/140/3, 86r; SP28/237/2, f. 479r; Bodl. Lib. Ms Eng. C14, f. 83v.

in providing these impressive quantities.[15] On 10 February 1646 the Committee for the Army ordered the Ordnance Office 'to deliver to Thomas Walker (commissary) out of the stores provided for Sir Thomas Fairfax his Army to be sent by him to Gravesend for the clothing of the Kentish recruits, 500 suits (viz. coats and breeches), 500 shirts, 500 pairs of stockings, 500 pairs of shoes and 500 snapsacks.'[16] These items were delivered seven days later. It is therefore likely that such recruits were meant for Colonel Ralph Weldon's regiment of foot as an order from the Commons issued the previous day to the former warrant instructed the Committee of Kent 'to send men that were raised and brought to Gravesend to Colonel Weldon ... and that the [same Committee] do pay the conduct of them, to be allowed them out of their assessments'.[17]

The distribution of clothing from the Ordnance Office stores to these Kent recruits – possibly impressed men – raises questions over the source of such items. The county's military forces had received some of their clothing in 1644 from Captain John Taylor of London, and in March 1645 he and others were remunerated for items furnished since 1 February 1644, in addition to 'bringing down the soldiers' clothes from London'. These included red coats costing 10s. 4d. apiece, with breeches, shoes, shirts, stockings, and snapsacks. The costs involved were, as was the case with the neighbouring county of Surrey, reimbursed from central funds. Hence, in 1644 the three Kentish foot regiments of Colonels Sir William Springate, John Birch, and Ralph Weldon were issued with quantities of red coats and other items of clothing by the Committee of Kent, which had procured them from Captain Taylor and additional London draper, Captain John Twistleton. Significantly too, Birch's regiment contained a large proportion of unwilling conscripts, while Weldon's passed into the New Model Army virtually unchanged in April-May 1645.[18]

Like other counties, Surrey had to provide money for the maintenance of Fairfax's Army as well as contributing recruits. By an Ordinance of 13 January 1645, the county had to pay £2,000 per month, and by an Ordinance of 1 February 1645, £2,100 each month for the Scottish Covenanter Army in England. All of this was in addition to the charges raised against the county for the upkeep of the local garrisons at Farnham and Guildford.[19] Nonetheless, the county committee informed the High Constables of Surrey that the £186 18s. 6s. disbursed by them 'for the providing of draught horses and impressed men, coat and conduct for Sir Thomas Fairfax's Army by order of Parliament, is to be deducted out of the first month's Assessment by order of Parliament.' This sum was duly reimbursed on 2 June 1645. Moreover, on 23 September 1645 the Committee at Kingston decreed that

> Whereas by Ordinance of Parliament all such monies as should be disbursed for the impressing of soldiers for Sir Thomas Fairfax, upon certificate thereof made by the Committee of this county ... should be deducted

15 TNA, SP28/199, ff. 1r–5v.

16 TNA, WO55/1646, unfol.

17 *CJ*, IV, p.104; *The Moderate Intelligencer*, 10–17 April 1645. TT, E278[14].

18 TNA, SP28/128, f. 25v; SP28/130/3, ff. 62r, 65v–67r, 156r-v.

19 *CJ*, IV, pp.17, 38.

> out of the Assessments for Sir Thomas Fairfax's Army. These are therefore to certify that Mr Gauson, Treasurer for the Middle Division of Surrey has disbursed the sum of £172 17s. 6d.[20]

Warrants from the treasurers of the Middle and West Divisions of Surrey, dated 15 May 1645, and another from the Eastern Division, issued on 19 June, ordered a total reimbursement of £315 12s. for 'red coats faced with orange, breeches, shirts, stockings, shoes and snapsacks, each provided for Sir Thomas Fairfax'. A further warrant from the county committee on 4 September ordered Gauson to

> forthwith pay unto Mr Jeremiah Whitworth the sum of £164 14s. for 137 coats, 137 pairs of breeches, 137 snapsacks, 138 shirts, 138 pairs of stockings, and 138 pairs of shoes at 24s in provision which was for the recruits of Sir Thomas Fairfax's and is to be deducted out of the Assessment for Sir Thomas Fairfax.[21]

These and the previous quantities are likely to have been for the 400 recruits ordered to be raised, on 4 June 1645, for Sir Hardress Waller's regiment in Surrey and Sussex.[22] On 13 August Gauson was compelled to pay Edward Bennet and William Kenman a total of £1 2s. 'for carrying the apparel and coats for the impressed soldiers to Reading'.[23] Other disbursements made for recruiting conscripts in Surrey include that by Thomas Heathfield, collector for Reigate hundred on 20 November 1645, who by 'an appointment for Sir Thomas Fairfax his Army disbursed £7 1s. for impressing, coating and conducting soldiers, and buying draught horses and other charges thereunto incident according to an Ordinance of Parliament dated 14 March 1645, which is to be allowed by the treasurers by warrant according to the said Ordinance'.

Moreover, the account of the Provost Marshal of the Surrey County Committee, dated 28 July 1645, records that among weapons and munitions received by him were 100 new muskets, 100 bandoliers and 100 new swords from a London armourer, although these may have been intended for the county forces rather than its conscripts, who were habitually equipped with weapons and accoutrements upon arrival at Reading or other garrison assembly areas.[24] The adjoining county of Sussex was divided into rapes or administrative areas. Jeremiah Whitworth supplied 100 sets of clothing for the impressed men from the Rape of Lewes, for which he received £120 on 19 June 1645. Similarly, Pevensey Rape, responsible for impressing 43 recruits, supplied 'suits of clothes for the said soldiers at 24s. per suit [comprising coat, breeches, shirt, stockings, shoes and snapsack]' at the first press of 9 April, costing a total of £52 16s., while at the second press on 17 July an additional 49 suits of clothes were distributed to recruits at the same rate and an overall price of £58 16s.[25]

20 TNA, SP28/244/1, ff. 470r, 472r.
21 TNA, SP28/244/1, unfol.; E179/187/468B, f. 55r.
22 *CSPD 1644–45*, p.563.
23 TNA, SP28/244/1, unfol.
24 TNA, SP28/31/6, f. 640r; SP28/224/1, unfol.
25 TNA, SP28/246, unfol.

The army commanded by Sir Thomas Fairfax during the period from its foundation in spring 1645 to the conclusion of the South-western campaign and siege of Oxford in 1646 has come under the orbit of various studies of the Civil Wars. But while scholars and researchers have more recently broken new ground in terms of more detailed information, context and understanding, a significant gap still remains in our knowledge. Two such areas are recruitment and unit strengths – the first integral to the second – especially among the regiments of foot. Thus, it has been largely accepted that, despite assumptions that Fairfax's infantry took the field in May 1645 something at or near their establishment numbers, documentary evidence suggests otherwise. The New Model Army's foot was drawn initially from Essex's, Manchester's and Waller's forces, but service in the infantry appears to have been less desirable than service in the horse. Many recruits for the foot regiments were conscripted and during the early months of its existence, the army was plagued with desertion. Despite Fairfax's best efforts, there remained a shortage of foot soldiers and his authority to impress recruits was repeatedly extended until mid-1646. A second quantity of recruits arrived in April 1645 and were transported up the Thames in boats to Windsor, where they were delivered to the army.

It is possible to suggest that the demarcation concerned which county the recruits were sent from (and this might only have applied to impressed men). Individual shires look to have retained some interest in their conscripts, including their clothing, certainly in 1645, perhaps wishing to distinguish their own men. How it worked in detail is problematic, however, especially given that the warrants from early 1646 instruct commissaries to issue clothing to drafts of recruits when they arrived at their rendezvous, such as Reading. Moreover, if counties had their own distinctive colours of facings for soldiers' coats it may have conformed to a system in which conducting officers and commissaries in the New Model could track which county quota had mustered and arrived. The army might also have been able to check that county committees had provided the rest of the required clothing for the recruits they sent. There is one hint in a contemporary newsbook about deserting conscripts being identified as such by their red coats, but the hue of their facings may have been just as prevalent. Assuming that the 'tapes' and 'ribbons' referred to in April 1645 contracts for New Model Army coats were in addition to facings – 'faced with baize or cotton, with tape strings'; 'with tape strings, and bound about with the same' – it is possible that when actual colours were given in sources they merely applied to impressed 'county recruits'.

When the armies of Essex, Manchester and Waller were merged into the New Model Army, there was a shortfall in the establishment of over 8,000 foot, which needed to be raised, largely by impressment. Hence, on 19 March 1645 warrants were issued to raise 8,460 men from London, Middlesex, Westminster, Essex, Suffolk, Norfolk, Norwich, Hertfordshire, the Isle of Ely, Cambridgeshire, Huntingdonshire, Kent, Surrey, and Sussex.[26] However, the clerk who drew up the document did not fill in the column headed 'coat colours', perhaps because he thought they were all to be red and it was unnecessary to do so. Of the various contracts and receipts for

26 TNA, SP21/120, f. 567r.

soldiers' coats in the brief weeks between the beginning of April and late May 1645 approximately 8,000 are given as 'coats' or 'cassocks', no colour of tapes and facings, nor further details are provided. However, the contracts of 3 April 1645 for '4,000 coats, the tape to be white, blue, green and yellow; 2,000 to be delivered by Saturday sennight and 2,000 before Saturday fortnight', and '1,000 coats with orange ribbon' are somewhat distinctive (and never repeated). Likewise, these 5,000 items were delivered and paid for within 11 days, thus giving the impression that they were in high demand. Given the county quotas of 19 March it is possible that these coats were to be issued to impressed men as per their county 'colours' or 'identifiers', possibly because so many were required, and the counties were unable to meet the demand. Various recruiting campaigns followed throughout 1645, as attempts were made to address significant reductions among the army's infantry regiments due to desertion and battlefield losses. On 22 January 1646 the Committee of Both Kingdoms issued the following, complete with quotas of recruits expected from each county:

> Circular from the same to the several Committees undernamed for recruits for Sir Thomas Fairfax's Army … In pursuance of the Ordinance of the 17th herewith sent to you, we in an especial manner recommend it to your care, that [the specified number] of men may be forthwith levied within your county by way of press, and may not fail to be at their rendezvous upon Friday 20 February, there to be delivered to such officers as shall be appointed by the Committee for the Army, from whom also you will receive more particular directions herein which we desire you to observe … The same to Colonel Rainborowe, or in his absence to the officer commanding that regiment. The Houses have appointed a press for recruiting the army, and the levy in Essex to the number of 500 are to recruit your regiment. Send such officers and sergeants as you consider fit to receive and conduct the recruits to the town of Waltham Abbey by 20 February, that place being the rendezvous for those who are to recruit your regiment. It is now desired by the Committee for the Army that the officers and sergeants above referred to may be sent forthwith to that Committee, in order to receive further directions.[27]

Hence, the Essex levy was intended for Colonel Thomas Rainborowe's regiment. It remains unclear how many of the required numbers were recruited, and how many reached the army's ranks. This county also contributed batches of voluntary recruits from an early stage. On 12 April 1645 it was reported, 'the Associated Counties are now making great preparations for the expeditious advance and completing of that gallant army under Sir Thomas Fairfax. Friday last [11 April] 500 volunteers, which were sent from the cordial county of Essex, lay at St Albans, and many other volunteers are upon their march out of Norfolk and Suffolk'.[28] Likewise, six surviving lists of soldiers (possibly impressed, though it is not made clear in the sources) 'for the recruit of Sir Thomas Fairfax's Army', record that 18 corporals, 6 sergeants, 6

27 *CSPD 1645–7*, p.319.
28 *The Kingdomes Weekly Intelligencer*, 8–15 April 1645.TT, E278[8].

gentlemen at arms and 587 private sentinels were paid at Abingdon on 9 April 1646 under six different captains. 210 of them were from Norfolk.[29]

On 30 August 1645 the Committee of Both Kingdoms wrote to the county committees responsible for maintaining the New Model, requiring them:

> to provide recruits for the army of Sir Thomas Fairfax now engaged in the siege of Bristol, where there must needs be a waste of men, and that therefore there is absolute necessity of speedy supplies. It is of great consequence that the army should leave the field in full numbers, both in regard of the many garrisons necessary to be kept against the enemy, and that they may be able to prevent the enemy by an early march into the field with an army formed of experienced and disciplined soldiers, and thus put a happy end to that work which they have thus far carried on with so good success. The Houses of Parliament have ordered that there shall be a present supply of men to be levied and brought to their rendezvous. The proposition for your county is [blank]. You are required to hasten the levies, so that they may be sent under conductors of your own, to their rendezvous at Reading on 20 September, where they shall find clothes and provisions ready for them. You are to deliver them to the officers there by indenture, and the charge to be defrayed as formerly. In the former impresses there have been so many miscarriages by retardings, defective numbers, and running away, that the army has never yet had the numbers assigned by the establishment.[30]

Two men impressed at Capel, near Dorking in Surrey on 16 April 1645 from 'the first press in or about Easter last' were given shoes and stockings for their journey to Kingston upon Thames, and thence to Reading, the shoes costing 3s. per pair. The constables also laid out 15s. for quartering three conscripts for five days, the sum of 12s. for 'conveying four men to Kingston and attending them', while an additional 3s. was given to the soldiers 'for their press money'. In the next (July) press, shoes were supplied to two men, though no stockings. Similar to before, 4s. was paid for quartering them for two days, 10s. upon 'charges of three men in conveying them to Kingston and the attendance of their quarter', 1s. each to the conscripts in 'pressed money', and another 2s. 8d. in pay. A receipt, dated 10 April 1646, from the parish of Peper Harow records the payment of £1 5s. 4d. for 6 yards of cloth for soldiers' clothes, and the making of them.[31] Such items, however, could have been provided months earlier. Similarly, in April 1645, the town of Colchester, in Essex, had paid £100 to provide 'coat and conduct money' for men raise in accordance with an Ordinance for the service of the army under the command of Sir Thomas Fairfax.[32] It is possible that the system in which county authorities provided clothing (including soldiers' coats) and footwear to conscripts before they were conducted to the New Model Army's headquarters at Reading was discontinued by August or September

29 TNA, SP28/123/2, unfol.; SP28/123/4, ff. 729r–730r.

30 *CSPD 1645–1647*, p.99.

31 TNA, E179/187/468B, ff. 81r, 149r.

32 BL, Ms Stowe 842, f. 7v.

1645, in favour of a more centralised issue made directly from the Ordnance Office to the men once they had arrived there, although conclusive evidence for this is lacking. Nevertheless, as impressment did not cease until the summer of 1646 the question must remain open.

On 16 July 1645, *The Moderate Intelligencer* reported:

> There are, and suddenly will be 4,000 for recruits for Sir Thomas Fairfax at the general rendezvous at Reading, who will suddenly march away, and order will be taken constantly to send monthly such a number, which will be a very good way to keep the Army always full, and send back the runaways as fast as they come home, that so many will be punished according to their merit. These supplies and money to pay the soldiers, so that the people are not dissipated, but encouraged to afford us; and all will go on well.[33]

It was ordered by the Commons on 13 February 1646 that:

> Mr Ball, a Member of this House, do forthwith repair to Reading, to take care of the soldiers that are to be levied by press, and appointed to be brought thither by the 20th of this month, for the recruiting of the Army under Sir Thomas Fairfax; and to see good order kept amongst them; and to order and direct the conductors of them, as occasion shall require. And it is further ordered, that Mr Ball shall have power, by warrant under his hand, to direct the Deputy-Treasurer at Wars, at Reading, to pay the said soldiers, and their conductors; and to recompense such officers as he shall think fit to employ; and to defray all extraordinary charges necessary for that service, according to such orders and instructions as shall be given him by the Committee of the Army; and likewise to assign quarters for the said recruits; and, by warrant, under his hand, to order the commissary of the ammunition for the delivery of clothes, arms, and ammunition, necessary for the said recruits.

This was repeated for recruits mustering at Northampton on 26 March 1646.[34]

There is some evidence, if only anecdotally, that some recruits attempted to sell their newly issued arms and equipment. The same newsbook recorded for 26 June,

> Recruits are still much desired, and arms. Soldiers will not be kept from converting these into their own profit, and will preserve a little in hand before three times as much upon ticket… Sir Thomas Fairfax continues for impressing men, the former being expired, and several orders for recruiting with horses and arms; likewise, care was taken that those that ran from [the New Model] Army be punished, but the question is, how they shall be

33 *The Moderate Intelligencer*, 3–10 July 1645. TT, E292[21].
34 *CJ*, IV, pp.438–439 & 490.

> known, for few are impressed but stragglers that had no dwelling who will never return to the place whence they came.[35]

There were, nevertheless, continued shortfalls in the expected numbers of conscripts arriving for duty. On 14 August 1645 the same source lamented, 'Sir Thomas Fairfax, as by letters this day from the West, of the 11th, is yet before Sherborne; he has at last whole cannon, and a demi-cannon come, which are planted ... the recruits are come likewise, which is good though not so good as was expected'.[36] Notes of stores supplied to the New Model Army provide an indication of the quantities of weapons involved. On 14 July 1645 Commissary William Botterell delivered 'out of his Majesty's Stores to Reading for the service of Sir Thomas Fairfax his Army' 1,000 pikes, 2,660 muskets, 3,000 collars of bandoliers, ½ ton of match, ½ ton of musket bullet, and 20 drums.[37]

In November 1645, *The Weekly Account* reported, 'the Commons taking into consideration the necessity of the foot soldiers, ordered 6,000 suits of apparel for Sir Thomas Fairfax, his army.'[38] Consequently, on 22 October a further 2,500 pairs of shoes and stockings were to be conveyed to the army. Although there is no indication of how these garments were distributed, on 30 January 1646 317 coats, 256 pairs of breeches, 474 shirts, 500 pairs of shoes, and 500 pairs of stockings were to be conveyed to Colonel Thomas Rainborowe's regiment, which arrived the next day. On 9 February 1646 a further 100 coats, breeches, shirts, pairs of shoes and stockings were also ordered to be delivered to the regiment, plus 150 snapsacks, which arrived on 16 February. Another Parliamentarian source declared in January 1646, 'letters from Sir Thomas Fairfax's quarters inform further thus much, that they have received the 5,000 pair of shoes and 5,000 pairs of stockings, which are a great comfort to the soldiery, but their want of other apparel is very great'.[39]

In February 1646 Rainborowe's regiment was further equipped with 200 pikes, and 450 muskets and bandoliers, in addition to 600 coats, 600 pairs of breeches, 600 pairs of shoes, 600 pairs of stockings, 100 shirts, 100 pairs of shoes, 650 snapsacks, 2 drums, 4cwt of match and 2 barrels of powder. Additionally, 4 drums, 2 colours, 8 halberds and 2 partizans were supplied to Captain Edward Mugford on 28 August 1645 'for the conducting of the recruits from Reading to the army out of the stores provided for Sir Thomas Fairfax his Army or otherwise'.[40] Whether the clothing received by Rainborowe's soldiers here included some or all of the quantities dispatched by the Ordnance Office stores the previous month in unclear, though it seems likely. On 8 September Commissary William Botterell was paid the sum of £10 'for his pains in attending at Reading to receive the recruits and mustering them to 9 September instant', in addition to a further £20 'for freight, and carriage of arms and ammunition to Sir Thomas Fairfax's Army, and other charges'. On the

35 *The Moderate Intelligencer*, 26 June–3 July 1645. TT, E288[37].
36 *The Moderate Intelligencer*, 10–17 July 1645. TT, E293[6]; 14–21 August 1645. TT, E297[12].
37 TNA, WO55/1646; WSL, Ms Salt 463, unfol.
38 *Weekly Account*, 3 November–3 December 1645. TT, E313[2].
39 *Perfect Diurnall of Some Passages in Parliament*, 12–19 January 1646. TT, E252[14].
40 TNA, WO55/1646, unfol.; WO55/1647, unfol.

Dutch Engraving of a musketeer *c.* 1645. It is interesting that he still carries a rest, an item that was already falling out of fashion in England, although it should be noted that rests also feature in many of the engravings of the Gardes Française depicted in *La Maréchal de Bataille* (Paris: Estienne Migon, 1647). His general appearance is probably little different from that of the New Model Army's musketeers, although his hat may be a little ostentatious and the breeches' decoration is personal adornment, not how such items would have been supplied. Artist not credited (Stephen Ede-Borrett collection, reproduced with thanks)

same day, 'for his care in looking to the stores and magazine at Reading' Botterell had 59 days' pay for himself at 5s. per day, while his clerk received 2s. 6d. for the same period, 'beginning 12 July past and ending on 8 September inclusive'. On 30 October Botterell and his clerk were paid the same for their services between 9 September and 6 October 1645.[41]

Further warrants issued by the Committee for the Army record the distribution of considerable quantities of arms, clothing and ammunition to the New Model Army and other Parliamentarian forces during the winter of 1645/1646. Moreover, the large quantities involved, and the frequency of such movements of matériel from the Ordnance Office stores illustrate the enormous logistical effort involved. On 13 February 1646 the Committee ordered that Sergeant Major John Browne's company (forming the garrison of Tenby) should be supplied with 150 bandoliers, 150 snapsacks, and 2 drums. This command received a further 100 matchlock muskets, 250 bandoliers, 50 long pikes, 100 coats, 100 pairs of breeches, 100 pairs of shoes, and 100 shirts on 26 February. On 13 February 1646 warrants were also issued to the Ordnance Office 'to deliver to Thomas Richardson [Waggon Master General] out of the stores to clothe and arm the new recruits at Reading for the supply of Sir Thomas Fairfax's Army' 1,700 suits (viz.) coats and breeches; 1,700 shirts; 1,700 pairs of shoes; 1,700 pairs of stockings; 700 pikes; 1,000 muskets with bandoliers; 1,700 snapsacks; and 8 drums. Richardson received another consignment, this time to clothe and arm the new recruits at Newport Pagnell, consisting of 1,500 coats; 1,500 breeches; 1,500 shirts; 1,500 pairs of shoes; 1,500 pairs of stockings; 650 pikes; 1,350 muskets; 1,300 bandoliers; and 2,000 snapsacks, in addition to 12cwt of match, 6 barrels of powder, and 6 barrels of musket bullet. This consignment, along with a further 300 suits, 300 shirts, 300 pairs of stockings, 300 pairs of shoes, and 8 drums were delivered on 18 February.[42]

More batches of clothing and weapons were sent out during March 1646. Thus, on 10 March Richardson took delivery of 500 matchlock muskets, 500 bandoliers, and 8 drums for new recruits at Reading, while on 18 March he received another 500 coats, 500 pairs of breeches, 500 shirts, 500 pairs of stockings, 500 pairs of shoes, 500 snapsacks, 400 matchlocks, 400 collars of bandoliers, 10 drums with cords, and 10 pairs of drumsticks 'to clothe and arm the new recruits at Reading for the supply of Sir Thomas Fairfax's Army'; these were delivered three days later. In clothing and equipping batches of recruits there Richardson distributed 2,189 coats; 2,179 breeches; 2,184 pairs of stockings; 2,180 pairs of shoes; 1,200 shirts; 1,770 muskets; 1,775 bandoliers; 168 long pikes; 36 drums furnished with cords; 1 ton of match; 10cwt of powder; and 10cwt of musket shot on 26 March 1646.[43] By any measure, such quantities – largely supplied for the clothing and arming of recruits – were extremely large. Consequently, during a period of six weeks in February and March 1646 a total of 3,889 coats; 3,879 pairs of breeches; 1,700 shirts; 2,680 pairs of shoes; 2,684 pairs of stockings; 868 pikes; 2,675 muskets and bandoliers; 500 snapsacks; 1cwt of match; 1 ton of powder; and 10cwt of

41 TNA, SP28/32/1, f. 116r; SP28/32/3, ff. 341r–343r.
42 TNA, WO55/1646, unf.
43 WO55/1647, unfol.; WSL, Ms Salt 463, unfol.

musket shot were transported and distributed to the army's recruits at Reading. Furthermore, 1,800 coats and breeches; 1,500 shirts; 1,800 pairs of shoes; 300 pairs of stockings; 650 pikes; 1,350 muskets; 1,300 bandoliers; 2,000 snapsacks; 12cwt of match; 6 barrels of powder; and 6 barrels of musket shot made their way to the recruits at Newport Pagnell.

Given that the expectation was to issue recruits with clothing and arms upon arrival at garrison distribution centres such as Reading, and their subsequent deployment to the foot regiments of the New Model Army, it must be assumed that the items were supplied by the Ordnance Office and stored in magazines in readiness for the arrival of these soldiers. The instructions issued by the Committee of Both Kingdoms to the County Committees on 19 March 1645 concerning the recruitment of conscripts, specified that 'the men may be brought on the day appointed to the rendezvous, where care will be taken for the arming and otherwise for them.'[44] Various warrants for the payment of batches of recruits and their conveying officers survive. For instance, on 26 July 1645 Colonel Thomas Rainborowe – who seems to have been especially responsible for recruitment – received the sum of £1,000 'towards the payment of recruits upon their march from Reading towards the army and for such officers as command these recruits.' On 26 August it was ordered that Captain Edward Mugford should be paid £16 6s. 'for his own entertainment', his lieutenant £8 8s. and 4 sergeants £3 3s. each, 'being to conduct the recruits now at Reading unto the army'. Likewise, *The Moderate Intelligencer* reported on 23 May 1645, 'divers we pressed in London and the suburbs, the city is the best magazine of men, take but those that may be best spared; theres need of a constant press they run away so fast'.[45] Six months later, on 28 October, the sum of £100 was disbursed to John Taylor, 'employed by the Militia of the City of London for conducting of the impressed soldiers and for the recruiting of Sir Thomas Fairfax's Army'.[46]

A modest quantity of muster lists of soldiers, made upon their arrival at garrisons in the Thames Valley area and elsewhere, offer an insight into the process in addition to the size and composition of drafts. A 'roll of recruits for Major-General Skippon's regiment' records that one corporal and 135 private sentinels were mustered at Newbury on 2 August 1645 under the command of Captain John Clarke, while another list, seemingly incomplete, containing the names of 35 soldiers, is appended to it. This officer duly testified that the men were held at Newbury for seven days, before being conveyed to the army, which at this time was situated at or near Sherborne in Dorset.[47] It is unclear whether such recruits had voluntarily enlisted or were conscripts, although lists made of drafts made the following year, in addition to payments to conducting officers and non-commissioned officers would strongly suggest that most drafts were of the latter category. Four lists by Thomas Barham, Muster-master to Sergeant-Major General Browne, contain the names of non-commissioned officers and conscripted men upon their arrival at Abingdon on 9 April 1646. Hence, a 'list of impressed soldiers for recruits for Sir Thomas Fairfax's

44 *CSPD 1644–5*, p.359.
45 *The Moderate Intelligencer*, 22–29 May 1645. TT, E286[9].
46 TNA, SP28/31/2, f. 26r; SP28/31/4, ff. 470r, 541r.
47 TNA, SP28/123/1, ff. 88r–89v.

Army under the command of Captain John Andrews' documents the names of three corporals, one drummer, one gentlemen of the arms, and 83 common soldiers.

A second list of conscripts commanded by Captain James Strachan has the same number of non-commissioned officers, plus 103 soldiers; Captain Taylor's company, the same with 92 private sentinels; and another three corporals, one drummer, one gentlemen of the arms, and 99 men led by another conducting officer, Captain John Ford. In addition to these, on 9 April a draft of impressed soldiers 'out of the City of Norwich and the county of Norfolk under the command of Captain Thomas Holland' comprising three corporals, one drummer, one gentlemen of the arms, and 106 soldiers was mustered by Barham. A further company of 104 recruits 'from the county of Norfolk' was brought into Abingdon by Captain Nicholas Kelk on the same day.[48] In all, 18 corporals, 6 drummers, 6 gentlemen of the arms, and 587 conscripted men assembled in the town on 9 April 1646 ready to be clothed, armed, allocated into individual companies and regiments and possibly to receive some level of military training before their transferal to Fairfax's Army.

Such batches of recruits were marched as ad hoc 'companies' and dispersed among Fairfax's regiments in the field. Likewise, Captains Kelk, Holland and others acted as conducting officers, rather than 'regular' officers in standard New Model units. Norfolk's drafts of recruits appear to have been in response to a circular sent out by the Committee of Both Kingdoms on 12 January 1646, which established quotas for 'the number of recruits to be supplied by them severally as Hants. 1,000, Wilts. 1,000, Dorset 600, Somerset 1,500, Gloucester 500, these to be sent to the army, to be there on 20 February; Essex 500, Suffolk 500, Norfolk 500, Norwich 50, Herts 250, Cambridge 100, Hunts. 100, Beds. 150, and Ely 50, these to be at Newport Pagnell on 20 February; Kent 500, Sussex 300, Surrey 200, London 400, Southampton 200, Middlesex without the line [of communication] 100, Westminster and Middlesex within the line 300, these to be at Reading on 20 February'.[49]

Soldiers' Coats

A report in the newsbook *Perfect Passages*, describing two brigades of the New Model Army's infantry as it marched out of Reading on 1 May 1645, stated 'The men are redcoats all, the whole army only are distinguished by several facings of their coats.'[50] However, what the writer observed (or thought he observed) can be questioned and may relate to the garb of the recently mustered county conscripts, rather than the rank and file of the standing volunteers. Moreover, none of the documents relating to the procurement and supply of soldiers' coats for the New Model between April 1645 and January 1646 mention the colour of their fabric. Even so, a contract agreed with Richard Downes (notified to the Ordnance Office on 14 February 1646) for the provision of 2,000 coats, 2,000 pairs of breeches and 2,000 pairs of stockings, stipulated in part, 'The coats to be of a red colour and of Suffolk, Coventry or

48 TNA, SP28/123/2, ff. 290r–299v; SP28/123/4, ff. 729r–731v.
49 *CSPD 1645–7*, p.319.
50 *Perfect Passages of each dayes proceedings in Parliament*, 30 April–7 May 1645. TT, E260[32].

Gloucester cloth, and to be made three-quarters and a nail long, faced with baize or cotton, with tape-strings according to a pattern delivered to the said Committee'.[51] Hence, a 'quarter' (or quarter of a yard) equates to nine inches, while a nail is two and a half inches, meaning that these coats were 29½ inches in length and supplied in a single size. A contract agreed with the same supplier was the one to supply 16,000 coats and breeches for soldiers in Ireland, drawn up on 16 October 1649, in which the coats were 'to be made of Coventry or Gloucester cloth of Venice colour, red shrunk in cold water'.[52]

Similarly, the breeches in the 1646 agreement were to be 'grey or some other colour and made of Reading cloth or other cloth, in length three quarters one eighth, well-lined and trimmed, suitable to the patterns presented, the said cloth, both of the coats and breeches to be first shrunk in cold water'. This means that these garments were 31½ inches in length and came in a single size. The 16,000 pairs of breeches included in a tender to supply the British forces in Ireland, dated 23 April 1648, are described as 'grey, or some other good colour, of broad cloth, or good kersey, in length three quarters, three quarters and a half, and three quarters and one nail, well lined, and with hooks; and the said cloth or kersey, both for the said coats and breeches, to be first shrunk in cold water'.[53] Furthermore, those agreed with Downes in 1649 were to be constructed of 'Reading cloth or other cloth', although here '12,000 to be three-quarters and a half in length, and 4,000 three-quarters and a nail, well lined, and with hooks and buttons'.

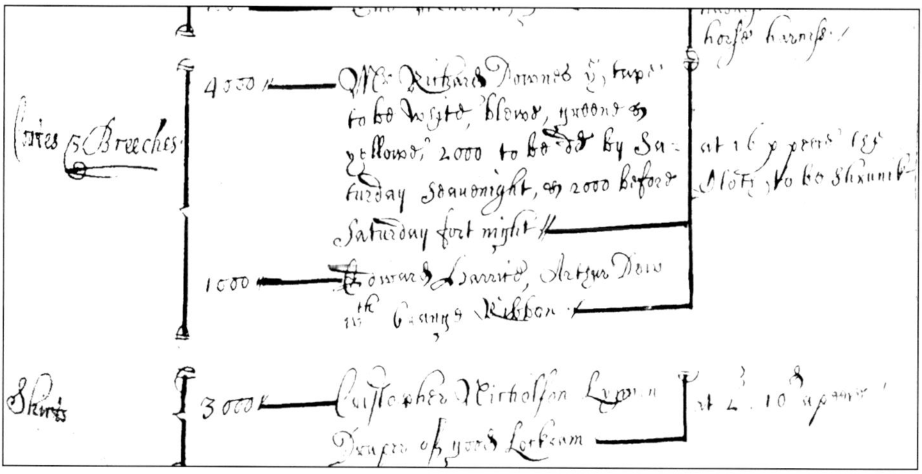

Notification of contracts for 5,000 coats with coloured tape from Richard Downes and Arthur Dew, 14 April 1645. (TNA, WO47/1, f. 209r)

It is conceivable that the coats issued to the New Model Army in April 1645 with coloured tapes and ribbons (possibly the same thing), in addition to the tape-strings

51 TNA, WO47/1, ff. 209r–210v; ML, Ms 46 78/708, ff. 27v–28r, 114r.
52 *CSPD Interregnum, 1649–50*, p.343.
53 *LJ*, X, pp.158–9.

mentioned in the Downes contract of February 1646 and the fellow magazine coats sent to Ireland, were for fastening them together. The New Model coats also, may have had linen tape bound around the edges of the garment, perhaps to reduce fraying and reduce the amount of woollen cloth needed as seams were then superfluous at the edges. Some of the musketeers depicted in the drill manual *Directions for Musters* (1638) have coats secured by tape-strings, while another is garbed in a cassock, which appear to have buttons down the side.[54] One indication that coat buttons were purchased separately comes from a payment in early 1644 of 6s. 2d. for such items for Lieutenant Colonel Massey's Parliamentarian command in Cheshire. However, some soldiers' coats made for men belonging to Sergeant Major Thomas Croxton's company of Sir William Brereton's infantry regiment were fastened by hooks and eyes.[55]

In fulfilment of his contract of 14 February 1646, Richard Downes delivered the initial consignment of 1,000 coats, breeches, and pairs of stockings to the Ordnance Office on 21 February, and the remaining quantities on 10 March.[56] No complete patterns associated with Downes' contract survive, however, and except for their length, the types of cloth to be used and the addition of 'tape-strings', the actual design and appearance of these garments remain unknown. As specified, the unlined soldiers' coats were to be made of Suffolk, Coventry, and Gloucestershire cloths. These were legally defined broadcloths in the early modern period, although much of the substantial broadcloth production in England was for the export market. Even so, large quantities were used for Elizabethan military coats and cassocks, in addition to coats and breeches for soldiers during the Civil Wars. In 1581, during the second Desmond Rebellion, 'a company of English soldiers, distinguished by their dress and arms, who were called redcoats, and being sent to war [in Ireland] by the Queen were overwhelmed near Lismore'. Similarly, on 4 June 1595, the Lord Deputy reported from Dublin that the Irish rebel Hugh O'Neill, Earl of Tyrone, had '300 shot in red coats like English soldiers'.[57] Moreover, red-dyed broadcloths were a significant export item to the Continent, red was generally considered a martial colour, and red dyes were easier to fix and thus a higher degree of consistency in terms of production was possible.

54 *Directions for Musters Wherein is shewed the order of drilling for the musket and pike* (Cambridge: University of Cambridge, 1638).

55 TNA, SP28/49, f. 100r.

56 TNA, SP28/140/3, unfol.

57 Philip O'Sullivan Beare, *Historiae Catholicae Iberniae Compendium* (Lisbon: 1621), II, book IV –translated in Matthew J. Byrne, *Ireland Under Elizabeth: Chapters towards a History of Ireland in the Reign of Elizabeth* (Dublin: Sealy, Bryers and Walker, 1903), p.27.; *CSPD Ireland*, 1592–1596, p.322.

Table 40: Notification of Contracts to the Ordnance Office for the Supply of Coats and Breeches to the NMA (TNA, WO47/1; SP28/140/3; Bodl. Lib., Ms Eng. hist. C14; Ms Eng. hist. C244; ML, Ms 46 78/708)

Date	Quantity and type	Price suit	Contractor
3/4/45	4000 coats, the tape to be white, blue, green and yellow; 2000 to be delivered by Saturday sennight and 2000 before Saturday fortnight. The cloth to be shrunk	16s.	Richard Downes
3/4/45	1000 coats with orange ribbon. The cloth to be shrunk	16s.	Edward Harris & Arthur Dew
3/8/45	2000 cassocks and breeches for foot soldiers, the cloth to be shrunk before making, all to be made of largest sizes	17s.	Richard Downes
3/8/45	2000 cassocks and breeches for foot soldiers, the cloth to be shrunk before making, all to be made of largest sizes	17s.	Richard Downes
3/8/45	2000 cassocks and breeches for foot soldiers as the first	17s.	Edward Harris & Arthur Dew
3/8/45	200 cassocks and breeches, the cloth to be wetted and shrunk before making up and of the largest size	16s.	Daniel Judd
18/9/45	2000 coats and breeches	17s.	Edward Harris & Arthur Dew
22/9/45	1500 cassocks and breeches	17s.	Edward Harris & Arthur Dew
22/9/45	200 coats and breeches	17s.	Daniell Judd
26/9/45	1500 coats and breeches	17s.	Edward Harris & Arthur Dew
9/2/46	4500 coats and breeches	17s.	Thomas Player, Tempest Milner, Stephen Eastwick, Maurice Gethin & John Pocock
14/2/46	2,000 coats and breeches	17s.	Richard Downes
26/2/46	1000 coats and breeches	17s.	Richard Downes
10/3/46	1,000 coats and breeches	17s.	Richard Downes
13/3/46	2,000 coats and breeches	17s.	Arthur Dew & Edward Harris

Table 41: Warrants for Payments to Contractors for the Delivery of Coats and Breeches to the Ordnance Office for the NMA (TNA, WO55/460; WO/55/1646; SP28/29/1-36/2; SP28/140/3)

Date	Quantity and type	Price suit	Contractor
7/4/45	2000 coats and breeches	16s.	Richard Downes
12/4/45	1000 coats and breeches in part of their contract	16s.	Edward Harris & Arthur Dew
14/4/45	4000 coats, the tape to be white, blue, green and yellow. Cloth to be shrunk	16s.	Richard Downes
14/4/45	1000 coats with orange ribbon. Cloth to be shrunk	17s.	Edward Harris & Arthur Dew

Date	Quantity and type	Price suit	Contractor
25/4/45	1000 coats and breeches in full of their contract	17s.	Edward Harris & Arthur Dew
25/4/45	2000 cassocks and breeches in full of his contract	17s.	Richard Downes
25/4/45	28 fine plunket coats for the Lifeguard	39s. 3d.	Richard Downes
15/5/45	1000 suits, viz.: cassocks and breeches at 3 months beginning the date hereof	17s.	Edward Harris & Arthur Dew
4/6/45	1000 suits, viz.: cassocks and breeches in part of their contract	17s.	Edward Harris & Arthur Dew
22/9/45	2000 suits in part of their contract, viz.: cassocks and breeches	17s.	Edward Harris & Arthur Dew
22/9/45	2000 suits in full of their contract, viz.: cassocks and breeches at 3 months beginning 18 September instant	17s.	Edward Harris & Arthur Dew
23/9/45	2000 suits, viz.: cassocks and breeches in part of his contract beginning 22 September instant	17s.	Richard Downes
23/9/45	2000 suits, viz.: cassocks and breeches in part of his contract	17s.	Richard Downes
29/9/45	1500 suits, viz.: cassocks and breeches, in full of their contract at 3 months and beginning 25 September instant	17s.	Edward Harris & Arthur Dew
29/9/45	1500 suits, viz.: cassocks and breeches, in part of their contract	17s.	Edward Harris & Arthur Dew
28/9/45	2000 suits, viz.: cassocks and breeches, in full of his contract	17s.	Daniel Judd
30/9/45	2000 suits, viz.: cassocks and breeches, in full of their contract at 3 months and beginning 28 September instant	17s.	Edward Harris & Arthur Dew
11/2/46	2000 suits, viz.: cassocks and breeches, in full of his contract	17s.	Richard Downes
14/2/46	2000 coats and breeches		Thomas Player, Tempest Milner, Stephen Eastwick, Maurice Gethin & John Pocock
21/2/46	1000 coats and breeches	17s.	Richard Downes
27/2/46	4500 coats and breeches	17s.	Stephen Eastwick et al
6/3/46	3500 coats and breeches	17s.	Stephen Eastwick et al
10/3/46	1000 coats and breeches	17s.	Richard Downes
10/3/46	1000 coats and breeches	17s.	Edward Harris & Arthur Dew

On 19 March 1639 the Deputy Lieutenants of Suffolk ordered the captains of the County's trained band and the chief constables of each parish to muster their 'proportional part of 600 able men, that out of them may be selected such and so many for his Majesty's service as we are commanded, and also your proportion of £1,500 according to former and usual levies, with your proportion of coats, to be

either blue lined with yellow, or grey lined with red, or red lined with white; the price not to exceed the sum of 10 or 11s.; all which charge shall be repaid you out of the general levy'. Likewise, the latter colour seems to have been preferred, because the following April they were to 'provide coats at 10s. or 11s. each, better than they were last year; and for the colour, we would have them red lined with white for 600 men levied out of the county trained bands'.[58]

In looking for precedents among other Parliamentarian armies during the Civil Wars for the colour and style of coats issued to the New Model Army's foot some caution needs to be adopted. On 30 October 1642 a warrant was issued to supply Colonel John Venn's regiment of foot, which had been recruited from London to serve as the Parliamentarian garrison of Windsor, with 1,200 coats, caps, shirts, and 'other necessaries'. Venn's acquittance, dated 21 December, records the receipt of 300 coats, 300 pairs of shoes, 300 shirts, and 630 snapsacks, while the coats were coloured grey lined with yellow.[59] Those soldiers' coats issued to Colonel Thomas Grantham's regiment of the Earl of Essex's Army in 1642 were described as 'tawny lined with white, and white and tawny straps'.[60] The latter could have been to fasten the coats together. Similarly, following its capture and stripping of its clothes at Brentford on 12 November 1642 Colonel Denzil Holles' regiment was re-equipped with red coats, breeches, doublets, caps, stockings.[61] Around the same time Sergeant Major Skippon's regiment, then part of the Earl of Warwick's forces, was supplied with red coats faced with yellow.[62] Essex's infantry would later benefit from two major clothing deliveries – one at Bierton, near Aylesbury in August 1643 and the other at Portsmouth in September 1644. As detailed in the accounts of the army's Waggonmaster General, Thomas Richardson, a total of 3,440 coats, 6,000 shoes, and 3,000 snapsacks were mostly supplied to 11 infantry regiments belonging to Essex's Army participating in the Gloucester campaign, probably to replace those issued a year earlier. The latter was part of the re-equipping of the army following its defeat at Lostwithiel, where many soldiers were subsequently robbed of their clothing by the victorious Royalists and local civilians.[63]

Nonetheless, there appears to be little correlation between the garments distributed in 1643 and those in 1644.[64] An undated letter from a London supplier lists the latter issue as 1,600 coats, comprising 540 grey with red lining, 500 grey coats with yellow lining, 560 grey with white lining; along with 740 red coats, 520 lined with red, and 220 lined with white. Such garments were issued in addition to 6,000 pairs of shoes, 1,200 snapsacks and 400 shirts.[65] On 15 October 1644 Sergeant Major Richard

58 HMC, *13th Report, App. IV*, pp.393 & 419.
59 TNA, SP28/261/2, ff. 294r–294v; SP28/262/2, f. 219r.
60 TNA, SP28/2A, f. 88r.
61 TNA, SP28/262, f. 374r; *CJ*, II, p.866.
62 TNA, SP28/3B, f. 412r; *Most Hapy Newes from the Earle of Essex. Wherein is declared the relation of two famous Victories obtained by the Parliament Forces* (London: 17 January 1643). TT, E85[30].
63 TNA, SP28/140/4, ff. 27r & 85v.
64 Stuart Peachey and Alan Turton, *Old Robin's Foot: Equipping and Campaigns of Essex's Infantry, 1643–45* (Leigh-on-Sea: Partizan Press, 1987), p.10.
65 TNA, SP28/93, ff. 183r, 187r, 211r; Bodl. Lib., Ms Tanner 62/2B, ff. 650r–650v.

Browne, the Parliamentarian governor of Abingdon informed the Committee of Both Kingdoms that owing to desertion, 'our strength instead of being augmented is of late much weakened, because those who are come back are not able to do duty for want of clothes and shoes. We have 500 fallen sick of late, and one or two being perished for want of clothes have died in the streets. I beg you to pity our sad condition and to think of ammunition so much wanted for this garrison'.[66] Moreover, one observer mentioned that at the same town on 14 January 1645 'my Lord General's army, whose red coats did show now as gallantly as at Newbury [presumably the second battle in 1644].'[67]

These garments could have represented a part or the whole of what Essex's infantry was wearing by early 1645. Even so, on 12 February 1644 a Royalist observer reported 'certain bluecoats of the Governor [Colonel Edward] Aldridge his regiment at Aylesbury'. This is likely to have been from a separate supply as soon afterwards, Aldridge wrote to the Speaker, describing his men as 'some much behind in their arrears, are not able to feed their bellies, nor clothe their nakedness, they may well be called ragged regiments.'[68] The garments supplied to Essex's Army in autumn 1644 were transported with other military hardware by waggon to Portsmouth, and by barge to Windsor.[69] Estimates by Simon Marsh of the contents of the packs of clothes and fatts of shoes carried to the army suggest that the 67 packs of clothes would have contained in excess of 9,800 coats, and that 'it is likely that the clothing provided was at least sufficient to re-equip the infantry and it is probable that some men in the train of artillery were also resupplied'.[70]

Additionally, the red, yellow, and white 'linings' of the 1644 coats are worthy of discussion, particularly as they are suggestive of the later 'coloured' tapes and 'facings' associated with some of the garments distributed to the New Model Army. Critically, Marsh observes:

> If the coats issued in late August 1643 were not of the same colour as those supplied earlier in the war, the lack of uniformity that this would have created would have made differences in the colour of new linings a minor issue by comparison. The colouring of linings may therefore have reflected the material available to make the new coats and was not a consideration in terms of establishing uniformity or distinction within and between regiments … it seems likely that the clothing supplies [in 1644] outlined in the letter to Skippon detailed what a single, unnamed contractor was intending to deliver to the army at Brierton and that the overall quantities issued there came from a range of different merchants. If this was the case, then it seems likely that suppliers would have been required to supply coats of red and grey but without concern for a specific lining colour.[71]

66 *CSPD 1644–5*, p.45.
67 *A Diary, or an Exact Journal*, 9–16 January 1645. TT, E25[2].
68 *Mercurius Aulicus*, 11–17 February 1644. TT, E35[27]; Bodl. Lib., Ms Tanner 62/2B, f. 582r.
69 TNA, SP28/140/4, ff. 69r–70r.
70 *'Exceedingly Toylsome'*, p.92; 'Disarmed Multitude', p.64.
71 Marsh, *'Exceedingly Toylsome'*, pp.88–9.

The New Model Army's soldiers' coats were faced rather than lined, and possibly edged with tape. Hence, facings could have meant a strip of material (specified as either baize or cotton), visible at the cuff and collar, or even inside the collar and cuff. Alternately, facings could have formed a strip of cloth attached to the inside of the front of the garment to reinforce fasteners. In March 1595 the 5,000 cassocks which were to be supplied by John and Thomas Bolton, along with Richard Catcher, 'drapers and merchant tailors,' for soldiers in the Low Countries, were to be 'made of very good cloth, lined with baize worth 2s. 6d. per yard, faced in the collar and sleeves with rich black taffeta and trimmed with silk buttons and loops, a thing far surpassing the standard.'[72] Interestingly, the term 'faced' is used here to describe the treatment of the collar and sleeves, and not just an area around the cuff. The accounts of the City of Leicester show that in 1595 it was charged with sending three soldiers to Ireland, for which payments were made for 'blue cloth for the coats ... 29 yards and a half yards of ribbon for the same coats... [plus] a yard and a nail of blue taffeta for the said coats.'[73] Similarly, in 1601 the Corporation of Bath laid out for 'two gross of lace to lace the soldiers coats 24s.'; the sum of 7s. 6.d was also paid to 'Richard Storie for new lacing of nine soldiers coats', with an additional 26s. 8d. for 'making of 16 soldiers coats'.[74]

The interpretation that the magazine coats supplied to troops in Ireland in the early 1640s and the New Model Army from spring 1645 onwards were closed with tapes is highly plausible. Another possibility is that these garments had no front opening and were pulled on over the head like a modern fishermen's smock or anorak, perhaps tied under the arm of down the sides with tape-strings. Various contemporary illustrations of soldiers show neither buttons nor other methods of fastening coats, although the limitations of such images limit their use as sources. Four musketeers depicted in the frontispiece of *The Loyall Sacrifice*, published in 1648 shortly after the siege of Colchester ended and the two Royalist commanders summarily executed in the aftermath, wear garments akin to cassocks with no central opening.[75] Cassocks and Gascon coats of the late sixteenth and early seventeenth centuries had neither central fastenings, nor methods of closure, and were pulled over the wearer's head.

In 1576 the county of Lancashire was charged with sending masons, carpenters, and labourers to Ireland. The sum of 33s. 4d. was to be levied towards their furniture, 'with which was to be provided for each man doublet, hose, shoes, dagger, and a coat of white cloth made of the fashion of a cassock, guarded with two laces of incle, the one of the colour of red, and the other green'. The following year, pikemen sent were to receive a 'coat of watchet, fashion Gascony, of Yorkshire broad cloth 1

72 *CSPD Elizabeth, 1595–1597*, pp.21–2.

73 Mary Bateson (ed.), *Records of the Borough of Leicester* (Cambridge: Cambridge University Press, 1905), III, p.320.

74 F. D. Wardle (ed.), *The Accounts of the Chamberlains of the City of Bath, 1568–1602* (Somerset Record Society, 1923), pp.178–179.

75 *The Loyall Sacrifice: presented in the lives and deaths of those two eminent-heroick patternes, for valour, discipline, and fidelity; the generally beloved and bemoaned, Sir Charls Lucas, and Sir George Lisle, knights. Being both shot to death at Colchester, five houres after the surrender* (London: 1648).

yard and three quarters 140d.; yellow and red broad cloth for two guards about the coat, and two guards down the hose, two fingers broad, one quarter and a half 30d.'[76] Correspondingly, a list of arms and equipment to be issued to the militia of Chester, dated December 1596, states that each company comprised 40 men armed with pikes or corselets, and 54 men armed with muskets or calivers. Each man was also issued with a sword and a coat with coloured guards according to his company.[77] Both the Lancashire and the Chester examples refer to guards or broad decorative stripes approximately 1½ to 2 inches wide, some with coloured tapes, sewn around the garment and possibly the cuffs in the manner of facings.

The specification in the Downes contract of February 1646 for soldiers' coats supplied to the New Model Army to be 'faced with baize or cotton' – very similar to the magazine garments sent to Ireland in 1642–1643 and 1646–1647 – present various problems of interpretation. The meaning of 'facings' has often been taken to mean 'turnback' sleeve cuffs, although there is no evidence for this and they could also have been a method of lining or strengthening the inside of collars and cuffs, or even the inside of the front of coats to reinforce fastening devices such as tapes. Hence, despite some assumptions, there remains no evidence that New Model Army infantry regiments were distinguished by the colour of the facings on their red soldiers' coats. Moreover, there is no hint in the records that when commissaries and their assistants bundled up coats and other garments at the army's magazine at Reading for onwards transportation, they either sorted these into coats with the same-coloured facing or with individual regiments in mind. Indeed, the numbers and letters daubed on each of the packs (for instance, 'C' for coats, with the quantity therein) suggests that such a practice was not adopted.

The earliest identifiable consignment supplied by Downes to the Ordnance Office 'for the use of Sir Thomas Fairfax his army', was for 2,000 coats and breeches at 16s. the set or 'suit', although he had previously provided clothing for troops in Ireland. Downes' order (and not the later one with coloured tapes) was delivered by 7 April 1645 when the warrant was drawn up to pay him £1,600 'in full of his contract'.[78] Accordingly, Skippon's promise of 6 April that 'there are clothes come down for the soldiers already' seems highly plausible.[79] On 3 April the Ordnance Officers were notified that Downes was engaged to provide '4,000 coats, the tape to be white, blue, green, and yellow. Cloth to be shrunk at 16s. apiece.' The Treasury Warrant drawn up for the full payment of £3,200 to him is dated 14 April 1645, although the contract for these garments, notified to the Ordnance Office on 3 April, specifies that the first 2,000 were to be delivered within a week (i.e., by 10 April) and the remainder in a fortnight's time (17 April). The entire order was fulfilled and delivered to the Ordnance Office by 14 April, when the warrant for Downes' payment was issued. Richard Downes continued to supply clothing to the New Model and Commonwealth armies in considerable quantities. Between April 1645 and March 1646, he delivered a further 8,000 coats and pairs of breeches, while between August

76 LA, DDKE/Box 122/1, ff. 50v–51r.

77 CRO, ZM/MP/8/48-49.

78 TNA, SP28/29/1, f. 189r.

79 *Mercurius Civicus*, 3–10 April 1645. TT, E278[12].

1648 and April 1649 he supplied 12,000 coats (also described as cassocks), 8,000 pairs of breeches, and 3,000 pairs of 'white cotton [undyed wool flannel] stockings' for distribution to troops in Ireland and Scotland.

In addition to these, on 25 April 1645 Downes had supplied '28 fine plunket [either a blueish grey or a sea-green colour, the same as Sir Thomas Fairfax's personal cornet] coats for the Lifeguard' at a cost of £1 19s. 3d. apiece.[80] According to the Woollen Cloths Act of 1606,

> all broad plunkets, azures, blues, and other coloured cloth, which shall be made within the shires of Wilshire and Somersetshire, or elsewhere of like making, shall contain, being thoroughly wet, between 26 and 28 such said yards and inches, as aforesaid, and in breadth 6 quarters and a half within the lists, and being clean scoured, thicked, milled, and fully dried, shall weigh 68lbs the cloth at the least.[81]

No details of buttons or lining for these garments are mentioned, and it must be assumed that they were purchased complete. Manchester's Lifeguard is known to have worn coats made of scarlet cloth, although it is unclear whether this refers to the colour, or a type of fine and expensive woollen fabric found in high status garments in the medieval and early modern periods. In March 1644 a bill presented for manufacturing such coats records 32½ ells of fine scarlet broad cloth at 12s. per yard; 33¼ yards of fine green London baize at 2s. 4d. a yard; 5 ordinary of grass green and crimson silk; 14 dozen, 7 yard of grass green and galloon costing 3s. per dozen; 15 dozen of grass green bobbin lace at 3s. a dozen; 10 grass green neck buttons; ½ yard of canvas; 15 gross, 3 dozen grass green and strawberry buttons at 4s. the gross; and 15 dozen large cloak buttons at 9d. the dozen.[82]

Items of clothing issued to civil war armies, and the New Model Army in particular, were often referred to as 'suits' or 'uniforms', which included coats and breeches, and perhaps other items such as stockings. The importance of providing soldiers in field conditions with complete suits is outlined in a letter from Lords Justices and Council to the Lord Lieutenant of Ireland, dated 7 June 1642, which stated 'we find that 1,000 coats, caps, stockings and shoes are to be brought in there weekly and sent hither, but therein we find no mention of breeches for the soldier, and therefore we must mind your Lordship to provide that their suits of clothes be entire, and such as may preserve them from cold as well in winter, when they must be put to hard duty in night watches, as now in their marches and services in the field'.[83] In May 1642 Parliament acknowledged that a group of suppliers had provided clothing that included 10,000 coats at 8s. 6d. each and 8,000 coats at 11s. apiece to Commissary George Wood for dispatch to Ireland. That the number of doublets and breeches

80 TNA, SP28/29/1, f. 252r; SP28/29/2, f. 254r; SP28/32/3, ff. 366r 367r; SP28/140/3, unfol.; Bodl. Lib., Ms Eng. hist. C244, f. 47r.

81 An Act for the True Making of Woollen Cloth (4 Jas. I c.2).

82 TNA, SP28/24/3, f. 334r.

83 *HMC Ormonde*, VIII, p.148.

Dutch Engraving of a musketeer *c.* 1645. Reminiscent of the men of the Gardes Françaises shown in *La Maréchal de Bataille* (Paris: Estienne Migon, 1647). As with the figure above, his general appearance is probably little different from that of the New Model Army's musketeers, although again the breeches' decoration is personal adornment, not how such items would have been supplied. His coat appears to be fastened with ties not buttons. His montero cap is of a more flamboyant style than is usually depicted. Artist not credited. (Stephen Ede-Borrett collection, reproduced with thanks)

provided in the same consignments is identical at 15,000, suggests that the suits referred to as being sent there are doublet and breeches combinations.[84]

Contemporaneous with the Downes indenture of 3 April 1645 was an order from the partners Edward Harris and Arthur Dew, who agreed to provide '1,000 coats with orange ribbon' at 16s. apiece. This was duly fulfilled within nine days.[85] It is possible that the 'tape' and 'ribbons' specified in each of these contracts were one and the same. Significantly, these two contracts – those agreed with Downes, and with Harris and Dew – from early April 1645 are the only ones that mention coloured 'tape strings', and or 'ribbons'. How this tape was to be attached to the coats is not mentioned, and no record of which foot regiments received them. A payment was also made to Harris and Dew 'in full of their contract' on 25 April 1645 for 1,000 suits of coat and breeches, costing 16s. for each set, but whether this was in connection with the same consignment, or an additional one is unclear, though the warrants do indicate that the coats with orange ribbon were brought in by 12 April.[86] Between May 1645 and March 1646 the partners delivered an additional 10,500 suits and 3,000 pairs of stockings to the Ordnance Office.[87]

The London merchant and plumber Daniel Judd was also engaged to supply coats and breeches for Sir Thomas Fairfax's Army in 1645. On 3 August the Ordnance Office was notified of an indenture agreed with him to provide 200 suits, 'the cloth to be wetted and shrunk before making up and of the largest size', at a cost of 16s. apiece. There is no record of a receipt of these items and there remains the possibility that the contract was terminated, perhaps to allow Judd to fulfil a separate order for 2,000 suits, which he did, half on 22 September and the rest six days later.[88] Nonetheless, a survey of the Treasury warrants issued by the Committee for the Army between April and December 1645 reveals that although a total of 6,700 coats and 6,770 pairs of breeches were issued to Fairfax's Army from the Ordnance Office land stores, a further 10,500 soldiers' coats and 12,500 pairs of breeches were procured, but not entered into the receipts books.[89] Such arrangements made with Daniel Judd for clothing were unusual. As plumber to the Ordnance Office, he delivered considerable quantities of musket shot and match for the use of the New Model, including 43 tons of musket shot, one ton of pistol shot, and 36½ tons of match between June and December 1645.[90]

During the winter of 1645–1646 the Committee for the Army procured quantities of clothing from additional suppliers, some of whom do not appear to have been used before. Hence, a consortium, headed by Stephen Estwick, but also including

84 TNA, SP28/139/4, f. 62r. Letter of Thomas Newburgh and George Wood, Commissaries, to the Irish Committee concerning consignments of clothing sent to Londonderry; SP28/139/9, ff. 103r–104v.

85 TNA, WO47/1, f. 209r; WO55/460, unfol.; WO/55/1646, unfol.; ML, Ms 46 78/708, f. 114r.

86 TNA, SP28/29/2, f. 252r.

87 TNA, SP28/30/4, ff. 355r, 369r; SP28/32/3, ff. 358r, 362r, 379r, 380r; Bodl. Lib., Ms Eng. hist. C14, ff. 48v, 51v; Bodl. Lib., Ms Eng. hist. C244, f. 2r.

88 TNA, WO47/1, f. 210v; SP28/32/3, f. 362r; ML, Ms 46 78/708, fol. 103r.

89 TNA, SP28/29-36, *passim*.

90 BL, Ms Add. 25585, f. 69r; TNA, WO49/82 ff. 2r, 5r, 69r-v; WO55/1662, ff. 76v–77v; WO55/1663 f. 83r.

Thomas Player, Tempest Milner, Maurice Gethin and John Pocock furnished 4,500 coats, breeches, shirts, and pairs of stockings costing 17s. per set on 9 February 1646. An acquittance signed by Estwick for £2,339 1s. 3d. shows that they obtained half of the sum on 6 March, and the remainder 21 days later. On 14 February a second consignment of 2,000 coats, breeches, shirts, and pairs of stockings was received from this syndicate, while a further 3,500 of each arrived at the stores on 6 March.[91] Although there appear to be no surviving contracts nor notifications of the same for these orders, at least the 4,500 coats and other clothing received on 9 February are recorded in one book of receipts 'containing certificates by the Officers of the Ordnance for the receipt of certain materials of war contracted for and supplied for Sir Thomas Fairfax's Army'.[92] Estwick was an important merchant who played a prominent part in the supply of clothing and footwear to the Parliamentarian forces, both through the Ordnance Office and otherwise. Between August and October 1642 Estwick received a total of £3,000 from the Army treasurer for the provision of coats, shirts, shoes, and knapsacks for the Earl of Essex's Army.[93]

Subsequently, on 4 October 1642 the Treasurer was ordered to pay £3,600 over the next three months to defray the cost of providing clothing, footwear, and knapsacks. A further £2,260 was disbursed to him between April 1643 and June 1644.[94] A damaged warrant, dated 24 February 1644, records the payment to an unidentified merchant for supplying 174 pairs of breeches to the Scottish forces in Ireland, at a cost of £30 11s. 8d. 'for the making of them [with] buttons, hooks, canvas for the waist and [missing] of them'. He also provided '40 suits, being cassocks and breeches'.[95] In September of the same year the English Parliament agreed to provide 10,000 suits (coat and breeches), 10,000 pairs of shoes and other items of clothing to the Scots Covenanter Army in England, although only 7,400 suits were delivered. The warrants pertaining to these show that most of them were provided by Arthur Dew and Edward Harris, who also supplied clothing for the New Model Army. The materials provided to the Scots were 6,215 yards of broadcloth at 5s. 8d. per yard; 1,170 yards of Yorkshire kerseys at 2s. 6d. per yard; an unspecified quantity of Yorkshire and Hampshire kerseys at 3s. 6d. per yard; and 11,500 yards of fine Hampshire cloth at 4s. per yard. The Covenanters were also supplied with 'linens for 7,400 suits', comprising 6,037 ells of white linens at 10d. per ell; 3,675 yards of brown linens at 12d. per ell; 1,662 yards of broad linens at 13d. per ell; 3,662 yards of broad brown linens at 15½d. per ell; 720 yards of broad brown linens at 14d. per ell; 22,200 dozen buttons at 1d. per dozen; 44,000 pairs of hooks and eyes at 5s. 2d. per 600 pairs; 7,400 pairs of leather pockets at 3d. per pair; and 740lbs of thread at 2s. 1d. per pound.[96]

Significantly, each suit – consisting of one coat and one pair of breeches – used approximately 2 yards of broadcloth or equivalent of kersey costing 11s. 4d.; 2 yards

91 TNA, SP28/140/3, unfol.
92 Bodl. Lib., Ms Eng. hist. C14, f. 78v.
93 TNA, SP28/1A; 28/2A; SP28/261; SP28/262, *passim*.
94 TNA, SP28/261, ff. 430r–431v, 433v.
95 TNA, SP46/106, f. 44r.
96 TNA, SP28/46/106, ff. 205r–223v.

of linen lining costing 2s. 2d.; 1 pair of leather pockets costing 3d.; 1.6 ounces of thread costing 2½d.; 36 buttons costing 3d.; and 6 pairs of hooks and eyes costing ½d. The total average price of the suits, without the cost of making up, was 15s. 9d. On 4 February 1645 the House of Commons instructed that '11,000 yards of broadcloth be forthwith provided upon account for the supply of the cloth formerly furnished and speedily sent down towards the clothing of the soldiers of the Army of the Earl of Leven'. This was to be made into clothing, and once more supplied by Dew and Harris. Three days later it was ordered that several of the members of the Committee of Goldsmiths Hall should furnish the Scots with 1,000 back, breast and pots, and the same number of pairs of pistols for their cavalry.[97] On 15 September 1645 3,000 swords, along with 5,000 muskets, 2,000 pikes, and 200 barrels of powder with a double proportion of match were supplied to the Scots Covenanter Army out of the Ordnance Office stores. Moreover, the Committee agreed on 2 December to supply the Parliamentarian forces in Lincolnshire with substantial military stores, including 400 swords and belts, 100 muskets and 400 collars of bandoliers for the garrison of King's Lynn; and 200 swords and belts, and 200 bandoliers for the foot at Boston.[98]

The soldiers' coats and other items of clothing detailed in the contracts for the troops in Ireland in 1642–1643 and the New Model Army in 1645–1646 are broadly like those laid out by Commissary George Wood in a projection of 19 December 1645. He outlined two specifications for 'the type of coats and breeches most often seen in magazines' to be sent to Ireland (given below), but whether these were ever intended for New Model units is unclear.[99] It is likely that part of the brigade of Scots troops sent to Ulster in 1642 were supplied with red coats. On 26 March 1644, the draper Anthony Fletcher provided 20 long red and green Coventry cloths costing £10 15s. with three plunkets of Suffolk cloth at £7 10s per cloth.[100] According to the Scottish writer John Spalding, in March 1645 there were anticipated back in Scotland '1,500 red coats out of Ireland, and some other regiment, yet there was but 650 red coats.' A few months later he described 'two regiments of red coats', one of which was the commanded by Lieutenant Colonel Robert Hume.[101]

The stores intended to be sent to the troops in Ulster in April 1645 had included 7,000 coats and breeches, 7,000 pair of shoes, 7,000 pair of stockings, 7,000 caps, and £4,000 worth of cloth.[102] Following their return to Scotland in 1645 to quell a Royalist uprising led by the Marquess of Montrose, at least two regiments of foot were wearing red coats. Such garments continued to be worn by infantrymen during the Commonwealth and Protectorate periods. On 16 February 1647 the Committee for the Affairs of Ireland ordered that '800 muskets, bandoliers, and swords, and 400 pikes and swords, to be ready, with Colonel Monck, by that time, or before his

97 TNA, SP23/2, ff. 48r–49v.

98 *CJ*, IV, pp.274, 363.

99 TNA, SP28/33/4, ff. 442v–443v; SP28/34/3, ff. 324v–325r.

100 TNA, SP46/106, f. 106v.

101 John Spalding, *The History of the Troubles and Memorable Transactions in Scotland 1624 to 1645* (Aberdeen: 1829), II, pp.287 & 301.

102 *CJ*, IV, p.120.

men shall be landed there; that they may be presently fitted for service. These to be provided and sent by the State'. Additionally, on 5 June the Committee for the Army ordered the issue to Colonel John Birch's regiment of foot of 1,050 'red coats', which, together 1,000 pairs of shoes, 1,000 pairs of stockings, 1,050 snapsacks and 408 shirts, were delivered five days later. The unit had been engaged in England for service in Ireland, but subsequently mutinied and was disbanded.[103]

During this period, as earlier, consignments of clothing for Parliament's troops in Ireland were inspected for defects before dispatch. Thus, on 2 February 1650 the Treasurers at War employed John Jackson, William Bottom, and Richard Mathews for 30 days' work examining 33,400 pairs of stockings for Ireland, whereas William Penny and Francis Easterly spent 30 days scrutinising 23,000 shirts. On 14 April John Matthews and Humphrey Hale received £3 10s. each. for 'viewing shirts, stockings, tent cloths, and other provisions for Ireland, and the following day John King and Andrew Vanly both had £6 13s. 4d. 'for viewing soldiers' clothes'. On 30 November 1650 Sergeant Major Robert Cobbet was paid a total of £2,598 8s. for 3,000 cassocks and breeches at 15s. a suit, for the army in Scotland, in addition to 800 cassocks at 9s. each, for Colonel Sexby's regiment. At least a portion of these garments were sub-standard, because the sum of £11 18s. 4d. was 'deducted for short measure'.[104]

On 16 December 1653 the Council of Officers and the Committee of the Commonwealth engaged Robert Molesworth 'to supply 5,600 yards of red broad cloth for clothing the foot soldiers in Ireland at 6s. per yard, amounting to £1,680'. Similarly, on 3 April 1654 the Commissioners for Customs and Excise were ordered to allow 1,600 yards of red cloth to pass free to Scotland for the use of Monck's regiment.[105] The Commissioners of Customs and Excise had agreed on 3 April 1654 to direct 1,600 yards of red cloth to the same regiment while it was serving in Scotland.[106] In August 1658 the same Committee certified the delivery of '6,000 red cloth coats at 9s. each for [the] soldiers, and four grey coats for the Marshal General's men, at £5 each'.[107] Similarly, in November 1658 the Dunkirk Committee reported that a contract had been agreed with Robert Walton to supply '150 red coats, breeches, stockings, and shoes, for the sick and wounded sent from Flanders to Dover, at 24s. a suit', according to previously supplied patterns. Walton also provided for the garrisons of Dunkirk and Mardyke 2,500 suits, consisting of coat, breeches, stockings, shoes, and shirts, at 24s. a suit, in addition to 100 gowns, at 14s. each, although the costs of such clothing remained unpaid.[108]

The London woollen draper, Richard Downes, was one of the leading suppliers of clothing to the forces of Parliament from 1642 to the late 1650s. As such, he provided considerable quantities of coats, breeches, and stockings to the army in Ireland (1642–1645), to the New Model Army, and to Commonwealth forces in both Ireland and Scotland. On 9 January 1660 an indenture with him was approved, whereby he

103 BL, Ms Add. 35332, ff. 49r–51v; *CJ*, V, pp.126, 176.
104 *CSPDI 1649–50*, pp.590–94; *CSPDI 1650*, p.601.
105 TNA, SP 28/98, unfol.; *CSPD Interregnum, 1654*, p.34.
106 *CSPD Interregnum, 1654*, p.440; *1657–8*, p.60.
107 *CJ*, V, p.465.
108 *CSPD Interregnum, 1659–60*, p.246.

was to deliver to the Tower stores 2,300 soldiers' coats and breeches, and 2,500 yards of broad cloth, 'if not equal to the patterns, defalcations to be made on the prices'.[109] Further contracts for garments agreed with Richard Downes in 1649 confirm their colour. On 23 January he agreed to supply 667 cassocks of 'Venice red cloth', which he brought into the Ordnance Office stores before 7 February, the date upon which a warrant for the payment of £300 3s. to him was issued.[110] In addition to these, Downes was also contracted on 23 January to provide '2,000 cassocks of red Venice cloth, 2,000 shirts and 2,000 pairs of stockings'. This order was fulfilled in two batches – on 21 February '1,000 coats, breeches, shirts and pairs of stockings' were received into the Tower stores, with the like consignment arriving on 10 March.[111]

Significantly, these indentures settled with Downes predate the one to supply 16,000 coats and breeches for soldiers in Ireland, drawn up on 16 October 1649, in which the coats were 'to be made of Coventry or Gloucester cloth of Venice colour, red shrunk in cold water'. These were delivered in full and paid for on 25 December 1649 – one batch of '6,000 soldiers' coats and breeches for Ireland' and another for 10,000 of the same. Seemingly, however, these did not fulfil the demand for garments, because on 7 January 1650 the Council of State decreed that 'finding the 16,000 cassocks and breeches provided for the foot forces in Ireland will not be sufficient, order should be given to the officers of the Tower, to deliver to William Dobbins, commissary, the 1,950 cassocks and breeches now in the Tower, to be sent to Sir Charles, on orders from the Irish Committee'.[112] Even so, an undated warrant for the payment of £1,640 10s. to Commissary William Dobbins for these items at 17s. a suit, mentions 'only 1,930 delivered, there being no more in the Tower'. A warrant for the payment of £290 that had been issued in November 1649 to Mr King and Andrew Wanley 'to view all soldiers' clothes delivered by Mr Downes, to see that they are according to his contract', indicates that such consignments were routinely checked by the Ordnance Office for compliance in terms of quantity and quality.[113]

On 14 March 1645 the Commons resolved that £1,519 9s. 4d. should be provided out of the £80,000 loan from the City, and 'put into the hands of Sir Thomas Fairfax and Sergeant Major General Skippon, upon account, for recruiting, and putting into pay, their respective regiments.'[114] Consequently, a warrant, endorsed by Sir Thomas Fairfax, was issued on 4 April for the disbursement of 14 days' pay to officers and soldiers enlisting in the nascent army. According to John Rushworth, Fairfax's secretary:

> The same third of April Sir Thomas Fairfax went from London to Windsor, where he appointed his general rendezvous, having caused proclamation to be made throughout London, for all officers and soldiers under his

109 *CSPD Interregnum, 1659–60*, p.306.
110 TNA, SP28/58, f. 468r.
111 Bod. Lib., Ms Eng. hist. C244, f. 52r; TNA, SP28/140/3, f. 120r; SP28/352/2, unfol.
112 *CSPD 1649–50*, p.471.
113 *CSPD Interregnum, 1649–50*, pp.343, 553, 576, 579, 582.
114 *CJ*, IV, p.77.

> command to give their attendance there on Monday the 7th and there he continued till the last of that month, diligently busy in modelling his army, wherein he was to encounter the discontents of those that were reduced under new commanders, and of those that wholly went off from employment. And besides fitting the Train for the field, and the attendance of the recruits from London, an entire new form was to be introduced into the whole army, the forces that remained of the old army being not only to be recruited, but reduced into new companies and regiments, as if they had been newly raised.

In similar vein, on 21 March 1645 the Commons had declared, 'each common soldier, that shall be pressed, shall be furnished with a coat, breeches, a shirt, a pair of stockings and shoes, and snapsack, by the several committees of the several countries ['counties']; so as the charge do not exceed 24s. for each, besides the conduct money'.[115] Furthermore, the Parliamentarian-leaning *The Kingdomes Weekly Intelligencer* reported for 4 April 1645:

> This day also the House of Commons brought up an additional ordinance to that of 27 February last, for the raising and impressing of soldiers for Sir Thomas Fairfax his Army, concerning the manner of securing, and disposing those that were pressed, and for the providing of money, clothes, stockings and snapsacks, and other necessaries for them, that so they might have all fit encouragement to go on in the service; also, that care might be taken to have their names and habitations, that so in case they shall desert the service they might be proceeded against.[116]

Sir Thomas Fairfax was aided by Major General Phillip Skippon, who on 6 April went to Reading, where five regiments of Essex's forces were rendezvoused. Skippon thus 'caused them to be drawn out into the field, and in the head of that which had been his Excellency's regiment' declared:

> There is (at present) a fortnight's pay to be paid to such officers as shall go off, which they shall presently have upon their muster. And as for the officers and soldiers that are continued (as soon as they shall be mustered and listed) they also shall have a fortnight's pay; and there are clothes come down for the soldiers already in part, and I assure you, that upon my life and honour there are more providing, and you shall be all furnished with coats, breeches, stockings, shoes, and such arms as you shall stand in need of, with all good usage and constant pay. And that as I have been with you hitherto, so upon all occasion of service to my God and country, I shall by the help of God, be willing to live and die with you.[117]

115 Ibid., p.85.
116 *The Kingdomes Weekly Intelligencer*, 1–7 April 1645.TT, E276[22].
117 *Mercurius Civicus*, 3–10 April 1645. TT, E278[12].

In a letter, dated 8 April 1645, Sir Phillip Skippon received reassurance from the Commons:

> The House, having received much satisfaction in the desired ordering and speedy delivering the foot soldiers you formed at Reading, have commanded me to return you thanks and to assure you that they will take care that whatsoever you have promised the soldiers in their names shall be ready performed, that all those that condescend in their service may lack no encouragement to go in cheerfully.[118]

Skippon's own foot companies from Essex's Army were stood down at Windsor and paid off a few days later, while two weak regiments from Manchester's army – Sir Thomas Horgan's and Sir Miles Hobart's – mustered the same day and were paid the day following. Moreover, many officers and non-commissioned officers accepted a reduction to the ranks principally due to the tact and persuasive skills of Fairfax and Skippon. On 8 April when the latter reformed his regiment, one cashiered officer complained that 'he had rather parted with his wife than his company'.[119] Those commissioned officers who were dismissed from the original formations were paid £148 14s. 4d.[120] On 10 April also, the Committee for the Army – responsible for contracting for all the arms, ammunition, equipment, and clothing required for the summer's campaign – issued a warrant to the Officers of the Ordnance 'to deliver to Mr Bond [commissary] or his deputy what coats and breeches are brought in for the supply of Sir Thomas Fairfax his Army, and also 3,000 shirts and 3,000 pairs of shoes, and what snapsacks you have.'[121] By 24 April the Tower stores had taken delivery from contractors of at least 8,000 coats, 5,000 pairs of breeches, 7,000 shirts, 9,000 pairs of shoes and 4,000 snapsacks (evidently the latter were slow coming in).

It is probable that unlike weapons, few, if any of these items remained in stock for very long at the Tower of London, because clothing and leatherware would become prone to dampness and mould. On 27 June 1645 a warrant issued to the Committee of the Navy informed its members that 'the storehouses of the said [Ordnance] Office are exceedingly out of repair, and it [the rain] comes into them so extremely that we can hardly keep anything dry'. Moreover, a schedule of repair work to the fabric of the stores was provided on the same day.[122] Prior to the Battle of Edgehill in 1642 some soldiers' coats issued to Essex's infantry remained in stores so that spare quantities could be distributed at a later point, though at least one bundle of coats became rotten due to them being kept in damp conditions. If the newly enlisted volunteers – mainly from the reduced infantry regiments of the armies of Essex, Manchester and Waller – were quickly issued their clothing, it remains possible

118 Bodl. Lib., Ms Tanner 60/1, f. 73r; *Severall Letters to the Honourable William Lenthall, Esquire, Speaker of the House of Commons* (London: 1645). TT, E277[8].
119 BL, Ms Harley 252, ff. 33r-v.
120 TNA, SP28/29/1, ff. 15r, 57r, 106r, 348r–349r.
121 TNA, WO55/460, unfol.
122 TNA, WO49/82, ff. 279v, 281r.

that some had to wait. In mid-July 1645 one newsbook reported, 'The grey coats of Colonel Morley's, and Colonel Leytons' are put in Colonel Pickering's and Colonel Waller's regiments.'[123] Whether these were immediately reclothed is unknown, but on 19 July John Pickering's and Hardress Waller's regiments were preparing to assault the east side of the Royalist defences at Bridgewater as part of an enlarged New Model Army brigade which also included Sir Thomas Fairfax's, Skippon's, Montague's, Rainborowe's, Hammond's and Harley's infantry regiments, the latter under the command of Lieutenant Colonel Pride.[124]

Brigades were fundamental to the organisation, composition and tactical nature of the New Model Army, and they are mentioned or alluded to by contemporary observers such as Sprigge. He relates that Colonel Thomas Rainborowe commanded a brigade at Bristol in September 1645, which contained his own, Skippon's, Harley's and Hammond's regiments. The same tactical unit served at the siege and capture of Basing House the following month. Similarly, the author of the London-based *Narration of the Expedition to Taunton ... Sent from a Commander in the Army, and dated at Chard, May 18. 1645* provides some useful observations of two brigades during Fairfax's march to relieve the town:

> ...our noble General Fairfax [he mentions], General Major Skippon, and that regiment which formerly was Barclay's [Colonel Harley's foot], were commanded back when we were at Blandford, which was a sad breakfast to most, both officers and soldiers, were after sad salutes, and watery eyes, like the parting of husbands from their wives, and dear friends, yet we were a thinking of nothing more than resolution to obey, and action to perform, that great work for the which we were sent, with four regiments of foot, to wit: Colonel Weldon, who as eldest colonel, a gallant, wise, and brave gentleman, commander-in-chief, Colonel Fortescue, Colonel Lloyd, and Colonel Ingoldsby's regiments.[125]

A particular impediment to our knowledge of how brigades operated on the battlefield stems from Robert Streeter's representation of the New Model foot at Naseby. He shows two clearly defined divisions of Parliamentarian foot: a front line of five regiments, supported by a second, 'reserve', line of three regiments. Streeter was not present at the battle however, and his interpretation is misleading. The eye-witness account of George Bishop, who described himself as 'a gentleman with the army' and was present, not only describes the initial dispositions of the army, but states, 'The infantry was thus ordered: in the right wing the General's, Colonel Montague's, Colonel Pickering's and Colonel Sir Waller's regiments; in the left, Major General Skippon's, Colonel Bartlett's [Harley's, commanded by Lieutenant Colonel Pride],

123 *The Moderate Intelligencer*, 17–25 July 1645.

124 Sprigge, *Anglia Rediviva*, pp.69–70.

125 *A Narration of the Expedition to Taunton: The Raising the Siege before it, and the Condition of our Forces, and the Enemies, at this present in the West. Sent from a Commander in the Army, and dated at Chard, May 18. 1645*. TT. E285[10].

Colonel Rainborowe's and Colonel Hammond's'.[126] This is supported by Sprigge, who stated that at the beginning 'The General, together with the Major-General, put the several brigades of foot into order.'[127] If Bishop viewed the action from the top of Windmill Hill, or at least from an easterly point, then it is likely that he witnessed Skippon's regiment leading the second wing or body of infantry, before the deployment of his own regiment to the front left of the line in order to match Sir Bernhard Astley's battalia on the opposing flank – Bishop stated 'that the two armies arrayed in a direct line equal to both parts'. This interpretation is critical since it demonstrates that the New Model Army's foot at Naseby was formed of two brigades of roughly equal strength, and not the formations shown by Streeter.

Among the first batches of clothing intended for New Model infantry recruits were '4,000 coats, the tape to be white, blue, green and yellow' delivered to the Ordnance Office stores by Richard Downes, and '1,000 coats with orange ribbon' from Edward Harris and Arthur Dew before 14 April.[128] These coats were likely seen by a correspondent of the newsbook *Perfect Passages*, who reported the movements of Sir Thomas Fairfax on 30 April, and the marching out of eight regiments of New Model Army foot and other units from Reading the following day intending to raise the siege of Taunton:

> From Windsor he marched on Wednesday (with about 1,000 horse and foot) to Reading, where he lay that night, and Thursday night his soldiers expressing (with him) so much joy and alacrity in their advance, as was enough to raise the courage of any dull spirit, which were such amongst them; and put valour into every coward, to see how they did unanimously rejoice at their advance, and they marched so much modesty and civility, that not a man amongst them durst offer wrong to any man, woman or child.
>
> The manner of Sir Thomas Fairfax's march is thus: (not to speak of Sir Thomas his own place in the march, for that is where he pleases) Major General Skippon marched in the van of the foot and leadeth the General's own regiment, Sir Thomas Fairfax's colours are blue; the men are redcoats all the whole army, only are distinguished by several facings of their coats, the firelocks (only) some of them are tawny coats; and thus the regiments of foot march one after the other.
>
> Between every regiment is drawn four pieces of ordnance, and four the next, and so all through the army. The horse march some before, and some behind; some on the one wind, and some on the other as there is occasion, or as is most convenient, the carriages and train is drawn in the middle of the army; between the regiments and the pioneers; who march before the train, and make way as occasion serves, some of the pioneers also going in every place with the ordnance.[129]

126 *A More Particular and Exact Relation of the Victory obtained by the Parliament's forces under the command of Sir Thomas Fairfax* (London: Richard Cotes, 1645). TT, E288[38].

127 Sprigge, *Anglia Rediviva*, pp.34–5.

128 TNA, WO47/1, f. 209r; WO55/460, unfol.; WO/55/1646, unfol.

129 *Perfect Passages*, 30 April–7 May 1645. TT, E260[32].

This passage – which is given in full – throws up several ambiguities and problems of interpretation, and we must question what the writer saw or thought he saw. The comment 'Sir Thomas Fairfax's colours are blue' has been taken that New Model officers wore blue scarfs, corresponding with his 'colours' (presumably his personal standard, rather than the 'flags' of the infantry), or perhaps his cornet only. In May 1647 agitators in Fairfax's own regiment called themselves 'private soldiers of the green regiment of foot', very probably referring to the hue of their colours.[130] Similarly, 'the men are redcoats all the whole army, only are distinguished by several facings of their coats': while the meaning of soldiers' coats (red and unlined) with 'tapes', 'tape strings' and 'facings' are debatable, it is possible that the writer observed recently arrived batches of recruits, clad in their new clothing, including red coats with corresponding 'colours' supplied to them by their respective county associations (including blue from Essex, and orange from Surrey and Sussex).

It is mentioned by this observer that 'the firelocks (only) some of them are tawny coats': the New Model firelock guard originated in Essex's Army, where it was issued with tawny-orange coloured coats. The inference here is that 'some of them' were seen at Reading in such garments. This could be interpreted in two ways, both integral to the other: these men might have been the modest number of firelocks who appear to have re-enlisted immediately into the New Model Army and were wearing the tawny coats when they came in; or those recruits who were added to the two companies of firelocks in late April 1645 were not among those described above, and had not yet been issued with any (hence, 'only (some) of them' were thus garbed). Whatever clothing the firelocks wore from early May 1645 onwards remains open to question as there is no evidence of coats of any hue being issued to them, nor are there any other contemporary narrative descriptions of them in wearing soldiers' coats. However, like the dragoons, these could have been provided by their officers and not recorded in any documents.

The possibility remains that in general terms, what the writer observed (or thought he observed) on 1 May, as part of Fairfax's forces left Reading were batches of infantry recruits, clad in their new clothing, including red coats with coloured tapes in the colour supplied to them by their respective county committees. It was reported by a news correspondent on 23 April 1645:

> Sir Thomas Fairfax is yet at Windsor, all possible preparations are making for his speedy advance; his foot were mustered on Monday and Thursday last, and then the horse on Thursday, upon Runsden Heath between Beaconsfield and Maidenhead. The number of horse and foot is said to be about 15,000, besides those which are since daily sent unto him from divers parts, so that his Train of Artillery being ready, you will shortly see him in the field with gallant army, able to encounter with the greatest of the King's power.[131]

130 *The copy of a letter sent to his Excellencie Sir Thomas Fairfax: With an account to the officers of the Generalls regiment, intended for satisfaction to their demands* (London: 1647). TT, E390[3].

131 *The Kingdomes Weekly Intelligencer*, 22–29 April 1645. TT, E279[11].

Likewise, *Mercurius Civicus*, for the same week stated, 'At the last muster of Sir Thomas Fairfax his forces, the number was about 15,000 foot, 400 and odd dragoons, between 4,000 and 5,000 horse besides four regiments employed abroad in service'.[132] However, the Scottish Presbyterian Robert Baillie reckoned that as the bulk of the New Model was being assembled in the days immediately prior to the Battle of Naseby, Fairfax had concentrated some 11,000–12,000 in Northamptonshire. Even though King Charles was understood to be weaker in foot, he noted, 'we were exceedingly afraid for the Parliament's forces: albeit lusty, well-armed, and well-paid men; yet without officers of experience'. Baillie added rather sourly, 'This new modelled army consists, for the most part, of new inexperienced soldiers; few of the officers are thought capable of their places.'[133]

Fairfax's secretary, John Rushworth, recounted, 'On Wednesday the 30th of April, Fairfax's Army marched from Windsor (hitherto his headquarters) to Reading (twelve Miles); from thence on Mayday to Theale (four Miles); and on May the second to Newbury (eleven Miles); whither Cromwell went to wait upon the General'.[134] By 7 May Fairfax and the part of the New Model Army had reached Blandford in Dorset, when they received instructions to abandon their march and to besiege Oxford instead. These troops were separate to the force commanded by Lieutenant General Oliver Cromwell. According to Sprigge, this consisted of cavalry and dragoons, 'and four regiments of foot besides, who were ordered, when their recruits were come up, to join with him to busy the enemy about Oxford.'[135] Pickering's regiment had been with Cromwell since early April, and it is likely that this infantry brigade, placed under the command of Major General Browne, contained this, Montague's, Hammond's and Rainborowe's, all former Eastern Association regiments, albeit topped up with recruits from other units.

This is confirmed by *The Moderate Intelligencer*, which on 2 May 1645 reported:

> This day, before the General advanced to Newbury, he dismounted 140 of Sir Miles [*sic.* – Michael] Livesey's men who were under a mutiny, Colonel Sheffield's men attended the action, punishments are inflicted, that the others might be terrified. The General said to him that commanded the regiment, it was not for his honour to have such thin troops, and they so mutinous. Sir Miles Livesey, seeing the disorder of his soldiers gave up his commission. Major Sedascue, a noble gentleman, commands the regiment *pro tempore*. The foot regiments that march with the General are his own, Major-General [*sic.* – Colonel] Fortescue's, Colonel Barclay's that was Floyd's [*sic.* – Harley's], Colonel Ingoldsby's, Colonel Weldon's, effective 8,000. The Horse, Sir Arthur Haslerig's now Colonel Butler's, Sir Miles Livesey's, Colonel Thompson's, Colonel Graves', Colonel Sheffield's, and Sir William Waller's its probable.[136]

132 *Mercurius Civicus*, 24 April–1 May 1645. TT, E.281[4].
133 Lang, David, (ed.), *The Letters and Journals of Robert Baillie, 1637–1662* (Edinburgh: Bannatyne Club, 1841), II, pp.116–117.
134 Rushworth, *Historical Collections*, VI, p.32.
135 Sprigge, *Anglia Rediviva*, p.15.
136 *The Moderate Intelligencer*, 1–8 May 1645. TT, E282[10].

The specifications included in the Richard Downes contracts of February 1646 and October 1649 state that the breeches supplied to the army were to be lined and made of 'Reading cloth or other cloth'.[137] In March 1643 the 'clothing tradesmen' of the town of Reading petitioned Charles I, 'requesting that the cloths seized by Sir Arthur Aston may be kept in safe custody until they and the inhabitants of Somerset, Devon, Wiltshire and Gloucestershire have procured safe conduct from Parliament for the transport of their goods to London'.[138] The appeal included the claim that Reading 'is an ancient clothing town solely consisting of the traffic and trade with London, which your petitioners did enjoy until your Majesty made the town of Reading a garrison town'. Garrisoned for the King in late October 1642, it had been a clothing centre since the Middle Ages, although its declining economic prosperity was not assisted by Charles I's refusal to allow manufacturers to sell their goods in London. Although the writer of *A Catalogue of the Taverns in ten Shires about London* (1636) stated 'Reading is the prime and principal town in this county of Berkshire, for fair buildings, large streets for clothing and other blessings,' and the governing charter of the borough was granted by Charles I on 17 December 1638, the decline in the prosperity of the town followed this event with astonishing swiftness.[139] This was partly caused by a rapid deterioration in the fortunes of the local cloth trade, which faced increased competition from Northern and West Country manufacturers, but also the self-serving members of the corporation. A 'petition from the mayor and burgesses to James I's Commissioners for Grievances, relating to the unemployment due to the decline of clothmaking in Reading,' dated *c.* 1623 foreshadowed the situation:

> Due to a sudden decay of clothing in our town many poor families, men, women and children who had their means and livelihood from the work of the clothier, to which only they have been trained, are now for want of work exposed to great misery, and have in woeful manner complained to your petitioners expostulating with them why they did not now as in former times furnish the poor people of the town with work. Their answer is they cannot because they have not that sale for their cloth as heretofore, they have had which causes them to make a less quantity of cloth; and so by consequence theirs is a necessity of the failing of work to the poor.[140]

Hence, the clothiers attributed the inability to sell cloth to 'the small number of merchants to whom they are limited to sell their clothes', and their inability to transport their cloth as cheaply as northern merchants, who 'have also recently altered the size of their cloths from twelve yards to the same length as Reading cloth and sell it under the name of Reading cloth.' They might be restored to their former position and supply the poor with work if merchants of white cloth were required to

137 TNA, WO47/1, ff. 209r–210v; ML, Ms 46 78/708, ff. 27v–28r, 114r.
138 BRO, R/Z3/36.
139 John Taylor, *A Catalogue of the Taverns in ten Shires about Lond*on (London: Henry Gosson, 1636), unpag.
140 BRO, R/Z3/24.

purchase at least one coloured cloth for every ten white ones, as the manufacture of one coloured cloth requires as much labour, and yields as much profit to the King, as six white ones. This would relieve 'many hundreds of poor people distressed for want of work [who are] ready to perish, and relief of whom will be insupportable for the town'.

On 4 November, from Oxford, Charles I instructed the mayor and aldermen of his permission to the clothiers of Reading to continue in their trade and vowed to take no more garments from them without payment, if they send none to London. An earlier order to the inhabitants 'to bring to the town hall all their arms and armour' for the use of Royalist troops appears to have achieved limited success, however, as they needed to be reminded that unless it was adhered to by 1pm on 7 November, 'any house in which such weapons are discovered thereafter shall be immediately given unto the soldiers to plunder'.[141] It is evident, nevertheless, that significant quantities of clothing continued to be produced in the town for the King's Oxford Army. On 8 November, 16 days after the Battle of Edgehill, Charles I issued a warrant to the mayor to impress all the tailors within a six-mile radius of the town to employ them in 'making clothes for the King's Army'.[142]

The following day the King ordered the tailors and merchants of Reading to supply 1,000 suits of clothes for soldiers, the town of Abingdon having sent the mayor 137 cloths (sufficient at 2½ yards per suit to make 1,644 suits). The sum of £1,500, being the cost of 'dying, drying and making cloth into suits for the King's soldiers, the cloth (valued at £1,000) having been freely given by the borough' was levied on the population. However, as this erroneous figure was found to be impossible to raise, the entire county of Berkshire petitioned Charles I to be permitted to shoulder the burden, to which the Council of War later agreed.[143] In addition to this, on 12 November a further warrant was issued to the mayor and aldermen which authorised them to 'take up [requisition] such carts, boats or barges as shall be most convenient' to deliver the clothes and victuals to be provided by the town for Charles I's army throughout the county of Berkshire.[144]

141 BRO, R/Z/6/1/5; R/Z/6/1/19.
142 BRO, R/Z3/27/1–7.
143 BL, Ms Harley 6851, f. 219r; BRO, R/Z3/29; R/Z3/38/1.
144 BRO, R/Z/6/1/3.

9

Clothing II

Shirts were an essential item of clothing during the early modern period. As such, they were regarded as a barrier against disease, something that was especially prevalent as many soldiers were subjected to relatively unhygienic living conditions and infection caused by battlefield wounds. Though a commissioned officer, the Royalist Captain Richard Atkins remembered from his participation at Roundway Down in July 1643, 'for want of a shirt, my wound having bloodied my linen, I became so lousy in three or four days that I could not tell what to do with myself. And when I had got a shirt, which was not till we took Bath, my blood and the sweat of my body had so worn it, that it fell off into lint'.[1] Made of linen cloth, soldiers' shirts may have been collarless. Several probate inventories of the inhabitants of Ipswich between 1583 and 1631 record shirts separately to neck bands (the collar of a shirt) and falling bands (a band or collar worn falling flat round the neck).[2] Likewise, a list of shirts and linens in the possession of the gentleman John Willoughby (1571–1658) of Leyhill, Devon in June 1645 includes, '3 bands and 3 pairs of falls [possibly cuffs], 2 of them plain and 1 of them with lace and 4 plain.'[3]

On 27 May 1642 the Commissioners for the Affairs of Ireland contract with Richard Wollaston of London and Richard Aldworth of Bristol for 16,000 ells of lockram [a coarse plain-woven linen] to be dispatched to Dublin for the making of 6,000 shirts in the city, and 8,000 ells to be sent from Bristol for 3,000 shirts for the soldiers in Munster. A further 6,000 ells were to be transported to Carrickfergus for the construction of 2,250 shirts for the English soldiers of the garrison, at the rate of 11d. the ell. An additional agreement was entered into by the same parties on 11 July:

> by the certificate of George Wood, commissary for sending of clothes into Ireland for the soldiers there ... to supply 4,000 fine Osnaburg [a coarse linen originally produced in Osnabrück, Germany] shirts, white and well-conditioned, for the use of the soldiers in Ireland, suitable to a pattern for the size and goodness showed and remaining to be seen, at the rate of

1 Peter Young and Norman Tucker (eds), *Military Memoirs of the Civil War: Richard Atkyns and John Gwyn* (London: Longmans, 1967), p.33.

2 Michael Reed (ed.), *The Ipswich Probate Inventories 1583–1631* (Woodbridge: Boydell, 1981), pp.19, 26, 42, 47, 51, 77.

3 Todd Gray (ed.), *Devon Household Accounts 1627–59*, Devon and Cornwall Record Society, New Series, 38 (1995), I, pp.90–1.

> 2s. 9d. the shirt; 8 ells being allowed to three shirts; the said 4,000 shirts amounting, at that rate, to the sum of £550.[4]

A later document reported that while this consignment was delivered in full before 4 August, 'the said contract was to be paid at the end of three and three months next after the delivery of the said shirts. Forasmuch as the first three months is already expired and no part of the said moneys is yet paid him [Wood].'[5]

In September 1642 Parliament ordered clothing for 7,000 infantrymen in Ulster, at a total cost of £15,937 10s. or 42s. 6d. per set of clothes. This provided each soldier with a cap, canvas doublet, cassock, breeches, two pair of stockings, two pair of shoes and two shirts.[6] Moreover, a tender to supply the British forces in Ireland, dated 27 March 1648, included '16,000 shirts, at 2s. 10d. per shirt. The shirts to be made of Lockram, good Osnaburg or Lübeck cloth'.[7] Unfortunately, however, the extent of the 1642 contracts presented some suppliers with the chance to profit from war and for the unscrupulous with the means of creating more through sharp practice. The clothing industry was particularly vulnerable to fraudulent activities. The contractors of the 1590s and 1642, for instance, were accused of the same abuses that Davies allegedly perpetrated in 1644–1645.[8] Informants testifying in December 1645 regarding the 1644 contractors, John Davies (an Irishman and friend of the Irish Adventurer and soldier Sir John Clotworthy), and his partners mentioned the poor quality of the cloth, the skimping of the material used and the inferior workmanship, in addition to the shirts being made of the coarsest linen. Apparently, these shirts 'were so short as that they did not cover their privy parts'.[9] Nevertheless, it is likely that the same type of shirts supplied to Parliament's forces in Ireland in 1642 and 1643 were obtained for the New Model Army.

On 1 or 3 April 1645 the Ordnance Office was informed of a contract with the London draper, Christopher Nicholson for '3,000 shirts of good lockram at 2s. 10d. apiece'. These were delivered on or before 8 April when a warrant for the payment to Nicholson was issued, though he received his money two days later.[10] Henry Pettit at the White Bear in Newgate Market was engaged on 3 April to provide 4,000 shirts costing 2s. 6d. each, 'the one half [to be paid for in] ready money the remainder in 3 months'. Accordingly, 2,000 were delivered on 19 April, and the remainder not until 29 September. Within the same time frame an associate of Pettit's, William Smith, was contracted to supply 2,000 shirts at the same rate, being 1,000 on 19 April and the other 1,000 on 29 September. Moreover, before 10 April 1645 Pettit agreed to supply 1,000 shirts, 'the one-half ready money, the other in three months' at 2s. 6d.

4 *CJ*, II, p.671.
5 Bodl. Lib., Ms Rawlinson A/110, ff. 27v–28r.
6 TNA, SP28/35/1, f. 106r; *LJ*, V, pp.347 & 556.
7 *LJ*, X, pp.158–9.
8 James Hogan, James (ed.), *Letters and Papers Relating to the Irish Rebellion between 1642–46* (London: HMSO, 1936), p.72; John McGurk, *The Elizabethan Conquest of Ireland* (Manchester: MUP, 2009), pp.211–12.
9 TNA, SP28/253B/2, ff. 75r–95v.
10 TNA, WO47/1, f. 209r; SP28/29/1, f. 200r; Bodl. Lib., Ms Eng C14, f. 6r; ML, Ms 46 78/708, f. 114v; WO47/1 dates this to 1 April 1645, while ML, Ms 46 78/708 gives 3 April.

apiece, although he fulfilled his contract in full on 7 May.[11] Thus, if the Ordnance Office debentures and receipts correspond, between early April and late September 1645 a total of 10,000 shirts were delivered by contractors, although further quantities could have been procured from other sources. For instance, on 15 January 1646 the Goldsmiths' Hall Committee directed the sub-committee for Scottish Affairs to convey to the 'Scottish army at Newark' 4,000 shirts, along with 29,000 suits of clothes, 300 pairs of boots, 3,000 pairs of stockings, and 1,000 pairs of pistols and holsters.[12] The shirts procured for the Protestant troops sent to Ireland in 1642–1643 and the New Model Army evidently were constructed of white Osnabrück linen, however, on 14 January 1651 a warrant was issued for the payment of £214 6s. 8d. to Richard Thorogood, linen-draper, 'for 5,362½ ells of white and brown Osnabrück to make 1,950 shirts for Sir Charles Coote's soldiers'.[13]

During early 1646 some 7,500 shirts were received by the Ordnance Office for the use of the New Model Army. On 9 February Stephen Estwick, and his partners Thomas Player, Tempest Milner, Maurice Gethin and John Pocock delivered 4,500 shirts at 2s. 8d. each as part of a larger batch including 4,500 coats, 4,500 pairs of breeches and 4,500 pairs of stockings. In accordance with their contract, 2,000 of each were delivered by 27 February, and the outstanding 2,500 on 6 March.[14] Similarly, 3,000 shirts were acquired from Richard Thorogood at 2s. 6d. apiece; these were brought in on 20 March 1646 and he received payment in full on 2 April.[15] Substantial quantities of shirts were likewise purchased for and distributed to Cromwellian troops in Ireland. Thoroughgood provided 16,000 shirts in December 1649, whereas the same quantity was received 'for the army in Ireland' from five suppliers on 19 April 1650. Shirts, like other items of clothing destined for Ireland, were quality tested by craftsmen employed by the Ordnance Office before they were paid for and dispatched. Thus, in February 1650 William Penny and Francis Easterly received £10 for spending 30 days examining 23,000 shirts, while on 17 June they had £4 10s. 'for viewing 16,000 shirts for Ireland'.[16]

Table 42: Notification of Contracts for Shirts to the Ordnance Office for the NMA (WO47/1; ML, Ms 46 78/708)

Date	Quantity and type	Price each	Contractor
8/4/45	3000 shirts of good lockram	2s. 10d.	Christopher Nicholson
3/4/45	4000 shirts the one half in ready money the remainder in 3 months	2s. 6d.	Henry Pettit
3/4/45	2000 shirts at the same rate	2s. 6d.	William Smith
10/4/45	1000 shirts, the one-half ready money, the other in three months	2s. 6d.	Henry Pettit at the White Boar in Newgate Market

11 TNA, WO/47/1, f. 235v; SP28/30/4, f. 200r; Bodl. Lib., Ms Eng C14, f. 51v; ML, Ms 46 78/708, ff. 44r, 103r.
12 *CJ*, IV, p.509; Mary A. Green (ed.), *Calendar, Committee for Compounding: Part 1*, (London, 1889), p.31.
13 *CSPD Interregnum 1651*, p.542.
14 TNA, SP28/36/2, unfol.; SP28/140/3, ff. 79v, 81v, 96r; Bodl. Lib., Ms Eng C14, f. 78v.
15 TNA, SP28/140/3, f. 102r; Bodl. Lib., Ms Eng C244, f. 14v.
16 *CSPD 1649–50*, p.369; *CSPD Interregnum 1649–50*, pp.591–594.

Table 43: Warrants for Payments to Contractors for the Delivery of Shirts to the Ordnance Office for the NMA (TNA, SP28/29/1-36/2; SP28/140/3; Bodl. Lib., Ms Eng C14; Bodl. Lib., Ms Eng C244)

Date	Quantity and type	Price each	Contractor
8/4/45	3000 lockram shirts in full of his contract	2s. 10d.	Christopher Nicholson
7/5/45	1000 shirts	2s. 6d.	Henry Pettit
19 & 26/9/45	6000 shirts	2s. 6d.	Henry Pettit & William Smith
9/2/46	4500 shirts	2s. 8d.	Stephen Estwick, et al
9/2/46	4500 shirts	2s. 6d.	Thomas Player, Tempest Milner, Stephen Eastwick, Maurice Gethin & John Pocock
20/3/46	3000 shirts	2s. 6d.	Richard Thorogood
4/4/46	73 shirts	2s. 6d.	Jeremiah Whitworth
8/4/46	76 shirts	2s. 6d.	Mr Walker, agent employed by Parliament
21/3 & 11/4/46	3,000 shirts	2s. 6d.	Richard Thorogood

Details of the distribution of items such as shirts to the foot regiments of Sir Thomas Fairfax's Army, can be found in the numerous warrants issued by the Committee for the Army to the Officers of the Ordnance, and various commissaries and carriers, in addition to the records of receipts and storage. These are by no means comprehensive, however, and often list shirts among substantial loads of military clothing and equipment. On 12 April 1645 3,000 shirts were issued to Commissary Bond of the train of artillery for immediate distribution to the army. These may have been the 3,000 lockram shirts delivered by Nicholson to the Ordnance office 4 days previously.[17] On 20 October 1645 3,510 shirts were stored at the New Model's magazine in Reading, ready for transportation. While at Reading on 15 December one of the commissaries, Robert Emerson, certified the receipt of 'several packs and vats of clothes' that had been prepared for dispatch to Portsmouth 'for the receipt of Sir Thomas Fairfax's Army'. This encompassed 'shirts six packs (50 bundles) weighing about 6cwt 28lbs marked: SH500', and 'shirts one pack (51 bundles and 2 shirts) about 6cwt 30lbs marked: SH512.'[18]

On 18 September 1645 5,000 shirts, along with other quantities of clothing and weapons, were delivered to Commissary Thomas Futter 'to be sent to Reading for Sir Thomas Fairfax's Army'. Eight days later 3,000 shirts were ordered to be supplied, and on 26 September instructions were given by the Committee for the Army for the distribution by Futter of 6,000 shirts, with 550 Spanish pikes, 1,400 matchlock muskets, 5,700 coats, 5,700 breeches, 6,500 pairs of shoes, 5,000 pairs of stockings, 4,000 bandoliers and 5,000 snapsacks 'by virtue of warrants dated 18

17 TNA, WO47/1, f. 209r; WO55/1646, unfol.; SP28/29/1, f. 200r.
18 TNA, SP28/31/4, f. 341r; SP28/126/1, ff. 2r–3r.

and 26 September 1645'.[19] In some cases shirts – like other items of clothing and arms – were distributed to specific units, such as Colonel Rainborowe's men, who received 600 on 13 February 1646 'to clothe and arm the old soldiers of his regiment'. However, substantial quantities were supplied to recruits upon their arrival at the army's rendezvous points. For instance, on 17 February 1646 500 shirts, 500 pairs of stockings, 500 pairs of shoes, 500 snapsacks and 500 suits were distributed by Commissary Thomas Walker 'out of the stores provided for Sir Thomas Fairfax's Army' Army to be sent by him to Gravesend for the clothing of the Kentish recruits [probably of Colonel Weldon's regiment]'. The following day Waggon Master Thomas Richardson delivered 1,500 shirts; 1,500 coats and breeches; 1,500 pairs of shoes; 650 pikes; 1,350 muskets with bandoliers; 2,000 snapsacks, 12cwt of match; 6 barrels of powder; and 6 barrels of musket bullet 'to clothe and arm the new recruits at Newport Pagnell' for the supply of the New Model.[20]

Evidence for the logistical system involving the storage, transportation, and distribution of stocks (such as clothing and rations) employed by Commissary Orpin, Commissary General of Victuals to the New Model, from the Ordnance Office in London, via the army's foremost magazine at Reading to be conveyed by sea and land to the West between August 1645 to January 1646 can be gleaned from his accounts.[21] On 21 December 1645 Mr Hazelwood, master of the *Jonas* was paid 'for waiting for 3 days in earnest for the hire of his ship to bring the clothes to Lyme, being informed they were come to Weymouth', while in early January 1646 the sum of 16s. was disbursed by Orpin 'for bringing the coats, breeches, shirts, shoes and stockings into the magazine at Tiverton'. Similarly, among the charges for 17 wain loads of clothing carried from Weymouth to Tiverton on 8 and 9 January were £1 12s. 6d. disbursed for '14 men and 7 teams, 5 horses in each team, one day at Weymouth', and a further £1 2s. 6d. paid to '9 men and 5 teams, 5 horses in each team' for the same journey.

Land transportation of loads of clothing, weapons and ammunition for the New Model Army required a significant logistical operation. Thus, on 18 January Orpin laid out the following:

> …for charges for 17 horse loads of clothes from Tiverton to Chard, containing 722 coats, 622 pair of breeches, 216 pair of stockings and 800 snapsacks: 5s. for carrying pack cloths from Tiverton to Chard; 3s. 6d. for 5 pack boards; 5s. for bringing horses; 10s. for making packs; 10s. for hay for 30 horses for one night; 3s. for 2 guides; £2 11s. for 17 pack horses; 10s. for 5 drivers for 2 days; 2s. 6d. for carrying the clothes up into the magazine at Tiverton.

Five days later, he paid 'for charges for bringing clothes from Tiverton to the Fairfax's advanced headquarters at Chudleigh, [comprising] 2,598 coats; 2,952 pairs of breeches; 2,082 shirts, being brought upon 100 State's horses.' This encompassed

19 WSL, Ms Salt 463, unfol.; TNA, WO55/1647, unfol.
20 TNA, WO55/1646, unfol.
21 TNA, SP28/147/2, ff. 352r–357r.

disbursement for things such as 'cords, packthread and needles to pack them up', 'loading and unloading them 3 times', 'hay for 4 wagon horses for 2 nights', 'watching them by the way several nights and at Chudleigh until the same delivered', 'bringing in 1 horse with the clothes which was gone out of the way', and 'straw to lay under the clothes sent to several regiments.'

Stockings

The stockings supplied to the New Model Army in 1645–1646 are variously described in the Ordnance Office contracts and receipt books as 'Irish stockings', 'stockings' or 'stockings of good Welsh cotton'. One order placed for 2,500 pairs of stockings with Francis Butcher on 9 October 1645 states that they were 'to be of the largest sizes [and] equal goodness of cloth'.[22] The most numerous purchases for the New Model – particularly in 1645 – were for Irish stockings, which cost 12d. a pair. Given that this price remained consistent, it must be presumed that batches referred to as 'stockings' were also of this type. Such items were cut from woven cloth and sewn. In 1595 the drapers and merchant tailors negotiating with the English Council of State 'for appareling the forces in the Low Countries' complained that they 'had been showed us the stockings for the private soldiers, made of good Devonshire kersey, worth 2s. 6d. a pair, while Her Majesty's allowance is but 15d.'.[23]

On 4 October 1650 three merchants were contracted to supply 3,000 pairs of stockings for horsemen and 1,000 pairs of stockings for foot soldiers, though how these items differed from each other is unknown.[24] In January 1660 John Harvey agreed to supply 2,300 pairs of stockings for the army in Flanders, 'to be made of good Welsh cotton to be doubled sewed, and of a size and goodness answerable to the patterns left in the Office of the Ordnance at the rate of 7d. a pair'.[25] In early 1642 3,000 pairs of 'grey knitted' stockings were issued to soldiers going to Ireland and costing between 15d. and 17d. per pair.[26] On 9 May 1642 a London syndicate agreed to supply the Commissioners for the Affairs of Ireland with 10,000 pairs of cotton stockings at the rate of 12d. a pair – 2,000 pairs were to be delivered each week, and on 14 May the first batch of 1,000 pairs of stockings were ready to be inspected. Six days later these were dispatched with 1,000 soldiers' coats to Dublin, by way of Chester.[27] By June 1643 orders had been placed to supply soldiers in 'the several provinces' of Ireland with 18,000 coats, 15,000 breeches and 23,000 pairs of stockings.[28]

During the initial outfitting of Sir Thomas Fairfax's Army in April 1645, a total of 10,500 pairs of stockings were received into the Ordnance Office stores. Out of

22 Bodl. Lib., Ms Eng. hist. C14, f. 53r; ML, Ms 46 78/708, f. 4r.
23 *CSPD Elizabeth, 1595–97*, p.22.
24 TNA, SP25/11, f. 3r.
25 TNA, SP25/115, f. 5v.
26 TNA, SP28/139/4, ff. 62r–62v.
27 *PJLP*, I, pp.442–443 & 448.
28 TNA, SP28/35/1, f. 106r; *LJ*, V, pp.347 & 556.

these 8,500 pairs – described as 'Irish stockings', and 'to be of the largest sizes [and] equal goodness of cloth' – were from the merchant Francis Butler. His first notified contract for '2,000 pairs at 12d. apiece' came by 14 April, though another of 8 April for '1,500 pairs to be delivered by 12 April' may have been delayed and included in the delivery of 6,500 pairs of Irish stockings delivered before 29 April 1645. Any record of the debentures for the outstanding 5,000 pairs appears to be missing, unless that for the like quantity 'according to the first contract' recorded as 3 September 1645 are those, and have been erroneously dated in the documents.[29] Between 8 August and 28 October 1645 Butler delivered a further 10,000 pairs.[30] On 29 May 1645 1,500 pairs of Irish stockings had been delivered to Commissary Thomas Futter for distribution to the army, while in February 1646 Colonel Rainborowe's regiment of foot was issued with 600 pairs of stockings. Additionally, 2,184 pairs were sent to Northampton on 24 March to clothe new recruits.[31] These, along with 'cotton' stockings previously sent to Ireland were probably constructed of Irish frieze – certainly not linen, for which there is no evidence.

According to Eric Kerridge, 'Friezes had a hard, rough feel. They were best suited to winter gowns and rough overcoating but were also used for doublets and jerkins.'[32] In 1549 William Baldwin remarked, 'The coarsest frieze best pleases the finest of them in winter', whereas William Stafford in 1581 reflected on serving men being content to go in 'a Kendal coat in the summer, and a frieze coat in winter.'[33] Welsh frieze was described by Thomas Fuller in the 1660s as 'a coarse kind of cloth, than which none warmer to be worn in winter.'[34] A memorandum to the Duke of Buckingham 'on the raising of more men from Ireland', probably written in 1627, stated that 'clothes, jerkin or cassocks, may be bought of whitish grey frieze. It is very good at 12d. a yard though only half a yard broad; but 12s. or thereabouts will make a cassock and breeches … if the money is carefully spent 20s. should clothe each man in shoes and shirt, cassock and breeches of whitish grey frieze, and white [undyed] stockings.'[35] Likewise, a tailor's bill of 2 October 1643, for suits and riding coats for Captain William Stukeley's troop of Sir William Brereton's Cheshire forces states that they were made of frieze 'at 4s. per yard'.[36]

From February 1646 onwards the Committee for the Army began procuring stockings of a more expensive, and perhaps more suitable fabric. On 14 February 1646 Richard Downes agreed to provide '2000 pairs of stockings of good Welsh

29 TNA, WO47/1, ff. 209v, 211r; SP28/29/1, f. 239r; SP28/32/3, f. 382r; ML, Ms 46 78/708, ff. 4v, 112r, 115r.

30 TNA, SP28/29/1, ff. 194r, 239r; SP28/32/3, fol. 382r; WO47/1, f. 209v; Bodl. Lib., Ms Eng. hist. C14, ff. 11v, 50r, 53r 54v, 78r.

31 TNA, WO55/1646, unfol.; Bodl. Lib., Ms Eng. hist. C14, f. 82v.

32 Eric Kerridge, *Textile Manufacturers in Early Modern England* (Manchester: Manchester University Press, 1985), p.19.

33 *The Canticles or Ballads of Salomon, phrase like declared in English Metres, by William Baldwin* (London, 1549), p.4; F. J. Furnival (ed.), *William Stafford's Compendious or Brief Examination of Certain Ordinary Complaints of Divers of Our Country Men in these our days* (London, 1876), p.64.

34 Thomas Fuller, *The History of the Worthies of England* (London, 1840), III, p.485.

35 *CSPI 1647–1660*, p.107.

36 TNA, SP28/8, f. 17r.

cotton' at 13½d. apiece'.[37] These were delivered in two batches of 1,000 pairs each, one within a week of his contract and the other on 13 March. Such items continued to be provided to Parliament's armies, because among the tender to supply the English forces in Ireland in March 1648 was £1,000 to be expended on '16,000 pair of stockings, made of Welsh cotton, at 15d. per pair'.[38] Moreover, on 9 January 1660 the Council of State approved a contract with the merchant John Harvey for 2,300 pairs of 'good Welsh cotton stockings', costing 1s. a pair.[39] Additionally, on 20 August 1648 a consignment of 3,000 pairs of 'white cotton stockings' was received into the Ordnance Office stores from the regular supplier, Richard Downes.[40] It might be assumed from other early modern examples of 'white' clothing – including doublets of white fustian and white kersey stockings supplied to Lancashire trained bandsmen for service in Ireland in 1578 – that the material used in the Downes order was akin to undyed grey woollen cloth produced in Somerset and Wiltshire, known as 'West Country whites'.[41]

Table 44: Notification of Contracts to the Ordnance Office for the Supply of Stockings for the NMA (WO47/1; ML, Ms 46 78/708)

Date	Quantity and type	Price pair	Contractor
1/4/45	2000 pair of Irish stockings	12d.	Francis Butcher
8/4/45	1500 pair of Irish stockings to be delivered by 12 April	12d.	Francis Butcher
3/9/45	5000 pair of stockings according to the first contract	12d.	Francis Butcher
9/10/45	2500 pair of stockings, to be of the largest sizes equal goodness of cloth	12d.	Francis Butcher
14/2/46	2000 pair of stockings of good Welsh cotton	13½d.	Richard Downes

Table 45: Receipts of Stockings by the Ordnance Office for the NMA (TNA, WO47/1; SP28/29/1-32/1; Bodl. Lib., Ms Eng. hist. C14)

Date	Quantity and type	Price pair	Contractor
8/4/45	2000 pair cotton stockings in full of his contract	12d.	Thomas Butcher
14/4/45	2000 pair Irish stockings	12d.	Francis Butcher
16/4/45	1,500 pair Irish stockings	12d.	Francis Butler
29/4/45	1500 pair Irish stockings in full of his contract	12d.	Francis Butcher
29/4/45	5000 pair cotton stockings in full of his contract	12d.	Francis Butcher
18 & 23/9/45	5000 pair stockings	12d.	Francis Butcher

37 TNA, SP28/140/3, unfol.; WO47/1, ff. 209r-210v; ML, Ms 46 78/708, ff. 27v–28r.
38 *LJ*, X, pp.158–159.
39 *CSPD Interregnum, 1659–60*, p.306.
40 TNA, SP28/140/3, unfol.; Bodl. Lib., Ms Eng. hist. C14, f. 47v.
41 LA, DDHK/10/1/6; Peter J. Bowden, *The Wool Trade in Tudor and Stuart England* (London: Palgrave Macmillan, 1962), p.48; J. H. Bettey, *Wiltshire Farming in the Seventeenth Century* (Trowbridge: Wiltshire Record Society, 2005), p.280.

Date	Quantity and type	Price pair	Contractor
10/10/45	2500 pair stockings	12d.	Francis Butcher
28/10/45	2500 pair stockings	12d.	Francis Butcher
9/2/46	4500 pair stockings	12d.	Thomas Player, Tempest Milner, Stephen Eastwick, Maurice Gethin & John Pocock
26/2/46	1000 pair stockings	12d.	Richard Downes

During the early modern period cotton meant a woollen fabric with the characteristics of frieze. It was produced in Lancashire, Westmorland, and Montgomeryshire in mid-Wales. The term 'cotton' was used to describe a type of weave, rather than a kind of fabric, in that it was a woollen cloth with a raised nap, possibly for improved insulation. Hence, the process of raising the nap was called cottoning or frizzing.[42] An Act of Edward VI stipulated that 'all the cottons called Manchester, Lancashire and Cheshire cottons, full wrought to the sale, shall be in length twenty-two yards and contain in breadth three-quarters of a yard in the water and shall weigh thirty pounds in the piece at least.' William Camden, writing in 1610, spoke highly of the clothing industry in Manchester, saying 'it has the best trade of any in these Northern parts [and] surpasses the towns hereabouts in woollen manufacture.'[43] Cloth appropriated in North Wales by Sir William Brereton's soldiers in April 1645 consisted of 16½ yards of *gwlanen* (a Welsh flannel), a fabric probably akin to cottons. The consignment consisted of 4 yards of rough *gwlanen*, 4¼ yards of red, 4 yards of green, 1¼ yards more of green and 3 yards of white in 2 pieces.[44]

There are no records of headwear, doublets and waistcoats being provided to the New Model Army. It seems likely that like its drafts of conscripts, all foot soldiers enlisting in the army were meant to come 'adequately provided for', in other words, wearing the basic items of civilian dress. Sir Thomas Fairfax's men could also have purchased headwear, doublets and other garments from merchants and markets accompanying the army, or their commissioned officers procured the item(s) for them from other sources. One of these was by the issue of contracted purchase orders from the governing authority, which might allocate money to the individual military units, who then located and bought their requirements themselves. On 4 March 1647, Colonel James Castle's regiment of foot, being detailed for service in Ireland, was to be given money 'wherewith to buy shoes and other necessaries', while in addition 300 muskets and 100 pikes were to be supplied for arming the same unit, the money for which was 'to be sent down by this Committee for the purpose'.[45] In late 1643 civilian tailors and merchants in Chester were asked to donate clothing to recently arrived troops from Ireland:

42 Eric Kerridge, *Textile Manufacturers*, p.104; Norman Lowe, *The Lancashire Textile Industry in the Sixteenth Century*, Chetham Society, 20, 3rd Series (Manchester, 1972), pp.25 & 29.

43 E. Gibson (ed.), William Camden, *Britannia* (London, 1695), II, p.963.

44 CRO, DDX/428, f. 85v.

45 *CSPI 1647–1660*, p.734.

> The Irish English soldiers came to Chester to rest and repose themselves for they were weary and out of clothing, the mayor sent through all wards to get apparel from the citizens who gave freely, some whole suits, some two, some doublets, others breeches, others shirts, shoes, stockings and hats to the apparelling of about 300. When they were refreshed, they marched to besiege Nantwich.[46]

Thus, the haphazard accounts of Edward Russell, beginning in November 1643, record the purchase of 1,022 pairs of stockings at 17s. per dozen and 408 pairs of shoes costing 2s. 8d. a pair, presumably for these troops or for the soldiers of the garrison of Chester. Further sums were disbursed to city merchants, tailors and other craftspeople for just over 480 ells of canvas (possibly for doublets), to John Pronton and Richard Haswell 'for dying cloth for the soldiers', and 10 individuals for 'making soldiers' clothes'. A later entry stated 'Sent in by the Lord Byron's order, cloth and cottons from Mr Sproston, Mr Reynolds, Mr Shaw and others, which was made into clothes for the soldiers' use.'[47]

Among Parliament's regional military forces, much of their clothing and footwear seems to have been procured locally, either by serving officers or by the sequestration committees of various hundreds. At Beverley on 7 September 1640 it was ordered, 'that whereas the trained band in Yorkshire are to attend His Majesty in the service now intended [the Second Bishops' War], that every common soldier for this town shall have a grey coat for the value of 8s. or thereabouts at the discretion of Mr Mayor'.[48] Although this was ordered for the East Riding trained bands, it is possible that other Yorkshire units were clad in coats of the same colour. On 12 October 1643 the Deputy Lieutenants of Lancashire ordered the supply of 200 grey coats to Colonel Alexander Rigby, but as the same issue included snaphaunces and cartridge boxes the soldiers could have been dragoons.[49] In March 1646 the Committee of Both Kingdoms ordered the same body to 'clothe Colonel [John] Booth's regiment, and make them fit to march with all expedition' to North Wales, although no there is no indication of what colour the uniforms were meant to be.[50]

Various examples of the supply of soldiers' coats and other clothing to Sir William Brereton's Parliamentarian army in Cheshire are known. Probably in early 1643 Captain John Bramhall received from Commissary William Hinde 52 coats for his dragoon company 'which were accordingly disposed of'. Bramhall also paid various sums to local tailors in May 1643 for the making of suits of clothes for his drummers, as well as laying out £1 4s. 3d. for another suit.[51] Four Nantwich tailors, Peter, John and William Burstow, and Thomas Greenall made 344 soldiers' coats and 55 troopers' coats during the winter of 1643–1644 and delivered them to

46 BL, Ms Harley 2125, f. 136r.
47 TNA, SP28/152/12, unfol.; David Eastwood, 'The Accounts of Edward Russell, the storekeeper of the Royalist garrison in Chester Castle', *TLCAS*, 106 (2010), pp.1–22.
48 ERA, BC/II/7/4 Minute book of the Governors and Beverley Corporation, 1597–1660.
49 *HMC 10th Report*, IV, p.67.
50 *CSPD 1645–7*, pp.408–409.
51 BL, MS Harley 2128, ff. 23v, 26v, 34v.

Hinde on 22 February 1644.[52] They were paid 1s. 2d. per soldiers' coat and 1s. 8d. per trooper's coat for making them up and transporting them to the army. On 24 December 1644 Brereton paid £100 'to William Barratt of Ridgeway in Cheshire to purchase cloth, 'which was accordingly bought and disposed of for the soldiers' coats'.[53] A rough estimate of the number of garments this might have produced is not straightforward, especially as the price of woollen cloth depended largely on its type. However, the frieze purchased to clothe Captain Robert Stukeley's troopers in October 1643 cost 4s. per yard. Given that as a rule of thumb a yard and a half of broadcloth was enough for a soldiers' coat, this could equate to enough fabric to make up over 300 garments.

On 5 April 1645 Colonel Robert Duckenfield paid £85 to John Gaskell, a Manchester draper 'for new uniforms for my regiment'.[54] At the rate of 18s. each, this might compute to over 90 sets of coats and breeches. Similarly, on 5 July 1645 the army's treasurer, James Croxton disbursed to John Acton the sum of £40 for cloth, 'which was part of moneys of the sequestration of saltworks in Middlewich, being held to pay for coats for Nantwich [for] 2 foot companies'.[55] Hence, much of the fabric for this clothing was locally made and procured. Further payments for cloth for Duckenfield's regiment included £5 disbursed to 'Henry Bradshaw, draper in Manchester' for Captain Richard Brereton's company, sometime between 13 November 1643 and 4 July 1644, and a further £30 laid out for 'arms to furnish my Irish company and some clothes for them' in March 1644.[56] The following month, when Duckenfield's infantrymen were besieging Adlington Hall the sum of £1 was paid to Roger Ridgeway, a local tailor for making up soldiers' coats.[57] Moreover, between October 1642 and October 1643 the constables of Mere in Northwich Hundred paid the sum of £2 14s. 10d. for grey coats delivered to Knutsford garrison, most probably for soldiers under Colonel John Leigh, whose infantry regiment was recruited from the area, while some of its companies were billeted in the town.[58] In April 1645 the Staffordshire Committee laid out £30 12s. 11d. for grey coats for Captain Thomas Monke's company of Brereton's own regiment, which was seconded to that county's forces.[59] Three months before, the same body had laid out £9 6s. for the making up of soldier's coats, which could have been an earlier batch.[60] In this light, it is possible to suggest that a proportion, if not most of the Cheshire foot were clothed in grey coats.

The Yorkshire sheep farmer Henry Best reported that 'three or four black sheep do well in a flock, to furnish one with wool for grey stockings and other uses; but many black sheep in a keeping are neither seemly nor profitable, for their wool is

52 TNA, SP28/49/1, f. 100v.
53 TNA, SP28/152/7, f. 16r.
54 BL, MS Harley 2130, f. 91v; Andrew Abram, 'The Civil War Account Book of Colonel Robert Duckenfield', *TLCAS*, 114 (2023), pp.5–35.
55 TNA, SP28/144, unnumbered account books, f. 15r.
56 TNA, SP28/128/10, f. 7v; BL, MS Harley 2130, f. 89r.
57 TNA, SP28/128/10, f. 5r.
58 BL, MS Harley 2128, f. 60r.
59 TNA, SP28/134/12, f. 395r; Lich. RO, MS Lichfield 24, f. 83r.
60 TNA, SP28/134/12, f. 391v.

usually hairy, scarce vendible.'[61] If Brereton's army obtained significant amounts of cloth and uniforms from north of the Mersey, so did other Parliamentarian forces in Lancashire and the midland counties. As Edwards asserts, 'Lancashire clothiers, especially those from Manchester, supplied Cheshire and Staffordshire forces, as well as their own troops with cloth'.[62] On 25 December 1643 the Staffordshire Committee purchased 118 yards of grey cloth from Thomas Hanson of Manchester at 2s. a yard for soldiers' uniforms; in March 1644 they paid the figure of £48 4s. to Yorkshire clothiers, and seven months later £54 14s. was disbursed to Lancashire suppliers.[63] On 2 May 1644 the Staffordshire committee ordered 'that the grey cloth in the treasurer's custody shall be delivered to such as Colonel Rugley shall appoint to make coats forthwith for his regiment. And the treasurer to keep a note of the number of yards delivered'.[64] Moreover, the Staffordshire Order Book records that in May 1645 8½ yards of grey cloth were delivered to Captain Roper's quartermaster.[65]

Outer clothing, such as coats and breeches, were usually made by tailors in their own workshops, although for supplying the Cheshire Parliamentarian soldiers a magazine or factory might have been set up (perhaps in Nantwich). Captain Bramhall, probably a mercer before the war, produced garments with his mother in the town, charging his soldiers various amounts for their supply, which would be deducted from their pay. This doubtless involved the purchase of cloth, which was followed by cutting-out from patterns, before being made up by tailors or finishers. In this fashion on 20 May 1643, he paid – among a range of disbursements – £1 4s. 3d. 'for cloth to make my drummer a suit of clothes', 3s. to a tailor for making it up, 11s. 1d. to Thomas Mottershaw for completed coats and breeches, 5s. 4d. to Henry Meeke for trimming a suit, and a further 9d. for buttons.[66]

Shoes

The shoes supplied to the New Model Army in 1645 and 1646 were almost entirely procured from members of the Livery of the Cordwainers Company in London. On 1 April 1645 the Ordnance Office was notified of an agreement entered into with Jenkin Ellis and Francis Marriot for '4,000 pair of shoes of neates leather, three soles only, two in each dozen of two soles of the sizes 10, 11, 12, 13 by Saturday next fortnight' at 2s. 3d. per pair'. Two thousand pairs were provided by Marriot six days later (for which he was paid £225), but the first recorded delivery from Ellis is dated

61 G. Andrews (ed.), Henry Best, *Rural Economy in Yorkshire in 1641: Being the Farming and Account Books of Henry Best, of Elmswell, in the East Riding of the County of York*, SS (Edinburgh: Blackwood, 1857), p.84.
62 Edwards, *Dealing in Death*, p.138.
63 TNA, SP28/134/12, ff. 357r & 384v.
64 D. H. Pennington and I. A. Roots (eds and intro.), *The Committee at Stafford, 1643–1645* (Manchester: Manchester University Press, 1957), p.110.
65 TNA, SP28/134/12, f. 394v.
66 BL, MS Harley 2128, ff. 26v, 23v, 28v, 31r.

11 July.[67] He was the most important contractor for footwear for the New Model. Sometimes his name appears by itself, sometimes with other suppliers and at the head of a consortium. Thus, Ellis and his associates provided 19,500 of the 32,000 pairs of shoes provided to Fairfax's forces during 1645 and 1646, bringing in some 12,500 pairs by October 1645 alone. Moreover, he and fellow cordwainers had previously supplied shoes to Sir William Waller's army and the Scottish Covenanters in 1644.[68] Occasionally the contracts are in his name only, but generally there are others designated with him, while phrases such as 'Jenkin Ellis and partners' suggest a reasonably stable consortium. He appears to have continued to supply footwear to the Commonwealth and Protectorate forces. On 16 November 1658 he petitioned the Council of State to provide 3,000 pairs of shoes 'made for the soldiery' in Flanders, asserting that he had 'served the State with shoes for many years.'[69]

Shoes worn by infantrymen, dragoons and others during the Civil Wars were generally low and open-sided. The provision of shoes, manufactured principally in London, to the infantry regiments of the New Model Army began in late March and early April 1645. Early notifications of contracts to the Ordnance Office include one of 3,000 pairs; another, for '1,000 pair of shoes of neats leather upon the same terms and at the same times' was agreed with Robert Botley and John Jones. A more detailed contract was that agreed with Edward Griffith and partners in December 1645 his stipulated that the 2,000 pairs were to be:

> of good neates leather with good soles, of the several sizes of 10s, 11s, 12s and 13s of each size a like number, all of them to be punched and each pair tacked together, and marked on the soles with several marks hereafter mentioned, to be brought into the Tower of London within 4 weeks to be viewed by the officers, which it is contracted they shall be paid when they bring them.[70]

The reference in the Ellis and Marriot contract mentioned above, states that the shoes should have 'three soles only, two in each dozen of two soles'. This corresponds in many respects with an agreement made in June 1642 by a syndicate of London merchants agreed to provide the following for troops in Ireland:

> 10,000 pair of well-conditioned neats leather shoes (some black and some russet) of four sizes, viz. nines, tens, elevens, and twelves, the one half to be with three soles and the other with two soles according to the patterns left with Mr Willis, for which they are to be paid upon the delivery of each 1,000 pairs at the rate of 2s. 5d. for the dry leather shoes and 2s. 6d. for those

67 TNA, WO47/1, f. 209v; WO55/1662, ff. 21v, 67v; TNA, SP28/29/1, f. 195r; Bod. Lib., Ms Eng. hist. C14, f.48r; ML, Ms 46 78/708, ff. 86r, 114v. The date of 3 April is given in ML, Ms 46 78/708.

68 TNA, SP28/46/106, ff. 3r–4v, 29r, 35r; *LJ*, VII, p.192.

69 *CSPD Interregnum 1658–9*, p.183.

70 Bodl. Lib., Ms Eng. hist. C14, f. 81r; ML, Ms 46 78/708, f. 86r.

> that are lacquered, and further agreed that but 500 pair of the shoes above mentioned that shall be of the nines and 500 pair of thirteens.[71]

The 'russet' shoes mentioned above were probably made of natural tan leather, in the same fashion that russet woollen fabrics contained natural fleece hues of greys and browns.[72] It seems that most shoes issued during the Civil Wars were of this type. The dry or russet leather shoes lacked oils and were essentially unfinished and required currying or 'lacquering', the working in of a mixture of tallow (animal fat) and beeswax.

Table 46: Notification of Contracts to the Ordnance Office for the Supply of Shoes for the NMA (WO47/1; ML, Ms 46 78/708)

Date	Quantity and type	Price pair	Contractor
3/4/45	4000 pair of shoes of neates leather, three soles only, 2 in each dozen of 2 soles of the sizes 10, 11, 12, 13 by Saturday next fortnight	27d.	Jenkin Ellis & Francis Marriot
3/4/45	1000 pair of shoes of neates upon the same terms and at the same times	27d.	Robert Botley & John Jones
10/7/45	2000 pair of shoes the sizes 10, 11, 12 & 13	27d.	Jenkin Ellis
3/8/45	4000 pair of shoes according to the first contract	27d.	Mr Harris and Jenkin Ellis & his Company
3/8/45	1000 pair of shoes	27d.	Robert Botley
3/8/45	500 pair of shoes the sizes 10, 11, 12 & 13	27d.	Edward Griffith
4/10/45	2000 pair of shoes all neates leather of 10, 11, 12	27d.	Jenkin Ellis, subcontracted by Francis Marriot & John Minnes
4/10/45	500 pair of shoes all neates leather of 10, 11, 12	27d.	John Taylor
22/12/45	2000 pair of shoes of good neates leather with good soles, of the several sizes of 10s, 11s, 12s and 13s of each size a like number, all of them to be punched and each pair tacked together, and marked on the soles with several marks hereafter mentioned, to be brought into the Tower of London within 4 weeks to be viewed by the officers, which it is contracted they shall be paid when they bring them 335 to be marked thus (110); 333 to be marked thus (111); 333 to be marked thus (112); 333 to be marked thus (113); 333 to be marked thus (114); and the 333 pair marked (115)	27d.	Edward Griffith, Edward Chipperfield & William Conyers, and their partners Francis Smith, Richard Hamond and Thomas Brasier

71 TNA, SP28/1B, f. 672r; SP28/1C, f. 194v; V. F. Snow and A. S. Young (eds.), *The Private Journals of the Long Parliament* (New Haven, 1987), II, p.46; III, pp.388, 422.

72 Pat Poppy, 'Russet: the decline and disappearance of a fabric', paper presented to the *Materials of Early Modern Fashion*, online conference 7–8 October 2021 (https://costumehistorian.blogspot.com/2021/10/russet-decline-and-disappearance-of.html)

Date	Quantity and type	Price pair	Contractor
22/12/45	500 pair of shoes as above according to the former contract to be brought into the Tower of London at the time in the former contract mentioned, for which they are to be paid as they bring them in 150 of them to be marked thus (116) 200 to be marked thus (117) 150 to be marked thus (118)	27d.	Richard Crafter, William Smith & partners
5/1/46	4500 pair of shoes of good neates leather with good soles, of the several sizes of 10s, 11s, 12s and 13s of each size a like number, all of them to be punched and each pair tacked together, and marked on the soles with several marks hereafter mentioned, to be brought into the Tower of London to be viewed within one month now next following, for which it is contracted he shall be paid when he brings them in for performance, whereof he shall set his hand 500 pair marked thus (19); 500 pair marked thus (20); 125 pair marked thus (21); 500 pair marked with a hart (22); 200 marked thus (23); 200 marked thus (24); 200 marked thus (25) 300 marked thus (26); 100 marked thus (27) 100 marked thus (28); 100 marked thus (29) 315 marked thus (30); 305 marked thus (31) 170 marked thus (32); 170 marked thus (33) 115 marked thus (34) Made 600 pair of this contract of 4500 were delivered forwardly into the Tower unmarked	27d.	Jenkin Ellis
5/1/46	1000 pair of shoes according to the several contracts, to be brought into the Tower of London at the times in the several contracts mentioned and are to be paid for aforesaid 370 pair marked thus (35) 310 marked thus (36) 320 marked thus (37)	27d.	Thomas Taylor
24/2/46	3000 pair of shoes, each 750 pair. Marked thus (2), (3), (4), (5) All the said shoes to be of good neates leather with several sizes of 10s, size a like number all [damaged] marked on the soles with the several marks before mentioned to be brought into the Tower of London to be viewed within one fortnight next coming, for which it is contracted they shall be paid when they bring them in for performance, whereof they have set their hands and marks severally the day and year before written	27d.	Jenkin Ellis, John Minnes, Francis Marriot & Benjamin Harris
24/2/46	2000 pair of shoes, each 1000 pair Marked thus (6) [Contractual details as above]	27d.	Lawrence Stanley & Thomas Taylor

Date	Quantity and type	Price pair	Contractor
24/2/46	500 pair of shoes Marked thus (7) [Contractual details as above]	27d.	Edward Johnson
24/2/46	1000 pair of shoes, each 500 pairs Marked thus (8), (9) [Contractual details as above]	27d.	Robert Botley & Jeffery Badger
24/2/46	200 pair of shoes Marked thus (10) [Contractual details as above]	27d.	William Blissett
24/2/46	300 pair of shoes Marked thus (11) [Contractual details as above]	27d.	John Jones
24/2/46	500 pair of shoes Marked thus (12) [Contractual details as above]	27d.	Edward Griffith
24/2/46	500 pair of shoes Marked thus (13) [Contractual details as above]	27d.	Edward Chipperfield

Table 47: Receipts for Shoes by the Ordnance Office for the NMA (TNA, SP28/29/1-32/3; SP28/140/3; Bodl. Lib., Ms Eng. hist. C14)

Date	Quantity and type	Price pair	Contractor
7/4/45	3000 pair of shoes	27d.	Francis Marriot, John Jones & Robert Botley
8/4/45	2000 pair of shoes in full of their contract	27d.	Jenkin Ellis & Francis Marriot
14/4/45	4000 pair of shoes of neates leather, three soles only, 2 in each dozen of 2 soles of the sizes 10, 11, 12, 13 by Saturday next fortnight	27d.	Jenkin Ellis & Francis Marriot
14/4/45	1000 pair of shoes 'upon the same terms and at same times'	27d.	Robert Botley & John Jones
2/6/45	1000 pair of shoes in the sizes of 10, 11 and 12 in full of his contract	27d.	Jenkin Ellis
14/7/45	2000 pair of shoes in full of his contract	27d.	Jenkin Ellis
20/9/45	500 pair of shoes	27d.	Edward Griffith
22/9/45	1000 pair of shoes	27d.	Thomas Taylor
22/9/45	1000 pair of shoes	27d.	Robert Botley
22/9/45	500 pair of shoes	27d.	Edward Griffith
22/9/45	4000 pair of shoes	27d.	Jenkin Ellis
28/9/45	1000 pair of shoes	27d.	Robert Botley
21/10/45	500 pair of shoes	27d.	Thomas Taylor
27/10/45	2000 pair of shoes	27d.	Jenkin Ellis, subcontracted by Francis Marriot & John Minnes
9/2/46	4500 pair of shoes	27d.	Jenkin Ellis and partners
9/2/46	1000 pair of shoes	27d.	Thomas Taylor

Date	Quantity and type	Price pair	Contractor
17/2/46	2500 pair of shoes	27d.	Edward Griffith, Edward Chipperfield and William Conyers
20/3/46	7000 pair of shoes	27d.	Jenkin Ellis and partners
20/3/46	500 pair of shoes	27d.	Edward Chipperfield
20/3/46	500 pairs shoes	27d.	Edward Griffith
8/4/46	76 pair of shoes	27d.	Mr Walker, agent employed by Parl.
5/5/46	83 pair of shoes	27d.	Thomas Richardson

The sizes referred to in contracts and books of receipts equate roughly to modern British sizes between 7 and 10. In the seventeenth century the sizing system was based on a quarter of an inch per size, commencing at 8½ inches for adult size 1. Shoes were provided strung together in pairs and made of neats leather (any leather made from the tanned hide of a bovine animal, such as ox or cow). One of the earliest consignments received into the Ordnance Office, on 14 April 1645, was from Jenkin Elliot and Francis Marriot '4,000 pair of shoes of neates leather, three soles only, two in each dozen of two soles of the sizes 10, 11, 12, 13 by Saturday next fortnight.'[73] Moreover, the price agreed with contractors by the Committee for the Army largely remained at 2s. 3d. per pair between 1645 and the 1650s, although shoes contracted for troops in Ireland in October 1646 cost 2s. 10d. the pair, the same price as the '16,000 pair of shoes of neates leather' listed in a tender to supply the British forces there in March 1648.[74] The same specification for shoes is evident in a contract made by the Ordnance Officers (approved on 9 January 1660) with William Saul, shoemaker of London, for '4,600 pairs of neats leather shoes, well-tanned, dressed, and sewn, sizes 13 to 9, according to patterns, to be ready by 16 January for the forces in Flanders, at 2s. 8d. a pair, to be paid for 3 months after delivery.'[75]

On 7 April 1645 a consignment of 3,000 pairs for the New Model Army was received from Francis Marriot, Jones and Botley, while a further 2,000 were delivered by Marriot and Jenkin Ellis. Though each supplier was promptly paid in full the following day, neither order appears among the known contracts, so it must be assumed that they were commissioned around 26 March. However, the 5,000 pairs of shoes notified to the Ordnance Office on 3 April were received into the stores on 14 April, thus showing that the date of their original contract was 31 March. Nevertheless, by this date at least 10,000 pairs of shoes had been received into the Tower stores.[76] The earliest known issue of shoes to Sir Thomas Fairfax's infantry is contained in a warrant issued to Commissary Nicholas Bond on 10 April 1645 'to dispatch 1,000 coats, 1,000 pairs of breeches, 3,000 shirts, 3,000 pairs of shoes and 1,700 snapsacks to the army'; these were delivered two days later. The next delivery of 2,000 pairs by Bond appears to have been that dated 15 July, by virtue of an order

73 TNA, WO47/1, f. 209v.
74 *CJ*, IV, p.698; *LJ*, X, pp.158–159.
75 *CSPD Interregnum, 1659–60*, p.306.
76 TNA, SP28/29/1, ff. 192r; 195r; WO47/1, f. 209v; Bod. Lib., Ms Eng. hist. C14, f. 5v.

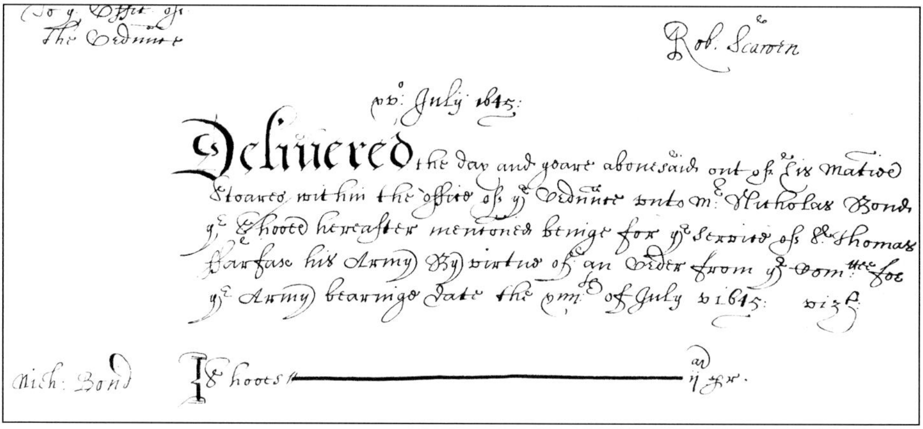

Delivery of 2,000 pairs of shoes by the Ordnance Office to Commissary Nicholas Bond, 15 July 1645. (WSL, Ms Salt 463, unf.)

from the Committee for the Army.[77] Even so, not all suppliers provided such large quantities. On 29 December 1645 Peter Moulson received payment of £5 8s. 6d. for 38 pairs of shoes and 10 pairs of boots.[78]

On 10 April 1645 the Commons instructed, 'That the Gentlemen of Kent do forthwith give order and directions, that the Kentish soldiers, now at Gravesend, may be speedily brought from Gravesend to Staines by water, to the rendezvous appointed by Sir Thomas Fairfax'. Likewise, he was 'to send men that were raised and brought to Gravesend to Colonel Weldon'.[79] They were here on 17 April, though on 25 April the regiment received £435 12s. 8d. for 14 days' pay, thus indicating that it was mustered into the New Model at Gravesend on 10 April.[80] This batch of conscripts (men between the ages of 16 and 60), being 470 in number, were rebellious and had been accompanied by guards. They were transported up the Thames in boats to Windsor, where they were delivered to the army.[81] This was a common method of moving troops and stores during the Civil Wars. *The Kingdomes Weekly Intelligencer* reported that on 3 May 1645 60 Royalists captured by Cromwell's forces near Oxford were 'brought in barges to London, and since dispersed to several prisons.'[82] The previously mentioned Kentish recruits, 'which were lately impressed in the county, taking their opportunity in their passage to Sir Thomas Fairfax his Army' mutinied and tried to flee, while four days later the same newsbook reported that other men in Kent:

77 TNA, WO55/460, unfol.; WO55/1646, unfol.; WO55/1647, unfol.; WSL, Ms Salt 463, unfol.
78 TNA, SP28/301/2, f. 307r.
79 *CJ*, IV, p.105.
80 TNA, SP28/29/1, f. 193r.
81 *CSPD 1644–5*, pp.411, 420, 426, 437; *Perfect Occurrences*, 11–18 April 1645. TT, E260[17]; *The Moderate Intelligencer*, 10–17 April 1645. TT, E278[14].
82 *The Kingdomes Weekly Intelligencer*, 29 April–6 May 1645. TT, E282[2].

> which were lately impressed in the county, taking their opportunity in their passage to Sir Thomas Fairfax his Army, fell upon their convoy about seven miles from Synnock, hurt divers of them, possessed themselves of Sir Percy Hart's horse, and since we hear, that divers of the discontented of that county are come to them, so that their number is increased to about 500.[83]

Such an alarming situation thus prompted the Committee of Kent to write the Speaker on 18 April 1645:

> By God's infinite mercy we are now past our third rebellion, the first two have yet passed without the punishment of any (except imprisonment only). If this pass so we must expect monthly rebellions if not hourly, when undoing well-affected men is held but a recreation. We shall therefore humbly desire that you will be pleased to let some of these to be made speedy examples of your justice, who have already so surfeited upon your mercy, that they grow wanton and insolent. This we are confident as well for the safety of the Kingdom as this county, you will grant to your humble servants, etc.[84]

Two days later, the Lords ratified an Ordinance prescribing the death penalty for any conscript who 'run away from their colours'.[85] Whether any of Weldon's men who arrived from Gravesend had been previously kitted out, either fully or in part with clothing, as requested, is unclear, given the level of turmoil in their own county. However, on 10 February 1646 Commissary Thomas Walker delivered to another batch of recruits 'out of the stores provided for Sir Thomas Fairfax his Army to be sent by him to Gravesend for the clothing of the Kentish recruits' 500 coats and breeches, 500 shirts, 500 pairs of stockings, 500 pairs of shoes, and 500 snapsacks. This issue corresponds with others of the time to supply new recruits for the New Model with clothing, arms and ammunition. For instance, on 18 February Thomas Richardson, the army's waggon master general, received a warrant from the Committee for the Army to convey 8 drums, 1,800 coats, 1,800 pairs of breeches, 1,800 shirts, 1,800 pairs of stockings, 1,800 pairs of shoes, 650 long pikes, 1,350 matchlock muskets, 2,000 snapsacks, 12cwt of match, 6cwt of corn powder, and 6cwt of musket shot to 'clothe and arm the new recruits at Newport Pagnell.'[86]

During what was a major winter refit of the New Model, at least 10,300 pairs of shoes were issued to the army between January and March 1646, along with 22,000 pairs of stockings. Though most of these went directly to the various regiments of foot – via the two commissaries specifically assigned to each for this purpose – substantial quantities were specifically issued to recruits. Hence, on 13 February one group assembled at Reading received 1,700 pairs of shoes, as well as 1,700 pairs of stockings, in addition to 1,700 suits, 1,500 shirts, 700 pikes, 1,000 muskets with

83 *The Kingdomes Weekly Intelligencer*, 8–15 April 1645. TT, E278[8].

84 Bodl. Lib., Ms Tanner 60/1, f. 99r.

85 *LJ*, VII, pp.334–5.

86 TNA, WO55/1646, unfol.

bandoliers, and 1,700 snapsacks. Correspondingly, on 26 March 2,180 pairs of shoes, 2,189 coats, 2,179 pairs of breeches, 2,184 pairs of stockings, 1,200 shirts, 1,770 matchlock muskets, 1,775 bandoliers, 168 pikes, 36 drums furnished with cords, 1 ton of match, 10cwt of powder, and 10cwt of musket shot was supplied to recruits in Northampton.[87] It would make sense that all or most of the 10,000 pairs of shoes received into the stores by 14 April 1645 were promptly issued to the infantry.

Though prone to exaggeration, some of the London-based Parliamentarian-leaning newsbooks report of May 1645 suggest that footwear remained in short supply amongst the ranks, yet this might to some extent, have been caused by difficulties encountered by commissaries in keeping up with the constant, rapid movement of individual regiments during a period when substantial parts of the army were either active around Oxford, or had been ordered to march to the relief of Taunton. The Royalist, Sir Edward Walker noted that 'Taunton was then besieged by us and brought to extremity; that Fairfax with his new army was then about Newbury, designing to relieve it, which, if he could effect, it would give him a reputation and enforce the keeping of an army in the West.'[88] For 13 May 1645 one Parliament-leaning newsbook reported, '[Sir Thomas Fairfax's and Sergeant Major General Skippon's regiments being about Newbury] where he stays some few days to refresh his wearied soldiers who were much tired out by long and tedious marches (sometimes 15 miles a day) till he receives a supply of shoes and stockings, whereof there is great necessity amongst his soldiers'. Another newsbook added, 'The House likewise taking into consideration that by reason of the late tedious and unwearied marches of Sir Thomas Fairfax's foot, they had worn out their shoes and were in great need of supply. It was further ordered that it should be referred to the Committee for the Army, and forthwith send down shoes for Sir Thomas Fairfax's foot.'[89]

On 14 May, as Weldon's brigade was resting at Chard, having relieved Taunton the previous day, the main body of the New Model Army arrived at Newbury. Sprigge, serving as chaplain to Sir Thomas, related the following, which speaks much of the commander-in-chief's steely discipline and quality of leadership:

> In their march, besides exemplary justice dome upon a rude soldier (as upon two before, in their march towards the West) and other things of particular note, there was one passage of great wisdom and condescension in the General, very remarkable: That when the duty became so hard to some of the regiments, as each other to bring up the rear, the General's own regiment, claiming a privilege to march always in the van, which was convenient now to be waved for the relief of the rest; but they being unwilling thereunto, the General instead of severe discipline, alighted himself, and marched on foot in the head of his regiment, about two miles, and so brought up the rear; and to this day, his own regiment takes the turn upon all duties. A thing if rightly considered, nothing to their dishonour (if it were to outvie others to

87 TNA, SP28/140/3, unfol.; WO55/1646, unfol.

88 Sir Edward Walker, *Historical Discourses upon Several Occasions* (London: 1705), p.122.

89 *The Kingdomes Weekly Intelligencer*, 13–20 May 1645.TT, E284[23]; *A Perfect Diurnall of Some Passages in Parliament*, 12–19 May 1645. TT, E260[38].

> do service) and resounding much to the good, and good success of an army, there being not any one thing that more frequently and certainly breeds distempers, and causes mutinies in an army, than claiming privileges, and insisting thereon it time of service.[90]

At Newbury, on 16 May 1645 Fairfax's and Skippon's infantry regiments were mustered by William Herbert, one of the Commissioners for Parliament. Five days later both units received 7 days' pay. On 16 May Colonel Robert Harley's regiment mustered at nearby Thatcham, and on 21 May 498 private sentinels under the command of Sergeant Major William Cowell of Colonel Barclay's regiment, who on 29 April were 'newly added to the recruit of the said regiment' [i.e., Harley's] were paid the sum of £275 19s. 6d., being 7 days' pay.[91] *The Moderate Intelligencer* recounted that on 5 July 1645:

> The wearisomeness of the foot forces of that brave chieftain, Sir Thomas Fairfax, as go by long march, 14 or 15 miles a day, almost to the tiring of the horse, yea the wearing out of draught horses, and to add to their weariness from Dorchester to Beaminster, is so craggy and unpassable, that the artillery was not able to pass, and so were forced to quarter on a hill with a good guard.[92]

As Sprigge wrote:

> The army marched that day from Dorchester to Beaminster, the train and most of the foot quartered on top of a hill, some few in Beaminster town, a place of the pitifulest spectacle that that man can behold, hardly a house left not consumed by fire; the town being fired by some of the enemy in five places at once, when Prince Maurice was there, by reason of a falling out between the French and the Cornish.[93]

Although the average daily marching distances of premodern infantry (and hence the general effectiveness of troops and the general wear placed upon footwear) are difficult to calculate to any degree of accuracy, it was often between roughly 5 and 20 miles. In Elizabeth I's army, for instance, a daily march of 12 to 15 miles was expected, whereas in October 1649 recruits at Chester for Colonel Robert Venables' regiment in Ireland were promised 6d. per day 'for every man not exceeding that number which he shall bring on board, for their marching money, allowing 10 miles a day, from the place where they were raised, to the places where they are shipped.'[94] The marching rates achieved by the New Model Army's infantry regiments between April 1645 and June 1646 as recorded by Sprigge show that over the 120 days of

90 Sprigge, *Anglia Rediviva*, pp.19–20.
91 TNA, SP28/30/3, ff. 218r, 221r–222v.
92 *The Moderate Intelligencer*, 3–10 July 1645. TT, E292[21].
93 Sprigge, *Anglia Rediviva*, p.60.
94 *CSPD 1649–50*, p.344.

actual marching the average mileage equates to 9.3 miles per day. On 5 May 1645 Fairfax's soldiers traversed 15 miles between Andover and Salisbury, while during the forced march from Ambersbury, Wiltshire to Bridgewater between 30 June and 11 July a total of 90 miles was covered.[95] It was *The Moderate Intelligencer* that reported on 14 May 1645, 'The letters that came last night speak of the sad and weary condition of Sir Thomas Fairfax's returned party Monday night [12th] to Alresford, having marched 15 miles back that day, the infantry so weary, that many of them to be carried in carts.'[96] Such distances, it must be remembered, largely reflect the operational requirements of the campaign and not necessarily the marching ability of the New Model.

In providing the logistical requirements of the New Model as its units progressed ever south-westwards during autumn 1645 a Council of War was held on 17 October, at which it was considered 'whether to march towards Exeter, and so towards Plymouth, or to take in Tiverton, in regard it lay upon a pass and might much annoy the army to leave it behind them unreduced, or at least blocked up; and if once taken, might be a Magazine, a place of strength and conveniency, either to secure anything in, or to retreat to upon occasion.' On 6 December Fairfax established the army's headquarters at Tiverton, where his troops paused until 8 January 1646. However, according to the same source, three days earlier;

> the stockings and shoes (which the poor foot had so great need of, and had so long expected) came to Tiverton most seasonably, to fit them for a march; wherewith they were so well satisfied, as they showed much forwardness to march, without staying for clothes, which they had great need of also, being many of them all to tatters, and the weather was extreme cold to boot. [adding on 8 January] All things being in readiness for a march, the horse and foot (with their ammunition on horseback) set forward to Crediton.[97]

As previously noted, the New Model Army generally received its shoes from London sources, though it is possible that some batches were obtained from local craftsmen. In comparison, the role and importance of Northampton – a town historically known for its footwear industry – in the supplying of shoes and boots to Parliamentarian armies during the Civil Wars remains to be comprehensively explored. In May 1642 the town's cordwainers provided 7,000 pairs of shoes at 2s. 4d. a pair for the troops in Ireland, while on 24 June a further 8,000 pairs were shipped there from Chester.[98] Moreover, when the Earl of Essex's Army was recruiting in the summer of 1644, ready to begin its drive on Oxford, the Northampton Commissioners supplied 2,000 pairs of shoes to be distributed to its regiments of foot.[99] According to P. R. Mounfield, 'it is clear that in 1642 Northampton was becoming an integral part of the system created by Parliament for supplying shoes to its armies. The town was acting as an

95 Sprigge, *Anglia Rediviva*, pp.331–5.
96 *The Moderate Intelligencer*, 8–15 May 1645. TT, E284[6].
97 Sprigge, *Anglia Rediviva*, pp.136–7, 157, 163.
98 TNA, SP28/1B, ff. 532r, 657r; SP28/170/1, ff. 26v, 29r, 44v.
99 *CSPD 1644*, p.285.

entrepot on the route between London and Chester, the major port for trade with Ireland'.[100] Nevertheless, Edwards suggested that the relatively modest quantities known to have been produced by the Northampton shoemakers 'may lie with the documentation rather than with the level of activity in the town', though Ben Coates emphasises that one reason why the trade played a minor role in supplying footwear was that it was 'disrupted by labour shortages during the war'.[101]

No form of headwear appears to have been supplied to soldiers of the New Model Army in 1645 and 1646, and it would be reasonable to think that they brought their own from home or bought them from market traders. This may have included monteros – round peaked caps constructed of panels of woollen cloth with a skirt running around the edge that could fold down for protection in bad weather. These were supplied to Royalist forces, especially the Oxford Army, in large numbers. The scholar Anthony Wood observed 1643, 'all the common soldiers then at Oxford were new apparelled, some all in red, coats, breeches and monteros; and some all in blue'.[102] In 1646 the Parliamentarian chronicler John Vicars related how at Naseby, Prince Rupert was mistaken for Sir Thomas Fairfax during the early fighting because they were both wearing similar hats:

> And, hear (as we have it from credible relation) a party of the enemy's broke through our left wing of horse, came quite behind our rear of our Train, the leader of them being a person somewhat in habit like our general, in a red montero, as our general had; he came as a friend, and our commander of the guard of the Train went with his hat in his hand, and asked him how the day went, thinking verily he had been our general. The cavalier (who wee since heard for certain was Rupert) asked him and the rest, if they would have quarter, whereupon, they cried no, gave fire instantly, and most bravely beat him off, making him flee for his life, and his companions.[103]

Unlike for the New Model Army, evidence shows that troops in Ireland were issued with hats. On 27 May 1642 Henry Paman and Edmund Hunt, haberdashers of London were contracted to:

> furnish the number of 20,000 caps for the service of the soldiers in Ireland at the rate of 23s. the dozen, according to certain patterns left in the hands of Mr Willis, whereof half are to be of one sort and half of the other sort, and of which number 2,000 are to be delivered by Whitsuntide and the rest by 1,000 or more every week after, for which they are to be paid in the manner following. Upon delivery of the first 5,000 caps as much money as

100 Mounfield, P. R., 'Moving the industrial flywheel: the origins of Northampton's footwear industry', *The Local Historian*, 40 (2010), pp.57–67, (p. 64).

101 Edwards, *Dealing in Death*, p.132; Ben Coates, 'The Impact of the English Civil War on the Economy of London, 1642–1650', PhD thesis (University of Leicester, 1997), pp.101–102.

102 Anthony Wood, *The Life and Times of Anthony Wood, antiquary, of Oxford, 1632–1695, described by Himself* (Oxford: Oxford Historical Society, 1891–2), I, pp.83–84.

103 John Vicars, *Magnalia Dei Anglicana, or England's Parliamentary Chronicle* (London, 1646), p.161.

> those 5,000 caps shall amount to at the rate aforesaid, and upon delivery of the next 7,000.[104]

Going by the accounts of George Wood, who laid out £16 15s. 10d. in April 1642 for the 'charge of the 3,000 Monmouth caps' sent to Ireland, these were the type of headwear.[105] However, as Stuart Peachey argues, 'Monmouth caps is a name and the first appearance and later use of the term can be noted relatively simply. What is far harder is deciding what a Monmouth cap was, its physical characteristics such as weight, materials, construction details and particularly what it looked like'.[106]

The production method involved in fashioning these caps was described by the Royalist Richard Symonds, who wrote of Bewdley in 1644, 'the only manufacture of this town is making of caps called Monmouth caps. Knitted by poor people at 2d. apiece, ordinary ones sold for 2s., 3s., 4s. First, they are knit, then they mill them, then block them, then work them with teasles, then they sheer them'.[107] Similarly, in 1661 Thomas Fuller stated, 'The best caps were formerly made at Monmouth ... But upon the occasion of a great plague happening in this town, the trade was some years since removed to Bewdley in Worcestershire, yet so that they are called Monmouth caps unto this day'.[108] It is possible that the design of hats worn by soldiers and Dutch seamen during the seventeenth century corresponded with those depicted in two Bewdley capper's tokens of 1656 and 1670. Possessing wide brims and relatively high-domed crowns, these share similar characteristics with those in English woodcuts produced no later than the 1640s, in addition to seventeenth century examples in the National Museum of Denmark in Copenhagen, and the 'Peter the Great' hat held at the Hermitage Museum in Saint Petersburg.

The Committee for the Affairs of Ireland confirmed on 11 February 1643 that:

> by the certificate of George Wood, Commissary for the clothing of soldiers in Ireland, that Edmund Hunt, according to a contract made with the Commissioners for the Affairs of Ireland dated 27 May last, and agreeable to an order of the Committee dated 10 December following, hath, upon several days between 11th July and 16 December last, delivered, for the service of Ireland, 3,750 Monmouth caps, at the rate of 23s. the dozen, which number, being part of the last 7,500 mentioned in the said contract, and amounting, at the rate aforesaid, to the sum of £359 7s. 0d.[109]

On 27 May 1643 Captain Edward Cooke, a troop commander in Waller's forces, acknowledged that he was indebted to William Beard, a tailor of Gloucester, 'for

104 Snow and Young (eds), *Private Journals*, III, p.461.
105 TNA, SP28/139, unfol.
106 Stuart Peachey (ed.), *Clothes of the Common People: Headwear* (Bristol: Stuart Press, 2013), p.13.
107 Charles Long (ed.), *Diary of the Marches of the Royal Army During the Great Civil War* (London: Camden Society, 1859), p.14.
108 Thomas Fuller, *The History of the Worthies of England* (London: 1661), p.432.
109 Bodl. Lib., Ms Rawlinson A/110, ff. 35r-v; *LJ*, V, p.600.

making clothes for my officers and troopers.' On the same day £10 14s was paid to John Cooke, a haberdasher, for hats for them.[110] Additionally, in early 1644 Captain Issac Ewer's company of dragoons in the Earl of Manchester's army had the sum of £10 10s. deducted from their pay for hats for the soldiers and non-commissioned officers, which they received from the merchant William Fenn.[111]

In the Commonwealth period, headwear was supplied to soldiers in Ireland in considerable quantities. A proposal to supply clothing to troops in Ireland, dated 27 March 1648, includes '16,000 hats for foot soldiers, at 1s. 10d. per hat, to be ready as soon as they can be got made; 4,000 hats for horsemen, at 2s. 2d. per hat, to be ready as soon as they can be got made; [and] 20,000 hatbands, at 1d. per piece.'[112] During the summer of 1648 5 dry fatts of hats and shirts were ordered to be shipped in the *Anne and Joyce* from London to Dundalk. Another 6 fatts containing 2,120 hats for the foot, along with shoes and stockings were apportioned to Colonel Monck's regiment, while quantities of hats, stockings, shirts, snapsacks, shoes, and 11 bales of cloth were landed at Dublin.[113] Similarly, on 12 May 1649 the governor of Dublin, Colonel Michael Jones, was requested by the Council of State 'to distribute the suits of clothes which we are sending [to Ireland], but reserve 2,000 suits for Colonel Monke and his proportion of horsemen's and footmen's hats.'[114] A Treasury Warrant of March 1651 ordered the payment of £958 6s. 8d. to Armiger Warner, felt maker, for 10,000 hats and bands delivered into the stores for Ireland, whereas on 17 December 1653 the Council of Officers and the Committee of the Commonwealth ordered Robert Molesworth to buy 8,500 Monmouth caps, which was part of the 17,000 Monmouth caps which were ordered to be sent to the stores of Ireland.[115]

Doublets, normally attached to a pair of breeches by hooks and eyes, and worn underneath soldiers' coats or buff coats, were a typical part of male attire, although references to them are not plentiful in military contexts. Nevertheless, on 23 August 1642 the Commissioners for Irish Affairs recorded:

> Whereas the lords and others [of] his Majesty's commissioners of the affairs of Ireland, authorised thereunto as a committee of both Houses of Parliament, have (amongst other things) taken into consideration the clothing of the regiments of horse and foot last taken into pay in the province of Ulster, they think fit that it be reported as their opinions to the House of Commons that 7,500 suits of clothes, viz., caps, doublets, cassocks, breeches, two pair of stockings, two pair of shoes, and two shirts for every soldier, are thought fit to be provided and sent to these regiments of foot, that is to say, 4,000 complete suits as aforesaid to be landed at Belfast and the rest at Londonderry or to the officers or their agents here, the charge whereof amounting to £15,937 10s. at the rate of £2 2s. 6d. the suit to be

110 TNA, SP28/299, f. 703r.
111 TNA, SP28/25/2, f. 445r; SP 28/128/8, f. 51v.
112 TNA, SP 28/353, f. 25r-v; *LJ*, X, pp.158–159.
113 TNA, SP21/28, unfol.
114 *CSPI 1647–1660*, pp.788–789.
115 TNA, SP 28/98, unfol.; *CSPD Interregnum 1651*, p.550.

afterwards defaulted upon the pay of every soldier at the rate of 2d. per day.[116]

In November 1642 Colonel Holles' regiment was re-equipped from the Ordnance Office stores with red coats, breeches, doublets, caps, and stockings.[117] On 14 January 1643 the linen merchant Richard Wollaston of London was appointed by the Committee for Irish Affairs to deliver clothes to Ireland for the soldiers, 'according to directions given him by the Lords and others his Majesty's Commissioners for the Affairs of Ireland for the furnishing of the magazines in the several provinces of that Kingdom, 15,000 doublets, at the rate of 6s. the piece, which in all amounts to the sum of £4,500, of which there is already ordered him £500, and the residue was to be paid him at three and three months next after the delivery of the said doublets'.[118] It is possible that these doublets were made of linen as Wollaston was also involved in the procurement of shirts and appears to have specialised in that fabric. In late 1643 civilian tailors and merchants in Chester were asked to donate clothing to recently arrived troops from Ireland. One observer recorded, 'The Irish English soldiers came to Chester to rest and repose themselves for they were weary and out of clothing, the mayor sent through all wards to get apparel from the citizens who gave freely, some whole suits, some two, some doublets, others breeches, others shirts, shoes, stockings and hats to the apparelling of about 300. When they were refreshed, they marched to besiege Nantwich'.[119]

Waistcoats appear to have been cold weather garments, worn close to the body in a process of layering and put on rather like a modern jumper or cagoule. According to Randle Holme, waistcoats were 'a close garment worn under a doublet, and within the waistband of the breeches'.[120] If the item was constructed of an open weave, air trapping, woollen fabric (cotton) it was probably used as an additional insulating layer. This might explain the lack of waistcoats in contemporary illustrations, as they would normally be worn under doublets, which were usually buttoned up. In March 1643 an order for 3,180 pairs of grey stockings, 1,200 caps, 861 pairs of breeches, 188 pairs of shoes, 1,600 cotton waistcoats, and 3,070 yards of cotton was delivered by the merchant John Davis to Viscount Conway's and Clotworthy's infantry regiments in Ireland. A further 800 waistcoats were provided for troops in Ulster on 18 December.[121] Sir Thomas Myddelton, the Parliamentarian commander in North Wales received from London manufacturers 36 red soldier's coats, along with white cloth to make draws and waistcoats in October 1644. Similarly, on 20 March 1645 compensation was paid for '360 waistcoats and 52 yards in a piece of red Welsh cotton', confiscated by mistake,

116 Vernon and Young (eds), *Private Journals*, p.428.
117 TNA, SP28/262, f. 374r; *CJ*, II, p.866.
118 Bod. Lib., Ms Rawlinson A/110, f. 27v; *LJ*, V, p.556.
119 BL, Ms Harley 2125, f. 136r.
120 Randle Holme, *The Academy of armoury, or, a storehouse of armoury and blason* (Chester: 1688), III, p.96.
121 TNA, SP 28/42, f. 723r; C. McNeil (ed.), *The Tanner Letters: Original Documents and Notices of Irish Affairs in the Sixteenth and Seventeenth Centuries* (Dublin, 1943), p.171.

which were intended for troops in Ireland.[122] Likewise, on 9 March 1645 a payment of £5 was made to the tailor John Wetherby for making 150 canvas waistcoats for the Earl of Manchester's soldiers.[123]

Clothing the New Model Army's Cavalry and Dragoons

Given the remit of the Ordnance Office and the train of artillery to clothe the foot, and the almost complete absence of references to clothing procured for and supplied to the mounted arm of Sir Thomas Fairfax's Army in 1645 and 1646, it remains largely unknown how the cavalry and dragoons were clothed, although it seems likely that items were procured, either in bulk by officers for their soldiers or individually from market traders or other sources. If the various parish loss accounts are to be believed, some items of clothing and fabric were stolen by troopers of the New Model Army during the Naseby campaign, perhaps to replace their threadbare garments. Thus, Henry Coppall of Gilsborough, Northamptonshire claimed that Captain Adam Lawrence's troop of Fairfax's own regiment took 11 yards of russet cloth worth £1 10s., in addition to 'linens and apparel' while being quartered upon him 'the night before Naseby fight'. Coppall's neighbour, Nicholas Hollis also complained of losing 'linens, clothing, a brass pan and firewood to the same troopers.[124] Moreover, following the movement of the New Model south-westwards through Warwickshire and beyond in late June 1645 various units were quartered upon, or passed though, the local population. John and Richard Mason of Brinklow Parish claimed, 'taken by his Excellency's Sir Thomas Fairfax his soldiers as the main body marched through town, taken in linens and other things to the value of £1 1s.'. Also, Robert Sedgley asserted that soldiers had pilfered 'linens and woollen cloths worth £2 10s.'.[125] The assumption would be that such textiles were turned into clothing for the cavalry and dragoons, although some could have been sold or bartered by the soldiers.

As alluded to, some mounted units in the New Model might have sourced their own items of clothing, or had them purchased by officers, the cost of which probably being stopped from their pay. From 1643 onwards Captain John Bramhall of the Cheshire dragoons, who was possibly a Nantwich mercer before the war, engaged in the supply and production of garments with his mother in the town. From January 1643 they outfitted his dragoons with quantities of cloth and made-up clothing, including coats, breeches and shirts, the costs of which were deducted from the soldiers' pay.[126] Bramhall also paid £1 4s. 3d. 'for cloth to make my drummer a suit of clothes' and a further 3s. to a tailor for making it up. He also disbursed the sum of 11s. 1d. to Thomas Mottershaw for made up uniforms, 5s. 4d. to Henry Meeke for trimming a suit, with a further 9d. for buttons. A further reference of 1645 to constructing coats includes

122 TNA, SP28/25, ff. 143v–144r; SP28/139, unfol.; SP28/211, ff. 130v–141r; SP28/300/1, f. 93v; SP28/346/1, unfol.

123 TNA, SP28/26, f. 19r.

124 TNA, SP28/173/6, unfol.

125 TNA, SP28/186/2, ff. 2r, 9r.

126 BL, MS Harley 2128, ff. 23v–26v, 28v, 31r; TNA, SP28/31/4, ff. 433r–434v.

'for making two suits together with linings, buttons and other necessaries for Colonel Jones' men'.[127] Lieutenant Colonel Michael Jones, the leader of the Parliamentarian horse in Cheshire also commanded some dragoons during this period.

Sizeable quantities of clothing for horsemen were supplied by London contractors for Commonwealth troops in Ireland and Scotland in the late 1640s and 1650s. On 7 January 1650 the merchant Nathaniel Andrews petitioned for a licence to transport shoes, boots, shirts, bridles, saddles, and other items for the army in Ireland. This was granted on condition that he paid 'the necessary customs and giving bond to the customs officers to carry such goods to the garrisons in Ireland obedient to Parliament'. Similarly, on 2 November 1649 an agreement was made between the Irish Committee and Richard Downes – who had supplied garments to the New Model from April 1645 onwards – for 15,000 yards of broadcloth for 'horsemen's cloaks', at 11s. 3d. per yard, and 1,178 yards of Spanish cloth for officers. He also provided '500 cloaks for the army in Scotland' on 21 October 1650, and a further 500 of the same the following month. These garments, described as 'cloaks' must have been riding coats, expressly issued to the cavalry to be worn in cold weather conditions.[128] In addition to shoes, large amounts of riding boots were also sent. For instance, on 29 November 1649 James Graves, Theodore Reynolds, Jenkin Ellis, and Francis Marriot, cordwainers, were contracted to supply:

> 2,000 pairs of boots of good neate's leather, well-tanned and waxed, viz., 600 pair of fourteens, 700 pair of thirteens, and 700 pair of twelves, at 14s. 10d. per pair, and deliver them into the stores at Botolph's Wharf, free of charge, within three weeks; all the boots to be approved by the master and warden of the Cordwainers' Company, and those not approved to be returned. £500 to be paid in advance to buy leather and warrant to be issued to the treasurers at war to pay it out of the 14 days' pay to be received by them out of the assignations for the Irish army. The residue to be paid upon certificate of receipt of the boots.

These were duly delivered and the sum of £1,450 was paid to them in full of their indenture. The consortium of Reynolds, Ellis, and Marriot provided another 3,000 pairs at a cost of £2,175 on 5 March 1650, while on 30 November Charles Graves and three others received an advance for the purchase of leather and 2,000 pairs of boots for troopers in Ireland, at 14s. 10d. a pair.[129] If they had them, then cavalry troopers and non-commissioned officers of Sir Thomas Fairfax's Army may have originally brought their buff coats with them when they re-enlisted from other Parliamentarian forces. According to Cruso, writing in 1632, all types of mounted soldiers were to have 'a buff coat with long skirts to wear between his armour and his clothes'. Additionally, he wrote that the harquebusier '(besides a good buff coat) is to have the back and breast of the cuirassier's armour, more than pistol-proof, [and the headpiece],' but condemned the practice of leaving off their armour 'and think

127 TNA, SP28/128/13, f. 30v; SP28/224, unfol.
128 *CSPD 1649–50*, p.740; *CSPD 1650*, p.374; *CSPD Interregnum 1650*, pp.591–2.
129 *CSPD 1649–50*, p.412; *CSPD Interregnum 1650*, pp.588–90.

themselves safe enough in a calf-skin coat'.[130] Evidently during the Civil Wars, it was desirable among the horse to wear buff coats as protection against sword cuts. Made of ox or bull hide, these tended to be purchased by officers and troopers themselves, although a good-quality officer's coat was considerably more expensive.

Writing in early 1642 the Lord Lieutenant of Devon had recommended that the county troopers 'be handsomely furnished [in] comely apparel with coat of buff with long skirts [and a] coat of cloth to keep both himself and furniture from the violence of the weather'.[131] Moreover, in 1642 Sir Samuel Luke, serving in Essex's Army, chose to supplement his allowance from Parliament for 64 horses and £538 to make his troop ready for service, by purchasing buff coats for his men with £58 15s. out of his own pocket. Equally, in 1644 Colonel John Fiennes paid £9 15s. 'to the troopers to buy them buff coats upon account'.[132] An inventory of the goods of the Cheshire gentleman, Edmund Jodrell, taken on 28 April 1643 by Captain Lieutenant Zankey of Brereton's troop, included two buff coats valued at £1 13s. 4d. each, 'one bull hide dressed buff-like' and three dressed buckskins, as well as 'two riding coats of broadcloth, the one set with plate [silver-gilt] buttons' at £2 10s. together.[133]

Trumpeters were an indispensable part of cavalry troops and armies in general. They acted like heralds in negotiating with enemy troops, discussing prisoners, delivering terms of surrender, or acting as messengers. Captains of horse could spend large sums of money on items such as trumpet banners and clothing issued to trumpeters. Markham described the more identifiable aspects of trumpeters:

> The trumpet is not bound to any arms at all, more than his sword, which in former times was not allowed, but with the point broken. He shall have a fair trumpet, with cords suitable to his captain's colours, and to his trumpet shall be made fast a fair banner, containing his captain's full coat armour; he may wear scarf and feather, and all other ordinary accoutrements of a horsemen, and for his horse it shall be a good hackney, with gentleman-like furniture'.[134]

There are few contemporary English illustrations of trumpeters to give an accurate picture of their appearance, although the two depicted in the Streeter schema of Naseby to the right rear of Fairfax's Army show them in what might be buff coats, with large waist scarfs and broad-brimmed hats.

A tailor's bill for trumpet banners and cornets for Sir William Brereton's troop, dated 30 May 1643, includes £10 for two trumpet banners of black taffeta at £5 apiece, and £10 10s. for two pairs of stirrups for the trumpeters at 15s. a pair. On 14 October 1645 Anthony Smith, a London supplier, was paid £4 for a trumpet banner and £2 for a trumpet for the same unit.[135] Another bill for 'fabric and trimmings' supplied

130 Cruso, *Military Instructions*, p.30.
131 TNA, SP16/492, f. 49v.
132 TNA, SP28/127, ff. 26r, 30r; SP28/147, f. 243v.
133 JRL, JOD/62c.
134 Markham, *Soldiers Accidence*, pp.44–5.
135 TNA, SP28/225/1, f. 3r; SP28/152/8, f. 3r.

to Captain Robert Stukeley's troop in Cheshire, dated 3 October 1643, includes '16 yards of frieze at 4s. per yard', costing £3 4s., which probably went into cassocks or other clothing for his trumpeters.[136] Similarly, in April 1644 Captain Enys, a troop commander under Sir Thomas Myddelton, purchased green taffeta for his cornet, with green and white fringing, and spent 14s. on a staff for it, for his own cornet and trumpet banners, although other captains of the regiment possessed cornets of other pigments. His brother officer, Captain Thomas Noakes received £150 a few weeks earlier 'to equip himself and his troop with sufficient horses for service in North Wales'. He received further sums in June 1644 for the pay of two corporals, two trumpeters and 62 troopers, and more in July 1644 for three corporals and 40 soldiers. Noakes himself spent £10 11s. for suits and coats for his trumpeters, another 18s. for hats and bands, £4 10s. for two trumpets, and £7 3s. for trumpet banners and cording.[137]

Direct references to the supply of soldiers' coats to civil war dragoons are few and none have come to light for Colonel John Okey's regiment of the New Model Army. In November 1642 Colonel Richard Browne's regiment received red coats, although in early 1645 its soldiers wore grey.[138] Colonel Richard Norton described a skirmish at Havant in January 1644 between his soldiers and Royalist dragoons belonging to Lord Crawford and Colonel Ennis' regiments. He defeated and captured several dragoons, reporting that they 'were most in red coats'.[139] In early 1643 Captain Bramhall of Sir William Brereton's Cheshire forces received 52 coats for his dragoon company 'which were accordingly disposed of'.[140] Four Nantwich tailors made 344 infantry coats and 55 troopers' coats during the winter of 1643–1644 and delivered them to the army's commissaries on 22 February 1644.[141] They were paid 1s. 2d. per soldiers' coat and 1s. 8d. per trooper's coat for their construction and carriage. On 24 December 1644 Brereton paid £100 'to William Barratt of Ridgeway in Cheshire to buy cloth for soldiers' coats in Cheshire, which was accordingly bought and disposed of for the soldiers' coats'. The sum of 3s. was paid to John Price, a local cordwainer on 12 August 1643, 'for one pair of shoes for Samuel Elliot', a dragoon in Captain Bramhall's company in Cheshire. Similarly, in November 1644 £9 9s. was disbursed by Brereton 'for stockings and shoes for soldiers who came out of Liverpool when it was besieged, took the Covenant and have done very good service for the Parliament under whom they formerly served in Ireland'.[142] These men – 50 in number – brought with them their arms and were formed into a new dragoon unit under Lieutenant Colonel Michael Jones. Hence, another payment of £5 14s. was made on 11 December 'to Lieutenant Colonel Jones to pay for shoes bought for some of his company of firelocks, 40 pair [at 2s. 8d. each]'.

136 TNA, SP28/8, f. 16r.
137 TNA, SP28/346/1, unfol.
138 TNA, SP28/144/2, f. 28v; BL, Ms Add. 18982, f. 409v.
139 *Good Newes from Portsmouth: declaring how Colonell Richard Norton Governour of Southhampton, met with my Lord Craford and Colonell Ennis regiments* (8 January 1644). TT, E81[7].
140 BL, MS Harley, 2128, f. 34v.
141 TNA, SP28/49/1, f. 100v.
142 TNA, SP28/152/7, ff. 16r & 25r.

In addition to their more general clothing, there is evidence to show that cavalry troopers in some civil war armies were supplied with riding coats (sometimes referred to in sources as long coats or smock coats) for cold and winter wear. During the siege of Chester Brereton's horse and dragoons were quartered in open terrain to the Welsh side of the city, and constantly engaged in patrolling and picket duty. On 8 November 1645 Sir William reported to the Speaker that in establishing such *perdues* (outposts) his soldiers had been hampered 'by extreme foul weather which is violent that our men cannot endure out of doors.' Similarly, the following month, Sir Richard Lloyd, the Royalist governor of Holt remarked, 'the river [Dee] is frozen, and can be passed over with horse and foot under this castle', while Brereton recounted on 9 January 1646 that 'Our duty is very hard; the weather extreme and piercing'.[143]

During the winter of 1643–1644 the Nantwich tailors Peter, John and William Burstow, and Thomas Greenall made 344 infantry coats and 55 troopers' coats, and delivered them to Commissary Hinde on 22 February 1644.[144] Instructions given in a tailor's bill of 2 October 1643 one of Brereton's officials, stated: 'we desire you to let Captain Stukeley and his cornet have so much frieze as will make 40 suits and smock coats, and we will see you satisfied for the same'.[145] Colonel Robert Duckenfield disbursed the sum of £41 8s. for '60 and odd new coats for the troop and for other clothes for some of them', in either November 1644 or April 1645 when troop was at Beeston.[146] In 1643 or 1644 Sergeant Major George Purefoy of the Warwick garrison paid £15 3s. 4d. 'to Mr Jarman of Warwick for cloth which made coats for the troop'.[147] Moreover, on 3 April 1644 the sum of £245 12s. 0d. was paid for coats and boots for the Earl of Manchester's regiment of horse, while a bill charged to the Eastern Association soon afterwards for soldiers' coats included the sum of £84 for '28 long coats with baize buttons and silk, and 28 pairs of breeches with lining and making'.[148]

Riding boots, issued to cavalry troopers, and in some instances to dragoons, were necessarily more expensive than shoes. In September 1644, a batch of 1,000 pairs of cavalry boots was delivered to the Eastern Association's agents at St Albans by the London shoemakers Richard Crofts and Edward Poole. Likewise, the army's treasurer employed agents to acquire boots and shoes in bulk – including 1,312 pair of shoes at 3s. 6d. per pair – which he issued to captains, 'deducting the costs from the sums owed to their companies for pay'.[149] While returning from London to Cheshire in June 1644, Sir William Brereton – who had been raising new troops of horse in the city – purchased quantities of cavalry boots from Thomas Pendleton at Northampton 'where boots are cheap', at a cost of 10s. a pair. He paid a further £5 'for carrying the above-mentioned boots from Northampton to Coventry, where they were distributed to the troopers.'[150] Boots were also purchased for 14s. and 15s.

143 BL, Ms Add. 11332, f. 59v; Ms Add. 11333, ff. 36r, 107r.
144 TNA, SP28/49/1, f. 100v.
145 TNA, SP28/8, f. 17r.
146 TNA, SP28/128/10, f. 8r.
147 TNA, SP28/136/37, f. 6v.
148 TNA, SP28/25, f. 570r; SP28/26, f. 186r.
149 TNA, SP28/25, ff. 143r–144v, 163v.
150 TNA, SP28/152/7, f. 6v.

a pair in early 1644 for Captain Vincent Potter's Parliamentarian cavalry troop in Warwickshire.[151] Moreover, in response to an order from the Commons on 3 February 1647, the sum of £393 6s. 8d. was disbursed four days later for boots for Colonel Rich's regiment of horse.[152] A further indication of the prodigious output of Marriott, Reynolds, and Ellis is that they supplied a total of 7,200 pairs of cavalry boots for the Commonwealth armies in Ireland and Scotland in 1650 alone.[153]

The assumption is that shoes must have been sourced for the New Model Army's dragoons, though there are no recorded instances of this. A few contemporaries felt that the most appropriate footwear for dragoons were shoes rather than boots and spurs, which might snag in the stirrup when mounting and dismounting, although such comments may reflect little more than their personal preferences. No widespread issue of boots to dragoons during the British Civil Wars is known, however. In 1642 Colonel Richard Browne's Parliamentarian regiment of dragoons benefitted from the disbursement of 9s. 6d. to 'Mr Wells for boots'; another 10s. 0d. was given to a carrier for transporting boots and spurs, whereas Bartholomew Grantham received the sum of £1 8s. 6d. 'for watering the horses for 7 days and delivering our boots'.[154] In Cheshire the sum of 9s. was distributed on 2 March 1643 'to a soldier of Captain Lea for boots', while the clothing and accoutrements provided for a dragoon by the constables of Hollingworth included boots and spurs.[155] Moreover, in March 1644 Captain John Holcroft's dragoon company from the Earl of Manchester's army had £42 14s. 9d. deducted for boots and shoes from their pay.[156] Wallhausen, writing in 1616, advocated that dragoons 'shall wear, if they so wish, cassocks and *gamaches* [gaiters] instead of boots, for greater ease in walking when necessary.'[157] Furthermore, the Royalist regiment raised and commanded by Sir Thomas Aston seems only to have been issued with shoes. One undated inventory of moneys 'lent to the dragoons' includes the sum of 2s. 6d. for shoes for Captain Thomas Newland, two sergeants, and 10 soldiers; 4s. 6d. and 3s. 10d. was furnished for shoes and stockings to another two dragoons, and shirts costing 3s. 10d. apiece were provided for five men.[158]

Many thousands of snapsacks were issued during the Civil Wars (including to the New Model Army's foot regiments), although direct references to their supply to dragoons are relatively uncommon. In November 1642 the London manufacturer, Mr Langham was paid £51 for supplying an unspecified number of snapsacks priced 8d. and 9d. for Browne's Parliamentarian regiment of dragoons. This seems a considerable sum of money, but his command was recently established with 7 companies of 100 men in each, besides non-commissioned officers, although Browne's accounts, drawn up on the raising of the unit, list at least 10 captains.[159]

151 TNA, SP28/136/27, f. 2r.
152 TNA, SP28/51, f. 215r.
153 *CSPD Interregnum 1649–50*, pp.587, 592, 596.
154 TNA, SP28/144/2, ff. 31r–32r.
155 TNA, SP28/196/3, f. 14v; BL, MS Harley 2128, ff. 29r, 8r.
156 TNA, SP28/25/2, f. 296r.
157 Wallhausen, *Kriegskunst*, pp.16–17.
158 BL, MS Add. 36913, ff. 118r-v.
159 TNA, SP28/144/2, ff. 1r–7r.

Bibliography

München, Bayerische Staatsbibliothek
Zeugbuch Kaiser Maximilians I – BSB Cod. icon. 222

Beverley, East Riding Archives
BC/II/7/4 Minute book of the Governors and Beverley Corporation, 1597–1660

Chester, Cheshire Archives
DDX/428 Letter Book of Sir William Brereton
DLE/89 Daybook of John Leche of Carden Hall, 1635–40
QJF/89/2 Petition of William Booth, 1661
ZBR/3/1 Register of Bishop John Bridgeman, 1619–1643
ZM/MP/8/48-49 Arms and equipment issued to Chester Trained Bands, 1596

Hull, History Centre
BRS/7/139 Inventory of armaments for the defence of Hull, 1643

Ipswich, Suffolk Records Office
HD36/A/137, HD36/A/142 Committee of Suffolk proceedings, 1645

Kew, The National Archives
E121 Trustees for the Sale of Crown Lands: Interregnum certificates
E179/187/468B Surrey Committee receipts and warrants, 1642–1649
PRO30/37/4 Ordnance Office records, May-December 1646
SP21/120 Records of the Committee of Both Kingdoms
SP28/1A-28 Musters, warrants issued by army committees, military commanders, 1642–1645
SP28/29-41 Pay warrants for supplies for the NMA, April 1645-December 1646
SP28/31/4 Clothing in Reading Magazine, October 1645
SP28/49 Warrants issued by army committees and military commanders
SP28/123/1-4 Lists of recruits to Sir Thomas Fairfax's Army, 1645–6
SP28/126/1 Clothing packed for transport from Reading to Portsmouth, 1645–1646
SP28/130/3 Payments to Colonel Ralph Weldon's regiment, 1644–5
SP28/139/4 & 9 Letters concerning consignments of clothing sent to Ireland
SP28/139/19 Accounts of Colonel John Fiennes, 1644–1645
SP28/140/1 Account of Sir Walter Erle relating to NMA artillery train
SP28/140/2 Account of John Rushworth for incidental charges of NMA
SP28/140/3 Ordnance Office receipts book, 1646–1649

SP28/140/4 Account of Thomas Richardson, waggon master general, 1642–45
SP28/140/7 Account of Commissaries John Smith and Thomas Richardson, 1645–1646
SP28/140/18 Account of Sir Walter Erle relating to NMA artillery train
SP28/147/2 Accounts of Edward Orpin, Commissary General of Victuals
SP28/173 Northamptonshire Parish Loss Accounts
SP28/182 & 4 Warwickshire Parish Loss Accounts
SP28/244 Surrey Committee Accounts
SP28/352 Warrants for payment to army contractors, 1645–1649
SP30/37 Ordnance Office warrants, 1645–6
SP33/443 Specification of Commissary George Wood, 1645
WO47/1 Ordnance Office minute book, 1644–1645
WO49/82 Ordnance Office debentures book, 1644–1650
WO55/460 Ordnance Office book of warrants for deliveries, 1643–1645
WO55/461 Ordnance Office book of warrants for deliveries,1648–1652
WO55/1646 Ordnance Office book of deliveries with corresponding warrants, 1644–1646
WO55/1647 Ordnance Office book of deliveries, June-October 1645
WO55/1662 Ordnance Office receipts book, 1644–1645
WO55/1664 Ordnance Office receipts book, March-September 1645
WO55/1754 Ordnance Office book of warrants for deliveries, August-October 1642

Lichfield, Lichfield Record Office
Ms Lichfield 24 Accounts of Lichfield garrison, 1643–5

London, British Library
Ms Add. 35332 Ordnance Office book of deliveries with corresponding warrants, 1646–50
Ms Harley 252 Diary of Military Proceedings of Sir Thomas Fairfax
Ms Harley 986 Notebook of Richard Symonds
Mss Harley 1943, 1999, 2130, 2137, 2166 Cheshire Sequestration Committee accounts
Ms Stowe 842 Committee for Colchester proceedings, 1644–56

London, Dr William Library
MS Modern 12.7 Parliamentary army officers' colours and standards

London, Museum of London
Tangye Collection Ms 46 78/708

Manchester, John Rylands Library (The University of Manchester Library)
JOD/62c Inventory of Edmund Jodrell of Yeardsley, 1643
TW/262 Sir William Brereton's commission as captain of a troop of harquebusiers, 1642

National Army Museum
6008-215 Receipt for colours

Oxford, Bodleian Library

Ms Add. C247 War materials delivered by the Ordnance Office, 4 April–2 May 1645

Ms Eng. hist. C14 Certificates from the Ordnance Office for the receipt of war certain materials contracted for and supplied for Fairfax's Army, 24 March 1645–4 March 1646

Ms Eng. hist. C244 Register of receipts for arms and supplies received into the King's Stores, mainly for the use of Sir Thomas Fairfax's Army, 1646–1649

Ms Nalson 4 Letters and papers, mainly addressed to the Speaker of the House of Commons, March-October 1645

Ms Rawlinson A/110 Orders of Parliament transferred to the Select Committee appointed to take care of the affairs of Ireland, September 1642-October 1644

Ms Tanner 60-1 Correspondence of Sir Thomas Fairfax and other New Model Army officers, 1645

Norwich, Norfolk Record Office

175P/38 Great Houghton parish records

Preston, Lancashire Archives

DDHK/10/1/6

Stafford, William Salt Library

Ms Salt 463 Warrant Book of the Ordnance Office, 1645–6

Ms Salt 477/11-2 Letters from Sir Arthur Aston to Prince Rupert

Stratford-upon-Avon, Shakespeare Birthplace Trust

Special Collections D98/1704 Accounts of Sir Edward Peto

Warwick, Warwickshire Archives

CR2017/9-10 Letter Books of the Earl of Denbigh

Worcester, Worcestershire Archives

BA 1714/899 (Townshend's Ms) Diary of Henry Townshend

Printed Primary Sources

Contemporary tracts and pamphlets

A glorious victory obtained by Sr. Thomas Fairfax, June, the 14. 1645 (London: 1645). TT, E288[21]

A letter from the Right Honourable Robert Earle of Warwicke, Lord High-admirall of England: to the Speaker of the House of Peeres. With an exact diurnall of all the most speciall and remarkable passages which have hapned during the siege of Lyme in Dorsetshire by Pr. Maurice his forces, from the 21 of February to this present (London: 11 July 1644). TT, E50[25]

A More Particular and Exact Relation of the Victory obtained by the Parliament's forces under the command of Sir Thomas Fairfax (London: Richard Cotes, 1645). TT, E288[38]

A Narration of the Expedition to Taunton: The Raising the Siege before it, and the Condition of our Forces, and the Enemies, at this present in the West. Sent from a Commander in the Army, and dated at Chard, May 18. 1645. TT. E285[10]

An Exact and Perfect Relation of the Proceedings of the Army under the Command of Sir Thomas Fairfax ... Dated at Sir Thomas Fairfax's Quarters at Middlesey July 11 (London: 1645). TT, E.292[28]

A Perfect Diurnall of Passages of the Souldiers, that are under the Command of the Lord Say in Oxford (London: 1642). TT, E122[13]

A True and Exact Relation of the Great Victories Obtained by the Earl of Manchester and the Lord Fairfax Against the Earl of Newcastle's Army in the North (London, 19 October 1643). TT, E71[5]

A True and Exact Relation of the...Red and Blue Regiments ... Who Marched Forth For the Relief of the City of Gloucester, Oct 2 1643 (London: 1643). TT, E69[15]

An Ordinance of the Lords and Commons assembled in Parliament ... Obtained against the Kings forces, nere Knasby in Northampton-shire the fourteenth of this instant Iune (London: 16 June 1645). TT, E.288[26]

A True Relation of a Victory Obtained over the Kings Forces (London: 1645). TT, E288[22]

Bishop, George, *A More Particular and Exact Relation of the Victory obtained by the Parliament's forces under the command of Sir Thomas Fairfax* (London: Richard Cotes, 1645). TT, E288[38]

Exceeding Joyfull Newes From the Earl of Essex Being a true and reall Relation of His incompassing the Kings Army neare the Citty of Oxford, Decemb. 7 (London: 1642). TT, E124[33].

Good Newes from Portsmouth: declaring how Colonell Richard Norton governour of Southhampton, met with my Lord Craford and Colonell Ennis regiments (8 January 1644). TT, E81[7]

Sir Thomas Fairfax's letter to the Honorable William Lenthall Esq: Speaker of the House of Commons; concerning the taking of Sherborn Castle (London: 15 August 1645). TT, E297[3]

The copy of a letter sent to his Excellencie Sir Thomas Fairfax: With an account to the officers of the Generalls regiment, intended for satisfaction to their demands (London: 1647). TT, E390[3]

The full and last relation, of all things concerning Basing-House: with divers other passages; represented to Mr Speaker, and divers members in the House (London: 1645). TT, E.305[8]

Newsbooks

Mercurius Civicus, 7–14 May 1646. TT, E337[21]

Mercurius Civicus, 12–18 June 1645. TT, E286[12]

Mercurius Civicus, 28 August–4 September 1645. TT, E229[7]

Perfect Diurnall of Some Passages in Parliament, 12–19 January 1646. TT, E252[14]

Perfect Passages of each dayes proceedings in Parliament, 30 April–7 May 1645. TT, E260[32]
The Kingdomes Weekly Intelligencer, 1–7 April 1645.TT, E276[22]
The Kingdomes Weekly Intelligencer, 8–15 April 1645.TT, E278[8]
The Kingdomes Weekly Intelligencer, 13–20 May 1645. TT, E284[23]
The Kingdomes Weekly Intelligencer, 10–17 June 1645. TT, E284[26]
The Kingdomes Weekly Intelligencer, 23–30 June 1646. E342[6]
The Moderate Intelligencer, 10–17 April 1645. TT, E278[14]
The Moderate Intelligencer, 23–29 April 1645. TT, E337[20]
The Moderate Intelligencer, 15–22 May 1645. TT, E285[7]
The Moderate Intelligencer, 22–29 May 1645. TT, E286[9]
The Moderate Intelligencer, 26 June–3 July 1645. TT, E288[37]
The Moderate Intelligencer, 3–10 July 1645. TT, E292[21]
The Moderate Intelligencer, 14–21 August 1645. TT, E297[12]
The Moderate Intelligencer, 6–13 November 1645. TT, E309[11]
The Scottish Dove, 27 November–5 December 1645. TT, E311[4]
The Weekly Account, 27 May–3 June 1646. TT, E339[14]

Books and Edited Collections

Anonymous, *Directions for Musters Wherein is shewed the order of drilling for the musket and pike* (Cambridge: University of Cambridge, 1638)
Barclay, Andrew, Wales, Tim and Morrill, John (eds), *The Letters, Writings, and Speeches of Oliver Cromwell*, vol. 1 (Oxford: Oxford University Press, 2022)
Bell, Robert (ed.), *Memorials of the Civil War*, 2 vols (London: Richard Bentley, 1849)
Birch, Thomas (ed.), *A Collection of State Papers of John Thurloe, Esq; Secretary to the Council of State*, 7 vols (London: 1742)
Boyle, Roger, Earl of Orrery, *A Treatise of the Art of War dedicated to the King's Most Excellent Majesty* (1677)
Buchanan, David, *Truth Its Manifest* (London: 1645)
Chadwick-Healey, Charles (ed.), *Bellum Civile: Hopton's Narrative of His Campaigns in the West Country, 1642–44* (Somerset Record Society, 1902)
Chamberlayne, Edward, *Angliæ Notitia, or the present state of England together with divers reflections upon the antient state thereof* (London: 4th edn, 1673)
Clarke, Andrew (ed.), *The Life and Times of Anthony Wood, antiquary of Oxford, 1632–1695* (Oxford: Clarendon, 1891)
Coates, Willson Havelock, Steele Young, Anne, Snow, Vernon F. (eds), *The Private Journals of the Long Parliament: 7 March to 1 June 1642* (Woodbridge: Boydell & Brewer, 1982)
Crocker, A. G., Crocker, G. M., Fairclough, K. R. and Wilks, M. J. (eds), *Gunpowder Mills: Documents of the 17th and 18th Centuries* (Surrey Record Society, 2000)
Elton, Richard, *The Compleat Body of the Art Military* (London:1650)
Evans, D. E., *Equipping a C17th Army* (March Publication, 1985)
Firth, C. H. (ed.), *The Clarke Papers: Selections from the papers of William Clarke, secretary to the Council of the Army, 1647–1649, and to General Monck and the commanders of the army in Scotland, 1651–1660*, 4 vols (London: Longmans, Green & Co., 1891–1901)

Firth, C. H. (ed.), *The Memoirs of Edmund Ludlow, Lieutenant General of the Horse in the army of the Commonwealth of England, 1625–1672*, 2 vols (Oxford: Clarendon Press, 1894)

Firth, C. H. and Davis, Godfrey, *The Regimental History of Cromwell's Army*, 2 vols (Oxford: Clarendon Press, 1940)

Firth, C. H. and Rait, R. S. (eds), *Acts and Ordinances of the Interregnum, 1642–1660*, 3 vols (London: HMSO, 1911)

Hahlweg, Werner, *Die Heeresreform der Oranier, Das Kriegsbuch des Grafen Johann von Nassau-Siegen* (Wiesbeden: Selbstverlag der Historischen Kommission, 1973)

Hall, James (ed.), *Memorials of the Civil War in Cheshire and the adjacent counties by Thomas Malbon, of Nantwich, Gent., and Providence improved by Edward Burghall*, Lancashire and Cheshire Record Society, 19 (1889)

Hodgson, John (ed.), *Original Memoirs, written during the great Civil War; being the life of Sir Henry Slingsby, and memoirs of Capt. Hodgson* (London: Ballantyne, 1807)

Hogan, James (ed.), *Letters and Papers Relating to the Irish Rebellion between 1642–46* (London: HMSO, 1936)

Lang, David, (ed.), *The Letters and Journals of Robert Baillie, 1637–1662*, 3 vols (Edinburgh: Bannatyne Club, 1841)

Lilburne, John, *Innocency and Truth Justified* (London: 1646)

Markham, Francis, *Five Decades of Epistles of Warre* (London: Augustine Matthew, 1622)

Marsh, Simon, *The Train of Artillery of the Earl of Essex: Vol. 2, 1644–1645* (Pike & Shot Society, 2022)

Marsh, Simon, *'Exceeding Toylsome': The Accounts of Waggonmaster General Thomas Richardson and the practice of Logistics and supply in the Earl of Essex's Army 1642–1645* (London: Pike & Shot Society, 2023)

Monck, George, *Observations upon Military and Political Affairs* (London: 1671)

Owen, G. Dyfnallt (ed.), *Calendar of the Cecil Papers in Hatfield House, 1612–1668*, 22 vols (London: University of London & History of Parliament Trust, 1971)

Philip, I. G. (ed.), *Journal of Sir Samuel Luke*, 3 vols (Oxford: Oxfordshire Record Society, 1947–53)

Roy, Ian (trans. and ed.), *The Royalist Ordnance Papers 1642–1646*, 2 vols (Oxford: Oxfordshire Record Society, 1964 and 1969)

Rushworth, John, *Historical Collections of Private Passages of State*, 8 vols (London: D. Browne, 1721)

Sprigge, Joshua, *Anglia Rediviva or England's Recovery* (London: 1647)

Trevelyan, W. C. and C. E. (eds), *The Trevelyan Papers* (Camden Society, 1872)

Turner, Sir James, *Pallas Armata: Military essayes of the ancient Grecian, Roman, and modern art of war written in the years 1670 and 1671* (London: Richard Chiswell, 1683)

Turner, Sir James, *Memoirs of His Own Life and Times* (Edinburgh: 1829)

Venn, Thomas, *Military Observations, Or the Tacticks Put into Practice* (London, 1672)

Vicars, John, *The Burning-bush Not Consumed. Or, The Fourth and Last Part of the Parliamentarie-chronicle* (London: 1646)

Vernon, John, *The Young Horse-man, or, The honest plain-dealing cavalier* (London, 1644)

Walker, Sir Edward, *Brief Memorials of the Unfortunate Success of His Majesty's Army and Affairs in the Year 1645* (London: 1705)

Wallhausen, Johan Jacob, *Kriegskunst zu Pferd* (Frankfurt: 1616)

Warburton, Eliot (ed.), *Memoirs of Prince Rupert, and the Cavaliers* (London: Richard Bentley, 1849)

Webb, T. W. (ed.), *Military Memoir of Colonel John Birch* (London: Camden Society, 1878)

Wrye, W. (ed.), *State Papers Relating to Musters, Beacons, Ship-money, &c. in Norfolk from 1626 chiefly to the beginning of the Civil War* (Norwich, 1907)

Young, Alan R. (ed.), *The English Emblem Tradition: Volume 3: Emblematic Flag Devices of the English Civil Wars, 1642–1660* (Toronto: University of Toronto Press, 1995)

Secondary Sources

Books

Abram, Andrew, *Dragoons and Dragoon Operations in the British Civil Wars, 1638–1653* (Solihull: Helion & Co., 2023)

Abram, Andrew, *More Like Lions than Men: Sir William Brereton and the Cheshire Army of Parliament, 1642–46* (Solihull: Helion & Co., 2020)

Barratt, John, *Cavalier Capital: Oxford in the English Civil War, 1642–1646* (Solihull: Helion, 2015)

Bull, Stephen, *The Furie of the Ordnance: Artillery in the English Civil Wars* (Woodbridge: Boydell, 2008)

Chartres, J. A., *Internal Trade in England, 1500–1700* (London: Macmillan, 1977)

Crofts, J., *Packhorse, Waggon, and Post: Land Carriage and Communications under the Tudors and Stuarts* (London: Routledge, 1967)

Denton, Barry, *Cromwell's Soldiers: The Moulding of the New Model Army 1644–1645* (Privately published: 2005)

Edwards, Peter, *Dealing in Death: The Arms Trade and the British Civil Wars, 1638–52* (Stroud: Sutton, 2000)

Edwards, Peter, *The Horse Trade of Tudor and Stuart England* (Cambridge: Cambridge University Press, 1988)

Evans, D. E., *Equipping a C17th Century Army* (Llanidloes: March Publications, 1985)

Everitt, Alan (ed.), *Suffolk and the Great Rebellion, 1640–1660* (Suffolk Records Society, 1960)

Everitt, Alan, *The Community of Kent and the Great Rebellion, 1640–60* (Leicester: Leicester University Press, 1966)

Firth, C. H. and Davies, Godfrey, *The Regimental History of Cromwell's Army, 2 vols* (Oxford: Clarendon Press, 1991 edn)

Foard, Glenn, *Colonel John Pickering's Regiment of Foot, 1644–45* (Whitstable: Pryor Publications, 1994)
Foard, Glenn, *Naseby: The Decisive Campaign* (Barnsley: Pen & Sword, 2004 edn)
Gentles, Ian, *The New Model Army in England, Ireland, and Scotland, 1645–1653* (Oxford: Blackwell, 1992)
Gerhold, Dorian, *Carriers and Coachmasters: Trade and Travel before the Turnpikes* (Chichester: Phillimore, 2005)
Hodgkinson, Robert, *Cromwell's Buffoon: The Life and Career of the Regicide Thomas Pride* (Solihull: Helion & Co., 2017)
Hopper, Andrew, *'Black Tom': Sir Thomas Fairfax and the English Revolution* (Manchester: Manchester University Press, 2007)
Kishlansky, Mark A., *The Rise of the New Model Army* (Cambridge: Cambridge University Press, 1979)
Langdon, John, *Horses, Oxen and Technological Innovation: The Use of Draught Animals in English Farming from 1066–1500* (New York: Cambridge University Press, 1986)
Lawrence, David R., *The Complete Soldier: Military Books and Military Culture in Early Stuart England, 1603–1645* (Brill: Leiden, 2008)
Lynn, John A. (ed.), *Feeding Mars: Logistics in Western Warfare from The Middle Ages to The Present* (Boulder: Westview Press, 1994)
Mendenhall, Thomas, *The Shrewsbury Drapers and the Welsh Wool Trade in the XVI and XVII Centuries* (Oxford: Oxford University Press, 1953)
Monaghan, Jason and Bound, Mensur, *A Ship Cast Away About Alderney* (Alderney Maritime Trust, 1997)
Parker, Geoffrey, *The Army of Flanders and the Spanish Road 1567–1659: The Logistics of Spanish Victory and Defeat in the Low Countries' Wars* (Cambridge: Cambridge University Press, 1972)
Peachey, Stuart, *Clothes of the Common People in Elizabethan and Early Stuart England*, 36 vols (Bristol: Stuart Press, 2013–14)
Peachey, Stuart, *The Soldier's Life in the English Civil War: Organisation, Food, Clothing, Weapons, and Combat* (Bristol: Stuart Press, 2016)
Peachey, Stuart and Turton, Alan, *Common Soldiers' Clothing of the Civil Wars 1639–1646*, I (Bristol: Stuart Press, 1995)
Price, Glenn W., *Soldiers and Civilians, Transport and Provisions: Early modern military logistics and supply systems during the British Civil Wars, 1638–1653* (Solihull: Helion & Co., 2023)
Privatsky, Kenneth L., *Logistics in the Falklands War: A Case Study in Expeditionary Warfare* (Barnsley: Pen & Sword, 2014)
Roberts, Keith, *Cromwell's War Machine* (Barnsley: Pen & Sword, 2005)
Robinson, Gavin, *Horses, People and Parliament in the English Civil War: Extracting Resources and Constructing Allegiance* (Farnham: Ashgate, 2012)
Ryder, Ian, *An English Army for Ireland* (Leigh-on-Sea: Partizan Press, 1987)
Scott, Christopher L. and Turton, Alan, *Hey for Old Robin!: The Campaigns and Armies of The Earl of Essex During the First Civil War, 1642–44* (Solihull: Helion & Co., 2017)
Stuart, Rob, *Wagons, Carts and Pack Animals 1580–1660* (Bristol: Stuart Press, 1996)

South, Robert, *Royal Castle, Rebel Town: Puritan Windsor in the Civil War and Commonwealth* (Buckingham: Barracuda, 1981)

Stuart, Rob, *Wagons, Carts and Pack Animals 1580–1660* (Bristol: Stuart Press, 1996)

Tomlinson, H. C., *Guns and Government: The Ordnance Office under the Later Stuarts* (London: Royal Historical Society, 1979)

Tibbutt, H. G., *Colonel John Okey, 1606–1662* (Bedford: Bedfordshire Historical Record Society, 1954)

Turton, Alan, *The Chief Strength of the Army: Essex's Horse (1642–1645)* (Leigh-on-Sea: Partizan Press, 1992)

Tylden, G., *Horses and Saddlery: An Account of the Animals Used by the British and Commonwealth Armies from the Seventeenth Century to the Present Day* (London: J. A. Allen, 1965)

Van Creveld, Martin, *Supplying War: Logistics from Wallenstein to Patton* (Cambridge: Cambridge University Press, 2004)

Wanklyn, Malcolm, *Reconstructing the New Model Army Volume 1: Regimental Lists April 1645 to May 1649* (Solihull: Helion and Co., 2015); *Volume 2: Regimental Lists April 1649-May 1663* (Solihull: Helion and Co., 2016)

Willian, T. S., *The Inland Trade: Studies in English Internal Trade in the Sixteenth and Seventeenth Centuries* (Manchester: Manchester University Press, 1976)

Wilson, John, *Fairfax: A Life of Thomas, Lord Fairfax, Captain-General of all the Parliament's Forces in the English Civil War, Creator and Commander of the New Model Army* (New York: John Murray, 1985)

Articles and Chapters

Abram, Andrew, 'The Civil War Account Book of Colonel Robert Duckenfield', *TLCAS*, 114 (2023), pp.5–35

Adams, Valerie, 'Logistics Support for the Falklands Campaign', *JRUSIDS* (September 1984), pp.43–9

Ailes, Mary Elizabeth, 'Camp Followers, Sutlers, and Soldiers' Wives: Women in Early Modern Armies (*c.* 1450-*c.* 1650)', in *A Companion to Women's Military History* (Leiden: Brill, 2021), pp.61–92

Atherton, Ian, 'Royalist finances in the English Civil War: the case of Lichfield garrison, 1643–5', *MH*, 33 (2008), pp.43–67

Barter, Sarah E., 'The Board of Ordnance: Some records recently acquired for the Tower of London', *JSA*, 3 (1966), pp.195–8

Blackmore, David, 'Counting the New Model Army', *ECWT*, 58 (2004), pp.3–5

Eastwood, David, 'The Accounts of Edward Russell, the storekeeper of the Royalist garrison in Chester Castle', *TLCAS*, 106 (2010), pp.1–22

Ede-Borrett, Stephen, 'Some Notes on the Raising and Origins of Colonel John Okey's Regiment of Dragoons, March to June, 1645', *JSAHR*, 87 (2009), pp.206–13

Edwards, Peter, 'The Supply of Horses to the Parliamentarian and Royalist Armies in the English Civil War', *HR*, 68 (1995), pp.49–66

Edwards, Peter, 'Turning Ploughshares into Swords: The Arms and Military Equipment Industries in Staffordshire in the First Civil War, 1642–1646', *MH*, 27 (2002), pp.52–79

Elliott, Katherine, 'Clothing Soldiers: Development of a System of Production and Supply of Military Clothing in England from 1645 to 1708', *Arms & Armour*, 10 (2013), pp.30–50
Gentles, Ian, 'The Choosing of Officers for the New Model Army', *Historical Research*, 67 (1994), pp.264–285
Gerhold, Dorian, 'Packhorses and Wheeled Vehicles in England, 1550–1800', *TJTH*, 14 (1993), pp.1–26
Higham, Robin, 'Some Thoughts on the Thirty Years War', *Bellum Tricannale* (Prague, 1997), p.340
Miller, D. P., Allsop, D. and Carr, D. J., 'The ballistics of seventeenth-century musket balls', *JCA*, 14 (2019), pp.25–36
Moore, Jonathan R., 'Oliver Cromwell and the English Experience of Manoeuvre Warfare 1645–1651, Part One', *Cromwelliana* (1993), pp.15–26; 'Part Two', *Cromwelliana* (1994), pp.24–36
Mounfield, P. R., 'Moving the industrial flywheel: the origins of Northampton's footwear industry', *The Local Historian*, 40 (2010), pp.57–67
Mungeam, Gerald I., 'Contracts of the Supply of Equipment to the New Model Army in 1645', *JAAS*, 6 (1968–70), pp.53–114
Nusbacher, Aryeh J. S., 'Civil Supply in the Civil War: Supply of Victuals to the New Model Army on the Naseby Campaign, 1–14 June 1645', *EHR*, 115 (2000), pp.145–160
Porter, Stephen, 'Farm Transport in Huntingdonshire, 1610–1749', *Journal of Transport History*, 3 (1982), pp.35–45.
Robinson, Gavin, 'Horse Supply and the Development of the New Model Army, 1642–1646', *War in History*, 15 (2008), pp.121–40
Southwick, Leslie, 'The London Cutler Benjamin Stone, and the Hounslow Sword and Blade Manufactories', *Arms and Armour*, 6 (2009), pp.12–61
Stern, W. M., 'Gunmaking in seventeenth century London', *Journal of the Arms and Armour Society*, I (1954) pp.55–100
Wanklyn, Malcolm, 'Choosing Officers for the New Model Army February to April 1645', *Journal of the Society for Army Historical Research*, 92 (2014), pp.109–25.
Wheeler, James Scott, 'Logistics and supply in Cromwell's conquest of Ireland', in Mark Fissel (ed.), *War and Government in Britain, 1598–1650* (Manchester: Manchester University Press, 1991), pp.38–56
Willard, J. F., 'Inland transportation in England during the fourteenth century', *Speculum*, 1 (1926), pp.361–74

Unpublished Theses

Crawshaw, Thomas, 'Military Finance and the Earl of Essex's Regular Army: 1642–1644', PhD thesis (York University, Toronto, 2013)
Price, Glenn William, 'Military logistics and supply during the British Civil Wars, 1638–1653', PhD thesis (Keele University, 2022)
Robinson, Gavin, 'Horse supply in the English Civil War 1642–1646', PhD thesis (University of Reading, 2001)

About the Author

Having joined the British Army in 1978 aged sixteen, Dr Andrew Abram served as a regular soldier in various theatres, including the South Atlantic. In 1997 he discovered that he could attend university, graduating with a first-class honours degree in history from the University of Wales, Lampeter, three years later. In 2007 he was awarded his doctorate by the same institution, being employed there as a teaching fellow and lecturer in medieval history until 2015. Andrew has subsequently acted as an associate lecturer in history at Manchester Metropolitan University, and historical consultant to museums and local groups. He has researched, written about, and taught on medieval and early modern warfare, and contributed journal articles and book chapters on related topics. More recently, Dr Abram's research interests in the civil war in Cheshire, the north-west of England and the Welsh borders, as well as seventeenth-century conflicts more generally, continues, and he is the author of books on Sir William Brereton's army, the 'Booth Rebellion' of 1659, Charles II's Army and Tangier, and Dragoons in the British Civil Wars for Helion & Company. Andrew lives with his family in the Peak District, where he enjoys travelling, brewing beer, climbing, hiking, and training for pilgrimages to holy sites. *Supplying the New Model Army* is Dr Abram's fifth book for Helion.

About the Artist

Patrice Courcelle was born in 1950 in northern France. He has been a professional illustrator for over 20 years. Entirely self-taught, he has illustrated many books and magazine articles, this is his second project for Helion. Patrice now lives in the town of Waterloo close to the famous battlefield.

Other titles in the Century of the Soldier series

No 29 *Home and Away: The British Experience of War 1618–1721*

No 30 *From Solebay to the Texel: The Third Anglo-Dutch War, 1672–1674*

No 31 *The Battle of Killiecrankie: The First Jacobite Campaign, 1689–1691*

No 32 *The Most Heavy Stroke: The Battle of Roundway Down 1643*

No 33 *The Cretan War (1645–1671): The Venetian-Ottoman Struggle in the Mediterranean*

No 34 *Peter the Great's Revenge: The Russian Siege of Narva in 1704*

No 35 *The Battle Of Glenshiel: The Jacobite Rising in 1719*

No 36 *Armies And Enemies Of Louis XIV: Volume 1 – Western Europe 1688–1714: France, Britain, Holland*

No 37 *William III's Italian Ally: Piedmont and the War of the League of Augsburg 1683–1697*

No 38 *Wars and Soldiers in the Early Reign of Louis XIV: Volume 1 - The Army of the United Provinces of the Netherlands, 1660–1687*

No 39 *In The Emperor's Service: Wallenstein's Army, 1625–1634*

No 40 *Charles XI's War: The Scanian War Between Sweden and Denmark, 1675–1679*

No 41 *The Armies and Wars of The Sun King 1643–1715: Volume 1: The Guard of Louis XIV*

No 42 *The Armies Of Philip IV Of Spain 1621–1665: The Fight For European Supremacy*

No 43 *Marlborough's Other Army: The British Army and the Campaigns of the First Peninsular War, 1702–1712*

No 44 *The Last Spanish Armada: Britain And The War Of The Quadruple Alliance, 1718–1720*

No 45 *Essential Agony: The Battle of Dunbar 1650*

No 46 *The Campaigns of Sir William Waller*

No 47 *Wars and Soldiers in the Early Reign of Louis XIV: Volume 2 - The Imperial Army, 1660–1689*

No 48 *The Saxon Mars and His Force: The Saxon Army During The Reign Of John George III 1680–1691*

No 49 *The King's Irish: The Royalist Anglo-Irish Foot of the English Civil War*

No 50 *The Armies and Wars of the Sun King 1643-1715: Volume 2: The Infantry of Louis XIV*

No 51 *More Like Lions Than Men: Sir William Brereton and the Cheshire Army of Parliament, 1642–46*

No 52 *I Am Minded to Rise: The Clothing, Weapons and Accoutrements of the Jacobites from 1689 to 1719*

No 53 *The Perfection of Military Discipline: The Plug Bayonet and the English Army 1660–1705*

No 54 *The Lion From the North: The Swedish Army During the Thirty Years War: Volume 1, 1618–1632*

No 55 *Wars and Soldiers in the Early Reign of Louis XIV: Volume 3 - The Armies of the Ottoman Empire 1645–1718*

No 56 *St. Ruth's Fatal Gamble: The Battle of Aughrim 1691 and the Fall Of Jacobite Ireland*

No 57 *Fighting for Liberty: Argyll & Monmouth's Military Campaigns against the Government of King James, 1685*

No 58 *The Armies and Wars of the Sun King 1643-1715: Volume 3: The Cavalry of Louis XIV*

No 59 *The Lion From the North: The Swedish Army During the Thirty Years War: Volume 2, 1632–1648*

No 60 *By Defeating My Enemies: Charles XII of Sweden and the Great Northern War 1682–1721*

No 61 *Despite Destruction, Misery and Privations..: The Polish Army in Prussia during the war against Sweden 1626–1629*

No 62 *The Armies of Sir Ralph Hopton: The Royalist Armies of the West 1642–46*

No 63 *Italy, Piedmont, and the War of the Spanish Succession 1701–1712*

No 64 *'Cannon played from the great fort': Sieges in the Severn Valley during the English Civil War 1642–1646*

No 65 *Carl Gustav Armfelt and the Struggle for Finland During the Great Northern War*

No 66 *In the Midst of the Kingdom: The Royalist War Effort in the North Midlands 1642–1646*

No 67 *The Anglo-Spanish War 1655–1660: Volume 1: The War in the West Indies*

No 68 *For a Parliament Freely Chosen: The Rebellion of Sir George Booth, 1659*

No 69 *The Bavarian Army During the Thirty Years War 1618–1648: The Backbone of the Catholic League (revised second edition)*

No 70 *The Armies and Wars of the Sun King 1643–1715: Volume 4: The War of the Spanish Succession, Artillery, Engineers and Militias*

No 71 *No Armour But Courage: Colonel Sir George Lisle, 1615–1648 (Paperback reprint)*

No 72 *The New Knights: The Development of Cavalry in Western Europe, 1562–1700*

No 73 *Cavalier Capital: Oxford in the English Civil War 1642–1646 (Paperback reprint)*

No 74 *The Anglo-Spanish War 1655–1660: Volume 2: War in Jamaica*

No 75 *The Perfect Militia: The Stuart Trained Bands of England and Wales 1603–1642*

No 76 *Wars and Soldiers in the Early Reign of Louis XIV: Volume 4 - The Armies of Spain 1659–1688*

No 77 *The Battle of Nördlingen 1634: The Bloody Fight Between Tercios and Brigades*

No 78 *Wars and Soldiers in the Early Reign of Louis XIV: Volume 5 - The Portuguese Army 1659–1690*

No 79 *We Came, We Saw, God Conquered: The Polish-Lithuanian Commonwealth's military effort in the relief of Vienna, 1683*

No 80 *Charles X's Wars: Volume 1 - Armies of the Swedish Deluge, 1655–1660*

No 81 *Cromwell's Buffoon: The Life and Career of the Regicide, Thomas Pride (Paperback reprint)*

No 82 *The Colonial Ironsides: English Expeditions under the Commonwealth and Protectorate, 1650–1660*

No 83 *The English Garrison of Tangier: Charles II's Colonial Venture in the Mediterranean, 1661–1684*

No 84 *The Second Battle of Preston, 1715: The Last Battle on English Soil*

No 85 *To Settle the Crown: Waging Civil War in Shropshire, 1642–1648 (Paperback reprint)*

No 86 *A Very Gallant Gentleman: Colonel Francis Thornhagh (1617–1648) and the Nottinghamshire Horse*

No 87 *Charles X's Wars: Volume 2 - The Wars in the East, 1655–1657*

No 88 *The Shōgun's Soldiers: The Daily Life of Samurai and Soldiers in Edo Period Japan, 1603–1721 Volume 1*

No 89 *Campaigns of the Eastern Association: The Rise of Oliver Cromwell, 1642–1645*

No 90 *The Army of Occupation in Ireland 1603–42: Defending the Protestant Hegemony*

No 91 *The Armies and Wars of the Sun King 1643–1715: Volume 5: Buccaneers and Soldiers in the Americas*

No 92 *New Worlds, Old Wars: The Anglo-American Indian Wars 1607–1678*

No 93 *Against the Deluge: Polish and Lithuanian Armies During the War Against Sweden 1655–1660*

No 94 *The Battle of Rocroi: The Battle, the Myth and the Success of Propaganda*

No 95 *The Shōgun's Soldiers: The Daily Life of Samurai and Soldiers in Edo Period Japan, 1603–1721 Volume 2*

No 96 *Science of Arms: the Art of War in the Century of the Soldier 1672–1699: Volume 1: Preparation for War and the Infantry*

No 97 *Charles X's Wars: Volume 3 - The Danish Wars 1657–1660*

No 98 *Wars and Soldiers in the Early Reign of Louis XIV: Volume 6 - Armies of the Italian States 1660–1690 Part 1*

No 99 *Dragoons and Dragoon Operations in the British Civil Wars, 1638–1653*

No 100 *Wars and Soldiers in the Early Reign of Louis XIV: Volume 6 - Armies of the Italian States 1660–1690 Part 2*

No 101 *1648 and All That: The Scottish Invasions of England, 1648 and 1651: Proceedings of the 2022 Helion and Company 'Century of the Soldier' Conference*

No 102 *John Hampden and the Battle of Chalgrove: The Political and Military Life of Hampden and his Legacy*

No 103 *The City Horse: London's militia cavalry during the English Civil War, 1642–1660*

No 104 *The Battle of Lützen 1632: A Reassessment*

No 105 *Monmouth's First Rebellion: The Later Covenanter Risings, 1660–1685*

No 106 *Raw Generals and Green Soldiers: Catholic Armies in Ireland 1641–1643*

No 107 Polish, Lithuanian and Cossack armies versus the might of the Ottoman Empire

No 108 *Soldiers and Civilians, Transport and Provisions: Early Modern Military Logistics and Supply Systems During The British Civil Wars, 1638-1653*

No 109 *Batter their walls, gates and Forts: The Proceedings of the 2022 English Civil War Fortress Symposium*

No 110 *The Town Well Fortified: The Fortresses of the Civil Wars in Britain, 1639-1660*

No 111 *Crucible of the Jacobite '15: The Battle of Sheriffmuir 1715*

No 112 *Charles XII's Karoliners Volume 2 - The Swedish Cavalry of the Great Northern War 1700-1721*

No 113 *Wars and Soldiers in the Early Reign of Louis XIV: Volume 7 - Armies of the German States 1655–1690 Part 1*

No 114 *The First British Army 1624–1628: The Army of the Duke of Buckingham (Revised Edition)*

No 115 *The Army of Transylvania (1613–1690): War and military organization from the 'golden age' of the Principality to the Habsburg conquest*

No 116 *The Army of the Manchu Empire: The Conquest Army and the Imperial Army of Qing China, 1600–1727*

No 117 *French Armies of The Thirty Years' War 1618–48*

No 118 *Soldiers' Clothing of the Early 17th Century: Britain and Western Europe 1618–1660*

No 119 *Novelty and Change: Proceedings of the 2023 Helion and ompany 'Century of the Soldier' Conference*

No 120 *Peter The Great's Disastrous Defeat: The Swedish Victory at Narva, 1700*

No 121 Royalist Newark, 1642–1646: Sieges and Siege Works

No 122 The Battle of Fribourg 1644: Eughien and Turenne at War

No 123 Science of Arms: the Art of War in the Century of the Soldier 1672–1699: Volume 2: Cavalry, Artillery & the Conduct of War

No 124 Supplying The New Model Army: Logistics, arms, ammunition, clothing, victuals and the matériel of war, 1645-1646

SERIES SPECIALS:

No 1 *Charles XII's Karoliners: Volume 1: The Swedish Infantry & Artillery of the Great Northern* War 1700–1721